NEW YORK

NATIONAL GEOGRAPHIC

TRAVELER

NEW YORK

Michael S. Durham

National Geographic
Washington, D.C.

CONTENTS

■ Pages 2–3: Illuminated in red, white, and blue, One World Trade Center (Freedom Tower) now dominates the New York skyline.
Opposite: The beaux arts beauty of Grand Central Terminal in Midtown Manhattan

TRAVELING WITH EYES OPEN

Alert travelers go with a purpose and leave with a benefit. If you travel responsibly, you can help support wildlife conservation, historic preservation, and cultural enrichment in the places you visit. You can enrich your own travel experience as well.

To be a geo-savvy traveler:

- Recognize that your presence has an impact on the places you visit.

- Spend your time and money in ways that sustain local character. (Besides, it's more interesting that way.)

- Value the destination's natural and cultural heritage.

- Respect the local customs and traditions.

- Express appreciation to local people about things you find interesting and unique to the place: its nature and scenery, music and food, historic villages and buildings.

- Vote with your wallet: Support the people who support the place, patronizing businesses that make an effort to celebrate and protect what's special there. Seek out local shops, restaurants, and inns. Use tour operators who love their home—who love taking care of it and showing it off. Avoid businesses that detract from the character of the place.

- Enrich yourself, taking home memories and stories to tell, knowing that you have contributed to the preservation and enhancement of the destination.

That is the type of travel now called geotourism, defined as "tourism that sustains or enhances the geographical character of a place—its environment, culture, aesthetics, heritage, and the well-being of its residents." To learn more, visit National Geographic's Center for Sustainable Destinations at *nationalgeographic.com/maps/geotourism.*

TRAVELER

NEW YORK

ABOUT THE AUTHORS

Michael S. Durham, born and raised in New York City, now lives far from those streets in rural upstate New York. His continuing interest in the city is reflected in his writings, particularly the Mid-Atlantic volume of the Smithsonian Guides to Historic America. He has been an editor at the American Heritage Publishing Company and a correspondent, writer, and editor for *Life* magazine in both Paris and New York City.

His books include *Desert Between the Mountains* (Henry Holt, 1997); *Miracles of Mary* (HarperCollins, 1995); and *Powerful Days* (Stewart, Tabori & Chang, 1991), based on his coverage of the civil rights movement in the 1960s.

Patricia Shaw, Matt Hannafin, and **Justin Kavanagh** updated and wrote new features for the later editions.

Shaw has spent twenty-plus years wandering New York City and is still charmed and energized by it. In addition to a career as a senior production editor at Random House, Workman, Simon & Schuster, and others, she has performed as a singer-songwriter, sold her jewelry design creations, and done freelance editorial and illustration work. She is a competitive runner and recently completed her first half-marathon in Central Park.

Hannafin is a freelance writer and editor, a musician, a husband, a father of two, and a New York native now based in Portland, Oregon. Author of numerous travel guidebooks as well as blogs and newspaper columns, he's written on topics ranging from speed traps and genealogical travel to minimalist art, risk management, and the 2008–09 world financial crisis. He's provided writing and editing services for global finance and consulting firms, congressional candidates, UN agencies, and most of the major book publishers. He has performed concerts for audiences of 2 to 2,000. In 2010, he was honored with an SATW Foundation Lowell Thomas Travel Journalism award in the Marine Travel category.

Kavanagh has had a long career as a writer and editor, starting in his hometown of Dublin, Ireland, and has worked in cities such as London, Washington, D.C., and New York. Since he first ventured warily down the 42nd Street of "smoke, coke, and switchblades" in 1985, he has constantly returned to the Big Apple, often to write on its districts and denizens for a variety of sports publications, and in his role as National Geographic International Editions editor.

CHARTING YOUR TRIP

With untold thousands of iconic sites, museums, shops, and restaurants to explore, you can take in scores of New York's offerings in an action-packed week. You will also surely absorb the city's unique vibe—as author Thomas Wolfe wrote in the early 20th century, "One belongs to New York instantly, one belongs to it as much in five minutes as in five years."

How to Visit

Like many other great cities, there's no better way to experience New York than by using your own two feet. A car in Manhattan is more of a hindrance than a help, as traffic is always heavy and on-street parking hard to find. If you do drive into town, park your car at your hotel or a public garage ($20–$50 or more per day) and use the city's taxis, subways, and buses—they're the most convenient ways to get around the city.

If you have just a week, begin on **day one** where the immigrants began: with a trip to **Ellis Island** and the **Statue of Liberty.** Excursions depart from **Battery Park** at Manhattan's southern tip. (Go early—the experience takes about five hours.) Afterward, explore historic Lower Manhattan: Battery Park and the surrounding streets were home to the first Dutch settlement and several colonial-era sites. Then walk down nearby **Wall Street** to see where America's money is made (and lost). About a half-mile north, head east onto the **Brooklyn Bridge** for exceptional views of the city. Back in Manhattan, walk north another half-mile or so into the colorful neighborhoods of **Chinatown, Little Italy,** and **SoHo,** where dozens of fine restaurant options await for dinner.

On **day two,** plan a walkabout in Midtown, the city's commercial and business hub. Start like the morning commuters at beautiful **Grand Central Terminal** (*42nd St. & Park Ave.*); then explore the **Chrysler Building's** gorgeous lobby next door and the **Public Library**—with its stately Reading Room and shady Bryant Park—just west on 42nd Street. A few blocks north from the library is the art deco masterpiece, **Rockefeller Center.** The **Museum of Modern Art (MoMA)'s** outstanding art collection stands just two blocks north, on 53rd Street. From MoMA, window-shop up **Fifth Avenue** at classic retailers like Tiffany's and Saks before cutting west across Central Park South to **Columbus Circle's** mix of great new architecture, shopping, and restaurants. Then stroll down **Broadway** to **Times Square,** which literally and figuratively lights up after dark, and take in a show. End your day at the **Empire State Building,** on 34th

▪ **The Statue of Liberty and its supporting infrastructure**

Street eight blocks south of Times Square. The 86th-floor Observation Deck is open every night until 2 a.m.

On **day three,** enjoy New York's version of the great outdoors: **Central Park.** Enter at the southeast corner, at 59th Street by the elegant **Plaza Hotel.** From here, you can easily explore all but the most northern sites of the park. Don't miss the Lake with its pretty (and rentable) boats and the paths of the wild, 37-acre (15 ha) Ramble. Then head to Fifth Avenue, on the eastern edge of the park, where at 82nd Street stands the massive **Metropolitan Museum of Art.** Snack on a hot dog from a vendor out front, then spend the rest of the day immersed in high art.

Day four takes you downtown again to New York's bohemian villages. Begin at the **Lower East Side,** an old neighborhood turned superhip. The popular **Lower East Side Tenement Museum** (*103 Orchard St., S off Delancey*) demonstrates how poor immigrants in the area lived a century ago. From here, make a long northwesterly arc of about 2 miles (3.2 km) through the trendy **East Village,** and then onto Bleecker Street for a jolt of **Greenwich Village** and 1960s folkie nostalgia and a stop at the brand-new **Whitney Museum of American Art** (*99 Gansevoort St.*). In nearby Washington Square Park, performers often do their thing near the central fountain. Wander west through the Village's street maze to the elevated **High Line Park** (*main entrance at Hudson & Gansevoort Sts.*), another bit of old New York with a hip new identity. At 20th Street, descend to street level and explore **Chelsea**'s many art galleries.

Day five can be your day to visit the tony Upper East Side. Start at **Bloomingdale's** renowned department store at 59th Street and Lexington Avenue. Then visit some of the outstanding museums on or near Fifth Avenue, a few blocks west. The **Guggenheim** (*at*

Getting Around, Part 1: Orienting Yourself

For the most part, the city's basic street grid makes it easy to navigate.

Numbered cross streets run east-west from First Street down in the East Village to 220th Street at the island's northern tip. Avenues run north-south and are numbered from First to Twelfth, increasing as you progress west. However, Lexington, Madison, and Park Avenues fall between Third and Fifth Avenues, superceding Fourth Avenue. And, although maps and street signs refer to the "Avenue of the Americas," most native New Yorkers still call it by its former name, Sixth Avenue.

Broadway meanders along the route of an old Indian trail and has little relation to the grid. And in much of Lower Manhattan, you'd do well to bring a compass: Streets angle off every which way, as they were laid out before city planners took over.

Manhattan is divided into the East and West Sides—Fifth Avenue is the central axis. If you're looking for a particular address, remember that address numbers advance out from Fifth Avenue on either side. So make sure you know what you're looking for: 300 East 23rd Street, for example, is very different from 300 *West* 23rd Street.

Rockefeller Center ice rink becomes a cosmopolitan winter wonderland in the holiday season.

89th St.) or the **Whitney** (*at 75th St.*) will appeal to fans of modern art, while the **Frick Collection** (*at 70th St.*) displays classic art treasures from throughout the centuries.

On **day six,** you can take in the fine residential areas of the **Upper West Side.** Perhaps a concert or ballet matinee is scheduled at **Lincoln Center for the Performing Arts** (*Broadway & 65th St.*)? Less than a mile north, drop into **Zabar's** market (*Broadway & 80th St.*) for gourmet deli treats. Next door, **H&H Bagels** sells some of the city's best. Farther uptown, off the northwest corner of Central Park, lies the century-old-yet-unfinished **Cathedral Church of St. John the Divine, Columbia University's** beautiful campus, and **Grant's Tomb.** End your day at the far western reaches of Manhattan at **Riverside Park,** with views over the Hudson River.

Day seven can be the day to zero in on museums that most suit your interests—the city has a cultural repository for almost every taste. Consider the **Museum of Natural History** or the **New-York Historical Society** on the Upper West Side, the **Cooper-Hewitt Smithsonian Design Museum** or the **Jewish Museum** on the Upper East Side, or the **Museum of the American Indian** downtown.

Visitor Information

New York City's Visitor Information Centers (*tel 212/484-1200, nycgo.com*) offer travel tips at several sites (see Travelwise p. 236). For a personalized introduction, contact Big Apple Greeter, (*tel 212/669–8159, bigapplegreeter .org*), a nonprofit organization that matches knowledgeable locals with visitors. Call two to three weeks in advance. Useful publications include *New York* magazine (*nymag.com*) and *Time Out New York* (*timeout.com/newyork*): Both offer listings of restaurants and entertainment. If you are lost (in any way) in New York, simply dial 311 and ask for assistance.

Getting Around, Part 2: Public Transportation

A few helpful hints about New York's extensive public transportation system:

- MetroCards are available at all subway stations and at many newsstands—the $2.75 fare is deducted each time you enter the subway or ride a bus. Subways require MetroCards; buses take either MetroCards or exact change.
- Some trains and buses are local, some express. Know where you're getting off to avoid overshooting your mark or waiting through many local stops unnecessarily.

- Between Houston and 42nd Streets, any subway you catch (except the L and S; see sidebar below) will be going north-south. If you want to get across town in that area, a bus is your only public transit option.
- Buses only stop when someone wants to get on or off: Push the yellow strip along the wall to alert the bus driver your stop is coming up.
- You'll find free subway maps at all stations and bus maps on the buses. Complete information is available at *mta.info*.

If You Have More Time

After a week in New York's central areas, head for the periphery. A wonderful day can be spent around Prospect Park in **Brooklyn,** visiting the Brooklyn Museum, the Brooklyn Botanic Garden, the historic Park Slope neighborhood, and the beautiful park itself. You can also stroll through the charming Brooklyn Heights neighborhood, where some homes are nearly 200 years old.

Or, head way north, to the very tip of Manhattan, where **The Cloisters,** the medieval art branch of the Metropolitan Museum of Art sits perched above the Hudson, nestled in Fort Tryon Park "like a jewel in velvet," in the words of novelist Teju Cole. Another northern option takes you to the **Bronx,** where the Bronx Zoo, the New York Botanical Garden, and the Italian neighborhood of Arthur Avenue all beckon. Another Bronx option? A game at Yankee Stadium to see New York's iconic baseball team.

Lastly there's the **Staten Island Ferry,** a bus on water, catering to commuters. But it's also a free ride across New York Harbor, and how can you beat that? Try to make time for it—getting out on New York's waterways is a must.

Getting Around, Part 3: Key Subway Routes

1: The 1 train takes you to sites on Broadway between 42nd Street and Manhattan's northern tip (including Times Square, Lincoln Center, Columbus Circle/Central Park, and the Cathedral Church of St. John the Divine).

R: This train is good for sights on Broadway from 42nd Street south to City Hall (including Times Square, Union Square, the Villages, and SoHo). It continues on to Wall Street and the island's historic southern tip.

C: The C is good for sites on the West Side between W. 4th and 168th Streets

(such as High Line Park, Columbus Circle/Central Park, and the Museum of Natural History). The legendary A train travels the same route, though it runs express between W. 59th and 125th Streets.

6: This is your best option for sites on the East Side, from City Hall to 125th Street (including the East Village, Grand Central, the Met, and the Guggenheim).

L: The L runs east-west along 14th Street between First and Eighth Avenues.

S: This train runs east-west on 42nd Street from Grand Central Terminal to Times Square.

HISTORY &
CULTURE

Above: NYPD's finest enjoy the city's St. Patrick's Day Parade. Opposite: The art deco Chrysler Building, the world's tallest brick building

NEW YORK TODAY

Wall Street's delirious early 2000s prosperity (before its equally delirious downturn) put the city into overdrive. Daring neo-modernist buildings rose amid the world's most famous skyline, bringing an exciting new wave of architecture to a city that has always known how to rebuild itself.

But these days the emphasis seems as much on recycling as rebuilding: Witness Times Square, where hundred-year-old theater facades front otherwise ultramodern multiplexes; or the far West Side, where a defunct elevated railway called the High Line has been transformed into one of the world's most distinctive public parks. Witness Columbus Circle, where two underused landmark structures—the Hearst Building and the Huntington Hartford Gallery—have been turned into bionic fusions of noble past and visionary future. And witness the drives by former mayor Michael Bloomberg to reduce New York's carbon footprint—in part by adding wind turbines to skyscrapers and bridges.

Neighborhoods, too, have gotten the fusion treatment: Chelsea's once gritty western perimeter turned into art gallery central; the Meatpacking District (between 15th & Gansevoort Sts.) has become a fashionista capital, where the hip and the famous come out to play at night.

A global nexus of creativity and commerce, the Big Apple is now more than ever the nation's heartbeat—this despite the fact that, at times, the place can seem like a chaotic jumble of worn infrastructure, feuding politicians, gridlocked traffic, and bags of garbage piled on sidewalks because there was no thought to build alleys when they laid out the street grid. Whatever its problems, though, New York's victories are of such magnitude, its achievements so grand, its human spectacle so astonishing, that nothing ever makes it stop—not Superstorm Sandy, not 9/11, not stultifying summer humidity, not economic havoc, not even transit strikes. For two hundred years, the city has been the nation's mighty engine, first of shipping and trade, then of industry, arts, and ideas—and always of people.

Countless millions trace their ancestry to or through New York City, and people from all corners of the world keep coming, to seek a better life or realize a personal dream. Immigrants and itinerants, dreamers and schemers, students and professionals, these and more transplant themselves "beside the golden door," propelling change and

Hailing a Taxi

To flag down one of New York's 13,437 licensed yellow cabs, station yourself along any busy avenue or street and start scanning for a rooftop light with its number illuminated. If it's out, the cab's taken. If the "off duty" light is lit, the cabbie is going home. A raised arm is usually enough to get a cab, though you may be competing with other people. If somebody's got an arm up for an oncoming cab, don't try to steal it; the unwritten rule is first come, first served. Once inside, you'll find that your cabbie's expertise regarding side streets and traffic patterns is probably a lot better than his English. By the way, those annoying backseat TVs do have an off switch.

■ **A gift from France in 1886, Lady Liberty still holds her torch aloft over New York Harbor.**

■ **Times Square by night is a dazzling kaleidoscope of commerce and American culture.**

creativity, making the city endlessly fascinating. Whether you are Irish, Italian, Chinese, Russian, Jamaican, Greek, Arab, or Iroquois, you can find a neighborhood waiting for you, or you can start your own. The essence of New York is its ever changing population base, but there is tremendous stability within all that change. People come here with their traditions intact. They find niches in the workplace, settle, and assimilate, but they don't forget or discard their heritage. Cultural festivals and parades are frequent, some large and loud, others intimate. The Puerto Rican Day Parade and St. Patrick's Day Parade sweep along Manhattan's broad avenues, while old-world Italian processions, with saints carried aloft, wind through narrow Brooklyn streets.

It's that kind of coexistence—of old traditions and new—that gives New York its simultaneous sense of timelessness and fresh newness. Decades coexist, with old-timers hanging on in the haunts they opened in the 1940s, '50s, or '60s, even as newcomers arrive to make their own New York on top of the old, like strata in a river canyon. Young and old, these kindred spirits have had their hearts tuned to the city's vibe and know bone deep that New York really is what the marketers and admen say: the capital of the world. It is without question the city that never sleeps, a place where

at any time of day or night it is possible to find food, entertainment, drugstores, transportation, and architectural spectacle all around. Perhaps John Updike best summed up how New Yorkers feel about New York: They think that people who don't live there have to be, in some way, kidding

Maybe this is what separates a New Yorker from those who find the city is not for them: To survive in New York City, one must be aware of one's surroundings, ready to adapt, eager to excel, willing to be constantly tested in every way, and—most importantly—in the know, about anything and everything. If New Yorkers are anything, they are "up to speed." In New York you can have a fascinating conversation with anyone you meet, from the street panhandler trying to sell you a poem to the hot dog vendor, waiter, doorman, cabbie, shop owner, or even the person crammed in next to you on the subway. Not only are they all in the know, but they know they are in the know, and they are strongly opinionated about what they know.

New York, New York

Who might be New York's power players today? Bill de Blasio, Senator Charles Schumer, developers Jerry Speyer and Bruce Ratner, Rupert Murdoch, and any number of on-the-ropes financial titans—we can make a very long list. But the power players are also the subway conductor on your trip uptown to the zoo, the park ranger at Ellis Island who brings history to life, and the baker who makes those bagels that you seek out. Firemen, policemen, and emergency workers who put themselves in harm's way are New York power players as well.

Power players can be musicians, writers, actors, and artists, forging inspiring works—the films of Woody Allen and Martin Scorsese, the books of Paul Auster and Richard Price, the journalism of Tom Friedman and Maureen Dowd, Tina Fey and friends in *30 Rock,* or the current comedic crew of *Saturday Night Live:* All show truths about New York, from the romantic to the hard-nosed.

The point is that each and every resident has been, and is, vital to the New York mix, part of its incredible, unfolding, and ever shifting destiny. More than eight million people live in New York. It takes all of them to light up the metropolis to a voltage that casts its light upon the rest of the world. The energy of New Yorkers crammed together produces an incandescent phenomenon that makes the city such a bright beacon for travelers.

21st-Century NY: Taller, Greener, Healthier

New York City is always changing, forever morphing toward the future. Since 2001, when Michael Bloomberg became mayor, to the end of his administration in 2013, certain shifts were noteworthy: Eight of the city's 20 tallest buildings were built, including One World Trade Center (see p. 63) and the New York Times Building (see p. 157). Some 757,386 trees were planted in the city and approximately 800 acres (324 ha) of parkland added. Also, smoking among adults dropped by roughly 33 percent, following the 2003 ban on smoking in restaurants and bars.

Eating Out in New York

No city in the country comes close to being New York's culinary equal. Nowhere can you find so many different things to eat and places to eat them. You can buy a hot pretzel or a hot dog from a street vendor, or sit down for a six-course meal created by one of the world's greatest chefs. You can sit at a sushi bar and dine on raw fish, or get a slice at any of 48 different, unrelated pizzerias named "Ray's." New York has seafood and soul food—and Chinese, Japanese, Korean, Thai, Middle Eastern, Middle Western, South American, and South Indian restaurants galore.

New York's taste in food has been shaped by its immigrant population. Here, plain down-home American cooking is considered exotic, and the city's few genuine diners are chic. Many foods and drinks familiar to the rest of the country originated here. The recipe for the round doughy bagel, which is boiled, then baked, was a closely held secret in the Jewish community. In the 1960s the rest of the country discovered bagels, but somehow they still taste better in New York.

Vichyssoise, another all-American favorite with a French name, was invented at the now-extinct Ritz-Carlton Hotel. The egg cream is a blending of seltzer, chocolate syrup, and milk (but no eggs or cream) known only in New York. On the other hand, the Reuben sandwich—a daunting combination of corned beef, swiss cheese, and sauerkraut (on New York rye, of course)—has a national following.

Delmonico's restaurant (see Travelwise p. 239) claims to have invented Lobster Newburg and Baked Alaska, and it gave its name to the Delmonico steak. It was America's first fine Parisian restaurant when it opened in 1837. The first restaurant

EXPERIENCE: Exploring Riverside Park South

Riverside Park South features a meandering boardwalk along the Hudson River as well as railroad-themed spots that hark back to the area's railroad history. The park adjoins Riverside Park to the north at 72nd Street and runs south to 57th Street, where it connects with Hudson River Park, another recreational greenway. To reach Riverside Park South, enter Riverside Park near the Eleanor Roosevelt monument at 72nd Street and Riverside Drive. Through the underpass tunnel, a sloping roadway or stairs leads you down to the river. Head south past the baseball and soccer fields to recreational **Pier I**, a 715-foot (218 m) pier. Public programs such as outdoor films and music concerts are held during summer months (*check the current calendar of events: tel 212/870–3070, nyc.gov/parks/soh or riversideparknyc.org*). An open-air café

(*open seasonally*) is located across from the pier. Stroll farther south to Riverside Park South. Amid tall wild grasses, rosebushes, and weeping willows, many seating areas are available for a picnic or a quiet read. A restored locomotive, **"No. 25"** (built in 1946), can be found and climbed upon at 62nd Street. At dusk, visitors can watch No. 25's headlamp light up, while the lights of the George Washington Bridge sparkle to the north.

For a unique experience, view the park and the Manhattan skyline from a kayak. Between May and October, the **Downtown Boathouse** (*downtownboathouse.org*) offers free kayaking programs on the Hudson River. You will find helpful volunteers and kayaks at three locations (*open weekends & holidays*): 72nd Street; Pier 96 (*at 56th St.*); and Pier 40 (*at Houston St.*).

to print its menu in French and to allow women in the dining room, it is still operating at the downtown location it has occupied since 1891.

No culinary tour of New York would be complete without a meal in a delicatessen and a coffee shop. Here the food is hearty, the service brusque, and the amenities few. The delicatessen came with immigrants from Germany and central Europe. Some are strictly kosher, and their specialties—pastrami, whitefish, matzo-ball soup—might be exotic to some palates, but their huge menus have something for every taste. Try Katz's Delicatessen, on the Lower East Side, Ben's Kosher Delicatessen on 38th Street, or Zabar's on the Upper West Side. Coffee shops, most of them

■ Zabar's market and delicatessen on the Upper West Side serves an array of irresistible comestibles.

run by Greeks, mix deli fare (bagels, lox, pastrami) with diner fare (omelets, burgers, meatloaf), and top it off with bottomless cups of coffee.

Each city neighborhood serves up delectable foods, from Brazilian and Cuban to Haitian and Vietnamese. Street festivals and markets offer chances to sample or just absorb the stimulating medley of sights and smells. In the "hot" neighborhoods, trendy restaurants open and close with lightning speed, though the many operated by Drew Nieporent in Tribeca, including Nobu, seem longer lived. No matter how extravagant you want to be, New York's restaurants can probably top your expectations. At the 26-seat Masa (*10 Columbus Circle*), for instance, the multi-course, seasonal prix fixe menu, prepared just for you, goes for a cool $450–$600 per person. ■

HISTORY OF NEW YORK

They call Rome the "Eternal City," but ask any New Yorker to think about this city in terms of time and you'll discover something: To its residents, New York has always been and will always be. Centuries of history are layered upon each other, as 21st-century advertisements in 20th-century frames hang on 19th-century buildings on streets first laid out in the 1700s.

To the average New Yorker, dating the city is both a nostalgic imperative and a functional nonstarter. Sure, everybody knows how long his favorite old bar has been in business, but when the city tried to celebrate its official centennial in 1988—a hundred years since it was incorporated within its present

■ A 1664 map of New Amsterdam shows the area that is today Lower Manhattan.

t' Fort nieuw Amsterdam op de Manhatans

boundaries—eight million New Yorkers responded with a giant, collective yawn. The consolidation added the boroughs of Brooklyn, the Bronx, Staten Island, and Queens to Manhattan, but how could that have not happened anyway? New York is, after all, the place everyone wants to be.

Besides, there are so many other dates more worthy of note. For example: 1609, when English explorer Henry Hudson passed Manhattan Island on his way up the river that now bears his name; 1625, when the first permanent settlement was established on Manhattan; 1639 (for Bronx residents), when a Dane, Jonas Bronck, settled just north of Manhattan. Anglophiles might celebrate 1674, the year the English took control of the city away from the Dutch, but patriots surely prefer November 25, 1783, when the British left New York City for good after the Revolutionary War.

> **Centuries of history are layered upon each other, as 21st-century advertisements in 20th-century frames hang on 19th-century buildings on streets first laid out in the 1700s.**

Of course, Manhattan and the surrounding region was first settled by Paleo-Indians about 11,500 years ago. Their descendants were living in the region when Giovanni da Verrazano became the first European to sail into New York Harbor, in 1524 (a year the city's many Italians honor, although da Verrazano was sailing for France). Other groups relate to other dates. Africans came to New Amsterdam as slaves in 1626, the year Peter Minuit purchased the island of Manhattan from the Indians. There would not be a serious attempt to free them until 1799, when the state legislature passed the Gradual Emancipation Act. Jews might well honor the year 1654, when 23 Sephardic refugees from Brazil arrived at the Dutch settlement and formed Shearith Israel—the first Jewish congregation in North America.

Dutch New Amsterdam

The first Europeans to spend any time on Manhattan Island were Adriaen Block, a Dutch navigator, and his crew, who passed the winter of 1613–1614 there after their ship burned offshore. Over the winter, Block built another ship before setting sail for home. On the way out, Block sailed through the tricky strait in the East River that he named Hellegat (Hell's Gate), into the body of water he called Long Island Sound, and on to Block Island, which he named for himself.

The same year, 1614, the colony called New Netherland was formed, with most of its

■ **Dwarfed by office buildings, Fraunces Tavern, now a museum and restaurant, evokes colonial days.**

activity centered up the Hudson River, near Albany. In 1625, some Dutch families from elsewhere in the colony were ordered to Manhattan Island, and the next year their leader, Peter Minuit, purchased it from the Indians with trinkets, blankets, cloth, and metal goods said to be worth about $24. And though Minuit is remembered as one of history's great bargainers, some might say that $24 would not have been a bad price for an island that was—except for the southern tip where the settlers were eking out a miserable existence—mostly wilderness.

Trade in beaver furs—to be made into felt hats back in Holland—was the colony's sole purpose. The number of pelts obtained from the Indians went from 7,520 in 1629 to almost 30,000 thirty years later. In 1628, when the first Dutch Reformed minister, Jonas Michaëlius, arrived, he was appalled by the ungodliness of the city's 270 residents, but the church he founded continues today as the Marble Collegiate Church (*29th St. at 5th Ave.*).

As the colony grew, its devotion to business and easygoing ways attracted such religious dissenters as Anne Hutchinson. Driven from Puritan New England, she came to New York in 1642, only to be killed by Indians the next year. In 1644 the 11 slaves who had come with the first settlers were declared to be "half free." That is, they were free and could own land, but their children remained in bondage.

English Quakers, who arrived in New Netherland in 1657, were made less welcome by Governor Peter Stuyvesant. When Stuyvesant ordered Quaker John Bowne arrested in 1662, Bowne appealed to the Dutch West India Company, whose directors ordered Stuyvesant to stop. Religious persecution, they sensibly believed, was bad for business. In other ways, Stuyvesant was an effective administrator: He encouraged trade, established a municipal government, and made and kept peace with the Indians. When threatened by the English presence, he built a wall stretching 2,340 feet (713 m), from the East River to the Hudson River, to protect New Amsterdam from invasion from the north. It's from this wall that the name of today's Wall Street derives.

English New York

When the English came, however, they came from the sea. On August 26, 1664, Col. Richard Nicolls, acting on behalf of the king's brother, James, the Duke of York, landed 450 soldiers in Brooklyn and placed the rest of his force aboard ships around Manhattan. Stuyvesant, with a handful of soldiers, made a brave show of resisting, but leading citizens persuaded him to surrender. Nicolls became the first English governor, naming the town after his patron, but the settlement was to change hands once more. Warring with the French and the English in 1673, the Dutch took New York back, then sued for peace the following year and returned it to England.

Under the English, New York grew from a mere trading port into a city, though not initially a prosperous one. British restrictions and ill-advised actions, such as paring away New Jersey as a separate colony, hindered commerce and growth. In 1683, under the new English governor, Thomas Dongan, a provincial assembly drew up a Charter of Liberties and Privileges, which included the freedom of religion and a right of self-government. By the time it reached England for approval, however, James, who as the Duke of York had charged Dongan with loosening the reins on New York, had become

Early Greenwich Village

Long before settlement, Canarsee Indians used the marshy area of what would become Greenwich Village for hunting and fishing. When the Dutch arrived, they grew tobacco along Minetta Brook, and the area became the best tobacco plantation in the colony. In 1644 slaves who had been given partial freedom by the West India Company settled near Minetta Lane, later part of the Underground Railroad. When the English took over, the section became Greenwich, meaning Green Village. The West Village attracted well-to-do New Yorkers fleeing yellow fever and cholera epidemics in the 1820s. Among the 19th-century residents was Henry James, who used his grandmother's house at 18 Washington Square North (now demolished) as the setting for his novel *Washington Square* (1881). The immigrants, intellectuals, writers, and struggling artists who gave Greenwich Village its bohemian reputation began to arrive at the end of the 19th century.

King James II. From his kingly perspective, the Charter of Liberties gave the colonists entirely too much liberty—so he nullified it.

The Glorious Revolution of 1688, which deposed the Roman Catholic King James, caused confusion about who was running New York. A German-born merchant and militia officer, Jacob Leisler, seized Fort George (Fort Amsterdam's English name) in May 1689 and proceeded to rule for most of the next two years. Leisler, an ardent member of the Dutch Reformed Church, ordered the arrest of "papists," dissolved the provincial assembly, and in 1690 attempted an unsuccessful invasion of Canada. When the new monarchs, William and Mary, sent a governor, Leisler was arrested for treason and hanged on May 16, 1691.

EXPERIENCE: Having a Drink at One of New York's 19th-century Taverns

There's nothing like an old bar, and New York has many classics. On the West Side, at 11th Avenue and 46th Street, the **Landmark Tavern** (*tel 212/247-2562, thelandmarktavern.org*) has been in business since 1868 and retains its old elegance. On 18th Street, the **Old Town Bar & Restaurant** (*45 East 18th St., bet. Broadway & Park Ave., tel 212/529-6732, oldtownbar.com*) opened in 1892 and boasts a fine mahogany bar. Two blocks east, **Pete's Tavern** (*129 East 18th Street, tel 212/473-7676, petestavern .com*) was established in 1864 and is (allegedly) where O. Henry wrote "The Gift of the Magi." In the East Village, **McSorley's Old Ale House** (*15 E. 7th St., near 3rd Ave., tel 212/474-9148, mcsorleysnewyork.com*) opened in 1854. In the West Village, the **White Horse Tavern** (*tel 212/989-3956*) has been at the corner of Hudson and 11th Streets since 1880, attracting writers like Dylan Thomas and Jack Kerouac. Farther downtown, the **Ear Inn** (*326 Spring St., near Greenwich St., tel 212/226-9060, earinn .com*) occupies a two-story federalist-style building dating from 1817.

In 1734, another test of colonists' rights occurred when John Peter Zenger, publisher of the *New-York Weekly Journal,* was arrested and jailed for libeling the British governor, William Cosby, with merciless parodies and diatribes. At his trial, Zenger's lawyer, Scottish-born Andrew Hamilton, persuaded the jury that Zenger's articles were not libelous because they were true. It was a milestone case that established the principle of a free press in America. Hamilton told the jury: "The question before the court ... is not of small or private concern. It is not the cause of a poor printer, nor of New York alone, which you are trying. No! It may in its consequences affect every freeman that lives under British government on the main of America! It is the best cause. It is the cause of liberty!"

The cause of liberty continued to be an undercurrent of this period, even infusing controversy into seemingly nonpartisan events like the founding of King's College (today's Columbia University) in 1754. After Britain emerged victorious from the French and Indian Wars, New Yorkers were rankled by having to support English troops headquartered in the city. To raise revenue for this purpose, the English Parliament passed the Sugar Act of 1764, which imposed strictly enforced duties on New York's molasses trade, and the Stamp Act of 1765, which required tax stamps for commercial transactions. In resistance, on October 7, 1765, New York convened a Stamp Act Congress in the city and sent a message to Parliament denying its right to tax the Colonies without their consent.

Mobs protesting the Stamp Act, led by the violence-inclined Sons of Liberty, attacked the homes and property of British officials. When the Sons erected a liberty pole in the Fields (now City Hall Park), the redcoats cut it down, starting a sequence of semi-comic events that kept both sides busy putting up and cutting down these symbols of dissent. Tension eased early in 1766, when Parliament repealed the Stamp Act and lowered duties on sugar and molasses. Suddenly King George III was a hero, and a statue lionizing the monarch as a Roman emperor was erected in Bowling Green.

The goodwill was short-lived. In 1767 Parliament's Townshend taxes on a variety of goods ignited more protests. Early in 1770, following a liberty pole incident, citizens and soldiers fought with bayonets, fists, and brickbats on a rise near John Street called Golden Hill, a clash that has been called by some the first blood of the Revolution. Then came the duties on tea, which led to the famous Boston Tea Party in December 1773 and the less well-remembered New York Tea Party on April 22, 1774. Dressed like Indians, as their Boston counterparts had been before them, the Sons of Liberty dumped 18 crates of tea into New York Harbor as crowds cheered.

In the two years that followed, there were lulls amid the tension as New Yorkers sorted out their loyalties in preparation for war. City merchants, believing prosperity depended on peace and stability, were reluctant to carry the conflict further. And New Yorkers were aware that their city would be a strategic prize and battleground in a war with Britain. George Washington, commander of the Continental Army, understood this, too, writing that British control of New York would "stop the intercourse between the northern and southern Colonies, upon which depends the Safety of America."

Revolution

With war on the way, Washington moved to reinforce the city. When the Declaration of Independence reached New York on July 9, 1776, Washington had it read to his men. Once dismissed, they tore down the statue of George III in Bowling Green and melted it down to make bullets. By then, the city was practically under siege. Nearly 500 British ships carrying 32,000 troops, commanded by Gen. William Howe, had arrived off New York and started disembarking soldiers on Staten Island.

Alexander Hamilton (1755–1804), influential shaper of an emerging New York, is buried in Trinity Churchyard, at Wall Street and Broadway.

On August 27, five days after Howe began moving men across the narrows to Brooklyn, the British met the Americans defending Brooklyn Heights and, in the Battle of Long Island, drove them back to their entrenchment, taking some 1,000 prisoners in the process. Fortunately for the Americans, Howe hesitated. During the night of August 29–30, under cover of dense fog, Washington ferried his entire force across the East River to Manhattan. Howe bided his time, waiting for an unsuccessful peace conference with the Americans on Staten Island to take place, before crossing to Manhattan at Kip's Bay (near today's 34th Street) on September 15. When the green and outnumbered American troops broke ranks and fled, Washington, in a rage, tried to rally them and had to be pulled out of the line of enemy fire by an aide.

Although the Americans were in flight and divided between the northern and southern ends of the island, Howe did not press his advantage. Legend has it that Mrs. Robert Murray, a patriotic woman residing near present-day 34th Street and Park Avenue, intentionally delayed him with an invitation to tea. More likely, the visit took place while Howe was waiting for his forces to land on Manhattan. The delay allowed the Americans in the south to sneak up the west side to rejoin Washington. The next day they drove back the British at about 125th Street in a two-hour battle that boosted morale, though it was clear the Americans could not hold the city. On October 16, Washington withdrew from Manhattan, leaving nearly 3,000 men to defend Fort Washington, which fell a month later.

The British occupied New York City for the rest of the war, from 1776 to 1783; during this time two serious fires destroyed some 600 buildings. Many Loyalists left at the outbreak of war, and during the frenzied summer of 1783 some 60,000 more left the country through New York. The city became the holding pen for American prisoners of war, with many kept in appalling conditions on prison ships in the harbor, where an estimated 11,000 prisoners died—far exceeding the 6,824 Americans killed in battle throughout the country.

The tide turned in favor of the Americans after Lord Cornwallis surrendered at Yorktown, Virginia, in 1781. Still, New York City would not be liberated until after the Treaty of Paris, signed on September 3, 1783, ended the hostilities and recognized American independence. The British occupation ended with an orderly withdrawal on

■ Mulberry Street circa 1900, the main artery of Little Italy's street trade

November 25, as Washington led his troops into the city. On the evening of December 4, Washington took leave of his officers in an emotional parting at Fraunces Tavern (see p. 55). He returned to be sworn in as the nation's first president in 1789. By that time, New York City was the capital of both New York State and the United States of America.

Recovery & Recognition

Although New York would not be a capital city for long—the federal government moved to Philadelphia in 1790, and the state to Albany in 1797—the city charged with characteristic energy into the 19th century. In a mere 30 years—from 1790, the year of the first federal census, to 1820—the city's population grew from 33,000 to 123,706, making it the largest city in the nation. This post-revolutionary period is the first from which many buildings survive. Castle Clinton (see p. 53) was built in preparation for the war with Great Britain in 1812. Commerce from the China and California trades caused the rise of the South Street Seaport (see pp. 64–65). City Hall was completed in 1812. Federal Hall, built on the site where Washington was inaugurated, dates from 1842. Trinity Church, its steeple now dwarfed by sky-scrapers, was completed in 1846.

> New York became the country's leading port after 1825, when the opening of the Erie Canal brought a vast wealth of farm products from the Midwest to New York's docks for export.

This period also saw the rise of such institutions as the New York Stock Exchange, which began after the American Revolution but started trading in earnest after the War of 1812. As early as 1784, Alexander Hamilton helped found the Bank of New York, today one of the country's largest financial institutions; later, as the country's first Secretary of the Treasury, Hamilton pursued policies that aided the growth of business in the city. (He died in the nation's most famous duel—with Aaron Burr on July 11, 1804.) New York became the country's leading port after 1825, when the opening of the Erie Canal brought a vast wealth of farm products from the Midwest to New York's docks for export.

Commissioners' Plan of 1811

In 1811 the city took steps to order its future growth by imposing a strict grid on the largely undeveloped region between 14th and 155th Streets. For a city that had grown haphazardly for almost three centuries, the Commissioners' Plan of 1811, as the grid was called, was remarkably forward looking.

Running north and south were 12 numbered, widely spaced (usually 920 feet/280 m) avenues. The 155 cross streets stretching from the East River to the Hudson River were closer together—200 feet (61 m). This purposeful configuration created long, rectan-gular blocks ideally suited, the planners believed, for "straight-sided and right-angled houses [that] are the most cheap to build, and the most convenient to live in."

Broadway, then called Bloomingdale Road, was the only thoroughfare allowed to cut across the grid. In doing so it created Manhattan's unusual triangular "squares"—Times Square, Herald Square, and the like. At the time, no one anticipated how fast the city would grow. Even the commissioners thought it would take time—"possibly centuries"—for the city to reach 155th Street.

The Commissioners' Plan, with its long, straight avenues and cross streets, did accomplish its stated purposes of providing for the "free and abundant circulation of air" and controlling growth. Otherwise, it has been criticized for its monotony, for not providing enough parks, for leveling much of the natural topography of Manhattan, and for narrow cross streets, which became a problem with the arrival of the automobile.

19th-century Setbacks: Epidemics & Wars

There were setbacks along the way to preeminence. The yellow fever epidemic of 1798 took more than 2,000 lives. The Great Fire of 1835 destroyed nearly 700 buildings in the heart of the city. The embargoes and blockades of the War of 1812 were hard on New York. When the British fleet threatened to invade in 1814, the city mobilized to strengthen its defenses and the mayor, DeWitt Clinton, announced he would prefer to "die in a ditch than tamely and cowardly surrender this delightful city." After the war, from which the city escaped unscathed, there were severe losses in the financial panics of 1837 and 1857.

New Yorkers were less militant than other northerners during the Civil War, particularly merchants who had profited doing business with the Southern states. Although New Yorkers had responded to the initial call for troops, by the summer of 1863, when President Lincoln instituted the first draft, that fervor had dimmed. Immigrant Irish laborers were outraged by the draft, particularly the provision that allowed a man to buy an exemption for $300, a sum way beyond their means. In general, they felt that the Civil War was not their war.

> **Of an estimated 23 million Europeans who came to America between 1880 and 1919, 17 million were processed through New York. Most settled in the city.**

July 11, the first day of the draft lottery, was quiet. But on July 13, when a second lottery was scheduled, the city exploded. A rampaging mob attacked police officers, wrecked draft offices, and ransacked the homes and offices of prominent Republicans and abolitionists. Then the violence turned against blacks: The Colored Orphan Asylum on Fifth Avenue at West 43rd Street was burned, and black men were brutally killed along Bleecker Street, then a black neighborhood. It took the combined efforts of police, politicians, Archbishop John Hughes, and five regiments of the Union Army to restore order. Over three days of rioting, at least 105 people were killed and immense amounts of property destroyed in what was the most violent urban riot ever to occur in the country.

After the Civil War

The city boomed in the post-Civil War era, in spite of a city government increasingly controlled by "Boss" Tweed and his Tammany Hall henchmen, which took municipal corruption and inefficiency to dazzling new heights. The addition of such enduring institutions as the American Museum of Natural History (1869), the Metropolitan Museum of Art (1870), and, in 1891, Carnegie Hall and the New York Botanical Garden gave the city the cultural dominance it had longed for. The dedication of the Statue of Liberty in 1886 came amid one of the greatest migrations in history. Of an estimated 23 million Europeans who came to America between 1880 and 1919, 17 million were processed through New York. Most settled in the city.

The city would never look the same after its first skyscraper, the Tower Building, was erected on lower Broadway between 1888 and 1889. This ushered in one of the most remarkable building booms in history, which lasted until the onset of the Great Depression of the 1930s. Characteristically—in a city that has often torn down as easily as it builds—the Tower Building did not last past 1913. But many steel-framed buildings from that era still stand: the triangular Flatiron Building; the 1904 New York Times Building, which marked the beginnings of Times Square; the grandiose Woolworth Building; and two art deco masterpieces, the Chrysler Building and the Empire State Building, each a symbol of the city.

Like all great cities, New York is subject to cycles, the ebb and flow of time and change. New Yorkers cannot count on continuity; the city changes even as words about it are written or read. No one could have predicted that one September morning in 2001 hijacked planes would crash into the twin towers of the World Trade Center. The city and nation reeled. But within a year, New York was back on its feet, honoring the tragedy while moving into the future.

Today, despite the 2008 Wall Street crash and the subsequent Occupy protests, the city's sparkle is as intense as ever. Cherished public spaces like the New York Public Library and Grand Central Terminal are buttressed for the future after huge restorations. The Museum of Modern Art continues to expand, while the Whitney is opening in a new downtown location. Madison

■ Spider-Man flies high above Macy's annual Thanksgiving Day Parade.

Square Garden has recently been renovated. And the project that started it all—the rejuvenation of Times Square in the 1990s, which transformed the legendarily grimy area into a family showplace—is now far enough in the past that only old-timers remember when "smoke, coke, switchblades" was 42nd Street's commercial mantra.

In Times Square, as throughout the city and its history, economics and commerce have been the driving forces for change. Those cities that endure, like New York, do so through imagination, courage, and readiness to adapt, without sacrificing their essential character. In the words of essayist E. B. White, written in 1949: "New York is nothing like Paris; it is nothing like London; and it is not Spokane multiplied by sixty, or Detroit by four."

New York is, and always will be, outstandingly New York. ■

THE ARTS

New York can be considered the art center of the world. Why? Is it the artists who live here? Or the city's lively galleries and museums? Is it because the money, patrons, and collectors are here? Or critics and commentators? Is it because New York itself is such a good subject for art? Perhaps it's all of these factors that have contributed to New York's preeminence in the arts.

Art

Always wild, diverse, and unpredictable, New York's tangible energy and spirit have made the city a magnet for artists and craftsmen for more than four centuries. In colonial times, portraiture occupied such successful New York artists as Gerardus Duyckinck (1695–1746). New York-born Abraham Delanoy (1742–1795) studied portraiture with Benjamin West in London, and, on returning to the city, painted members of the Livingston, Beekman, and Stuyvesant families. In the early republic, Robert Fulton and Samuel F. B. Morse were both accomplished painters before they turned to other pursuits—steamboats and the telegraph—that made them famous. John Vanderlyn (1775–1852) returned from Paris and created a panoramic painting of Versailles, which he displayed in a rotunda he had erected in City Hall Park; it now hangs in the Metropolitan Museum of Art.

> **Always wild, diverse, and unpredictable, New York's tangible energy and spirit have made the city a magnet for artists and craftsmen for more than four centuries.**

Painters of the Hudson River school, led by Thomas Cole and Asher B. Durand, believed they could capture the country's divine essence in glorious landscapes. Two of them, John Frederick Kensett and Thomas Worthington Whittredge, were among the founders of the Metropolitan Museum of Art in 1870, a time when no work by an American artist was considered museum-worthy.

Throughout the 19th century, New York artists banded together—and contentiously disbanded. In 1825 Morse and other younger artists rebelled against the conservative American Academy of Fine Arts and its president, historical painter John Trumbull, and founded the National Academy of Design. When the National Academy became stodgy, younger artists such as John La Farge and Albert Pinkham Ryder founded the American Society of Artists in 1877. This organization helped establish the Art Students League, the distinguished art school where Robert Henri, William Merritt Chase, and Thomas Hart Benton taught and had as pupils George Bellows, Rockwell Kent, Edward Hopper, and many other notables. The school still operates from its 1892 building (*215 West 57th St.*).

A group of New York-based impressionists known as The Ten also broke away from the National Academy of Design and set up their own gallery in 1898. Early in the 20th century, a different group, called The Eight, declared independence, and in 1908 put on a famous exhibit at the Macbeth Gallery: The paintings of William Glackens,

■ Frank Lloyd Wright's spiraling interior of the Solomon R. Guggenheim Museum

■ Lincoln Center's fully renovated Alice Tully Hall

George Luks, Everett Shinn, and John Sloan included realistic scenes of New York. The Macbeth Gallery show spawned the Exhibition of Independent Artists in 1910 and, in 1913, the Armory Show (see p. 83), which exhibited the work of younger New York artists such as Stuart Davis, Marsden Hartley, John Marin, Joseph Stella (known for his evocations of Coney Island and the Brooklyn Bridge), and Edward Hopper, whose vision of New York is lonely, alienated, and melancholy.

Photographer Alfred Stieglitz was another influential figure of the era. In his gallery at 291 Fifth Avenue, he exhibited John Marin, Max Weber, and others, and during the 1920s and '30s he promoted the work of Arthur Dove, Charles Demuth, and Georgia O'Keeffe, whom he married in 1924. To gain attention for their work, other New York painters formed the American Abstract Artists in 1936. Its members—among them Mark Rothko, Willem de Kooning, Robert Motherwell, and Jackson Pollock—went on to experiment with new forms and techniques that radically changed the direction of world art, and their style became known as the New York School, action painting, or abstract expression- ism. Starting in the mid-1960s, abstract art veered in new, realistic directions with Robert Rauschenberg and Jasper Johns. This led into pop art and the works of Roy Lichtenstein, Andy Warhol, and James Rosenquist, with their vivid use of advertising and popular images. Most of these artists used New York as a subject, but as a group, the action painters expressed the city best, and none better than Jackson Pollock. His wild canvases—with paint poured, flung, and dripped directly on canvas to pull beauty out of chaos—could serve as a painterly metaphor for New York City as a whole.

Classical Music

Talent from abroad has always bolstered the New York music scene. In 1833 Lorenzo Da Ponte, librettist for Mozart's *Don Giovanni* and a New Yorker since 1805, founded the Italian Opera House, one in a succession of halls that followed the city as it moved uptown. In 1850, P. T. Barnum brought the Swedish soprano Jenny Lind to New York to perform at Castle Garden (see p. 53). Antonín Dvořák was music director of the National Conservatory of Music on East 17th Street from 1892 to 1895. Tchaikovsky conducted at the opening of Carnegie Hall in 1891. Kurt Masur was director of a symphony orchestra in Leipzig before serving as music director of the New York Philharmonic (1991–2002).

Wealthy New Yorkers have patronized the musical arts, sometimes as a path to social status. In 1825, John Jacob Astor, a music shop owner before he became one of the richest men in America, arranged the production of Rossini's *Il Barbiere di Siviglia,* the first full-length Italian opera performed in the city. The original 3,700-seat Metropolitan Opera House at Broadway and 39th Street was founded in 1883 by wealthy New Yorkers who were denied boxes at the Academy of Music (built in 1854) on 14th Street. In 1891, Carnegie Hall on West 57th Street opened. Built by Andrew Carnegie, it became home to one of the world's greatest orchestras, the New York Philharmonic, founded in 1842. Although other halls were built, the Metropolitan and Carnegie Hall reigned supreme until 1961, when the Lincoln Center for the Performing Arts (see pp. 176–178) opened on the Upper West Side. Robert Moses, the city's master planner, had chosen the site in the 1950s as part of a slum-clearance program.

In the mid-19th century, diarist George Templeton Strong noted that he could attend a concert in New York most nights of the year. Had he lived today, it would

(continued on p. 36)

Discounts & Money-Saving Passes

It's possible to offset the high cost of culture in New York City by taking advantage of the many discount programs and free performances offered. Performance venues such as Carnegie Hall often offer reduced rates to children, students, and senior citizens, while some museums offer specific days or evenings of free admission (free Friday evenings at MoMA between 4 p.m. and 8 p.m.; and free Saturdays at the Jewish Museum, for example). Also note that if a museum lists a "suggested donation" for its entrance fee, you could actually pay a lesser amount than the one posted.

For reduced Broadway show tickets, try the **TKTS** booth at Times Square or South Street Seaport, websites such as *broadwaybox.com* and *nytix.com,* or popular mobile app *TodayTix.* Most Broadway shows sell discounted standing-room-only tickets right before a show, too, and some have daily lotteries for discounted front-row seats; check with individual theaters. If you plan on visiting multiple attractions (the Top of the Rock Observation Deck, Statue of Liberty, and Guggenheim Museum, to name a few), try a **City Pass** (*tel 888/330–5008*) or an **Explorer Pass** (*tel 866/629–4335*). If you want to get a good overview of the city, you can buy a Sightseeing Pass (*www.sightseeingpass.com/new-york*). Many tour companies offer organized and themed tours, as well as behind-the-scenes tours of a variety of entertainment venues.

THEATER

"The Broadway theater is dead!" "Long live the Broadway theater!" Variations of these two cries have been heard, together and separately, ever since there has been theater in New York City. And yet the Broadway theater persists, even thrives, much changed over the years but still alive and kicking nonetheless. Of all the institutions identified with New York, the theater is perhaps the most prominent.

■ A scene from Rodgers & Hammerstein's *South Pacific* at the Vivian Beaumont Theater

"To see a show" is the main reason many people come to the city. And to act, sing, or dance in the theater, or to write for it, is still a dream that brings many young people to New York.

The theater has always been a fragile institution, vulnerable to all sorts of pressures, such as the Great Depression, World War II, and the Wall Street crash of 2008. Motion pictures, radio and television, the spread of regional theater, and the rise of home video, DVDs, and the Internet have all caused

doomsayers to predict the New York theater's demise. Financially, the theater always seems to be on shaky footing. Today the cost of staging a production runs far into the millions, and as a result a single ticket can cost more than $100.

The dearth of serious or innovative new plays on Broadway is another recurring complaint, but the fact is that theaters elsewhere fill the gap. Ever since 1952, when Tennessee Williams's *Summer and Smoke* opened at the Circle in the Square Theatre in Greenwich

Village, the alternative theater known as Off Broadway has often been a better fit than Broadway for serious works. Circle in the Square dates to 1951, when it was founded as

a nonprofit by producer/director Theodore Mann and director Jose Quintero. Jason Robards, George C. Scott, and Geraldine Page all began their careers there. In 1971 the theater moved to 1633 Broadway between 49th & 50th Streets. As Off Broadway theater went mainstream, another phenomenon, Off-off Broadway, burgeoned in the 1960s as a testing ground for experimental theater. Playwright Sam Shepard is one of several who first had works performed at the Caffe Cino, a coffeehouse on Cornelia Street, which kick-started the Off-off Broadway phenomenon.

Theater has been a cultural force in New York City since the mid 18th century; the first known professional production was *Richard III*, staged in 1750 by an English company at a Nassau Street theater. The versatile William Dunlap—manager, producer, playwright—was the city's leading impresario in the beginning of the 19th century. He ran the dominant Park Theater on Park Row, importing popular actors from England. From Lower Manhattan, the city's theater district moved to lower Broadway and then, in the 1870s, to Union Square. There vaudeville got its start at Tony Pastor's New 14th Street Theater, and grand opera was performed at the Academy of Music. By 1900, the final shift to Longacre

Square, as Times Square was originally called, had taken place.

The legitimate theater thrived in the 1920s. Works by Eugene O'Neill and other American dramatists—Maxwell Anderson and Robert E. Sherwood, among them—were produced on Broadway. The American musical began its shift from gaudy revue to more dramatic and serious forms such as the 1927 hit *Show Boat*, by Jerome Kern and Oscar Hammerstein II. Today, lavish productions such as *The Lion King* and *Spider-Man: Turn Off the Dark* attract new family audiences. Broadway theater thrives.

The restoration of several venerated buildings has brought a new magic to Broadway. Nearly as remarkable was the resurgence of Off-Broadway theater on 42nd Street. In 2000, the Theater Row complex opened, with six small theaters under one roof (*410–412 W. 42nd St., tel 212/714–2442*). It sits along 42nd Street's western stretch. Nearby, at 422 42nd Street, the Little Schubert Theatre opened in 2002, staging larger productions from its digs at the base of a 39-story residential tower.

EXPERIENCE: Enjoy Youth Workshops

The **New Victory Theater** (*209 W. 42nd St., tel 646/223–3010, newvictory.org*) originally opened in 1900 with a play starring Lionel Barrymore. A refurbished version of the theater opened almost a century later, in 1995, and focused on family entertainment. In addition to simply watching a concert, dance recital, circus act, or puppetry, children and teachers can participate in one of the many workshops offered throughout the year. Recent ones have included "All the World's a Circus," "Storytelling and Music," and "Breakdancing." Check the theater's online calendar or call for a list of upcoming workshops and to reserve tickets in advance.

have been several concerts every night. Classical music pervades the city; it is performed in large halls and in intimate spaces—museums, schools, churches—and unique venues such as Bargemusic, a converted cargo barge moored near the Brooklyn Bridge (see pp. 207, 263), or outdoors at Lincoln Center. You can hear a musician scratching out a Beethoven sonata on a street corner or listen to the New York Philharmonic perform under "the stars" (rarely visible in the city) in Central Park.

Writers & New York

New York is a rich backdrop for literature. In 1791, Susanna Rowson published *Charlotte Temple, a Tale of Truth*, a lurid novel about a fallen woman. Edgar Allan Poe was inspired by a New York murder to write *The Mystery of Marie Roget* (1845). After coming to New York in 1866, Horatio Alger wrote inspirational novels chronicling the rise of street urchins to success through hard work. In 1842, poet Walt Whitman called New York "the great place of the western continent, the heart, the brain, the focus, the main spring, the pinnacle, the extremity,

the no more beyond of the New World." In the 1950s, Jack Kerouac and the Beats made poetry out of city life. Today, resident authors Joseph O'Neill (*Netherland*), Colum McCann (*Let the Great World Spin, This Side of Brightness*), Paul Auster (*The New York Trilogy, The Brooklyn Follies*), and Pete Hamill (*Forever, North River*) often make the city their subject matter.

New York has given other writers the perspective to write brilliantly about where they came from. For Willa Cather, 40 years a New Yorker, it was the Nebraska of her childhood. Thomas Wolfe described his youth in North Carolina in the novel he wrote in New York, *Look Homeward, Angel* (1929).

Washington Irving was one of the first city-born writers. His satirical *Knickerbocker's History of New York* was published in 1809. Herman Melville was born at 6 Pearl Street in 1819. He left to go to sea and returned to write such works as *Typee*. Novelist Henry James used his grandmother's Greenwich Village house as the setting for his 1881 novel

■ **Walt Whitman (1819–1892) heard America singing in the people of Manhattan and Brooklyn.**

Washington Square. His neighbor Edith Wharton wrote *The Age of Innocence* (1920) about the city's elite. Novelist Nathanael West was born Nathan Weinstein in 1903 on East 81st Street. Henry Roth based *Call It Sleep* on his immigrant childhood in New York.

Harlem has produced such important writers as James Baldwin, who wrote about black New York in his 1953 novel, *Go Tell It on the Mountain*. Although they were born elsewhere, Richard Wright, Ralph Ellison, and Langston Hughes drew on their Harlem experience in their writings. In the 1920s, the movement known as the Harlem Renaissance (see pp. 200–201) attracted black writers from all over the country, including Zora Neale Hurston, author of *Their Eyes Were Watching God* (1937).

New York writers have always gathered in literary groups, clubs, salons, or in association with publications. In the 1820s, Irving was a leader of the Knickerbockers, gentlemen who wrote "for no other earthly purpose but to please ourselves." A few years later, James Fenimore Cooper founded the Bread and Cheese Club. Herman Melville gravitated toward the Young Americans, dedicated to encouraging a national literature. At the turn of the 20th century, Greenwich Village was a hotbed of literary activity, centered on *The New Masses* and other journals, theater groups, and salons. While some Village writers struggled, others, like Mark Twain, lived in patrician comfort in a town house near Washington Square.

The Algonquin Round Table was a lunch group of writers and artists that met during the 1920s at the Algonquin Hotel. Its members—among them Dorothy Parker, *New Yorker* editor Harold Ross, and drama critic Alexander Woolcott—were known for their witty barbs and quips. In the East Village, the Poetry Project at St.-Marks-in-the-Bowery (*131 E. 10th St.*) has been presenting regular readings every week since the mid-1960s. And in neighborhoods like Park Slope, Brooklyn, you can't swing a cat without hitting at least three novelists, essayists, critics, or, increasingly, bloggers.

Even with the advent of the digital age and new ways to publish and market online, New York's foothold as the center of English-language publishing is certain. This is the place the industry began. The publishing houses, editors, agents, lawyers, reading venues, awards ceremonies, media—all the elements that swirl around the process of writing are entrenched here. As for writers, the next Philip Roth or Tom Wolfe (both New Yorkers, by the way) will sooner or later make the trek to this mecca, hoping for a deal—over lunch at the Four Seasons in Midtown, over drinks at Pete's Tavern in East Village. To be followed, of course, by appearances on the morning shows, "Live from New York!"

> ## EXPERIENCE: Attend Printing Workshops
>
> To learn how to set, block, and print type, take a one-day letterpress workshop at **Bowne & Co. Stationers** (*211 Water St., tel 646/315–4478, southstreetseaportmuseum. org*). Beneath atmospheric lighting evocative of the 19th century, you will become familiar with the letterpress tools of that era—such as uppercase and lowercase drawers in which letter forms were traditionally stored (the designations of "uppercase" and "lowercase" letters derive from this practicality)—and learn how to utilize metal spacers around letters before inking the blocked type and printing via a foot-pedal-operated machine. Walk away with handmade stationery and the experience of a historic printing shop.

New York in Film, Television, & Song

Question: What do "Take the A Train," *Taxi Driver,* and *Sex and the City* have in common? Answer: They are by New Yorkers, about New York, and products of New York's creative industries—popular music, film, and television. "A Train" is a jazz composition by Harlem musician Duke Ellington. *Taxi Driver* is a quintessential New York movie, directed by New Yorker Martin Scorsese, starring a New York actor, Robert De Niro, and filmed on the city's mean streets. *Sex and the City* was a phenomenally successful TV series (and later movie) featuring the kind of fashionable, successful, yet screwed-up characters that define New York.

Anyone wandering around New York will encounter, sooner or later, a street blocked by a crew in the process of making a film, television episode, or commercial. There will be cameras, trailers, lights, dozens of busy people, and occasionally a star or two. While several film production companies had their start in New York, relocating to Hollywood in the twenties, cinema enthusiasts never abandoned the city. The film industry, in particular, has a number of producers and directors who, by choice, do most of their work in New York, among them Scorsese, Spike Lee, and Woody Allen. In Allen's NYC-based films, the anxiety level of the neurotic characters rises whenever the plot requires them to leave Manhattan.

■ **Quiet please: one of the New York Public Library's famous stone lions**

From the turn of the 19th century, when filmmakers associated with Thomas Edison started in the city, to World War I, New York was the moviemaking center of the country. Even in 1920, as the industry began moving to Hollywood, Famous Players-Lasky Productions, the production company that would become Paramount, opened Astoria Studios in Queens and continued to produce features there until 1937. The studio was taken over by the military during World War II and closed in the 1960s. In 1975 it reopened; Bob Fosse's *All That Jazz* (1979) and Woody Allen's *Radio Days* (1987) were among the features made there. In 1988 the Museum of the Moving Image (see p. 225), which documents New York's film history, took over part of the facilities.

Television also came of age in New York City. In 1927, an image of then Secretary of Commerce Herbert Hoover was beamed from the AT&T labs in New York to a receiver in Washington, D.C. The first CBS broadcast, in 1931, featured New York Mayor Jimmy Walker and composer George Gershwin. By the late 1940s, New York had four networks and about two-thirds of the nation's television sets. In the early 1950s, situation comedies such as *I Love Lucy* and *The Honeymooners* were all New York produced. Soon afterward, the entertainment end of the business shifted to the West Coast.

Still, New York remains a force in television. Network news and shows like *60 Minutes* are produced here, as are *Saturday Night Live* and *The Tonight Show Starring Jimmy Fallon*, which rely on a typically biting New York style of humor. *Seinfeld* was so New York-oriented that it still brings out-of-towners to the Upper West Side in search of Tom's restaurant (*corner of 112th St. & Broadway*), where the characters hung out; while such police and legal dramas as *Elementary* and *Law & Order: Criminal Intent* present a grittier side of city life.

Architecture

Architecturally, New York is a proud but restless city. It is the city's nature to build, tear down, and build again, though in recent decades preservation efforts have increased—and for good reason. New York today has only a handful of buildings left from the colonial era. Most are remotely located in the outer boroughs—at Historic Richmond Town on Staten Island, for example.

Buildings from the years after independence are better represented, with many surviving examples of the row house and its cousin, the brownstone (New Jersey sandstone over brick). Those years also saw the construction of the Astor House (1836)—forerunner of the modern hotel—and A. T. Stewart (1846), the department store. The Gothic Revival style in church architecture arrived with the completion of the third Trinity Church (see p. 57) in 1846.

In 1857, Richard M. Hunt, Leopold Eidlitz, Richard Upjohn and his son, Richard M., and others founded the American Institute of Architects to put the practice of architecture on a professional footing. Cast-iron

New York City—Some of the Best Books to Bring

If you have time to read in New York, these titles are worth downloading:

Bonfire of the Vanities by Tom Wolfe: Wolfe's drama distills the essence of 1980s Wall Street excess.

Call It Sleep by Henry Roth: This 1934 novel dramatizes the violence and poverty of the tenements of NYC.

Falling Man by Don DeLillo: A haunting tale of post–9/11 New York.

Inside the Dream Palace by Sherill Tippins: The story of the legendary Chelsea Hotel (see sidebar p. 91).

Let the Great World Spin by Colum McCann: A stunning work of fiction about the weird realities of 1970s New York told via a chorus of characters.

Open City by Teju Cole: A modern-day take on the immigrant's search for identity in the city of anonymity.

The New York Nobody Knows by William B. Helmreich: An astonishing account of the author's 6,000-mile walk through all five boroughs.

The New York Stories by John O'Hara: The definitive collection from one of the city's best chroniclers.

Washington Square by Henry James: James's novel is a peerless study of New York in the mid-1800s.

Wonderful Town edited by David Remnick: Short stories from the *New Yorker* magazine; ideal for coffee stops.

Writing New York edited by Phillip Lopate: A fine anthology of writing on the city through the centuries.

buildings were introduced in the city around 1850 by the inventive James Bogardus, and the world's first passenger elevator—the innovation that would make the city's later skyward growth possible—began its vertical journey in the Haughwout Building (*Broadway & Broome St.*) in 1857.

In the post-Civil War years, the luxury apartment was introduced as a living option for the wealthy. One of the first was Richard Morris Hunt's Stuyvesant Apartments, constructed on East 18th Street in 1869. On the Upper West Side, the still fashionable Dakota Apartments were completed in 1884. For the poor, there was the tenement with windowless flats, preserved today in the Lower East Side Tenement Museum (see p. 68). The postwar years also heralded magnificent beaux arts public buildings—the Metropolitan Museum of Art, the New York Public Library, Audubon Terrace, and the Brooklyn Museum. And during this time, the millionaires' freestanding mansions on Fifth Avenue were built, including James B. Duke's 1912 mansion at Fifth Avenue and 78th Street, designed by Julian Abele, one of the city's first African-American architects.

Skyline Transformed

Then came the skyscraper, a word coined in the 1890s to describe an iron-framed building on which masonry was hung like a "curtain." The skyscraper was born in Chicago but came to full flower in New York. Manhattan's shallow bedrock is ideally suited for supporting tall buildings. In 1889 architect Bradford Gilbert built

■ **Manhattan's ever changing skyline, seen from Brooklyn Bridge Park across the East River**

New York's first skyscraper, the Tower Building, a structure so thin and tall (11 stories!) that New Yorkers thought it would blow over. In the ensuing race to build the world's tallest building, early record holders included architect H. H. Richardson's Park Row Building (1897, 30 stories), Napoleon LeBrun's Metropolitan Life Insurance Tower (1909, 50 stories), and Cass Gilbert's Woolworth Building (1913, 60 stories).

D. H. Burnham's triangular, 21-story Flatiron Building, when built in 1901–1903 the tallest building north of the financial district, remains a favorite with the public. The 1915 Equitable Building on lower Broadway blocked out so much sunlight that the city changed the zoning regulations to require setbacks—creating the so-called wedding-cake profile—on tall buildings. The race for height culminated in 1930 with the art deco Chrysler Building and the Empire State Building (see pp. 96 & 108); the latter, with 102 stories, was the city's record holder until eclipsed by the World Trade Center's twin towers (1970–1971, 110 stories), which were felled by terrorists 30 years later on September 11, 2001.

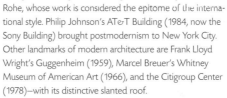

In 1889 architect Bradford Gilbert built New York's first skyscraper, the Tower Building, a structure so thin and tall (11 stories!) that New Yorkers thought it would blow over.

After World War II, form rather than height became the prime architectural concern. The unadorned, boxy international style is reflected in the UN Secretariat Building, Lever House, and the bronze-clad Seagram Building, the last designed by Ludwig Mies van der

Rohe, whose work is considered the epitome of the international style. Philip Johnson's AT&T Building (1984, now the Sony Building) brought postmodernism to New York City. Other landmarks of modern architecture are Frank Lloyd Wright's Guggenheim (1959), Marcel Breuer's Whitney Museum of American Art (1966), and the Citigroup Center (1978)—with its distinctive slanted roof.

The heyday of the skyscrapers may be over, but New York continues to both redesign existing structures and build anew, both in traditionally wealthy neighborhoods like Midtown and the Financial District, and in once sketchy areas like the Lower East Side and the Meatpacking District. Over the past decade and a half woefully underused Columbus Circle has been brought back to life by construction of the Time Warner Center, with its mix of offices, hotels, restaurants, shopping, theaters, and offices. The Museum of Modern Art got a fabulous redesign and enlargement in 2004, while westward on the same block, architect Jean Nouvel is planning Tower Verre, a 75-story tower that's one of the most anticipated—and controversial—additions to the New York skyline in decades. Near the shore of the Hudson River, projects such as Richard Meier's twin glass luxury buildings at 173 and 176 Perry Street and Frank Gehry's IAC Building (see p. 157), the new Whitney Museum of American Art, designed by Renzo

Piano (see p. 82) and the Hudson Yard Redevelopment Project have given new life to areas that were once run down. And never one to let go of the past. The city has plans to move some of the train service out of Penn Station into the 1913 James A. Farley Post Office, a beaux arts building akin to the grand old Penn Station that was demolished (see below). Although buildings may disappear in the city, their memory endures, and their grace and spirit often live on, echoed in creations blending old and new. And thus the city grows and endures.

Preserving & Tearing Down New York

Imbued with what Walt Whitman called "the pull-down-and-build-over-again spirit," early New Yorkers were not concerned about historic preservation. Particularly on Manhattan. Land is too scarce and valuable there to permit sentimentality over something as ephemeral as an old building.

So New York has done a lot of tearing down. The hope always is, of course, that the replacement will be better than what is lost. Sometimes that happens. In 1899–1900, the 45-foot-high (13.7 m) granite walls around the reservoir at Fifth Avenue and 42nd Street—a sterling example of "Egyptian architecture"— were torn down to make way for the New York Public Library, one of the city's most beloved buildings. The demolition of the majestic first Waldorf-Astoria Hotel is unlamented today because it made way for the incomparable Empire State Building. There was grumbling in 1939 when opulent brownstone residences on West 53rd Street were torn down to make way for the Museum of Modern Art, but that international-style building became a landmark in its own right—a worthwhile trade-off.

> **The old Penn Station's much lamented demolition marked the beginning of the historic preservation movement in New York City.**

However, there are certain buildings whose demise New Yorkers now regret. Ernest Flagg's great Singer Tower, at 47 stories, is remembered as the tallest building ever demolished. The Brokaw mansions that once stood at Fifth Avenue and 79th Street were emblems of wealth that are irreplaceable today. One loss that shocked New York was the demolition in 1963–1964 of Pennsylvania Station, a "monumental act of vandalism," as the *New York Times* called it. The two marble eagles outside the new Penn Station now remain as relics from what was one of America's most beautiful buildings. It was razed to make way for the new Madison Square Garden (see p. 99) and the new station underneath it. As one academic lamented: "One entered the city like a god; one scuttles in now like a rat."

Historic Preservation

The old Penn Station's much lamented demolition marked the beginning of the historic preservation movement in New York City. In 1965, the city created the Landmarks Preservation Commission to identify and protect landmark buildings and districts—and public interiors and scenic vistas—based on aesthetic, cultural, architectural, and historic criteria. Brooklyn Heights was one of the first neighborhoods to gain landmark status as a historic district. Today there are more than 1,000 individual landmarks, nine scenic landmarks, and 82 historic districts, encompassing nearly 21,000 buildings. There have been several tests of the commission's considerable powers.

When it rejected proposals to build a 54-story office tower over Grand Central Terminal or to squeeze in one adjacent to St. Bartholomew's Church on Park Avenue, opponents' appeals went to the Supreme Court. In both cases, the court upheld the landmark legislation and the city's right to protect its architectural heritage. In other battles, the Edgar Rice mansion at the corner of 89th Street and Riverside Drive, owned by a Jewish religious school, was saved after a battle involving charges of discrimination. There have also been compromises: One allowed the New York Palace Hotel to be tacked onto the rear of the Villard Houses on Madison Avenue. In another, the Preservation Board was only too happy to let the Museum of Arts and Design redo the exterior of the much reviled but familiar Huntington Hartford Gallery at Columbus Circle. And there have been defeats. There is no way, ever, to replace such New York fixtures as Luchow's, the ornate German restaurant on 14th Street, or the low-slung art deco Airlines Terminal Building at 42nd Street and Park Avenue South, or the Hotel Biltmore on Madison Avenue, or the crenelated 71st Regiment Armory on East 34th Street, or ...

Today's preservationist forces might have saved some of those monuments; going forward, the new civic vigilance—which saved Grand Central Terminal and rescued Times Square's historic theaters—bodes well for the future of New York's architectural treasures. ■

NYC Playlist: A Sound Track for the City That Never Sleeps

When walking in New York, it's fun to hear songs inspired by the city. Here are some suggestions:

"Angel of Harlem" by U2: "It was a cold and wet December day, as we touched the ground at JFK," exudes Bono in celebration of Billie Holiday and New York jazz & blues.

"Central Park West" by John Coltrane: Perfect for a walk in the park (see p. 167).

"Chelsea Hotel #2" by Leonard Cohen: An insider's report from New York's bastion of bohemianism (see sidebar p. 91).

"Dirty Blvd." by Lou Reed: The late bard of the Big Apple will take you down the city's meaner streets. If this walk on the wild side appeals, download all of his classic album, New York.

"Fairytale of New York" by The Pogues: The bittersweet Christmas ballad of Irish exiles in the city "where the wind blows right through you ..."

"New York City" by John Lennon & Yoko Ono: Two of the city's best known transplants pay their rock 'n' roll respects.

"New York City Serenade" by Bruce Springsteen: An early ode by the Boss.

"New York Minute" by Don Henley: A noirish tale of a Wall Street trader struggling to keep his sanity in the city that never sleeps. Check out the spoken-word version read by Hank Beukema too.

"New York, New York" by Frank Sinatra: Let Ol' Blue Eyes himself serenade you right through the very heart of it.

"New York State of Mind" by Billy Joel: The New Yorker plays a monthly residency at Madison Square Garden, if you want to hear this live (see p. 99).

"Positively 4th Street" by Bob Dylan: Dylan's bitter kiss-off to the folk scene of 1960s Greenwich Village (see pp. 80–81).

"Shattered" by The Rolling Stones: "Go ahead, bite the Bi-i-i-i-ig Apple," sneers Mick Jagger on this slice of 1970s NYC neurosis, "don't mind the maggots!"

"Stayin' Alive" by The Bee Gees: Strut through the city streets like it's 1977.

"Take the A Train" by Duke Ellington: The jazz standard that doubles as an early NYC rail schedule: "Take the A Train to go to Sugar Hill way up in Harlem / Listen to those rails a-thrumming (All Aboard!)."

ENTRANCES

Fly in or drive in, take a car, bus, train, ocean liner, or ferry, ride a bike or walk the George Washington Bridge: Any way you reach New York is dramatic. The city's exuberantly etched skyline is exhilarating. By day the city's buildings gleam, and by night, lights of bridges, traffic, and skyscrapers cut the darkness. Turn off the dark: You are entering the Big Apple.

■ The headlights of cars as they cross the Brooklyn Bridge at sunset with the Manhattan skyline in the background

Tunnels

It is impossible to drive into Manhattan without negotiating a bridge or a tunnel. The Holland and Lincoln tunnels, on the West Side, go under the Hudson to New Jersey. The Brooklyn-Battery and Queens-Midtown Tunnels, on the East Side, lead to their namesake boroughs and Long Island.

When the **Holland Tunnel** opened in 1927, it was the city's first vehicular tunnel and the world's longest. The 1950 **Brooklyn-Battery Tunnel,** at 9,117 feet (2,778 m), is North

America's longest continuous vehicular tunnel. The **Lincoln Tunnel,** built between 1937 and 1957, is, at 40 million vehicles a year, the world's busiest. The **Queens-Midtown Tunnel,** stretching 6,300 feet (1,920 m), holds no titles, but is a useful route to LaGuardia and Kennedy airports.

Bridges

The primary bridges, from Manhattan's tip and going uptown, are the Brooklyn Bridge, the Manhattan Bridge, the Williamsburg Bridge, the Queensboro Bridge, and the

Triborough Bridge (now renamed the Robert F. Kennedy Bridge) at 125th Street. High on the West Side, the George Washington Bridge connects the city to New Jersey.

The age of the great New York bridges began with the opening of the **Brooklyn Bridge** in 1883, joining Manhattan to Brooklyn, then a major city in its own right. Measuring some 3,580 feet (1,091 m), with a central span of 1,595.5 feet (486 m) between its two massive stone towers, the bridge was for years the world's longest, and it was the world's first steel suspension bridge.

In 1867 a steel suspension bridge was a radical idea, but this was John Augustus Roebling's plan. When the German-born engineer died, his son, Washington Roebling, saw the project through. Washington was crippled by the bends while working underwater in 1872, but he supervised the construction from a distance, using a telescope and passing instructions through his wife, Emily Warren Roebling.

Today, the Brooklyn Bridge is still a marvel and a symbol of the city. Walk across the pedestrian walkway (see p. 209) for a close-up view of the structure and harbor views; looking uptown, you will see the other major bridges. On the Brooklyn side, the riverfront promenade provides spectacular views of lower Manhattan.

Today, the five boroughs have 2,027 bridges, 76 of which cross water. New York's first bridge, the King's Bridge, was built by Frederick Philipse across Spuyten Duyvil Creek between Manhattan and the Bronx in 1693 and lasted until 1917. The city's oldest surviving bridge is **High Bridge,** constructed between 1837 and 1848 to carry water into Manhattan. It has recently been reopened as a pedestrian bridge.

The 1964 **Verrazano-Narrows Bridge** between Staten Island and Brooklyn provides a spectacular starting point for the New York City Marathon. It is also the last bridge designed by the city's master bridge-builder, Swiss-born Othmar H. Ammann, whose other projects include the **George Washington Bridge** (1931), the

Triborough Bridge (1936), the **Bronx-Whitestone Bridge** (1939), and the **Throgs Neck Bridge** (1961). The stately **Queensboro Bridge** (1909) will always be identified with F. Scott Fitzgerald's evocative words in *The Great Gatsby*: "The city seen from the Queensboro Bridge is always the city seen for the first time, in its first wild promise of all the mystery and the beauty in the world."

New York Harbor

Go out into New York Harbor any way you can: There is no better view of New York than from its beckoning waters. Odds are

EXPERIENCE:
Take a City Bus Tour

While New York is a city that demands to be explored on foot, a bus tour is an option if you're footsore or just want a good overview. The most ubiquitous company is **Gray Line New York Sightseeing** (*tel* 800/669-0051 ext. 4 or 212/445-0848, graylinenewyork. com), which operates red double-deck buses on both fully escorted tours and hop-on, hop-off sightseeing loops. A 48-hour pass covering all loops costs $64 (or $49 online). You can buy tickets online or at locations around town, including the **Times Square Visitor Center** (*1560 Broadway, bet. 46th & 47th Sts.*), the **Gray Line/New York Visitor Center** (*777 8th Ave, bet. 47th & 48th Sts.*), and **Grand Central Terminal** (*125 Park Ave., bet. 41st & 42nd Sts.*).

slim that you will arrive in Manhattan as the immigrants did, crowding the rail of a ship to watch the city rise gradually from the horizon. But once you are on the water, the excitement will build, whether you're on the Staten Island Ferry, Circle Line cruise, or in a kayak (see sidebar p. 18); whether passing the Statue of Liberty or en route to Ellis

Island—where millions of immigrants first touched American soil.

The Dutch settlers were quick to recognize the virtues of New York Harbor. It was wide, close to open ocean, and deep, providing both easy passage and safe anchorage. This natural harbor became a magnet for commerce beginning with the trade in furs. Peter Stuyvesant built the first wharf on the East River in 1648. The American Revolution, the War of 1812, the steamship, the industrial revolution, and the 1800s dredging of the Ambrose Channel all contributed to the Port of New York's rapid growth. For the first 50 years of the 20th century, it was the world's busiest port.

While cruise ships continue to sail from the city, parts of the Manhattan and Brooklyn waterfronts have been imaginatively

> **Since the turn of the millennium, Hudson River Park and Riverside Park have been extended, creating a greenway along the entire western edge of Manhattan.**

restored, such as the **South Street Seaport Museum** (see pp. 64–65) near Manhattan's tip. This "living" historic district on the site of the original Port of New York includes 18th- and 19th-century buildings and a marina. Along the Hudson is **Chelsea Piers,** once a port of call and now a sports-entertainment complex at the beautifully restored piers 59 to 62. The *Titanic* was en route here when it sank in 1912.

Since the turn of the millennium, **Hudson River Park** and **Riverside Park** have been extended, creating a greenway along the entire western edge of Manhattan. Meanwhile, on the other side of the island, the **East River Waterfront Project**

envisions a 2-mile (3.2 km) esplanade and park from the Battery to the Williamsburg Bridge.

Airports

You can dream about steaming into New York Harbor aboard a passenger liner, but if you are coming from any distance, you will probably fly. From a plane you get a view of the city in its entirety (see pp. 2–3); it brings home the fact that New York is a city of islands and waterways. You can reach New York via three major airports: LaGuardia handles domestic carriers; John F. Kennedy (JFK) International and New Jersey's Newark Liberty International are gateways for overseas flights.

Through the 1930s, **Newark Liberty International Airport** was the only airport serving the city. This so galled New York's feisty mayor, Fiorello La Guardia, that he once refused to get off a plane at Newark because his ticket read "New York." The city got the point. Shortly thereafter, in December 1939, **LaGuardia Airport** in north-central Queens opened.

John F. Kennedy International Airport opened in 1948 on Jamaica Bay, some 15 miles (24 km) from Manhattan. Then the largest airport in the world, it was named Idlewild until 1963. At JFK, airlines were allowed to design their own terminals, a decision that brought leading architects into airport design and produced such notable buildings as Eero Saarinen's TWA Terminal A (1956–1962), a winged masterpiece of curved concrete and glass, intended, in Saarinen's words, "to interpret the sensation of flying." It's now part of the JetBlue terminal.

In February 2017, the first phase of the ARK project (*arkjfk.com*) was launched. The 170,000-square-feet (16,000 sq m) facility offers assistance, full veterinary services, accommodations, and special aid for pets and large animals travelling with their owners, both before and after flights. In January 2018, Governor Andrew Cuomo announced the appropriation of 34 million dollars for Stewart International Airport, which will expand its international routes.

The fast-paced Financial District and the ever changing ethnic and artsy neighborhoods to the north

LOWER MANHATTAN

■ Downtown Manhattan reimagined: A futuristic view from the Hudson River

LOWER MANHATTAN

From anywhere else in Manhattan, go south, to the heart of Lower Manhattan. Here you start to understand all the changes the city has undergone through the ages: from fortification to thriving colony to seat of government to place of entry for immigrants to busy seaport to what it is today—the financial center of the world, and since September 11, 2001, a place of pilgrimage.

Those starting a downtown visit near the harbor will find a modern-day immigrant experience with sightseers from far and wide and a carnival-like atmosphere of vendors and performers. Many people will head directly to the Battery for tickets to Liberty Island or Ellis Island (see pp. 50–52) or the always-free Staten Island Ferry. Others may feel drawn to a historic walk up Broadway, guided by Heritage Trail markers and signs (see pp. 60–61). The federal-style James Watson House (7

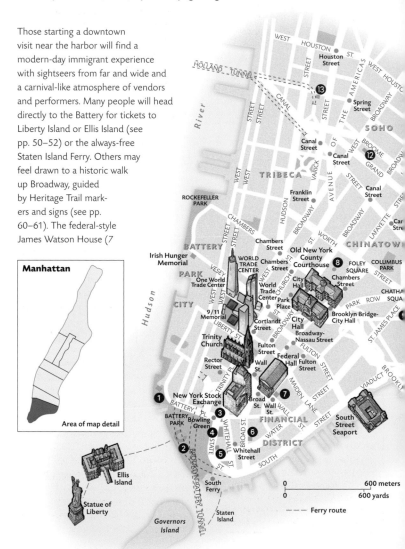

Manhattan

Area of map detail

State St., bet. Pearl & Whitehall Sts.) nearby, dwarfed by skyscrapers, is now the Rectory of the Shrine of St. Elizabeth Ann Seton (1774–1821), canonized in 1975 as the first American-born saint.

Farther north, on the site of the World Trade Center, the 9/11 Memorial draws visitors from around the globe. At the adjacent museum you can see two steel beams from the original towers. Next to the site is the entrance to the new, spectacular World Trade Center Transportation Hub (Oculus) designed by Spanish architect Santiago Calatrava.

One World Trade Center (Freedom Tower) now rises into the

Manhattan skyline to the symbolic height of 1,776 feet (541 m), to reflect the birth of the U.S.A.

The memorial grounds include two reflecting pools, with the names of the victims of the attacks memorialized in surrounding bronze parapets (see p. 63). The neighborhoods of Lower Manhattan from the Brooklyn Bridge north to Houston Street—Chinatown, Little Italy, the Lower East Side, SoHo, and Tribeca—are evocative of earlier times and foreign ways. Traditionally where immigrants lived and worked, these areas are now as likely to be inhabited by American-born artists or stockbrokers. At the turn of the 20th century, three-quarters of the residents of the Lower East Side were Jewish; today Hispanics and Asians make up the majority of the population. Boutiques, galleries, bars, and young entrepreneurs contemporize the flavor here. Even Orchard Street, New York's old immigrant shopping district, is changing. Clothes and bargains still clog the sidewalks. ∎

Lower Manhattan

❶ Museum of Jewish Heritage ❷ Castle Clinton ❸ Bowling Green ❹ National Museum of the American Indian ❺ New York Unearthed ❻ Fraunces Tavern ❼ Museum of American Finance ❽ African Burial Ground National Monument ❾ Shearith Israel Graveyard ❿ Lower East Side Tenement Museum ⓫ St. Patrick's Old Cathedral ⓬ The Drawing Center ⓭ New York Fire Museum

STATUE OF LIBERTY NATIONAL MONUMENT

Located in upper New York Bay, the Statue of Liberty is rarely seen by many New Yorkers, but even the most jaded have never tired of her. Nor have the words of Emma Lazarus that are inscribed on the base—"Give me your tired, your poor, your huddled masses yearning to breathe free"—lost their power. Dedicated in 1886, the statue was a gift to America from France to celebrate the alliance of the two nations in achieving U.S. independence.

■ The view from the torch

Staten Island Ferry
See p. 215

siferry.com

The French sculptor Frédéric Bartholdi modeled his statue on one of the seven wonders of the ancient world, the Colossus of Rhodes. The Statue of Liberty's torch symbolizes enlightenment; her seven-pointed headdress denotes the world's continents.

In her left arm is a tablet representing the Declaration of Independence. Lady Liberty stands 151 feet (46 m) tall, weighs 225 tons (204 metric tons), and has a 35-foot (10 m) waistline. Her index finger is eight feet (2.4 m) long.

Bartholdi's compatriot, the engineer Gustave Eiffel (who built Paris's Eiffel Tower between 1887 and 1889), helped on the project. He devised a way to hang 88 tons (80 metric tons) of thin copper sheeting on an iron frame so that the statue is flexible enough to withstand high winds. More help came from Paris-trained Richard Morris Hunt. He designed the base and pedestal that lifts the statue 165 feet (50 m) off the ground.

Once called Bedloe's Island, Liberty Island was chosen by Bartholdi for the site of construction. The massive statue was unveiled on October 28, 1886.

Facilities at the statue were updated in 2011, but it closed again in 2012 due to Hurricane Sandy, when Liberty Island and Ellis Island were badly flooded. It reopened on July 4th, 2013, and visitors have access to the

INSIDER TIP:

Forget the huge lines to board a boat heading to Lady Liberty or Ellis Island. Head to the Staten Island Ferry for great views and, better yet, it's free of charge!

—MARGIE GOLDSMITH
National Geographic writer

pedestal observation deck, the museum, and the Fort Wood level. Special tickets to access Lady Liberty's crown and pedestal must be reserved in advance. The new museum opened in 2019, with interactive displays, galleries, and a movie theater. It is possible to admire the statue from the building, which also has a roof garden (*libertyellisfoundation.org*). ∎

Statue of Liberty National Monument

🗺 Map p. 48

✉ Liberty Island, New York Harbor

☎ 212/363–3200 For ferry tickets: 877–LADY–TIX or 201/604–2800

🕐 Monument open daily 9.30 a.m.–3.30 p.m.

💲 $$$ (tickets online at statuecruises .com or at Castle Clinton)

🚇 Subway: 1 to South Ferry; 4, 5 to Bowling Green; R to Whitehall

⛴ Ferry leaves Battery Park every 30 mins.

nps.gov/stli

EXPERIENCE: Tour Historic Governors Island

Because of its strategic location in New York Harbor, Governors Island has had many roles as a military outpost, including in the Revolutionary War, the War of 1812, the Civil War, both World Wars, and the Gulf War. By early 2003, however, the U.S. federal government sold the island to the people of New York—for one dollar. The development of the island is ongoing, but it has much to offer: Castle Williams and Fort Jay; pre-Civil War arsenal buildings; Victorian and Romanesque Revival housing; and more. You can take a walking tour of the national historic district with National Park Service rangers or take advantage of a tram tour that circles the island. To explore on your own, rent a bike from **Bike and Roll** (*tel 866/RENTABIKE,*

bikeandroll.com/newyork) upon arrival or pick up a self-guided walking tour brochure at the ferry landing's bookstore. Open seasonally, the island is reached by a 10-minute ferry ride from lower Manhattan via the **Governors Island Ferry**, which departs from the Battery Maritime Building (*10 South St. at Whitehall St.; to reach the ferry terminal by subway, take the 1 to the South Ferry stop, the 4 or 5 to Bowling Green, or the R to Whitehall St.; by bus, take the M1, M6, M9, or M15*).

Past events on the island have included art fairs, a free concert by the New York Philharmonic orchestra, and "Battle of Brooklyn weekend." Check *govisland.com* or *nps.gov/gois* or call 212/825–3045 for more information.

ELLIS ISLAND NATIONAL MONUMENT

Some 100 million Americans have ancestors who passed through Ellis Island. Even if you are not one of them, a visit to the restored processing center, Ellis Island National Monument, is a moving experience. Stand in the Great Registry—a room 200 feet long, 100 feet wide, and 56 feet high (61 m x 30 m x 17 m)—and imagine the lines of anxious arrivals waiting to be processed. One-third of the 16 million who arrived here ventured no farther than New York.

A display of luggage at Ellis Island National Museum of Immigration

Ellis Island

🗺 Map p. 48

✉ New York Harbor

☎ 212/363–3200

💲 $$$ (includes ferry)

🚇 Subway: 1 to South Ferry; 4, 5 to Bowling Green; R to Whitehall

⛴ Ferry leaves Battery Park every 30 mins.

libertyellisfoundation. org

In 1907, its busiest year, 1,004,756 immigrants passed through Ellis Island; 75 percent were from Italy, Austria-Hungary, and Russia; the rest from northern Europe and countries all over the world, including China, Japan, Canada, and Mexico.

In 1924 Congress set strict quotas on immigration and the numbers passing through dwindled. The facility closed in 1954, but after lengthy restorations, the Ellis Island Museum of Immigration opened in 1990. Exhibits on three floors re-create the experience of the immigrants on Ellis Island and celebrate their contributions to America. Follow their journey through the entry inspections and health checks, see the dormitory and dining hall, and hear the voices of immigrants telling their stories.

On May 20, 2015, the galleries of The Peopling of America Center, at Ellis Island, opened to the public. The exhibits trace the history of immigration in America before the opening of Ellis Island in 1892 and after it closed in 1954. ■

The island is named for Samuel Ellis, who purchased it in the 1700s. Over the years it grew, with landfill, from 3 to 27 acres (1.2 ha to 11 ha). In 1892, the federal government opened an immigration processing facility on the island.

After it burned in 1897, it was replaced with today's French Renaissance-style building, which opened in 1900.

MANHATTAN'S HISTORIC TIP

Battery Park is a 25-acre (10 ha) swath of greenery at the southernmost tip of Manhattan. It is dotted with memorials honoring, among others, early Dutch and Jewish settlers, the Coast Guard, and the explorer Giovanni da Verrazano, who first sighted the Battery's shore. North of it, the winding streets of the oldest part of the city disappear into canyons of skyscrapers.

The Battery's principal building, **Castle Clinton,** is Manhattan's only existing fort. The circular structure was actually on an island just offshore when it was built before the War of 1812 with Great Britain. It took successive landfills to create the terrain that is Battery Park today. The fortification was named for DeWitt Clinton, who, as mayor of New York, was responsible for reinforcing the harbor defenses.

Castle Clinton, whose 28 guns never fired at an enemy, has had a varied history. In 1823 it was renamed Castle Garden temporarily and was converted into an entertainment arena. From 1855 to 1890 (before Ellis Island opened) it was the city's immigration center. Luis Sanguino's 1973 statue "The Immigrants" pays tribute to the 7.7 million new arrivals who

INSIDER TIP:

Hop on a Citi Bike to Battery Park for great views of New York Harbor and the Statue of Liberty.

—**KENNY LING**
National Geographic contributor

passed through Castle Clinton. In 1896 the building was transformed into the New York Aquarium, and so it remained until 1940. Castle Clinton was restored in the 1970s and opened as a historic site with a museum. Concerts and events are held here in the summer.

The 1907 Cass Gilbert–designed **U.S. Custom House** (*corner of Bowling Green & State St.*) stands on the site of Fort Amsterdam (later Fort George), built by the Dutch in 1625. The highlight

Castle Clinton
- Map p. 48
- Battery Park
- 212/344–7220
- Subway: 4, 5 to Bowling Green; 1 to South Ferry

nps.gov/cacl

New York Subway Etiquette

New York's subways may seem anarchic, but subtle rules do apply: 1) Make yourself small, especially at peak times. There's little enough room aboard, and nobody appreciates people who take too much space. 2) Don't expect privacy. Whether sitting or standing, expect to be pressed up against your neighbor as if he/she is your prom date. Just don't get fresh. 3) Keep it down. Nothing says "out-of-towner" like a shouted conversation. 4) Don't get in people's way. When boarding, move to the center of the car, away from the doors, so more people can pack in behind you. When standing, don't lean against the vertical handrails: Other people will be trying to hold on. 5) Don't be afraid to ask directions. New Yorkers are proud of their subway knowledge and happy to show it off.

of the monumental exterior is Daniel Chester French's "The Four Continents," four allegorical sculpture groupings, each dominated by a female figure. Asia appears serene; America radiates vigor; Europe is regal; and Africa slumbers. The **National Museum of the American Indian** (see p. 56) is located within.

Just north of the National Museum of the American Indian is tiny **Bowling Green,** with benches and a picturesque fountain. This became the city's first public park in 1733, when it was rented to three citizens for lawn bowling, at the yearly rent of one peppercorn. In 1770, the British erected a gilded statue of George III on the green, later pulled down by Revolutionary patriots.

An unusual attraction north of Bowling Green is the huge bronze bull statue. The gift of the sculptor Arturo Di Modica, it arrived unexpectedly at the New York Stock Exchange on Wall Street

Washington's Farewell

On December 4, 1783, following the nation's victory over the British, Gen. George Washington gave a farewell dinner at Fraunces Tavern (see p. 55) for his officers. He was unusually emotional and eloquent: "With a heart full of love and gratitude I now take my leave of you. I most devoutly wish that your latter days may be as prosperous and happy as your former ones have been glorious and honorable."

one evening in the 1980s. It was later moved to this spot here on Broadway.

History is preserved in street names here: Wall Street takes its name from the wooden barricade the Dutch erected in 1653 to protect the colony's northern

A bronze bull, sculpted by Arturo Di Modica, symbolizes a rising Wall Street stock market.

flank. Rector Street is a tribute to the rectors of Trinity Church. Beaver Street was once rich in beaver pelts, while Pearl Street marked the shore, named for the gleam of shells. Battery Park is named after the gun battery the British mounted in the 1700s.

Fraunces Tavern Historic District

The historic block that includes **Fraunces Tavern** is a passageway back to colonial times. The tavern dates from 1719 and is today one of the financial district's more atmospheric restaurants. Samuel Fraunces, a West Indian who, tradition says, was black, bought the brick building in 1762 and opened a tavern. It was saved for patriotic reasons— George Washington dined here (see sidebar opposite)—and,

somehow, the whole block has survived. Fraunces Tavern was rebuilt in 1907 in authentic Georgian style. Only the west brick wall is from the original building. The tavern reopened in 1907 as a museum and restaurant, including the Long Room, a re-creation of the site of Washington's farewell speech, and the Clinton Room, decorated with federal furnishings and 1834 wallpaper.

Today the whole block, which is bounded by Pearl, Broad, and Water Streets, and Coenties Slip, is a designated historic district with 19th-century buildings in the federal and Greek Revival styles. Coenties Slip, once a wharf, is now landlocked. The adjacent plaza (*55 Water St.*) holds the **New York Vietnam Veterans Memorial,** a rectangular glass prism. ∎

Fraunces Tavern Museum

🗺 Map p. 48
✉ 54 Pearl St.
☎ 212/425–1778
🕐 Open Mon.–Fri. 12 p.m.–5 p.m., Sat.–Sun. 11 a.m.–5 p.m.
💲 $$
🚇 4, 5 to Bowling Green; 1 to South Ferry; R to Whitehall

frauncestavern museum.org

EXPERIENCE: Bike Your Way Around New York

Mayor Bloomberg's sustainability drives (2002–2013) proved a boost for cycling in New York. The city now has more than 700 miles (1,125 km) of bike lanes, including parks and greenways, and cycling is a great way to explore the city.

The **Hudson River Greenway** runs 13 miles (20 km) from Battery Park in the south to Inwood Hill Park at Manhattan's northern tip, primarily through riverfront parks. This is part of the **Manhattan Waterfront Greenway,** a 32-mile (51.5 km) route that circumnavigates Manhattan. Bikers to Brooklyn can also use a lane on Warren Street and a bike path through the north end of City Hall Park to reach the Brooklyn Bridge. In Central Park, the **Park Drive** is a 6.1-mile (9.8 km) loop that's closed to cars on weekends and

between 10 a.m. and 3 p.m. on weekdays. Check *nyc.gov/html/dot* ("Bicyclists" section) for route maps.

Introduced in 2013, **Citi Bike** is New York's new bike-sharing system (*nycdot bikeshare.info*). This offers bikes at 330 stations across Manhattan and parts of Brooklyn (*member.citibikenyc.com/map*). Each station has a touchscreen kiosk, a map of the service area, and a docking system that releases bikes for rental with a card or key. You can buy a 24-Hour or a 7-Day Access Pass, and a $101 security hold is placed on your card. You can also rent bikes from **Danny's Cycles** (*75 Varick St., tel 212/334–8000, metrobicycles.com*) in Tribeca, the **Loeb Boathouse** (*bet. 75th & 76th Sts., Central Park, tel 212/517–2233*), and other locations around the city.

NATIONAL MUSEUM OF THE AMERICAN INDIAN

One million artifacts collected by wealthy New Yorker George Gustav Heye (1874–1957) during his journeys throughout the Americas form the cornerstone of this fascinating museum.

■ A museum cultural interpreter explains the significance of a traditional handwoven blanket.

National Museum of the American Indian

🗺 Map p. 48

✉ 1 Bowling Green

☎ 212/514–3700

🚇 Subway: 1 to Rector St. or South Ferry; 2, 3 to Wall St.; 4, 5 to Bowling Green; J, Z to Broad St.; R to Whitehall St.; Bus: M5, M15, M20

nmai.si.edu/visit/newyork

Displayed on a rotating basis in the sprawling beaux arts U.S. Custom House, the artifacts represent significant Native American places, from the American Southwest to Hawaii, Canada, and South and Central America. They include stone and wood carvings from the Pacific Northwest; feather bonnets and quilled hides from the North American plains; Navajo weavings; ceramics from Costa Rica, central Mexico, and Peru; Maya carved jade; featherwork from the Amazon; and the list goes on. One ongoing exhibit, "Infinity of Nations," illustrates the geographic and chronological scope of the museum's collection. The exhibit includes an Apsáalooke (Crow) robe illustrated with warriors' exploits; a Maya limestone bas-relief depicting a ball player; and an elaborately beaded Inuit *tuilli,* or woman's inner parka.

Since it opened in 1994, this free museum has become a popular attraction for millions of visitors. It comes under the auspices of the Smithsonian Institution, which opened an impressive adjunct museum in 2004 in Washington, D.C. ■

TRINITY CHURCH

In its 300-plus years at the head of Wall Street, Trinity Church has earned a prominent place in the life of the financial community. A good time to visit this lovely Episcopal church is during the week at midday, when—during services or concerts or on strolls through the historic graveyard—you can join Wall Streeters as they shake off the tensions of their fast-moving jobs.

Trinity is a very wealthy church, thanks to a land grant from Queen Anne in 1705 that gave it a huge chunk of Manhattan Island. The present building is actually the third church on the site. The first, completed in 1698, burned down in 1776. It was rebuilt in 1788. A year later a service was held honoring George Washington's inauguration as president. After this building was razed, Richard Upjohn

The main sanctuary is closed for a restoration that began in 2018, but the Chapel of All Saints and the cemetery are open to the public. Many influential New Yorkers are buried in the cemetery, including the founding father, Alexander Hamilton (see pp. 25, 27) and Robert Fulton, inventor of the steamboat. ■

Trinity Church

⬛ Map p. 48

✉ Broadway at Wall St.

☎ 212/602–0800; concert information 212/602–9632; museum 212/602–0872

trinitywallstreet.org

INSIDER TIP:

Visit St. Paul's Chapel [see pp. 60–61], a few blocks north of Trinity Church—an inspiring exhibit honors the relief efforts following the 9/11 attacks.

–LARRY PORGES
National Geographic Travel Books editor

---

designed the present church in the Gothic Revival style.

The 280-foot (85 m) steeple was, until the 1860s, the highest point in New York City. Richard Morris Hunt designed the three sculptured bronze doors as a memorial to a wealthy parishioner, John Jacob Astor.

■ **Trinity Church, a spiritual retreat amid towering skyscrapers**

NEW YORK STOCK EXCHANGE

At the New York Stock Exchange (NYSE), pandemonium reigns; people are invariably astonished that the business of trading securities, despite the mass of tickers, computers, and monitors, is still conducted by traders waving their arms and shouting orders. It wasn't always this disorderly. In the early days members were assigned chairs. Today's traders are too busy to sit down, but a membership is still called a seat on the exchange.

■ Once the opening bell sounds, the floor of the exchange is abuzz with frantic buying and selling.

New York Stock Exchange

🅰 Map p. 48

✉ 11 Wall St.

☎ 212/656–3000 (information)

🚇 Subway: 2, 3, 4, 5 to Wall St.; J, M, Z to Broad St.; R to Rector St.

nyse.nyx.com

Despite its recent rough times, the NYSE remains the world's largest equities marketplace, home to about 3,000 companies valued at some $16.6 trillion in global market capitalization. It is, in short, the epicenter of the global economy. No one could have imagined such magnitude when, in 1792, 24 investors gathered under a buttonwood tree at Wall and William Streets, and agreed to buy and sell stocks and bonds among themselves.

In 1903 the institution moved into its current two-million-dollar neoclassical building. The pediment sculpture, grandly titled "Integrity Protecting the Works of Man," was designed by John Quincy Adams Ward. Although the exchange is now strictly regulated, "integrity" has not always universally applied. Low points include the crash of October 1929 and the conviction and imprisonment of its president, Richard Whitney, in 1938 for bilking customers.

The NYSE is now permanently closed to visitors. ■

FEDERAL HALL

Federal Hall, possibly the city's first Greek Revival building, stands at the heart of the busiest financial district in the world. Every business day, hordes of Wall Streeters stream past a location rich in colonial history. The financiers probably know that the statue in front is George Washington, but many of them—even those who spend their lunch hours lounging on the steps—may not realize that this is where he took the oath as the country's first president.

The present Federal Hall, erected in 1842, was designed by Ithiel Town and Alexander Jackson Davis. Eight Doric columns, 32 feet (9.7 m) high, line the front and rear, on Pine Street. The statue of Washington, sculptured in 1883 by

INSIDER TIP:

Federal Hall houses a great museum with permanent and special exhibits on its role in New York and American history. Take a tour with a park ranger through the opulent building.

—BRIDGET ENGLISH
National Geographic editor

■ The statue of George Washington at Federal Hall stands near where the nation's first president took the oath of office.

J. Q. A. Ward, shows him lifting his hand from a Bible.

The original building on this site was home to the first United States Congress, Supreme Court, and Executive Branch offices. The present structure housed the Customs Service for 20 years. The building became a national monument in 1955, and reopened in 2006 after a two-year, $16 million renovation to repair damage from the World Trade Center attacks.

Nearby, the Bank of Manhattan Building, which is now the **Trump Building** (*40 Wall St.*), at 927 feet (282 m) was the world's tallest from 1929 until the Chrysler Building surpassed it the following year. The National City Bank Building, now **Citibank,** at No. 55 was built in 1840; it took 40 teams of oxen to haul its 16 Ionic granite columns up Wall Street. It was remodeled and enlarged in 1904–1910. ■

Federal Hall National Monument & Museum

- Map p. 48
- 26 Wall St.
- 212/825–6990
- Closed Sun. Tours offered Mon.–Fri.
- Subway: 2, 3, 4, 5 to Wall St.

nps.gov/feha

A WALK UP BROADWAY

If you would rather avoid fast-paced crowds, try this tour on a weekend, when the streets are quieter. It begins at the foot of Broadway, near Battery Park, going from the financial district to City Hall, convenient for shopping and restaurants.

Your downtown stroll begins on Broadway in front of the **National Museum of the American Indian ❶** (see p. 56; *Alexander Hamilton U.S. Custom House, One Bowling Green, 10 a.m.–5 p.m., Thurs. 10 a.m.– 8 p.m., free*). Then proceed to the Renaissance-style **25 Broadway,** the Cunard Building **❷** by Benjamin Morris. Built in 1921 as the Cunard Line's New York headquarters, it now houses financial businesses, but take a look inside the Great Hall, where tickets for ocean liners like the *Titanic* and *Lusitania* were sold; its murals and decorated domed ceiling were based on Raphael's Villa Madama in Rome. Continue up Broadway,

---

INSIDER TIP:

On Broadway, at the southeast corner of Trinity Churchyard, you'll find a unique photo op of the old church with One World Trade Center rising behind it.

–CHRISTOPHER AUGER-DOMÍNGUEZ
*National Geographic
International Editions photographer*

---

passing Arturo Di Modica's bronze bull (see p. 54). The building at No. 26, designed by Carrère and Hastings, has a pyramid tower; it was once the Standard Oil Building.

Return to Broadway. Just north of **Trinity Church** (see p. 57) and the head of Wall Street, the hulking 1915 **Equitable Building ❸** (*120 Broadway*) rises straight up for 38 stories. The protests of critics who feared that such buildings would make the city a sunless canyon led to zoning laws in 1916 requiring setbacks (in which upper stories are stepped

NOT TO BE MISSED:

Cunard Building • Federal Reserve Bank • Woolworth Building

back to allow more light to reach street level). Just beyond the Equitable Building, the sleek **Marine Midland Building ❹** (*140 Broadway*), built in 1967 by Skidmore, Owings & Merrill, has one of Lower Manhattan's finer plazas, set off by Isamu Noguchi's red cube sculpture (1973). The green space opposite is Zuccotti Park, site of the 2011 Occupy Wall Street protest camp. Turn right onto Liberty Street. Ahead, the **Federal Reserve Bank ❺** (*33 Liberty St., tel 212/720–6130 for free tours with advance reservation*), in the style of a Renaissance palace, holds the cash reserves of many banks plus gold bullion from countries throughout the world. The four-story Vermont marble building at No. 65, fronted by Ionic columns, was built in 1901 for the Chamber of Commerce of the State of New York. The organization was founded by 20 city merchants meeting at Fraunces Tavern in 1768. Turn left on Nassau Street, then right on John Street. The austere **John Street United Methodist Church ❻** (*44 John St., tel 212/269–0014*), built in 1841, replaced the 1768 Wesley Chapel, the first Methodist church in the United States. An early sexton was a slave who purchased his freedom from the chapel's trustees. He later founded the country's first black Methodist church.

Turn left on William Street. On the southwest corner of Fulton Street is the site of writer Washington Irving's birthplace (*131 William St.*). Turn left on Fulton, and right on Broadway.

St. Paul's Chapel ❼ (*tel 212/602–0800*) and its churchyard, between Fulton and Vesey Streets, has been in continuous use since it opened in 1766 as an adjunct of Trinity Church. George Washington worshipped here; his pew is marked by a plaque. The chapel now houses a memorial to victims of the 9/11 terrorist attack, including "The Unwavering Spirit," a permanent exhibit. Just beyond St. Paul's is the **9/11 Memorial** site, with One World Trade Center, a public memorial and WTC Transportation Hub (see p. 63).

Proceed up Broadway. No. 233, between Park Place and Barclay Street, is the 60-story **Woolworth Building** ❽. Topped by a golden crown, it was the world's tallest from 1913 until 1929, when the tower at 40 Wall Street outreached it. Its architect, Cass Gilbert, described it as a steel frame covered with masonry and terra-cotta. Take a walk through City Hall Park to **City Hall** (see p. 62) to end the tour. You can go back to Broadway or swing over to **South Street Seaport** (see pp. 64–65).

⛰	See also map pp. 48–49
➤	National Museum of the American Indian
↔	1.25 miles
⏱	2.5 hours
➤	City Hall

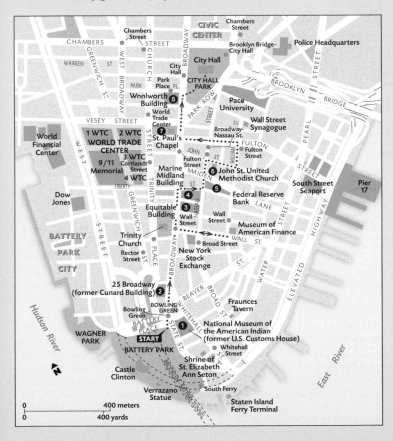

CITY HALL & CITY HALL PARK

City Hall Park, once a Dutch cow pasture and now pleasantly landscaped, surrounds the magnificent, federal-style City Hall. Frederick MacMonnies's bronze statue of patriot Nathan Hale on the green is a reminder that Americans once protested British rule here. For a liberating experience, stroll across the street to the imposing Brooklyn Bridge, with its wide wooden walkways and bike paths, and spectacular views north and south.

■ City Hall Park, a green oasis near Wall Street: City Hall is visible through the trees, and the Municipal Building is to the right.

Although the hall is sited in the middle of City Hall Park, its architects, John McComb, Jr., and Joseph Francois Mangin, faced the building south. This was because, when it was built in 1812, few thought the city would extend farther north.

Venture inside, where you will see in the lobby a bronze copy of a statue of George Washington, crafted from life by the French sculptor Jean-Antoine Houdon.

The **Governor's Room** is now a museum with George Washington's writing table on display. The paintings here include a portrait of Washington on Evacuation Day 1783, by John Trumbull, as well as works by John Wesley Jarvis, who painted the heroes of the War of 1812, and Samuel F. B. Morse, inventor of the telegraph, whose portrait of Lafayette was made during the marquis's triumphal return to the U.S. in 1824.

Northeast of City Hall, near Park Row, J. Q. A. Ward's statue of Horace Greeley shows the publisher seated with a newspaper over his right knee. For years Park Row was the center of Manhattan newspaper publishing. For a brief history of the park, seek out the circular tablet at the southern end that was added at the turn of the millennium to educate visitors. ■

City Hall

- 🅰 Map p. 48
- ✉ City Hall Park
- ☎ 212/788–3000
- 🕐 Group tours Mon.–Wed. from 10.30 a.m.; individual tours also Wed. 12 p.m.
- 🚇 Subway: 4, 5, 6 to Brooklyn Bridge; R to City Hall; 2, 3 to Park Place

Even strangers to New York will probably recognize City Hall from countless news shots of the mayor greeting visiting dignitaries and handing over the keys to the city on its steps. City Hall has also been the center of many celebrations and demonstrations. This is where ticker-tape parades up Broadway from the Battery usually end, a tradition that started in 1886 when office workers threw ticker tape out of windows during a parade celebrating the dedication of the Statue of Liberty.

GROUND ZERO & THE 9/11 MEMORIAL

When the twin towers of the World Trade Center (WTC) fell, the landscape of lower Manhattan changed forever. Yet in the years of reconstruction since, city planners' main aim has been to rebuild around Ground Zero while honoring the memories of the 2,983 people who died in the terrorist attacks of February 26, 1993, and September 11, 2001. While the new WTC has divided opinion, the 9/11 Memorial and Museum remembers the events with a quiet, graceful dignity.

Since 2001, Ground Zero has become the most visited site in New York, and a visit to the **9/11 Memorial and Museum** is a moving experience. The memorial, designed by Daniel Libeskind, opened on the tenth anniversary of the attacks. It features pools set into the footprints of the

INSIDER TIP:

Stop by the Callery pear tree known as the Survivor Tree, just west of the south pool. Its story of survival and resilience is inspiring.

–PETER GWIN
National Geographic writer

twin towers. Thirty-foot (9 m) waterfalls cascade into these, each descending into a center void. To the soothing sound of water, walk around the pools and read the names of the victims, inscribed in bronze parapets. To find a name, visit *names.911memorial.org* or download the 9/11 Memorial Guide app.

The eight-acre (3.2 ha) site is surrounded by a spiral of new towers, including **One World**

■ The South Tower pool of the 9/11 Memorial is built on the footprint of the fallen building. Names of the victims skirt the edge.

Trade Center, just beyond the north pool, with its spectacular observatory on the 102nd floor (*oneworldobservatory.com*). Standing at a symbolic 1,776 feet (541 m), this glass tower is the tallest building in the U.S.

Enter the museum through the impressive glass and steel pavilion building between the pools. Then descend to the memorial plaza, which uses the deep foundations of the original WTC as exhibition space. The focal points are the two steel tridents, the familiar forked columns from the facade of the old North Tower. ■

9/11 Memorial & Museum

🅼 Map p. 48

✉ World Trade Center, 1 Albany St.

☎ 212/266–5211
212/312–8800

💲 $$$$ (free Tues. 5 p.m.–8 p.m.)

🚇 Subway: A, C, J, Z, 2, 3, 4, 5 to Fulton St.; 2, 3 to Park Place; E to WTC; R, 1 to Rector St.; R to Cortland St.

911memorial.org

SEAPORT DISTRICT & SOUTH STREET SEAPORT MUSEUM

For a trip back to the days when New York Harbor was the world's busiest port, visit the 11-square-block historic district along the East River at South and Fulton Streets. Here you'll find the South Street Seaport Museum, a restoration of the early 19th-century waterfront. The damage done by Hurricane Sandy (2012) are no longer visible. The area is once more in the throes of historic changes, as it seeks to reinvent itself once again.

Seaport District: This designated historic district has many 19th-century landmarks.

Prior to the storm, the entire seaport area had become an outstanding maritime museum, in and among important 18th- and 19th-century buildings. The **Titanic Memorial Lighthouse** at the intersection of Pearl, Water, and Fulton Streets marks its entry point. The seaport divides into two areas ahead of you, with F. D. R. Drive perpendicular to Fulton Street in between. West of the drive, in front of the lighthouse, are complexes of joined buildings. These housed the seaport's museums, exhibits, offices, and small stores. East of F. D. R. Drive you'll see the pier, with its historic ships.

Fulton Market Building, which suffered severe storm damage, has yet to reopen at publication time. As you walk along the piers, the Seaport offers superb views of the river and Brooklyn Bridge.

Exploring the Seaport

While the South Street Seaport Museum is under reconstruction,

INSIDER TIP:

Having a hard time fig-
uring out which bridges
you're looking at as you
gaze up the river from
the seaport? The order
from south to north is
BMW: Brooklyn, Man-
hattan, Williamsburg.

–LARRY PORGES
National Geographic
Travel Books editor

the building at Water Street is
worth a visit. The new location
has a collection of 26,500 works
of art that document New
York's development as a port
city and the economic center of
the United States. Some of the
objects on display came from
the Fulton Fish Market. **Bowne
& Co. Stationers** (*211 Water St.,
tel 646/315–4478*) is a working
restoration of a 19th-century
print shop (see sidebar p. 37).
From Water Street, head for the
piers via the main Fulton Street
corridor. Lined with shops and

restaurants, here you can shop in
10 Corso Como (*1 Fulton Street*),
an Italian design and fashion
trademark, inaugurated in 2018.
The 12-building complex on the
right is historic Schermerhorn
Row, dating from 1812 and
comprising 12 federal-style brick
buildings. Walk around it to John
Street, once an entrance for
ships from China that unloaded
their wares into the counting-
house of the **A. A. Low Building**
(*171 John St.*).

Turn back to the harbor, near
the intersection of South and
Fulton Streets, where Pier 16
and historic ships await. Here
you can buy tickets for harbor
cruises at the visitor center. Be
sure to wander **Piers 15** and
16. Outings include Circle Line
tours, a speedboat ride, and
seasonal tugboat rides (*information: tel 212/748–8786*). The fleet
includes the *Ambrose* (1908),
a lightship used in New York
Harbor; the *Peking,* a 1911 four-
masted ship built in Germany;
and the *Pioneer* (1885), a former
cargo schooner popular for its
twilight sails. ∎

South Street Seaport Museum

- 🗺 Map p. 48
- ✉ Fulton & South Sts.
- 🕐 Closed Mon. year-round, Mon.–Thur. Nov.–Mar.
- 💲 $$
- 🚇 Subway: 2, 3, 4, 5, J, Z, M to Fulton St.; A, C to Broadway/ Nassau

seaportdistrict.nyc

South Street Seaport Visitor Center

- ✉ Pier 16
- ☎ 212/748–8600 (main); 212/732–7678 (events)

Hurricane Sandy & Its Aftermath

The Howard Hughes Corporation's reno-
vation of the area includes the reconstruc-
tion of seven buildings for a total of
400,000 square feet (37,000 sq m) dedi-
cated to cuisine, fashion, entertainment,
and culture. The 17,000-square-foot (1,600
sq m) rooftop of the new Pier 17 offers
magnificent views of the New York skyline,
as well as signature restaurants, an open-
air bar, and spaces for concerts and special
events. The Tin Building was reconstructed
and reconverted to its original function as
a covered market. In fact, it was here that
the historical Fulton Fish Market opened in
1835 and operated for more than a cen-
tury. Recently, the market moved to Hunts
Point in the Bronx, where it still operates,
while the new building is home to a food
market managed by world-famous chef
Jean-Georges Vongerichten. Nearby, you
can find Carla Sozzani's concept store and
an iPic Theater.

THE NEIGHBORHOODS

Many immigrants began their new American lives in the lower Manhattan neighborhoods. Today these areas strive for balance as gentrification and high-rises introduce change.

■ On Chinatown's busy Mott Street, signs are in English and Chinese—and tourists mix with residents.

Chinatown

For the center of old Chinatown, head for Mott and Pell Streets below Canal Street. New York's first Chinese settlement developed in the mid-1870s along Mott Street, and today the area is filled with restaurants, cafés, curio and antique shops, and bookstores. Try one of the many fine restaurants and then explore.

There are daily masses in Cantonese and English at the 1801 **Church of the Transfiguration** (*25 Mott St., tel 212/962–5157*). The church was built for English Lutherans, sold to an Irish Roman Catholic congregation in 1853, and attracted an Italian community before becoming primarily Chinese.

The most visible symbols of Chinatown are the Chinese shop signs and the pagoda-style roofs that top anything from banks to telephone booths. At 41 Mott Street stands the only wooden pagoda roof left in Chinatown. The **Eastern States Buddhist Temple** (*64 Mott St., tel 212/966–6229*) is filled with candles and offerings to more than a hundred gold Buddhas, while the small **Museum of Chinese in America** holds fascinating exhibits.

You may seek out enclaves such as Doyers Street, once a dead-end alley known as the

Bloody Angle, where warring tongs ambushed one another. Confucius Plaza at Chatham Square is graced by a bronze statue of the ancient philosopher.

Chinatown's most colorful event is the five-week-long Lunar New Year Festival, kicked off with a mammoth celebration on the official New Year's Day in January or February (varies each year).

Chinatown today has expanded into Little Italy. Canal Street, once the division between Chinatown and Little Italy, has a bustling sidewalk market and Chinese groceries stocked with curious roots, herbs, and vegetables. West on Canal, closer to Broadway, shops teem with Chinese souvenirs and fashions as well as knock-off designer clothes and perfumes. All of Chinatown is fun to shop.

Historic Sites

The **Edward Mooney House** (circa 1785–89), at 18 Bowery, recalls an era when the area was known for its fine residences. Stanford White designed the Bowery Savings Bank (1895) now a Cipriani luxury restaurant and event space—at 130 Bowery, in the classical style of a Roman temple. **St. James Roman Catholic Church** (*32 James St.*) is the city's second oldest Roman Catholic church. Nearby, the **First Shearith Israel Graveyard** (*55–57 St. James Place*) is the burial ground of the first Jewish congregation in North America, formed in 1654 by Sephardim from Brazil.

Little Italy

Mulberry Street north of Canal is the pulse of what remains of Little Italy. Here you'll find Italian restaurants, cafés, delis, shops, and legendary Mafia sites. Start off with a cappuccino and a treat on Mulberry or at **Ferrara** (*195 Grand St.*), a hundred-plus-year-old pastry shop just around the corner.

Little Italy's annual gala is the Feast of San Gennaro, held for eleven days in mid-September. A statue is paraded through the

---

INSIDER TIP:

At Sara D. Roosevelt Park, in Chinatown, on any fair morning between spring and fall, you'll find Chinese men showing off their colorful songbirds in bamboo cages. Listen for the yellow hua-mei, a thrush whose song conjures romance.

–KENNY LING
National Geographic contributor

---

streets and there are food stalls, music, and dancing, with activity centered around the courtyard of the **Church of the Most Precious Blood** (*109 Mulberry St.*). Mulberry Street is also connected to organized crime. Before being jailed, mobster boss John Gotti frequented the Ravenite Social Club at No. 247. Gangster Joey Gallo was shot to death in

Museum of Chinese in America

✉ 211–215 Centre St., bet. Howard & Grand Sts.

☎ 855/955–6622

🕐 Closed Mon.

💲 $$

🚇 Subway: B, D to Grand St.; J, M, N, R, Q, Z, 6 to Canal St.

mocanyc.org

Lower East Side Tenement Museum

✉ 97 Orchard St.

Museum Visitor Center

✉ 103 Orchard St.

☎ 212/982–8420

💲 $$$

🚇 Subway: F to Delancey St.; B, D to Grand St.; J, M, Z to Essex St.

tenement.org

New Museum

✉ 235 Bowery at Prince St.

☎ 212/219–1222

🕐 Closed Mon.

💲 $$$$

🚇 Subway: N, R to Prince St.; 6 to Spring St.

newmuseum.org

1972 on his birthday, at No. 129, Umberto's Clam House.

Some historic sites have little original connection with Italian residents. Gothic **St. Patrick's Old Cathedral** (*260–264 Mulberry St., tel 212/226–8075*) is one of the city's oldest churches (1815), largely rebuilt after a fire in the 1860s. Its first congregation was Irish; a smaller Italian congregation developed in the 1880s. The **Stephen Van Rensselaer House** (*149 Mulberry St.*), with its brickwork front, gambrel roof, and dormer windows, was built in about 1816. The beaux arts-style 1909 New York City Police Building (*240 Centre St.*), once a proud symbol of the city's modern police force, was converted into luxury apartments in the 1980s.

Lower East Side

Street names are all that remain of the Lower East Side's rural, colonial past. Orchard Street ran through fruit trees. The Bowery, a principal north-south thoroughfare, once led to Peter Stuyvesant's *bouwerie,* or farm.

Some of the city's finest houses were on the Bowery, but once the immigrants arrived—Irish in the 1830s, then Germans, and, in the 1880s, thousands of Eastern European Jews, Poles, Italians, Romanians, Russians, and Greeks—the Lower East Side became a place of tenements and slums. How that has changed with escalating rents!

To travel back in time, visit the **Lower East Side Tenement Museum,** in a preserved and restored tenement building. Purchased by the museum in 1988, the six-story brownstone was built in 1863 before the advent of housing laws. Living conditions were appalling—tiny, windowless rooms, without electricity or plumbing. Some 10,000 people are estimated to have lived in the building until it was condemned in 1935. Visitors can see immigrants' apartments and educational displays, and the shop sells gifts and books on immigrant life.

Founded in 1977, the **New Museum** has the mission of

EXPERIENCE: Party on the Streets at a New York Street Fair or Festival

Between late spring and autumn, you very likely will stumble upon a street fair in New York City. Large fairs will have foods such as corn on the cob, fruit smoothies, and sausage sandwiches, with vendors selling everything from jewelry to bonsai plants. One of the most popular street fairs is the **Feast of San Gennaro** (*sangennaro.org*), in historic Little Italy each September. Also extremely popular

is the annual **Ninth Avenue Food Festival** (*ninthavenuefoodfestival.com*), known for its wide array of international foods, held in May along Ninth Avenue from 42nd to 57th Streets. More than a million people visit each of these festivals annually, so be prepared for large crowds. For a current list of upcoming street fairs and festivals, check the Mayor's Community Affairs Unit website: *nyc.gov/caucalendar.*

■ Shoppers browse the informal displays along Orchard Street on the Lower East Side.

promoting new art and new ideas. Thirty years later, the museum relocated to a new seven-story building (meant to evoke stacked boxes shifted off-axis) on the Bowery, where the opening exhibit of "Unmonumental: The Object in the 21st Century" showcased more than 100 works by artists who used found, fragmented, and discarded materials. An outdoor terrace on the top floor provides a panoramic view.

The recently restored **Eldridge Street Synagogue** belies the belief that the entire Lower East Side was impoverished. Completed in 1887, the Moorish Revival building cost $100,000, a stupendous sum at the time.

As the population changed, synagogues took over churches. The 1826 **Bialystoker Synagogue** (7–11 Bialystoker Pl., tel

---

INSIDER TIP:

Don't miss the Lower East Side Tenement Museum for insight into the tough beginnings that many U.S. immigrants experienced after entering through Ellis Island.

–BARBARA A. NOE
National Geographic Travel Books senior editor

212/475-0165) was built in 1826 as the Willett Street Methodist Episcopal Church and it became a synagogue in 1905. The **Forward Building** (175 E. Broadway), a ten-story classical revival structure that is now a residential building, was completed in 1912 for the *Jewish Daily Forward,* a widely read

Eldridge Street Synagogue

✉ 12–16 Eldridge St. at Canal St.
☎ 212/219-0888
🕐 Closed Sat.
🚇 Subway: B, D to Grand St.

eldridgestreet.org

■ Boutique shops and cafés line the streets of trendy SoHo.

Yiddish newspaper. The building is decorated with flaming torches, symbols of the socialist causes the paper supported. Nearby, the Educational Alliance at No. 197 was founded in 1889 to ease the process of Americanization. Comedian Eddie Cantor, sculptor Chaim Gross, and broadcasting pioneer David Sarnoff studied here; they are just a few of the talented people who grew up in the neighborhood.

Traditional Jewish shops bring former residents back to the "old neighborhood" for religious items—and especially for food. The **Essex Street Market** (*120 Essex St.*), filled with a vibrant mix of food merchants, originally housed pushcart peddlers. You can make a stop at Russ & Daughters (*179 E. Houston St.*), a New York institution for kosher food that opened in 1914. Also here are Kossar's Bialys (*367 Grand St., tel 212/473–4810, closed Sat.*) and Katz's, the popular delicatessen (*205 E. Houston St., tel 212/254–2246*). Meg Ryan's memorable moment in the 1989 film *When Harry Met Sally* was filmed at Katz's, and yes, the food really is that good.

SoHo & Tribeca

SoHo, an acronym for "South of Houston (Street)," lies between Houston and Canal Streets, West Broadway, and Lafayette Street. Famous for its concentration of fine cast-iron buildings (see pp. 72–73), its main thoroughfare, West Broadway, is lined with specialty shops, high-end shoe stores, antiques stores, trendy restaurants, and art galleries—though many have relocated to Chelsea or Midtown.

In the 1970s SoHo's lofts and low rents attracted young artists. As the area was "discovered," rents soared, and artists sought affordable space elsewhere. Many moved

INSIDER TIP:

Dinner and a movie at the Tribeca Film Festival? Enjoy fine traditional Japanese cuisine at Nobu [195 Broadway, 212/219–0500, noburestaurants .com/new-york], the flagship of Chef Nobu Matsuhisa, followed by a show at Tribeca Cinemas.
—SEAN EGAN
Film Writer,
Chelsea Now/The Villager

to an industrial section between Canal and Chambers Streets.

The area acquired a chic new name, Tribeca ("triangle below Canal"), and the SoHo phenomenon repeated itself, with building conversions and an influx of shops, galleries, restaurants, and nightclubs.

Into the 1990s, the transformation of Tribeca picked up speed, led by actor Robert De Niro's 1989 renovation of a warehouse into the **Tribeca Film Center** and the **Tribeca Grill** (*tel 212/941–3900*). From Sixth Avenue to Hudson Street there are now upscale furniture stores, unusual shops, and restaurants

in all price ranges, from Bâtard establishments to Bubby's (*120 Hudson St., tel 212/ 219–0666*), where brunch is an institution. The Roxy Hotel Tribeca (*2 Avenue of the Americas, tel 212/519–6600*) caters to the entertainment industry, and celebrities frequent the public lounge. The Tribeca Film Festival (see sidebar below), was established in 2001. As the neighborhood's transformation continues, it guards its architectural treasures, including the federal-style Harrison Street Houses (*25–41 Harrison St.*). ∎

Tribeca Film Center

✉ 375 Greenwich St

☎ 212/941–2000

tribecafilmcenter .com

Tribeca Film Festival

The film world comes to Lower Manhattan every spring for the Tribeca Film Festival (*tribecafilm.com/ festival*). Founded in 2002 by film producer Jane Rosenthal, her husband Craig Hatkoff, and Academy Award winner Robert De Niro, the festival was designed to rejuvenate the Tribeca area, economically and culturally, after the 9/11 attacks. While screenings are primarily in the flagship **Tribeca Cinemas** (*54 Varick St., tel 212/941–2001*), festival events have mushroomed all over the downtown area. These include not only premieres from new talents and veterans, but also family programming, post-screening discussions, and lively panels with directors and actors.

WALK: CAST IRON IN SOHO

This walk through SoHo's historic cast-iron district begins on West Broadway, goes south, then briefly touches on Canal Street before swinging back north on Broadway to West Houston. You will see outstanding examples of the cast-iron style, which were prefabricated, shipped to the building site, and bolted onto the structures. The result was highly ornate architecture with the appearance of stone carving.

Start on West Broadway, between Prince and Spring Streets. You can pick up a free gallery guide at any gallery nearby. Start at 421 West Broadway, the **Crown Fine Art Gallery ❶** (*tel 212/757–8255, sohogallery. com*) for fine contemporary art. Here you can pick up a print at a reasonable price, or maybe consider spending $88,000 ("negotiable!") on a Warhol depicting the Brooklyn Bridge, the pop artist's only official NYC commission. A few doors down, at No. 419, photography

> **NOT TO BE MISSED:**
>
> Queen of Greene Street • King of Greene Street • Haughwout Building

buffs will enjoy a stroll through **Lik Soho** (*tel 212/941–6391, lik.com*), with many fine art photos of New York. Just before you enter the cast-iron district, stop by **Cipriani Downtown** (*376 W Broadway, tel 212/343–0999*), a French bistro offering cozy tables indoor and out, with heated lamps for winter.

Turn left (east) at Broome Street. No. 489 was built in 1873. Turn right (south) on Wooster Street to No. 33, the **Performing Garage** (*tel 212/966–9796*), home of the avant-garde Wooster Group of actors. Crossing Grand Street, look back at the Grecian-style Nos. 68–70 Grand St., designed by George da Cunha. Go south a block to Canal Street and turn left, and then left again, onto Greene Street, heading uptown.

This is SoHo's premier cast-iron district, with an unbroken expanse of ten buildings, Nos. 8 through Nos. 32–34. Isaac F. Duckworth designed the Empire-style Nos. 28–30, known as the **Queen of Greene Street ❷**; its mansard roof is a fitting crown. But the true cast-iron king is Henry Fernbach, who designed most of this block. Note the variations in the exterior staircases, columns, and windows, with repetitive identical elements that suggest their origin in a cast-iron mold. One of the most extravagant structures, also by Duckworth and aptly dubbed the **King of Greene Street ❸**, is Nos. 72–76, with stacked porches and Corinthian pillars.

Renovated cast iron-fronted buildings along Greene Street

Turn right (east) on Spring Street, then right (south) on Mercer. Turn left (east) on Broome Street. One block east, turn left (north) onto Broadway. The 1857 **Haughwout Building ❹** (*488 Broadway at Broome St.*) is the oldest and best preserved cast-iron building in the city, and the first to have a passenger elevator, designed by Elisha Otis.

On the left, between Broome and Spring Streets, 521–523 Broadway is all that remains of the elegant **St. Nicholas Hotel** (1854), which closed in the 1870s. Alfred Zucker built 555 Broadway in 1889 for wholesaler Charles Rouss, a real-life Horatio Alger story. A sign on the construction site read: "He who builds, owns, and will occupy this marvel of brick, iron, and granite, thirteen years ago walked these streets penniless and $50,000 in debt." The green structure at 561 Broadway is known as the **Little Singer Building ❺**, designed in 1903 by Ernest Flagg for the Singer Manufacturing Company. Note the terra-cotta facade, wrought-iron balconies, and windows. No. 560 Broadway houses several top galleries, including Janet Borden and Staley-Wise.

At Prince Street, bibliophiles will want to take a right and then a quick left to 126 Crosby Street, **Housing Works Used Book Café** (*tel 212/334-3324, housingworks.org/bookstore*). Then retrace your steps and go north on Broadway to

⛰ See also map pp. 48–49

▶ Crown Fine Art Gallery

↔ 1.1 miles (1.7 km)

🕐 1.5 hours

▶ Angelika Film Center

INSIDER TIP:

Avoid the easily made mistake of confusing West Broadway with Broadway. Check your map.

—MIKE McNEY
National Geographic Maps

---

the crossroads at Houston Street. Across the way at 610 Broadway is a seven-story modern office building by Christian Amolsch. West along Houston, the structures at Nos. 19–35 and No. 55, by H. Thomas O'Hara, represent the "gateway to SoHo." The **Angelika Film Center ❻** (*18 W. Houston St., tel 212/995-2000, angelikafilmcenter. com*), one of the city's best independent cinemas, has a fine public café.

Places of Interest Off the Beaten Path

African Burial Ground National Monument

The African Burial Ground (*bet. Duane & Elk Sts.*) is the most important urban achaeological project in the U.S. Human remains dug up in 1991 by workers turned out to have come from a five-acre (2 ha) graveyard, where 20,000 African Americans were buried between 1712 and 1794. *nps.gov/afbg* ✉ 290 Broadway ☎ 212/637–2019 🕐 Closed Sun.–Mon. 🚇 Subway: 2, 3 to Park Place; 4, 5, 6 to Brooklyn Bridge; R to City Hall

The Drawing Center

The center has been a unique part of the city's cultural life since 1977. It was founded to promote drawing as an art, and its excellent contemporary and historical exhibits feature everyone from Picasso to contemporary cartoonists and street artists. Called by the *New York Times* "one of the city's most highly respected small art museums." *drawingcenter.org* ✉ 35 Wooster St. ☎ 212/219–2166

Irish Hunger Memorial

Just west of the World Trade Center site, on the bank of the Hudson River, the Irish Hunger Memorial commemorates the Irish Famine of 1845–1852, which killed a million Irish and drove another two million to emigrate. The memorial takes the form of a hillside, comprising grasses and stones brought from each of Ireland's 32 counties. A path leads past the ruins of a stone cottage, a symbol of all the lives left behind. From the hilltop, visitors can view Ellis Island (see p. 52), through which so many of the refugee Irish came to America. The memorial stands at the western end of Vesey Street (see map p. 48).

🕐 Closed Mon.–Tues. 🚇 Subway: A, C, E, Q to Canal St.

Museum of American Finance

This display is based on the personal collection of founder John E. Herzog and is the nation's only public museum of finance. Its collection includes an 1880 stock ticker invented by Thomas Edison. *moaf.org* ✉ 48 Wall St. ☎ 212/908–4110 🕐 Temporarily closed. Consult the website for information regarding the event calendar 🚇 Subway: 2, 3, 4, 5 to Wall St.

Museum of Jewish Heritage

A living memorial to those who perished in the Holocaust, the museum opened in 1997, with a new wing dedicated in 2003. It provides poignant insight into 20th-century Jewish history. *mjhnyc.org* ✉ 36 Battery Place, Battery Park City ☎ 646/437–4202 🕐 Closed Sat. & Jewish holidays 💲 $$ 🚇 Subway: 1 to South Ferry; 4, 5 to Bowling Green

New York City Fire Museum

This rich collection of historic fire-fighting equipment and memorabilia, housed in a former fire station in SoHo, includes fire engines dating back to 1765. The first floor houses a permanent 9/11 memorial. *nycfiremuseum.org* ✉ 278 Spring St., bet. Hudson & Varick Sts. ☎ 212/691–1303 💲 $$ 🚇 Subway: 1 to Houston St.; C, E to Spring St.

The Skyscraper Museum

Through exhibitions, programs, and publications, this museum celebrates New York's rich architectural heritage and the forces and individuals that have shaped its successive skylines. *skyscraper.org* ✉ 39 Battery Place, Battery Park City ☎ 212/968–1961 🕐 Closed Mon.–Tues. 💲 $ 🚇 Subway: 1 to South Ferry; 4, 5 to Bowling Green

Narrow streets and quaint low-rise buildings that have been home to New York's finest families, its immigrants, and some of America's best artists and writers

THE VILLAGES

Old Glory flies on an Astor Place building in the East Village.

THE VILLAGES

Greenwich Village is one of New York's legendary neighborhoods. Centered around and west of Washington Square Park, it extends from Houston Street north to 14th Street and from Broadway west to the Hudson. Encompassing the Meatpacking District, it is often called the West Village to distinguish it from the equally vibrant East Village, which until the 1950s was viewed as part of the Lower East Side.

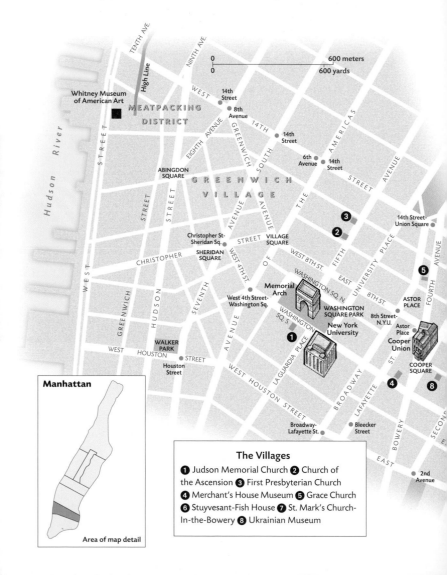

Manhattan

Area of map detail

The Villages

❶ Judson Memorial Church ❷ Church of the Ascension ❸ First Presbyterian Church ❹ Merchant's House Museum ❺ Grace Church ❻ Stuyvesant-Fish House ❼ St. Mark's Church-In-the-Bowery ❽ Ukrainian Museum

The West Village's reputation as a haven for freethinkers, free-lovers, artists, poets, writers, rebels, and revolutionaries dates back to the turn of the 20th century; and that reputation applies now equally to the East Village (east of Broadway). Even the street plan of the West Village is bohemian—the diagonal streets defy the grid plan imposed on the rest of the city north of 14th Street. West Village streets follow divisions that once marked farms and are lined with low-rise houses and green courtyards.

Today, in addition to poets and artists, you will find students, skateboarders, women pushing baby carriages, and men playing chess in Washington Square Park in the West Village or Tompkins Square Park in the East Village, along with that dreaded fixture of urban life, the drug dealer. Washington Square Park is well protected by the New York City police, and Tompkins Square, renovated and free of squatters, is now a community-oriented park.

Nothing keeps away visitors and new residents able to pay the ever soaring rents. The West Village is unique and alluring, an attraction for New Yorkers from all over the city and tourists from all over the world. Drawn

by the Italian groceries, antique stores, and outdoor art shows, they seek the past in coffeehouses, bars, and streets where the now legendary once hung out. Bob Dylan sang his folk songs in the early 1960s in Washington Square Park. Writers haunt the White Horse Tavern, an 1880s saloon at the corner of Hudson and West 11th Streets. Here the Welsh poet Dylan Thomas had his final drink. In the East Village, you'll find McSorley's Old Ale House on East Seventh Street, founded in 1854 and dedicated to "Good Ale, Raw Onions, and No Ladies" (until 1970 when women were finally admitted). The legendary CBGB closed in 2006, but the new Bowery Poetry Club (*308 Bowery, tel 212/614-0505, bowerypoetrystudios.com/club*) hosts open mics, readings, and events. ■

WASHINGTON SQUARE PARK

Extensive reconstruction of Washington Square Park began in 2007, including relocation of the fountain and expansion of unpaved green space; the first phase was completed in 2011. Since the 1960s, when the park closed to traffic, it has been one of the city's great gathering places—for students, performers, dog walkers, tourists, and, to keep an eye on things, police. The focal point is the landmark 86-foot-tall (26 m) Washington Arch, dedicated in 1895.

■ Washington Square Park on a rare quiet day during a snowstorm

Washington Square Park
🖼 Map p. 76

NOTE: Washington Square is the center of New York University (NYU; *70 Washington Sq. S., tel 212/998–1212*); its library, law school, and administrative buildings line the park. Founded in 1831, NYU was intended as a nonsectarian alternative to Columbia University (see p. 193).

The city used the almost-ten-acre (4 ha) parcel of land as a potter's field, public gallows, and parade ground before redesigning it in 1826 as Washington Square Park. With it came chic town houses, like the 12 exquisite Greek Revival brick houses (1831–1833) known as "the Row."

Although the Row and its northern environs housed writers and artists—Edith Wharton, Willa Cather, John Dos Passos, and Mark Twain, among others—there was never anything bohemian about this neighborhood. Writer Djuna

Barnes described the difference between the north and south sides of the square in early 20th-century terms: "satin and motorcars on this side, squalor and pushcarts on that." Even today, the square separates two very different neighborhoods. Along the northern side, near the arch, the streets are quiet, tree-lined, and patrician. Two churches a short distance north of the arch on Fifth Avenue continue the sense of restraint. At West Tenth Street, Richard Upjohn designed the 1841 Gothic Revival **Church of the Ascension** (*10th St.*

& 5th Ave., tel 212/254–8620). The stained glass and altar mural are by John La Farge. The 1846 **First Presbyterian Church** (*12 W. 12th St., tel 212/675–6150*) has a tower that is based on one at Oxford's Magdalen College.

Across from the arch, in the direction of Bleecker Street, the atmosphere becomes more ethnic and earthy. **Judson Memorial Church** (1892) is still known for its political activism. This Romanesque basilica has stained-glass windows by John La Farge and a marble relief by Augustus Saint-Gaudens. Its social and political mission was to bring together the square's aristocratic northern residents with immigrants on the south side.

Struggling writers and artists moved here, too. Mrs. Branchard's boardinghouse at 61 Washington Square South—the "house of genius"—was home to writers Stephen Crane, Theodore Dreiser,

and Frank Norris. Provincetown Playhouse (*139 MacDougal St.*) was where Eugene O'Neill's works were first produced. Writer John Reed (1887–1920), resident at 42 Washington Square South between 1911 and 1912, celebrated the Village as a place where "nobody questions your morals, and nobody asks for the rent." ∎

Judson Memorial Church

⬛ Map p. 76
✉ 55 Washington Square South
☎ 212/477–0351

EXPERIENCE: Hit the Hot Spots of the Meatpacking District

On the northwest fringes of Greenwich Village, the Meatpacking District has transformed from industrial to hip. From serving the city with 250 slaughterhouses and packing plants in 1900 to having barely three dozen a hundred years later, the area has now shifted to a concentration of high-fashion shops. Among them are **Helmut Lang** and **Diane von Furstenberg** on the stretch of West 14th Street from Ninth to Tenth Avenues. Also tucked away on this block is the **Ground Zero Museum Workshop** (*420 W. 14th St., tel 212/924–1040, groundzeromuseumworkshop.com*), where visitors can view images and artifacts of the recovery period after 9/11. On the northwest corner of Ninth Avenue and West 14th Street, across from the 1868 **Old Homestead Steakhouse,** a huge Apple store (*401 W. 14th St., tel 212/444–3400, closed Sun.*) stands as a three-story glass beacon. Heading towards the entrance of the High Line, you'll find the Woodstock, a new, 1960s-themed bar with 24 original Salvador Dalí paintings. The French bistro, Pastis, is reopening on Gansevoort Street with new cuisine created by McNally and Starr (*www.pastisny.com*). For a homey feel, try Serafina Meatpacking (Italian; *meatpacking. serafinarestaurant.com*).

A WALK IN GREENWICH VILLAGE

This 90-minute walk around the West Village historic district wends through quiet residential areas, charming nooks and enclaves, and busy thoroughfares.

The picturesque streets of Greenwich Village echo with artistic and bohemian history.

Your walk begins at Sixth Avenue (Ave. of the Americas) and Ninth Street, by the landmark **Jefferson Market Courthouse Library ❶**. Its name derives from a market named for President Thomas Jefferson that opened on the site in 1833. The present building is a redbrick Gothic structure (1877). In the 1960s, crusading Villagers saved the structure from demolition.

NOT TO BE MISSED:

Gay Street • Sheridan Square • Father Demo Square

Go left on West Tenth Street to **Patchin Place ❷**, a cul-de-sac of ten brick houses from 1848, built to house waiters from the Hotel Brevoort. Poet E. E. Cummings lived at No. 4 for 40 years until his death in 1962. Look for a plaque with his verse. At the end of the street you'll find the last gaslight lamppost in New York.

Turn left on Greenwich Avenue, right onto Christopher Street, and left again on **Gay Street ❸**. This short curving street is a perfect introduction to the irregular street pattern in the Village, which refused to adopt the grid plan imposed on the city north of 14th Street. Gay Street became famous as the birthplace of *My Sister Eileen* (1938), a book about life in zany Greenwich Village. The author, Ruth McKenney, was a young woman from Ohio who lived here with her sister, Eileen, a struggling actress, at 14 Gay Street, midway down on the right.

Turn left on Waverly Place. Edgar Allan Poe, master of the macabre, lived at No. 137. When ill, he walked down the street for treatment— to follow his path, turn back, walking west on Waverly Place. The triangular building ahead is the 1827 **Northern Dispensary ❹**, where Poe could get free medical care.

Turn left on Stonewall Place (a segment of Christopher St.), named after the **Stonewall Inn ❺**, where the gay liberation movement began on June 27, 1969. The present bar occupies part of the space of the original inn (*53 Christopher St.*). Next door is the **55 Bar,** a Prohibition-era bar that also serves up a good selection of live jazz, funk, and blues music. **Christopher Park,** across from the bars, has a George Segal sculpture of gay couples, and a statue of the Civil War general, Philip Henry Sheridan.

Ahead is Seventh Avenue. This area is known as **Sheridan Square ❻**, a pulse of Village life. Early in her career, Barbra Streisand appeared at the **Duplex** cabaret (*61 Christopher St. at 7th Ave. S., tel 212/255–5438*). The **Village Vanguard** (*178 7th Ave. S., tel 212/255–4037*), three blocks north on Seventh Avenue, has been preeminent among jazz clubs since 1935.

Go south on Seventh Avenue and turn right on Grove Street. Revolutionary-era writer Thomas Paine lived for a time at No. 59, where an 1839 building now houses **Marie's Crisis Café** (*tel 212/243–9323*), a sing-along piano bar.

Continue to Bedford Street and turn right to No. 102, Twin Peaks, remodeled in 1926 after a building in Nuremberg as an inspirational home for artists. Continue to Christopher Street and turn left, then left again on Hudson Street to No. 485, **St. Luke in the Fields Episcopal Church ❼**. At the southwest corner of Hudson and Barrow is the gate to a peaceful public garden path with benches.

Turn left on Barrow Street and right on Bedford Street (or detour onto Commerce Street to see Cherry Lane Theater). Actor John Barrymore lived at **75½ Bedford** in 1915. Just 9.5 feet (2.8 m) wide, it is the city's narrowest house.

Turn right on Morton Street, left on Hudson, and left onto St. Luke's Place. New York mayor Jimmy Walker lived at No. 6 from 1886 to 1934. Resident writers included Theodore Dreiser (No. 16) and Marianne Moore (No. 14).

Cross Seventh Avenue to Leroy Street. This takes you to Bleecker Street, the Village's main street, with many funky shops and restaurants. Music lovers should make a detour towards Washington Square, to the Café Wha (*115 MacDougal St., tel. 212/254–3706*) where you can enjoy young artists with the talent of Jimi Hendrix and Bruce Springsteen. Benches and a fountain await you at Bleecker Street and Sixth Avenue in **Father Demo Square ❽**, named for a priest of the 1926 **Church of Our Lady of Pompeii** (*Carmine & Bleecker Sts.*).

Cross Sixth Avenue and pilgrimage down Bleecker to the legendary coffeehouse district, and onward to the **Bitter End** (*tel 212/673-7030*) at No. 147 (three and a half blocks east of Sixth Ave.), a springboard for comics and musicians such as Woody Allen, Bob Dylan, and Lady Gaga.

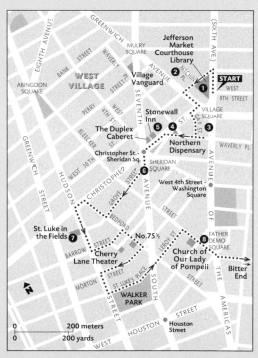

- See also map pp. 76–77
- Sixth Avenue and Ninth Street
- 1.5 miles (2.4 km)
- 1.5 hours
- Father Demo Square

WHITNEY MUSEUM OF AMERICAN ART

The Whitney Museum is one of the few museums anywhere founded by an artist, in this case, Gertrude Vanderbilt Whitney. A member of two of New York's most prominent and wealthy families, she was also a sculptor with a taste for the avant-garde. The Whitney is still one of the few museums dedicated to American art of the 20th and 21st centuries.

■ Edward Hopper's "Early Sunday Morning," a cornerstone of the Whitney collection

Whitney Museum of American Art

 Cartina p. 76

 99 Gansevoort St., bet. 10th Ave. & Washington St.

☎ 212/570–3600

🚇 Subway: A, C to 14th St.

whitney.org

The Whitney Museum was founded in 1966, a period in which the United States did little to encourage its artists. It played an important role in changing that mentality. After trying to expand the historical display space on Madison Avenue for years, the Whitney family decided to move the museum to a new location. The new structure, designed by architect Renzo Piano, is in a strategic position, at the entrance to the new High Line park. The display space has

been increased considerably and it better highlights the museum's priceless collections. The building, with its asymmetrical lines and dynamic, futuristic shape, has indoor galleries as well as open-air spaces and terraces that overlook the High Line. Its cantilevered entrance along Gansevoort Street provides a sheltered public space with a splendid view of the river, the park, and the industrial structures of the Meatpacking District. In fact, one of the goals of the project was to create a visual connection to the neighborhood, which has traditionally been tied to industrial activities. The building's nine floors are also home to an educational center for artists, classrooms, projection rooms, and two theaters, one of which has a capacity of 170. Its floors of reclaimed wood and LED light illumination with an advanced system of sun shading and natural refraction are some of the elements that make it an eco-friendly structure with low environmental impact. A restaurant on the ground floor and a bar on the top floor enliven the museum's atmosphere. Both were conceived by restauranteur Danny Mayer, who also managed the bar and restaurant in the old structure on the Upper East Side. A long-term collaboration with the Metropolitan Museum of Art has been planned for the temporary exhibits that alternate in the museum. The permanent collection is the richest and most important ever dedicated to American artists of the 20th and 21st centuries.

The Permanent Collection

Whitney's permanent collection has over 19,000 works that include paintings, sculptures, drawings, prints, photos, and multimedia installations. The galleries offer a significant selection of art dating from 1900 to 1950: works of Edward Hopper, Marsden Hartley, Georgia O'Keeffe, Stuart Davis, Arshile Gorky, and Alexander Calder. Some of the most admired masterpieces are "Circus" (1926–1931), a playful sculpture by Calder, O'Keefe's "Flower Abstraction" (1926), and "Early Sunday Morning" (1930) by Hopper. In 2000, the Mildred & Herbert Lee Galleries opened the door to key works of the collection from the postwar and contemporary periods, including the art of Willem de Kooning, Andy Warhol, Jasper Johns, Philip Guston, Alex Katz, Joseph Stella, Jackson Pollock, Louise Nevelson, and Kiki Smith. Look for "Green Coca-Cola Bottles" (1962) by Warhol, "Three Flags" (1958) by Johns, and "Black Majesty" (1955) by Nevelson. ∎

Whitney Pushing the Boundaries of Art

In 1913, Gertrude Whitney helped sponsor the Armory Show and afterward expanded her own studio into exhibition space and an artists' club. In 1929, she offered to give her collection to the Metropolitan Museum of Art. Her collection was refused—too new, too modern for the Met at the time—and she established her own museum, in four town houses at 8–14 West Eighth Street. This was the first museum in the world devoted to American art, and the origin of the Whitney Museum. Today, the museum still pushes the line of accepted forms of art, energetically seeking out independent artists in fields other places overlook, such as film and video. Its invitational spring Biennial, first held in 1932, continues to stir up controversy with its exhibition of emerging American artists and trends.

EAST VILLAGE

Once part of the ethnic Lower East Side, the East Village has attracted artists, musicians, writers, and political activists since the 1960s. Large numbers of immigrants still live here as well. Explore the many bookstores, record stores, and specialty shops. Eateries—from two-table storefronts to Jewish delis, Polish coffee shops, an entire street of Indian restaurants (East Sixth Street), and atmospheric gourmet restaurants—reflect the area's zesty ethnic mix.

■ Tompkins Square Park hosts the annual Howl Festival, featuring East Village art.

Cooper Union

🅐 Map p. 76
✉ 30 Cooper Sq.
☎ 212/353-4100
🚇 Subway: 6 to Astor Place

cooper.edu

Astor Place

Astor Place is at the center of a lively student-filled neighborhood formed by the junction of exotic St. Marks Place, businesslike Fourth Avenue, the once derelict Bowery, and the architecturally distinguished Lafayette Street.

Historically, Astor Place is identified with the 1849 Astor Place Riot that took place where an opera house once stood on the plaza. When an English actor named William Macready was hired over Irish-American actor Edwin Forrest to play Hamlet, more than 10,000 Irish Americans gathered in protest. Police fired on the crowd, killing and wounding many. Today many know the area as the home of the Italianate redbrick building housing the highly respected Cooper Union for the Advancement of Science and Art, commonly called **Cooper Union.**

Founded in 1857–1859 by Peter Cooper to provide a free higher education for worthy sons

INSIDER TIP:

If you like to lose yourself in a labyrinth of literature, head to the Strand Book Store, just south of Union Square [see p. 86]. But be warned, you might not surface for days.

—WILL KATINSKY
National Geographic contributor

and daughters of the city's poor, Cooper Union is still a tuition-free institution to this day. Almost every American president since then has spoken here. Cooper, who built the country's first steam locomotive engine, was a self-taught entrepreneur and reform-minded politician. His statue, by Augustus Saint-Gaudens, stands at the school's entrance.

Astor Library opened in 1854 as the city's first free library, thanks to a bequest from multi-millionaire and philanthropist John Jacob Astor. It is now **The Public Theater,** which was founded by the late Joseph Papp, the dynamic producer who, in 1965, persuaded the city to convert the building into theaters. Excellent plays and films are regularly scheduled. Also worthy of note is the 1886 **De Vinne Press Building** (*393–399 Lafayette St.*), which is built in the Romanesque Revival style, and **Colonnade Row** at Nos. 428–434, four houses remaining from a row of nine 1833 marble-fronted Greek Revival residences.

St. Marks & Alphabet City

At the heart of the East Village's is Tompkins Square Park, named for Daniel Tompkins (1774–1825), a governor of New York and later U.S. vice president. The Dutch governor Peter Stuyvesant (1602?–1672) is buried behind **St. Mark's Church-In-the-Bowery** (*E. 10th St. at 2nd Ave., tel 212/674–6377*) and some say his ghost walks the grounds, tapping his wooden leg. The church is a center of activism and the arts, featuring contemporary dance

"Right Makes Might"

On the snowy evening of February 27, 1860, 1,500 people packed Cooper Union to hear Abraham Lincoln, soon to be president, speak about slavery. Arguing that the Constitution gave the federal government power to control slavery in the federal territories, he closed with these now-famous words: "Let us have faith that right makes might, and in that faith, let us, to the end, dare to do our duty as we understand it."

and weekly readings (*Danspace Project, tel 212/674-8112*).

Directly across from the church stands a classic federal-style structure, known as the **Stuyvesant-Fish House** (*21 Stuyvesant St., not open to the public*), built in 1803.

The Public Theater

✉ 425 Lafayette St.
☎ 212/539–8500
🚇 Subway: 6 to Astor Pl.; N, R to 8th St.

publictheater.org

Merchant's House Museum

- Map p. 76
- 29 E. 4th St.
- 212/777-1089
- Open 12 p.m.– 5 p.m. Fri.–Mon. & 12 p.m.–8 p.m. Thur.
- $$
- Subway: 6 to Astor Place; N, R to 8th St.

merchantshouse.org

Ukrainian Museum

- Map p. 76
- 222 E. 6th St., bet. 2nd & 3rd Aves.
- 212/228-0110
- Open 11.30 a.m.–5 p.m. Wed.–Sun.
- $$
- Subway: N, R to 8th St.–NYU; 6 to Astor Place

ukrainianmuseum .org

INSIDER TIP:

The Caracas Arepa Bar, on Seventh Street near First Avenue, is unmissable—whether you're an arepa connoisseur or tasting the stuffed Venezuelan corncakes for the first time.

–SETH KUGEL
Former New York Times *travel writer*

Architect James Renwick built the 1861 Italianate town houses that are here (Nos. 23–35) and also at 114–128 East Tenth Street, comprising Renwick Triangle.

To the south of St. Mark's Church-In-The-Bowery, performers such as Janis Joplin and the Doors appeared at Bill Graham's psychedelic Fillmore East (*2nd Ave. at 6th St.*). Rock fans should also check out 98 St. Marks Place, where Mick Jagger and the Rolling Stones were filmed "waiting on a friend," and which featured on the cover of Led Zeppelin's *Physical Graffiti* album.

To the west of the church is an 1846 Renwick Gothic Revival masterpiece, Episcopal **Grace Church** (*802 Broadway & E. 10th St., tel 212/254-2000*). The interior of the church has exquisite stained glass and a mosaic floor. North of Grace Church is a must for bibliophiles, the **Strand Book Store** (*828 Broadway, tel 212/473-1452, strandbooks. com*), "home of 18 miles of books" and bargains galore.

The **Merchant's House Museum** dates from 1832 and provides visitors an authentic look into 19th-century New York life. The **Ukrainian Museum** is an impressive 25,000-square-foot (2,320 sq m) building with extensive collections and exhibitions on all things Ukrainian. ■

EXPERIENCE: Seek Out the Sweet Spots for Gourmet Chocolates & Hot Chocolate

Engage your senses and observe chocolates being crafted at the SoHo location of **Jacques Torres** (*350 Hudson at King St., tel 212/414-2450, mrchocolate.com*). "Mr. Chocolate" sells hot chocolate variations and artistically molded chocolates, from rabbits to skyscrapers. Head to the heart of SoHo to **Vosges Haut-Chocolat** (*132 Spring St., tel 212/625-2929, vosgeschocolate.com*) for exotic flavor combinations of chocolates, *haut chocolat*, and chocolate ice cream. At **MarieBelle** (*484 Broome St., tel 718/599-5515, mariebelle.com*), pick up tins of Aztec hot chocolate and handmade candies. Try the handmade bonbons at Stick With Me (*202A Mott St., tel. 646/918-6336, swmsweets.com*) or the delicacies of **Li-Lac Chocolates** (*162 Bleecker Street, tel. 347/609-0941, li-lacchocolates.com*), a traditional pastry shop since 1923. Near Union Square, try the popular thick hot chocolate at **City Bakery** (*3 W. 18th St., tel 212/366-1414, thecitybakery.com*) or, farther uptown at 30 Rockefeller Center, indulge in French truffles or savor a rich hot chocolate at **La Maison du Chocolat** (*30 Rockefeller Center, W. 49th St., tel 212/265-9404, lamaisonduchocolat.com*).

Quiet enclaves, libraries of unsurpassed riches, one of the city's busiest shopping districts, and two of New York's favorite skyscrapers

MIDTOWN SOUTH

The High Line, an elevated park built on an old freight rail line

MIDTOWN SOUTH

Midtown South has areas of frenzied activity along with pockets of tranquillity, quiet enclaves where the bustle of a modern city hardly penetrates. The busier sections include Herald Square, home to Macy's, and the Garment District, where traffic and crowds are among the densest anywhere in the city.

Most Midtown South buildings predate New York's famous skyscrapers, but they are no less significant. In its 19th-century heyday, this was the center of the city, boasting everything that New York's finest areas have today: the best hotels, restaurants, theaters, opera houses, department stores, and the residences of the rich and powerful.

The New York Public Library was erected in 1911 on the site of an 1842 walled reservoir that was part of the Croton Aqueduct. Madison Square Garden is still a Midtown South fixture. The first "Garden" (1879) stood in a converted

NOT TO BE MISSED:

railroad depot on the east side of Madison Square Park, near 23rd Street. Stanford White's elaborate replacement, on the same site, was demolished when the Garden moved in 1925. The present-day Garden (*7th Ave. bet 31st & 33rd Sts.*) replaced the famed Penn Station, a massive beaux arts structure that was demolished in 1968 to make way for the new arena. What we know of as Penn Station today is completely underground.

In the 19th century, Midtown South became the center of the city's clothing factories. From its beginnings on the Lower East Side, the garment industry moved first to the Madison Square Park area, then to the now famous Garment District in the West 30s. A statue by Judith Weller, "The Garment Worker" (1984) honors the Jewish immigrants who helped build the industry. The Fashion Institute of Technology (*7th Ave. at 27th St., tel 212/217-7999*), a training ground for the trade, hosts frequent fashion exhibits and operates a museum.

The past two decades have seen renewal in the region, with new stores, restaurants, nightclubs, and businesses moving in. The area around the Flatiron Building is now known as the Photo District: Photographers converted lofts to studios, and galleries followed. ■

Manhattan

Area of map detail

Midtown South

❶ Jacob K. Javits Convention Center
❷ General Theological Seminary ❸ St. Peter's Episcopal Church ❹ Church of the Holy Apostles ❺ General Post Office
❻ Madison Square Garden ❼ Holy Communion Church ❽ New Amsterdam Theater ❾ Macy's ❿ Flatiron Building
⓫ Worth Monument ⓬ Museum of Sex
⓭ T. Roosevelt Birthplace N.H.S. ⓮ Con Edison HQ ⓯ N.Y. State Supreme Court
⓰ N.Y. Life Insurance Co. ⓱ American Radiator (Standard) Building ⓲ Church of the Incarnation ⓳ Daily News Building

CHELSEA

Chelsea, along the West Side from 14th Street to 30th Street, has blossomed into one of the city's most dynamic neighborhoods. Now home to approximately 300 art galleries plus chic shops and restaurants, it retains its past aura in 19th-century row houses and well-preserved churches. The former Ladies' Mile along Sixth Avenue (see pp. 96–97) bustles with new stores, while on Eighth Avenue high-tech companies occupy buildings long vacant.

■ A venerable city landmark, the Chelsea Hotel has a history rich in legend, literature, and scandal.

Dia: Chelsea

✉ 535 W. 22nd St.
☎ 212/989–5566
🕐 Closed a.m. & Sat.–Sun.
💲 $$
🚇 Subway: C, E to 8th Ave. & 23rd St.; 1 to 7th Ave. & 23rd St.

diaart.org

The innovative **Dia Art Foundation** opened its 40,000-square-foot (3,716 sq m) exhibition facility on West 22nd Street (*bet. 10th & 11th Aves.*) in 1987, leading the way for droves of galleries to follow. At Dia you can see modern art that is too big to be shown elsewhere.

Prominent in Chelsea's lavish banquet of art venues, the **Rubin Museum** (*150 W. 17th St., tel 212/620–5000, rubinmuseum.org, closed Tues., $$$*) is the first museum in the Western Hemisphere dedicated solely to Himalayan art. Six floors of lovingly curated works are installed around a central spiral staircase.

Art galleries of **David Zwirner** (*533 W. 19th St., bet. 10th & 11th Aves., tel 212/727–2070, davidzwirner.com*), on 19th, 20th, and 69th Streets mix shows of historical figures and movements with exhibits by international contemporary artists.

Heating up the mix is the **Museum of Sex** (*233 5th Ave. at 27th St., tel 212/689–6337, museumofsex.com, $$$*), the country's first major cultural institution devoted to the subject of human sexuality.

Chelsea has played a central role in New York's art scene since the mid-1990s, boasting veritable gallery franchises (Gagosian) as well as tiny spaces. In addition to its galleries and museums, the area is home to the Fashion Institute of Technology (*7th Ave. & W. 27th St.*), the School of Visual Arts (*209 E. 23rd St.*), and the Dance Theater Workshop (*219 W. 19th St.*).

Chelsea Historic District

The Chelsea Hotel (*222 W 23rd St., bet. 7th & 8th Aves.*), famous for its wrought iron balconies, was built in 1884 and converted to a hotel in 1905 by Philip Hubert, the architect who designed it. It soon became an incubator of artistic talent, as you can see from the commemorative plaques dedicated to some of the hotel's guests who stayed and worked here, including, among others, Mark Twain, Tennessee Williams, Arthur Miller, Brendan Behan, and Dylan Thomas. In the 1960s and '70s, the hotel became the cradle of counterculture, thanks to the songs of Bob Dylan, Leonard Cohen, and Joni Mitchell, all of whom contributed to the hotel's international fame. The marble staircase has hosted exhibits and among the many works that were written here, in the "Dream Palace," as Sherill Tippins defines it (see sidebar p. 39) are *2001: A Space Odyssey,* by Arthur C. Clarke, and *Netherland,* by Joseph O'Neill. In 2011, the Chelsea closed for a long period of reconstruction that forced many of its residential guests to move. It will reopen with 130 hotel rooms, 50 apartments, two restaurants, a spa, a rooftop gym, and many works of art. The historical

EXPERIENCE: Learn to Fly–on a Trapeze

Ever wanted to soar through the air? Fulfill that dream with a flying trapeze class at **Trapeze School New York** (*353 West St. & seasonally atop Pier 40, near W. Houston St., tel 917/797–1872, newyork.trapezeschool .com*). Beginners, including children, are welcome. Reservations are recommended. Take the A, C, or E subway to 34th Street or the M34 bus to 10th Avenue, then walk south and west. For the Pier 40 location, take the 1 subway to Houston Street, then walk west to Hudson River Park.

district in the area is worth a visit, particularly Cushman Row (*406–418 W 20th St.*), a series of 7 neoclassical residences, some decorated with window wreaths or pineapples on the staircases, as a sign of hospitality. The nearby James N. Wells Row (*400–412 W. 22nd St.*), a street lined with narrow Italian-style houses, was named for another important builder of the era. ∎

The Chelsea Piers Sports & Entertainment Complex

Visiting the 28-acre Chelsea Piers Sports & Entertainment complex (*tel 212/336–6666, chelseapiers.com*) is like entering a small village that is always abuzz with sports and activities.

Located along the Hudson River between W 17th and W 23rd Streets, Chelsea Piers features a golf driving range at **Golf Club** (*tel 212/336–6400*) at Pier 59 and a bowling alley at **Bowlmor** (*tel 212/835–2695*); there's the **Chelsea Piers Fitness** (*tel 212/336–6000*) and spa (*tel 212/336–6780*) at Pier 60; or try ice-skating at the **Sky Rink** (*tel

212/336–6100*) at Pier 61; and the **Field House** (*tel 212/336–6500*) for gymnastics, soccer, basketball, and rock climbing at Pier 62. Take the M23 bus across 23rd Street or the M14-D across 14th Street; the last stops are near the northern and southern entrances.

Fans of the hit TV series *Law & Order* should also check out Pier 62's **Silver Screen Studios,** which has been featured in several episodes. The studios are Manhattan's largest center for film and television production, with more than 200,000 square feet (18,580 sq m).

THE HIGH LINE

New York is a city usually viewed from within the fast-flowing human stream of the streets or from the rarefied air atop a skyscraper. Since 2009, however, a public park built on a disused rail line has given pedestrians a whole new way of experiencing Lower Manhattan. In the process, the High Line has fused history with modern urban planning, and elevated the environmental index for downtown dwellers.

A stroll over the Falcone Flyover at 26th Street affords vistas of Chelsea and Midtown skyscrapers.

The High Line story begins in 1929, when the city built an elevated rail line to shuttle cargo from the docks to its meatpacking plants. Rising 30 feet (9 m) above ground on iron bridges, it snaked through the West Side, over streets and through buildings. When the last train stopped in 1980, the line became an abandoned relic. For the next two decades, many New Yorkers wanted it demolished, as Chelsea was gentrified with galleries, restaurants, and lofts.

In 1999 writer Joshua David and artist Robert Hammond formed the **Friends of the High Line** (*tel 212/500–6035, thehighline.org*) and ran a contest to garner support. Eventually they convinced the city of the High Line's potential, and plans for a public park were announced in 2002.

Landscape architect James Corner designed the park, fusing the serenity of nature with the industrialized structure of the High Line. The design included wooden benches for reading or reflection, and retained many of the original train tracks. Running 1.45 miles (2.3 km) north from Gansevoort Street to 34th Street, High Line Park is now a 30-foot-wide (9 m) corridor of calm in the clamor of New York City. Its paths meander amid beds of grasses, perennials, and shrubbery.

A new public plaza marks the park's south entrance at Gansevoort Street, next to the new branch of the **Whitney Museum of American Art** (*whitney.org*). Walk through **Gansevoort Woodland** up to the **14th Street Passage.** Look out for the **Diller - Von Furstenberg Sundeck** between West 14th and 15th Streets. Chelsea's vibrant **Meatpacking District** is on your right, and to the left, between old buildings with their New York-style water towers and sleek new edifices you catch glimpses of the Hudson River.

The **Chelsea Market Passage** runs alongside another wonder of urban renewal, the old Nabisco factory that now houses **Chelsea Market** (*bet. 9th*

The Prototype for the City of the Future: Hudson Yards

Hudson Yards is a 1.2 million-square-foot (113,000 sq m) rail yard on the Long Island Rail Road (LIRR), a suburban train system that connects Manhattan and Long Island, transporting about 350,000 commuters every day. The yard extends from south to north (W. 30th St. to W. 33rd St.) and east to west (10th Ave. to 12th Ave.). It is the site of the biggest private real estate development in the history of the United States, after Rockefeller Center.

To build the project, two platforms were suspended over 30 actively operating LIRR tracks. The buildings stretch the length of the rail yard, overlooking it. The foundation for load-bearing support columns was laid in the middle of the tracks.

The "neighborhood" will have over 17 million square feet (1.6 million sq m) of residential and commercial space with more than 100 shops and restaurants, 4,000 apartments, an innovative arts center, 12 acres (5 ha) of open public space, and a luxury hotel. Integrated buildings, streets, parks, and public spaces make up a community that is efficient, clean, safe, and connected. Fiber optics optimize data transmission and guarantee satellite connections, mobile networks and radio communications, and stable wireless or cable internet connections from anywhere in the area. An advanced technological platform with a sensor system monitors the surrounding environment, traffic, electricity demand, and pedestrian flow.

er 10th Aves. and 15th er 16th Sts., chelseamarket. com), the historical closed market that has always been a point of reference for the area. Farther north along the High Line, the path crosses Tenth Avenue and morphs again into an amphitheater-like space suspended over **Tenth Ave. Square.** Rest at the **23rd Street Lawn,** or hop off the High Line to visit the **Chelsea Hotel** (see sidebar this page) three blocks west. The **26th Street Viewing Spur** looks down though a huge white

frame. Beyond this, the **Wildflower Field** adorns a long stretch of promenade. Continue as far as the **Radial Bench,** which starts at W. 29th St. Make a small detour at W. 30th St. to admire two, very particular buildings that are part of Hudson Yards, the new futuristic arts center, and The Vessel, an oval-shaped structure designed by Thomas Heatherwick, composed of 154 flights of steps, connected by platforms. The last part of the High Line ends at the Javits Center.

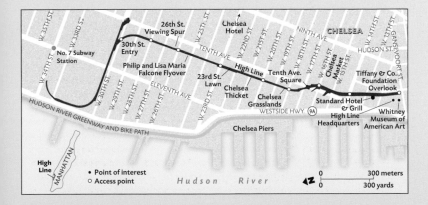

GRAMERCY PARK

Gramercy Park is Manhattan's only private park, surrounded by a tasteful but formidable iron fence, and unless you live in the immediate vicinity or know someone who does, you will not be able to go in. The rule restricting the use of the park to residents was relaxed only once—when troops were bivouacked there during the Draft Riots of 1863 (see p. 28). The picturesque area has often been the site of film shoots.

■ Exclusive and private Gramercy Park

Writers of Renown

One of the city's first cooperative apartment buildings, the 1883 Gramercy (*34 Gramercy Park E.*), has housed such prominent figures as playwright DuBose Heyward and the late actors James Cagney and Margaret "Wicked Witch of the West" Hamilton.

On the south side of the park, 144 East 20th Street was built in 1859 as a Quaker meetinghouse and now serves as a synagogue. At the corner of Irving Place, the 1845 brick building at 19 Gramercy Park South was owned in the 1880s by financier Stuyvesant Fish; more recently the house was home to actor John Barrymore and, later, the colorful public relations genius Ben Sonnenberg.

Actor Edwin Booth (see sidebar opposite) gave his home at 16 Gramercy Park South to the **Players Club;** Stanford White remodeled the 1845 brownstone in 1888. Next door, Calvert Vaux remodeled No. 15 in the 1870s for Samuel Tilden, a former New York governor. Fearful of populist revolt, Tilden had an underground escape tunnel dug to 19th Street. The restored brownstone is now the **National Arts Club,** where literary events and performative shows often take place.

National Arts Club

✉ 15 Gramercy Park St.

☎ 212/475–3424

🚇 Subway: 6 to 23rd St.

nationalartsclub.org

The original name was Dutch, Krom Moerajse, meaning "little crooked swamp," which the English, somehow, anglicized to Gramercy. In 1822, Samuel Ruggles purchased and drained the swamp, laid out the park, and sold lots. Early residents included lawyer and diarist George Templeton Strong and James Harper, a publisher and New York City mayor (1844–1845), whose home at 4 Gramercy Park West still has the traditional outdoor lampposts that marked it as the mayor's residence.

INSIDER TIP:

Visit the penthouse bar at the Gramercy Park Hotel. The hotel lobby and alfresco bar do double duty as galleries for a rotating collection of paintings by Andy Warhol, Julian Schnabel, and Jean-Michel Basquiat.

—DAISANN McLANE
National Geographic writer

The **Gramercy Park Historic District** extends several blocks in each direction beyond the park itself. Developer Ruggles named the six-block-long street between the park and 14th Street Irving Place, after his friend, writer Washington Irving. The gesture led to the misconception that Irving lived on the street; however, he did visit his nephew who lived at 45 Irving Place. In the early 20th century, the house was the home of the society interior decorator

Elsie de Wolfe, who was famous for the mix of high society and bohemia at her salons and her open relationship with her lover, literary agent Bessie Marbury. Another well-known Gramercy Park figure, William Sydney Porter (pen name: O. Henry) did much of his writing and drinking at Healy's (today called Pete's Tavern) at Irving and 18th Street, where—in the second booth from the right—he supposedly penned his most famous short story, "The Gift of the Magi."

West of Gramercy Park, the **Theodore Roosevelt Birthplace National Historic Site** is a careful replica—right down to the slate shingles on the mansard roof—of the original 1845 building, which was demolished in 1916. Roosevelt was born here in 1858 and lived in the house until 1872; he later recalled the "gloomy respectability" of the building's library. Operated now by the National Park Service and open to the public, the birthplace was rebuilt in 1923 by Theodate Pope Riddle, the country's first woman architect. ■

Gramercy Park Hotel
- ✉ 2 Lexington Ave.
- ☎ 212/ 920–3300

**gramercyparkhotel
.com**

Theodore Roosevelt Birthplace N.H.S.
- 🅰 Map p. 88
- ✉ 28 E. 20th St.
- ☎ 212/260–1616
- 🕐 Closed Mon.–Tues.
- 🚇 Subway: 6, N, or R to 23rd St.

nps.gov/thrb

The Melancholy Thespian

Inside locked Gramercy Park, but visible through the fence, stands a bronze statue of Edwin Booth (1833–1893), the most famous American actor of his day. In April 1865, he received unwanted notoriety when his actor brother John Wilkes Booth assassinated President Abraham Lincoln in Washington, D.C., and died trying to elude capture. After the assassination, Edwin retired temporarily, then built his own theater to stage his own productions. In 1888 he founded the Players Club for actors at 16 Gramercy Park South.

Twenty-five years after his death, the club commissioned the statue of Booth, a small, lithe figure, as Hamlet, a role at which he excelled—perhaps because the prince's melancholy matched his own after his brother's murderous deed.

WALK DOWN LADIES' MILE

In the relatively short distance covered by this walking tour—which spans two pleasant parks, Madison Square on the north and Union Square on the south—you will see a neighborhood that is constantly rejuvenating itself on a walk that will take about an hour, depending on stops.

In the 1870s, so many of the city's fashionable retailers were located along this stretch that it became known as Ladies' Mile. The stores moved northward, but many neglected buildings survived and today they are being renovated and reinhabited. Businesses, among them many fashion outlets, have

> **NOT TO BE MISSED:**
>
> Madison Square Park • Flatiron Building • Union Square

The elegant and unmistakable Flatiron Building

returned, bringing with them bars and restaurants. The Ladies' Mile Historic District also includes Fashion Row on Sixth Avenue, a cluster of late 19th-century structures centered between 18th and 19th Streets.

Start at the north end of **Madison Square** ❶ near East 26th Street. The park contains excellent sculpture, notably the 1881 "Admiral Farragut Monument" by Augustus Saint-Gaudens, with a base by Stanford White.

Midtown Skyscrapers

Three eminent skyscrapers abut the park. Cass Gilbert designed the block-long neo-Gothic **New York Life Insurance Company Building** ❷ (*51 Madison Ave., bet. E. 26th & E. 27th Sts.*) in 1928. Another massive building is at the north corner of East 25th Street and Madison Avenue, the 1900 beaux arts **Appellate Division of the Supreme Court.** Napoleon LeBrun's tower for the huge art deco **Metropolitan Life Insurance Company Building** ❸ (*1 Madison Ave., bet. E. 23rd & E. 24th Sts.*) was built in 1909. Note the tower's clock and elegant gold crown. Walk south to Fifth Avenue and East 23rd Street to see architect Daniel Burnham's 22-story **Flatiron Building** ❹ (1902); it was called Burnham's Folly by those who feared high winds would blow it over.

The 778-feet tall (237 m) Madison Square Park Tower was constructed one block to the east in 2017.

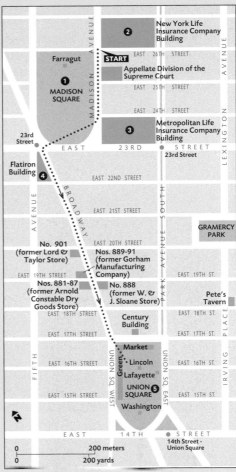

⚠ See also map pp. 88–89
▶ Madison Square
↔ 0.5 mile (0.8 km)
🕐 1 hour
▶ Union Square

Head downtown (south) to **901 Broadway** (*at E. 20th St.*), an Empire-style cast-iron building that was, until 1914, the Lord & Taylor store. It now houses Brooks Brothers' Flatiron Store. One block south you'll pass three other 19th-century survivors. The Queen Anne-style 1884 building at 889–891 Broadway was once a retail outlet of the Gorham Manufacturing Company, an American silver manufacturer. The **Arnold Constable Building** (*881–887 Broadway at E. 19th St.*) is an 1869 building; its cast-iron extension up to Fifth Avenue has an impressive mansard roof. On East 19th Street, **888 Broadway** once housed W. & J. Sloane, purveyors of rugs, curtains, and fabric. Today the ABC Carpet & Home store attracts New York's modern homemakers. Note the striking cast-iron storefront and carved columns.

Continue south for three blocks to **Union Square ❺**, renovated in 1986 and 2008 and now a popular park. On its north side, at 33 East 17th Street, the **Century Building** (1881), faced with red brick and white stone, housed *Century* magazine, an illustrated publication devoted to U.S. reunification after the Civil War. It is now a Barnes & Noble bookstore. The Blue Water Grill, No. 31 Union Square West, at East 16th Street, now serves fine sea food in the original 1903 Bank of Metropolis building, designed by Bruce Price, an innovative architect of skyscrapers. On the square's east side (*Park Avenue S.*), the imposing Greek temple was built in 1907 as the Union Square Savings Bank.

Opened as a park in 1831, Union Square has long been a stump for political orators, from the Civil War until recent times. Today the square holds the year-round **Greenmarket** (*open Mon., Wed., Fri., & Sat.*), where farmers sell local produce. The park's statuary includes heroic statues of Abraham Lincoln, the Marquis de Lafayette, and George Washington. You'll find places to eat on all sides of the square and going north along Park Avenue South, and famous Pete's Tavern is just two blocks away at 129 East 18th St.

EMPIRE STATE BUILDING

The tallest in the world for more than 40 years, the Empire State Building will always be the quintessential skyscraper. A high-speed elevator whisks you to the 86th-floor outdoor observation deck. The view from the top, uptown and down, is matchless and essential to understanding Manhattan's lay of the land.

■ The Empire State Building, an art deco marvel in Midtown

Empire State Building

- ⓐ Map p. 88
- ✉ 350 5th Ave.
- ☎ 212/736–3100
- 💲 $$$$$
- 🚇 Subway: B, D, F, N, Q, R to 34th St.

esbnyc.com

The 102-story building is 1,250 feet tall (381 m) with 6,400 windows. The five-story base covers two acres (0.8 ha) along Fifth Avenue. The metal-and-glass tower on top, 16 stories tall, was intended as a mooring mast for dirigibles but was only used twice. Some said it detracted from the building's beauty, but that was before a giant ape used it as a perch in the 1933 film *King Kong*.

INSIDER TIP:

If you're only going to make it to the top of the Empire State Building once, choose to go after the light has faded for the most spectacular views of the city's brightly lit skyline.

—ALLY THOMPSON
National Geographic contributor

Work on the building proceeded at unprecedented pace, with an average of four and a half stories added every week. The Empire State Building opened May 1, 1931, ahead of schedule and five million dollars under its $50 million budget. It was an instant hit with tourists, but during the Depression half of the two-million-plus square feet (185,806 sq m) of floor space was unrented, hence its nickname, the Empty State Building.

The Empire State Building lost its title as the world's tallest building in the 1970s. But that has not diminished its grace, its popularity, or its place in the city's consciousness. As one critic once said in its praise, "That it is the world's tallest building is purely incidental." ■

HERALD SQUARE

In 1904, when songwriter George M. Cohan wrote the famous line "remember me to Herald Square," it was the merchandising center of the city. Most of the original stores have disappeared, but the area—where Broadway and Sixth Avenue cross at 34th Street—retains a grimy vitality and attracts the masses and popular retail shops.

The square is named for the *New York Herald*, headquartered here in a Renaissance-style building from 1894 to 1921. All that remains of the building is the ornamental clock, located where Broadway meets Sixth Avenue. On the hour, two bronze bell ringers, nicknamed Stuff and Guff, appear and strike the bell with mallets. **Macy's**, still the world's largest department store, opened in Herald Square in 1902.

To the west, **Madison Square Garden** (see sidebar right) stands on the site of the former Pennsylvania Station, a beautiful beaux arts building torn down in the 1960s to maximize the revenue potential of the space above it. Today's **Penn Station,** serving long-distance Amtrak trains and commuter trains to Long Island and New Jersey, is housed in a labyrinth underground.

At 2 Penn Plaza, the entrance to the present Penn terminal, are Adolph A. Weinman sculptures from the 1910 Penn Station: a ten-foot-high (3 m) statue of a railroad president and two large granite eagles from the cornice. The present Penn Station is meant for grander quarters. Senator Daniel Patrick Moynihan spearheaded the effort in the 1990s to move the terminal into the monumental **General Post Office,** on the west side of Eighth Avenue between 31st and 33rd Streets. The firm of McKim, Mead & White designed the building in 1912 to visually blend with the old Penn Station's grander entrance across the avenue.

Farther west, on 11th Avenue between 34th and 39th Streets, is the **Jacob K. Javits Convention Center,** a modernistic all-glass pavilion designed by I. M. Pei. There is currently a project to expand the Center that will cost 1.5 billion dollars. The 7 Subway extension project is an extension of the IRT Flushing Line from the Times Square terminus to the new western terminus at 34th Street-Hudson Yards, inaugurated in 2015. ■

Macy's
- 🅜 Map p. 88
- ✉ 151 W. 34th St.
- ☎ 212/695–4400
- 🚇 Subway: B, D, F, N, Q, R to 34th St.

macys.com

Jacob K. Javits Convention Center
- 🅜 Map p. 88
- ✉ 655 W. 34th St.
- ☎ 212/216–2000
- 🚇 Subway: A, C, E to 34th St.; 7 to 34th St.-Hudson Yards.

javitscenter.com

Tour the Garden

Want to dance where Michael Jackson and Mick Jagger strutted their stuff or shadowbox where Ali fought Frazier? Madison Square Garden (*4 Pennsylvania Plaza, bet. 7th & 8th Aves., 31st to 33rd Sts., thegarden.com*) **is the world's best known arena and worth a visit. To see the New York Knicks or Rangers in action, or maybe to catch the Barnum & Bailey Circus, head to the Garden. An All Access Tour** (*tel 866/858–0007, $$$*) **takes you behind the scenes at the venue that was recently renovated to the tune of $1 billion.**

THE MORGAN LIBRARY AND MUSEUM & AROUND

Named for Quakers Robert and Mary Murray, who owned an estate here in colonial times, the Murray Hill neighborhood extends, north to south, from 40th to 34th Street and east to west, from Third to Madison Avenue. Although it intrudes on Manhattan's busy Midtown, its tree-lined side streets are reminiscent of a more tranquil era when some of the city's richest lived here. Among them was financier John Pierpont Morgan (1837–1913), one of the world's richest men in a time when there were few restraints on making money.

■ Three tiers of rare books, accessible by catwalks, line the opulent East Room of the Morgan Library.

Morgan began collecting books and manuscripts, and expanded to sculpture, Renaissance painting, old master drawings, and music manuscripts. When his collection grew too large for his mansion, Morgan commissioned Charles McKim to design the one-story, neoclassic building on East 36th Street.

The library was built, in classical fashion, from marble blocks put together without mortar. Adolph A. Weinman created the sculptured panels on the exterior representing the arts and other disciplines; Edward Clark Potter's lions at the entrance are forerunners of those he made for the New York Public Library. The interior consisted of the Rotunda at the original entrance, the book-lined East Room, the North Room (an office), and Morgan's study, called the West Room.

The Collection: Morgan's son opened the library to the public in 1924. Four years later, Morgan's home at the corner of 36th Street and Madison Avenue was torn down and replaced by an annex. Hans Memling's "Portrait of a Man

The Morgan Library

Map p. 88

225 Madison Ave. at E. 36th St.

212/685–0008

$$

Closed Mon.

Subway: 6 to 33rd St.

themorgan.org

The Morgan Library

J. P. Morgan was also a leading collector of the Gilded Age. His library, quipped its first director, "contains everything but the original tablets of the Ten Commandments," and it is recognized as one of the world's great collections. Wander amid the artistic and literary treasures on view in this marble palace.

with a Pink" (ca 1475), perhaps the most famous painting in the collection, is displayed on the red damask walls of the West Room. One of three Gutenberg Bibles Morgan acquired is on display in the East Room. This room, with its spectacular domed ceiling and stone fireplace, is lined with three tiers of bookcases.

The collection continues to expand through acquisitions: in 1992, a signed copy of Lincoln's Emancipation Proclamation and other historic American documents; in 1998, the Carter Burden Collection of American Literature, with more than 80,000 volumes dating from 1870. In 1988, the library purchased Morgan House (37th St. and Madison Ave.), the 45-room home of Morgan's son, which was renovated as the education center and bookstore. A garden court connects the library and Morgan House. The largest renovation yet was completed in 2006, more than doubling the exhibit space. Italian architect Renzo Piano connected the old and new structures with a central piazza and added a new entrance at Madison Avenue.

Around Murray Hill

The federal style townhouse, hidden by a garden, at 152 E. 38th St. was built in 1857. It's the oldest building in the area. Nearby, **De Lamar Mansion** (No. 233 Madison Ave.), now the Polish Consulate, was built in 1905 for a Dutch-born businessman. At Nos. 205 and 209 (at 35th St.), the 1864 **Church of the Incarnation** (1906) and its

rectory contains stained-glass windows by William Morris, Louis Comfort Tiffany, and John La Farge, and sculpture by Daniel Chester French and Augustus Saint-Gaudens.

A block east on Park Avenue, No. 57 was designed by Philadelphia architect Horace Trumbauer, with sculptured friezes, for socialite Adelaide L. T. Douglas. The 1911 building now houses the Guatemalan Consulate and related offices. No. 23, the former Advertising Club, now apartments, is another McKim, Mead & White structure designed as a millionaire's mansion. Near the eastern border lies **Sniffen Court** (150–158 E. 36th St.), which is the city's smallest historic district. This intriguing mews of ten brick carriage houses dates from the 1850s. ∎

Church of the Incarnation

🅰 Map p. 88

✉ 205–209 Madison Ave.

☎ 212/689–6350

🕐 Open Mon.–Sat. 11:30 a.m.– 2 p.m.; Sun. 8 a.m.–1 p.m.

🚇 Subway: 6 to 33rd St.

churchofthe incarnation.org

EXPERIENCE:
Listen to Literary New York at Free Events

You can't swing a cat without hitting a writer in New York, and those who are lucky enough to have secured a book deal can often be found giving free readings at the city's bookstores. There are also a number of literary series held regularly in bars and cafés around town. The "Books" sections of TimeOut New York (timeout .com/newyork/books) and New York magazine (nymag.com/arts/books) list bookstore readings, lectures, literary series, and special events. Barnes & Noble (barnes andnoble.com), the city's dominant brick-and-mortar bookseller, lists forthcoming author events online as well.

EXPERIENCE: Choose Your Toppings—NYC's Best Pizza

Pizza may be the ultimate New York food: Invented by immigrants, adopted by everybody, and not very good for you—but fold it just right and you can eat it while walking, because you've got things to do, and places to be.

It originated in 1905 exactly where you'd expect: on Spring Street in Little Italy, where grocer Gennaro Lombardi began selling a specialty from his hometown of Naples, Italy—"tomato pies" made from fresh tomatoes, melted mozzarella cheese, olive oil, and a little basil and garlic on oven-baked flatbread. A hit in Italy, it went over just as well in the New World, and New York pizza was born.

The real experience doesn't involve a lot of froufrou choices. You have your average pizzeria that serves quick slices and your sit-down restaurant that serves only full pies. You have your Neapolitan style and your Sicilian, the latter a deep-dish pie employing a thicker and breadier crust. For toppings, think pepperoni, sausage, black olives, mushrooms, onions, and/or peppers.

Debate rages over who makes the best in town, but a good bet is **Patsy's,** in Spanish Harlem (*2287 First Ave. at 117th St., tel 212/534–9783, thepatsyspizza.com*). Open since 1933, it's totally traditional, totally historic (it was Sinatra's favorite), old-time friendly, and delicious, due to the slightly sweet sauce and perfectly baked crusts.

Near Union Square, **Artichoke** (*321 E. 14th St., tel 212/228–2004, artichoke pizza.com*), by cousins Francis Garcia and Sal Basille, has been a hit and now has shops in Chelsea, Greenwich Village, and even one in Berkeley, California.

Also in Greenwich Village, **John's of Bleecker Street** (*278 Bleecker St., tel 212/243–1680, johnsbrickovenpizza. com*) serves a classic pie at

---

INSIDER TIP:

Most people think of New York pizza as the thin, foldable Neapolitan slice, but there's also Sicilian style: square, on thick, focaccia-like crust, and saucy, with mozzarella cheese. A must-try.

—PHILIP SPIEGEL
National Geographic contributor

---

booths and tables that have been carved and graffitied by more than eight decades of patrons. A newer Greenwich Village entrant, **Numero 28 Pizzeria** (*28 Carmine St., tel 212/463–9653, numero28. com*), uses fresh, natural ingredients in its traditional elongated pies.

In Little Italy, **Lombardi's**

(*tel 212/941–7994, firstpizza .com*) is still mining the gold it struck in 1905, serving from a touristy new location at 32 Spring Street.

Over in Brooklyn Heights, **Grimaldi's** (*1 Front St., tel 718/858–4300, grimaldis-pizza. com*) merges a similar recipe to Patsy's (the place was opened by Patsy's founder's nephew in 1990) with a more accessible location in the shadow of the Brooklyn Bridge. You'll have to wait in line, but it's worth it. At **Di Fara Pizzeria** (*1424 Ave. J, tel 718/258–1367, difarany. com*) in Brooklyn's Midwood neighborhood, every pie is an individual, handmade masterpiece. In Coney Island, **Totonno's** (*1524 Neptune Ave., tel 718/372–8606, totonnos. com*) was the city's oldest continuously-operating pizzeria, open since 1924—until devastated by Hurricane Sandy. It reopened in 2013, serving its delicious thin-crust pies.

Those are the best of the best—and most of the rest, weirdly, seem to be named Ray's—or maybe Famous Ray's, or Ray's Famous, or Original Ray's, or Famous Original Ray's, Ray's Real, World's Famous New York Ray's, Ray Bono, New York Ray's ... at last count, there were about 50 "Rays" in the city, and no one really knows why. Just enjoy it and fuggetaboudit! Pizza is part of New York's charm.

NEW YORK PUBLIC LIBRARY

Guarded by Edward Clark Potter's sculptured lions "Patience" and "Fortitude," the New York Public Library is one of the world's great cultural institutions. Founded in 1895, it grew out of the consolidation of two private libraries, those of millionaire John Jacob Astor and real estate heir James Lenox. There are now 92 branch libraries throughout the boroughs.

■ The library's Rose Main Reading Room

History &
the Collection

The New York Public Library opened its doors in 1911 on the site of the old Croton Reservoir. The broad steps and terraces leading up to its grand exterior entrance, framed by Corinthian columns, have become a favorite gathering place for New Yorkers. The library is widely considered the greatest example of beaux arts design in the country. What's more, it works. In an enlightened move, librarians themselves assisted the

architects Carrère & Hastings in designing a building that was not only beautiful but also functional. The behind-the-scenes system for moving its more than nine million books is still state of the art.

The library's collection includes some 21 million other items, among them priceless manuscripts, recordings, periodicals, historical maps, prints, photographs, and family histories. The contents of the regular, changing exhibitions held by the library are drawn from these.

**New York
Public Library**

🅰 Map p. 88

🖼 5th Ave. & 42nd St.

☎ 212/930-0830; 917/275-6975 for exhibits & events

🕐 Some areas closed Sun.

🚇 Subway: B, D, F to 42nd St.; 4, 5, 6 to Grand Central; 7 to 5th Ave.

nypl.org

American Radiator (Standard) Building

 Map p. 88

✉ 40 W. 40th St., bet. 5th & 6th Aves.

🚇 Subway: B, D, F to 42nd St.; 4, 5, 6 to Grand Central; 7 to 5th Ave.

Rooms throughout the library display elegant design and clever use of natural light. The **Rose Main Reading Room,** which is lined by windows adjoining interior courtyards, is two blocks long, with chandeliers and a magnificent wood-paneled ceiling. The skylit Bartos Forum and the Periodicals Rooms, with murals by Richard Haas, are also superb, and the gift shop has many unusual items.

Bryant Park

Stretching behind the library to Sixth Avenue, Bryant Park is named for the poet and editor William Cullen Bryant (1794–1878); beautifully restored in the 1990s, there are public benches and a fine indoor-outdoor restaurant, Bryant Park Grill (*25 W. 40th St., tel 212/840-6500*). To the south, stands the landmark 1924

INSIDER TIP:

Between late October and late January, the center of Bryant Park is transformed into The Pond (*wintervillage .org*), a free, outdoor ice-skating rink, open morning to late night. Skate rentals are available.

—MATT HANNAFIN
National Geographic contributor

American Radiator (Standard) Building, distinct for its black and gold exterior. The building houses the Bryant Park Hotel (*tel 212/642-2200, bryantpark hotel.com*), opened in 2001, which features a theater and a swanky restaurant and bar. ∎

EXPERIENCE: Enjoy Outdoor Concerts & Plays

In summer, New York's parks, piers, and public areas fill up with reasons to stay outside. **Central Park SummerStage** (*tel 212/362-6000, cityparksfoundation.org/ summerstage*) offers pop, jazz, and world music, dance, poetry, and films (*June–Aug.*) at its huge stage at Rumsey Playfield, near the park's 72nd Street entrance from Fifth Avenue. Most shows are free. At the park's **Delacorte Theater,** mid-park at 80th Street, **Shakespeare in the Park** (*tel 212/967-7555, publictheater.org*) presents free performances (*June–Aug.*), sometimes actually Shakespeare, sometimes "other." At 62nd Street and Amsterdam Avenue, **Lincoln Center Out of Doors** (*tel 212/875-5000, lcoutofdoors.org*) presents world-class free

music, dance, and family events throughout August. In Bryant Park (*42nd St., bet. 5th & 6th Aves.*), the **Bryant Park Summer Film Festival** (*212/512-5700, bryantpark.org*) screens a series of free classic films on Monday nights (*June–Aug.*). On the Hudson River, **Hudson Riverflicks** (*hudsonriverpark.org*) presents classic and cult movies on Wednesday nights at Pier 63 (*West 26th St.*) and family classics Fridays (*July–Aug.*) at Pier 46 (*West St. at Charles St.*) at dusk. Popcorn is free.

Farther downtown, the southern end of Manhattan from the Hudson to the East River hosts literally hundreds of music, theater, dance, and other cultural events as part of the **River to River Festival** (*June–Sept.; rivertorivernyc.com*).

The city's grandest district—from the East River to the Hudson—with restaurants, music, theater, art, and enduring architecture

MIDTOWN NORTH

 Atlas holds the world in his arms at Rockefeller Center.

MIDTOWN NORTH

The entrance court to Rockefeller Center's International Building features a massive statue of Atlas supporting on his broad shoulders an open sphere representing the world. To many, it is a symbol of Midtown North, that slice of Manhattan running river to river between 42nd and 59th Streets. This is the nerve center for business, culture, and entertainment. Grand Central Terminal has long welcomed visitors from all over the country, and the United Nations Plaza hosts the entire world.

You can even live here, and New Yorkers pay a great deal of money to do so. Beekman Place and Sutton Place, on and near the East River, are among the city's most expensive addresses. Another is Central Park South along 59th Street, Midtown's northern edge.

No places better illustrate the diversity of Midtown North than frenetic Times Square in the 40s (where Broadway and Seventh Avenue cross) and staid Rockefeller Center in the 50s (between Fifth and Sixth Avenues). In Times Square you will be assaulted by traffic, noise, pedestrians,

NOT TO BE MISSED:

The famed vaulted ceiling of Grand
  Central Terminal   108–109

A tour of United Nations Plaza   111

A dazzling Broadway show and
  the lights and crowds of Times
  Square   112–118

Discussing literature in the Round
  Table Room of the Algonquin
  Hotel   114–115

Ice-skating at Rockefeller Plaza's
  outdoor rink   120

Shopping in Fifth Avenue's marquee
  stores   125

Monet's mesmeric "Water Lilies"
  at the Museum of Modern
  Art   126–130

1 Museum of Arts and Design
2 Carnegie Hall 3 Trump Tower
4 Sony Building 5 Citigroup Center
6 Waldorf-Astoria 7 Former McGraw-Hill
Building 8 Lyceum Theater 9 Algonquin
Hotel 10 International Center of
Photography 11 New York Public Library
12 Chanin Building 13 News Building

and the constant presence of gigantic animated signs. At Rockefeller Center the atmosphere is more proper and restrained, its buildings radiating a conviction that all is well with the world.

Midtown North was created as the wealthy elite led the city northward. Fifth Avenue was chosen as the site for St. Patrick's Cathedral in 1848 by a bishop who wanted to put his Roman Catholic congregation on an equal footing with the Protestant Establishment. In 1926 the Metropolitan Opera selected a nearby area for its new home. When the plan floundered, one of its key investors, John D. Rockefeller, Jr., instead built one of the world's great urban centers. Park Avenue developed into prime residential property—and later a business district—after 1903, when the New York Central decided to put the railroad tracks serving Grand Central below ground.

Midtown's southern boundary, 42nd Street, has long been a major crosstown street. Still, the *New York Times*'s 1904 decision to move to its western part was considered daring. Then called Longacre Square, it was a red-light district with stables and shops catering to the carriage trade. *Times* publisher Alfred Ochs persuaded the city to run the subway there, ensuring development. The newspaper's building became Times Tower, the area Times Square. A decade later, the *Times* moved to West 43rd Street and Times Tower became One Times Square: The name was there to stay. Completed in 2007, the New York Times Building at 620 Eighth Avenue is the present home to the *Times* (see p. 157).

As the theater district developed in the area in the early 1900s, Times Square also became the "Great White Way." ■

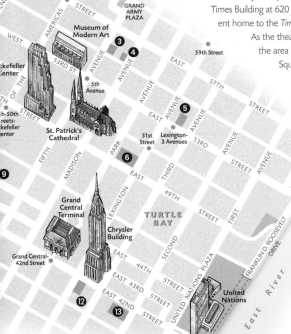

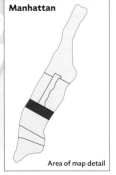

Manhattan

Area of map detail

GRAND CENTRAL TERMINAL & ALONG 42ND STREET

Stand on the balcony on Grand Central Terminal's Vanderbilt Avenue side and enjoy the view of the Main Concourse; witness the ebb and flow of New York, timed to the rhythm of the daily rush hours. Grand Central Terminal is a major gateway to the city, used by 750,000 people daily for travel, dining, and shopping.

Grand Central Terminal, a landmark building with a practical purpose

Grand Central Terminal

Map p. 106

42nd St. & Park Ave.

212/532-4900

Subway: 4, 5, 6, 7, S to Grand Central

grandcentral terminal.com

The terminal opened in 1913. Warren Whitney designed the beaux arts facade facing south on 42nd Street. Atop the entrance is a clock topped by the figure of Mercury, whom sculptor Jules-Felix Coutan described as "the god of speed, of traffic, and of the transmission of intelligence." The firm of Reed & Stem, architects, made the station work by devising a rail system that brings trains in on two levels.

As part of a $196 million, nine-year restoration, the East Waiting Room was completed in 1992, followed by an impressive overhaul of the Main Concourse. This immense space—measuring 120 feet by 275 feet (36 m x 82 m) with arched windows soaring 60 feet (18 m) on either end—has a floor of Tennessee marble and

125-foot-high (38 m) vaulted ceilings, which are painted to resemble the constellations. Between the two levels is the historic **Oyster Bar,** opened in 1913, famous for its oyster stew, extensive menu, and raw bar. Its marvelous decor includes a ceiling of Guastavino tiles, which were restored after a major fire in 1997.

Along 42nd Street

The following are a few sights to help orient you as you visit 42nd Street.

The former **McGraw-Hill Building** (*330 W. 42nd St.*) is a 1931 avant-garde skyscraper by architect Raymond Hood. You can visit its art deco lobby, which is green like the exterior terra-cotta tiles, hence the building's nickname, "The Jolly Green Giant." Across the street is the **Holy Cross Church** (*329 W. 42nd St., tel 212/246–4732*), an 1870 Byzantine-style building and the parish church of Father Francis P. Duffy, chaplain of the Fighting 69th in World War I. Duffy Square (see pp. 112, 116) is named for him.

Past the renovated theaters (see p. 117) is the former **Knickerbocker Hotel** (*tel 855/865–6425, 142 W. 42nd St.*). Built in 1906 by John Jacob Astor, the hotel's Maxfield Parrish mural now hangs in the King Cole Bar in the St. Regis Hotel. In 1924 George Gershwin's "Rhapsody in Blue" premiered at a concert hall across from the New York Public Library. Next door, the contoured **W. R. Grace Building** (*41 W. 42nd St.*) is a rarity in a city where horizontal and vertical

lines are the architectural norm. Pass Grand Central Terminal, then continue to the **Chanin Building,** at No. 122. This 56-story, 1929 skyscraper was the first in the area; the interior bronze art deco grillwork is by Rene Chambellan, whose sculptures also grace Radio City Music Hall (see p. 120). Across Lexington is the **Chrysler Building** (see p. 110), and across Third Avenue, the art deco **Daily News Building** (*220 E. 42nd St.*), home until 1995 of the city's first tabloid, and another 1930 Raymond Hood classic. The building is the fictional *Daily Planet* in

---

INSIDER TIP:

Head to the Oyster Bar at Grand Central for the secret "whispering gallery" in front of the restaurant. Stand at one of the arched columns, have your friend stand opposite you, both face the wall, and whisper. You will hear each other perfectly.

–MARGIE GOLDSMITH
National Geographic writer

---

the *Superman* movies. Cross to the **Ford Foundation Building** at No. 320, a 1967 glass box enclosing a public plaza and atrium. Reachable by steps near First Avenue is Tudor City, a Tudor-Gothic self-contained community, celebrated as the first residential skyscraper complex in the world. ∎

Oyster Bar

✉ Grand Central Terminal at 42nd St. & Park Ave.

☎ 212/490–6650

🚇 Subway: 4, 5, 6, 7, S to Grand Central

oysterbarny.com

CHRYSLER BUILDING

The art deco Chrysler Building is the favorite skyscraper of many New Yorkers and visitors alike. A historic landmark since 1971, it was built for automobile magnate Walter P. Chrysler, who wanted a corporate headquarters that reflected the glory of America's automotive industry.

■ A block away from Grand Central Terminal, the Chrysler Building's famous spire dominates the sky.

Chrysler Building

🗺 Map p. 106

✉ 405 Lexington Ave. at 42nd St.

☎ 212/682–3070

⊕ Closed Sat.–Sun.

🚇 Subway: 4, 5, 6, 7, S to Grand Central

In order to meet Walter P. Chrysler's lofty aspirations, architect William Van Alen adorned the facade of the building with symbols such as wheels and radiator caps, even adding iconic stainless steel gargoyles that resemble the hood ornaments of Chrysler automobiles.

The stainless-steel pinnacle, called the vertex, is an art deco version of a radiator grill. And, as indicated below, in the race for the skies that was taking place in the New York of the 1920s, the vertex of the Chrysler Building had more than purely aesthetic purposes. The lavish granite and marble lobby, with its Edward Trumbull ceiling mural, was once a Chrysler showroom.

From the start, artists were taken with the building. Georgia O'Keeffe rendered it as a painting, and a famous photograph of Margaret Bourke-White, taken by her "unsung partner" Oscar Graubner, shows her perched on a gargoyle high above the city. ■

Ever Higher

In the late 1920s an architect had only to announce a new skyscraper and he made the front page. In this charged atmosphere, the competition between the Chrysler Building's architect, William Van Alen, and his rival, H. Craig Severance, whose Bank of Manhattan building at 40 Wall Street was going up at the same time, was big news. Van Alen started at 56 floors, then, to top Severance, went to 65. Severance countered by adding a tower and, looking like a sure winner, finished at 71 stories. Van Alen, however, had secretly assembled a 185-foot (56 m) steel spire within the Chrysler Building's fire shaft. At his signal, he recalled, "the spire gradually emerged like a butterfly from its cocoon." The Chrysler Building won, with a height of 1,048 feet (319 m). Opened in 1930, it was also briefly the world's tallest building, surpassing the Eiffel Tower. But Van Alen's triumph was short lived; a few months later the Empire State Building opened. However, the Chrysler Building remains a jazz age masterpiece, and its spire, lit since 1978, is a distinctive skyline presence in Manhattan night and day.

UNITED NATIONS PLAZA

In 1946 the year-old United Nations Organization decided to locate its headquarters in the United States. Although other cities were in the running, it was a John D. Rockefeller gift of $8.5 million, for the purchase of an 18-acre (7.2 ha) plot on the East River, that made New York the chosen site.

The entrance is lined with flags of the 192 member nations. At the heart of the complex is the 39-story **Secretariat Building,** designed by France's Le Corbusier. Stretching north is the **General Assembly,** with its concave roof and central dome. The **Conference Building,** where the Security Council meets, extends east over FDR Drive. Guided tours leave from the General Assembly lobby, and there is a gift center and postal counter selling unique stamps.

Augustincic's statue "Peace" and the Japanese Peace Bell. Inside the Secretariat Building's Dag Hammarskjöld Memorial Chapel you can see Marc Chagall's stained-glass windows.

Construction began in 1947. The library is a 1963 addition. Other buildings surrounding the plaza include the office-hotel complex and UNICEF Building.

United Nations Plaza

- Map p. 106
- 1st Ave. & 46th St.
- 212/963–4475
- Closed Sat.–Sun.
- $$$ (tours)
- Subway: 4, 5, 6, 7, S to Grand Central

un.org/tours

■ The General Assembly of the UN can accommodate representatives of the 192 member nations.

INSIDER TIP:

After hoofing it to the UN, rest at nearby Greenacre Park. Complete with a 25-foot-high [7.6 m] waterfall and a lunchtime snack bar, it's New York's prettiest landscaped "pocket park" [a park built in an empty lot].

–MARGIE GOLDSMITH
National Geographic writer

Artwork donated by member nations is throughout. Barbara Hepworth's bronze monolith rises from a fountain at the entrance; see also Croatian Antun

Steps at 43rd Street lead to **Ralph Bunche Park,** dedicated to the African-American UN delegate and Nobel Peace Prize laureate. Upon its Isaiah Wall are engraved the words "They shall beat their swords into plowshares," fitting for this area, a symbol of world peace and freedom. ■

Greenacre Park

- On 51st St., bet. 2nd & 3rd Aves.
- Subway: 4, 5, 6, 7, E, F to 51st St./Lexington Ave.

TIMES SQUARE

Stand at Duffy Square between 46th and 47th Streets, to the north of Times Square, to admire the much-photographed scene of cars and pedestrians that shoot across the intersection of Boadway and Seventh Avenue. This is the Crossroads of the World. Night or day, gigantic illuminated signs blaze their messages. Such splendor is the gateway to the city's newest extravaganza, a revitalized 42nd Street.

■ Times Square, the world's most visited tourist attraction, hosts more than 39 million visitors annually.

Times Square

- Map p. 106
- Information Center: 1560 Broadway; entrance is at 7th Ave. bet. 46th & 47th Sts.
- 212/452–5283
- Subway: 1, 2 3, 7, N, R, S to 42nd St.–Times Square

timessquarenyc.org

Times Square today is a very different place from the tawdry tenderloin it had become by 1989. A newly designed **Duffy Square** opened in 2008 and features a new **TKTS** booth with glowing glass stairs. Buildings have sprouted, including one on Duffy Square designed especially for electric billboards. The new building at Four Times Square, housing the Condé Nast offices of *Vogue*, *Vanity Fair*, and the *New Yorker*, has been nicknamed the "citadel of chic." Just a few years ago, the thought of a *Vogue* editor in Times Square would have been inconceivable.

Two decades ago, 42nd Street between Seventh and Eighth Avenues, known as the "deuce," was somewhat dangerous, a place of hustlers, deteriorating second-run X-rated movie theaters, peep shows, and sex shops. Times Square had become a blot on the city's image and a place to steer clear of. Today it is clean, policed, and visitor friendly. Commuters, tourists, and school groups on class trips to New York are much in evidence, as are sightseeing New Yorkers, proud to see this neighborhood reclaimed.

Before leaving Duffy Square, give your regards to the statues of actor-producer George M.

Cohan and Father Francis P. Duffy, chaplain of the 69th Regiment during World War I and pastor of Holy Cross Parish, then get your bearings. At the TKTS booth, with its red steps, you can buy discount tickets for same day performances. Take a Broadway Walking Tour, which leaves from the Actor's Chapel (*239 49 St. bet. Broadway & 8th Ave.*), to discover the backstage secrets of New York Theater. The building that was once the **Embassy Theater,** the first to operate as an all

INSIDER TIP:

If you're willing to leave it to chance, try getting discount tickets at TKTS a half hour before showtime, when the lines have diminished. See Times Square or have dinner close by and be right there for the show.

–EDWARD BELLING
Broadway box office expert

newsreel theater, is now home to the Times Square Information Center.

The tower straight ahead (south) of Duffy Square is One Times Square, where the glittering ball drops on New Year's Eve. Remember that between 45th and 42nd Streets, both Broadway and Seventh Avenue have Broadway addresses. East at 43rd and Broadway, the seven-story-high

---

EXPERIENCE: New Attractions in Times Square

If you're looking for something other than Broadway theater performances, Times Square has an array of alternatives, all of which are exciting and unique. **Gulliver's Gate** (*tel. 212/235–2016, gulliversgate.com*) has over 300 miniature buildings, more than 1,000 train and car models, 3D models of the Big Apple's historical landmarks, and reproductions from around the world.

If you're a sports buff, the **NFL Experience Times Square** (*tel. 646/863–0088, nflexperience.com*) is for you. You can experience NFL videos in 4D, study training sessions and game plans using interactive displays, and measure your strength with those of professional players.

MarketSite Tower dominates the corner, illuminating the area 24 hours a day. It houses a state-of-the-art digital broadcast studio transmitting 100 live market updates from major networks: CNN, CNBC, BBC, and more. You may forget the occupants, but not the high-tech electronic display wrapping the cylindrical building with up-to-the-minute NASDAQ information.

Landmark Buildings

You can also seek out landmarks. The theaters (see pp. 117–118) are architectural gems. The 1931 **Brill Building** (*1619 Broadway at 49th St.*) was part of Tin Pan Alley. In this building many of America's most popular songwriters honed their craft, including Burt Bacharach, Paul

---

TKTS

✉ Broadway at W. 47th St., in Duffy Square

🚇 Subway: 1, 2 3, 7, N, R, S to 42nd St.–Times Square

tdf.org/TKTS

Sardi's

✉ 234 W. 44th St.

☎ 212/221–8440

🚇 Subway: 1, 2, 3, A, C, E to 42nd St.

sardis.com

Simon, and even Lou Reed. At street level the **Paramount Building** (*1501 Broadway*), a 1926 landmark with setbacks, towers, and clocks, once housed the Paramount Theater. An opulent movie palace of the day, it is also remembered for a 1944 concert when bobby-soxers, as teenage girls were then called, went into a frenzy over a young singer called Frank Sinatra.

Experience "hotel as theater" at the **Paramount Hotel** (*235*

its walls and for the low-priced "actor's menu" it offers to members of Actors' Equity.

There have been casualties of changing tastes and times. Some might argue that renewal has washed away Times Square's distinctive character, but even naysayers have now accepted a renaissance long overdue, a boon to tourism and the city economy, and a catalyst to revitalization elsewhere. The area has recently undergone a restyling that expan-

---

At the Stroke of Midnight

It was the opening of the Times Tower on New Year's Eve 1904 that first brought the crowds into Times Square. Marked by fireworks, the celebration was reported in the newspaper: "The instant the first flash on the Times Tower showed, a great shout went up, and an ear-splitting blast was sounded from the horns of the myriad merrymakers on the streets below." Thus the *Times* unwittingly gave birth to a tradition that continued after it moved out of the building in 1913. Today, a million people pack Times Square on New Year's Eve to watch a lighted ball begin its countdown fall one minute before midnight. Millions more watch on TV.

Algonquin Hotel

🗺 Map p. 106

✉ 59 W. 44th St.

☎ 212/840–6800

💲 $$$$$

🚇 Subway: B, D, F to 42nd St.

algonquinhotel.com

W. 46th St., tel 212/764–5500, nycparamount.com), where a light tableau animates the sweeping lobby staircase. The hotel is home to Sony Hall, a concert venue with avant-garde audiovisual technology and a capacity of 500 seats and standing room for 1,000. The hall is located in what was once the historical Diamond Horseshoe, a theater famous for its variety shows founded by entrepreneur Billy Rose in 1938. Blue Note and Sony have preserved much of the classic look and feel of the venue. Less ostentatious is **Sardi's,** a theatrical restaurant and landmark. Opened in 1921, it is famous for the caricatures of celebrities on

ded the pedestrian zone and its event spaces. Even so, in Times Square the pulse of New York beats as strong as ever.

43rd & 44th Streets

For a break from busy Times Square, sample West 43rd and 44th Streets (between Fifth and Sixth Avenues), streets of impressive dignity, whose buildings hold wonderful interiors.

Start with the 1902 **Algonquin Hotel** (see Travelwise p. 246), still in its original grandeur. The hotel is the famed home of the literary Round Table. This 1920s group included Dorothy Parker, Robert Benchley, and other writers and

INSIDER TIP:

No visit to the Big Apple is complete without a hot dog, pretzel, or knish (all with mustard!) from a food cart. Then follow your nose to a stall selling roasted nuts, the quintessential New York street aroma.

—JUSTIN KAVANAGH
National Geographic International Editions editor

artists. The venerable Oak Room, Blue Bar, and Rose Room (now the Round Table Room)—no longer rose—are open for dining and periodic cabaret shows. The lobby, delightful for tea, remains genteel: Ring a bell for the waiter.

Celebrity spotting is better across the street at the 1898 **Royalton Hotel** (see Travelwise p. 246), renovated in 1988 by Philippe Starck. Nearby, a plaque identifies the building that housed the offices of the *New Yorker* (25 W. 43rd St.). The **Mossman Lock Collection** is housed at the General Society of Mechanics and Tradesmen building. It has a unique collection of 400 locks, keys, and tools. Some buildings from the end of the 19th century are host to exclusive associations. The limestone-clad 1896 **Association of the Bar of the City of New York Building** runs through the block and has two addresses (*42 W. 44th St., 37 W. 43rd St.*). More fanciful is the 1899 **New York Yacht Club** (*37*

W. 44th St., tel 212/382–1000, nyyc.org), home of the America's Cup from 1857 to 1983. Its beaux arts window bays have a nautical air. Architects McKim, Mead & White designed the 1894 brick-faced **Harvard Club** (*35 W. 44th St.*), as well as the 1891 Italianate-style building for the **Century Association** (*7 W. 43rd St.*), a men's dining club.

If tranquility isn't what you're looking for, dive into the new **National Geographic Encounter** attraction, the Ocean Odyssey, a virtual aquarium where you can use touchscreens and enjoy 3D marine world videos and images, simulators, holograms and a play area. The visit lasts about 90 minutes. ∎

Oak Room at the Algonquin Hotel

✉ 59 W. 44th St.
☎ 212/840–6800
🕒 Seasonally Tues.–Sat., dinner; Sun. brunch

**algonquinhotel.com/
oak-room-supper-club**

National Geographic Encounter: Ocean Odyssey

✉ 226 W. 44th St.
☎ 646/308–1337
🕒 Open Sun.–Thur. 10 a.m.–9 p.m., Fri.–Sat. 10 a.m.–10 p.m.
💲 $$$
🚇 Subway: A, C, E, 7 to 42nd St.

natgeoencounter.com

EXPERIENCE: Eat NYC Specialty Street Foods

To sample some of New York's finest street food, keep an eye out for falafel from **Moishe's Falafel** cart (*94 W. 46th St.*); artisanal ice cream from the **Van Leeuwen** truck (*tel 718/701–1630, vanleeuwenicecream .com*); freshly baked cookies and cupcakes from the **Treats Truck** (*tel 212/691–5226, treatstruck.com*); and Belgian waffles with toppings from **Wafels and Dinges** (*tel 646/257–2592, dinges.nyc*). The chain, which was mandated by King Albert II of Belgium, has food trucks all over Manhattan; check their website. For great Japanese street food, go to **Otafuku x Medetai** at 220 East 9th Street (*tel 646/998–3438, otafuku.ny. com*); the *okonomiyaki* (savory crêpes) and *takoyaki* (octopus balls) are delicious. Finally **MUD Coffee** (*tel 212/228–9074, mudnyc. com*), the East Village's "anti-establishment" coffee shop, sells its own blend out of the MUDTRUCK. It's usually found on weekdays at the Astor Place Uptown 6 subway line.

THE GREAT WHITE WAY

O. J. Gude, whose company did many of the early Times Square signs, coined the term the Great White Way around the turn of the century. This referred to Broadway's appearance when lit up by signs that used only white lightbulbs. Gude saw the effectiveness—and art—of electric signage: "Everybody must read them, and absorb them, and absorb the advertiser's lesson willingly or unwillingly."

Gude was right. Here, in Times Square, a distinctly urban popular art form evolved, one that wedded beauty, communication, architecture, and technology. Times Square's premier signmaker for much of the last century has been Artkraft Strauss. To view the Great White Way, start at Times Square's southern perimeter, by the subway entrance on 42nd Street and Seventh Avenue, and look north to Broadway's main stem. Across from you, on your left, the latest fabulous sign will wrap the corner; to your left the

---

INSIDER TIP:

Stage doors still exist and, if you hang out long enough after the show, you may meet some of the cast. You may also bump into the actors in restaurants adjacent to the theaters.

—GARY McKECHNIE
National Geographic author

---

marquees of the newly restored theaters fan out toward the multiplex cinemas. Cross 42nd Street and look back toward the subway station and teeming streets. Streaming, biking, horse-drawn crowds create their own energy field. The vibe is contagious. Proceed uptown, choosing your favorite signs. At Duffy Square, the signs soar skyward. A latter-day favorite here was an electronic delight: The cap lifted off a 42-foot-tall (12 m) Coke bottle and its contents disappeared through a straw.

The first electric sign was an 1898 advertisement for Coney Island, erected at 38th Street and Broadway. The 1904 move of the *New York Times* created Times Square, where electric signage would enjoy its brightest days and nights. In 1910 the *Times* introduced its popular news ribbon for the Jim Jeffries–Jack Johnson heavyweight title fight in Nevada. This blow-by-blow account ran along the outside of Times Tower, the words rendered by 15,000 bulbs flashing 72,000 times a second. The technique is still used today, in digital ribbons known as zippers.

In 1917, Wrigley erected what it claimed was the world's largest electric sign. Eighty feet tall (24 m) and 200 feet (60 m) long, the Spearmint Gum ad featured animated spear-thrusting elves. In the 1920s, neon lighting brought color to the Great White Way. Everyone with memories of Times Square recalls specific signs. Many cite the Pepsi-Cola extravaganza of the 1950s, an immense waterfall flanked by huge Pepsi bottles. Douglas Leigh, responsible for the lighting of many of the city's buildings and signs over his lifetime, created the Pepsi sign and other landmarks such as the Camel man who blew gigantic smoke rings, one every 20 seconds. The smoke was an illusion: It was really Con Edison steam.

The 1950s were the heyday of the Great White Way. Today, colors are more intrusive. Many signs advertise imports. The contrast between past and present creates a nostalgia for the old days. On assignment to shoot Times Square, Jack Pierson made his photos blurry: "I still like to believe that the signs say 'Franks One Nickel' not 'Casio' or 'TDK'—so, if they're out of focus, I've got my New York Dream."

BROADWAY THEATERS

If you have heard that the Broadway theater is dead, don't believe it. In one recent year, 11,890,000 people paid $666 million for tickets and had a choice of more productions—close to 40—than at any other time in recent memory. Since 1880, "Broadway" has been a term for large-scale theater that opens in New York and often travels elsewhere; since 1929, most plays have opened not on Broadway but on the streets off Times Square.

You can still step back into the past wandering these streets. Begin with the **Belasco Theater** (*111 W. 44th St.*) and walk west to the theaters along "Rodgers & Hammerstein Row," from the **Shubert** (*225 W. 44th St.*) to the **Broadhurst,** the **Majestic,** the **Helen Hayes,** and the **St. James.** Farther along is the **Actors Studio** (*432 W. 44th St., not open to the public*), founded by Elia Kazan in 1947. Here director Lee Strasberg taught his students, including Marlon Brando, Marilyn Monroe, and Al Pacino.

Starring on the next block is the **Lyceum** (*149–157 W. 45th St.*), a beaux arts masterpiece dating from 1903. Note the graceful marquee, ornate columns, and theatrical masks across the entablature on the grandiose facade. Two blocks away, Marlon Brando debuted in *A Streetcar Named Desire* in 1947 at the **Barrymore** (*243 W. 47th St.*).

Although the architecture of many theaters is a show in itself, the wonder is what happens onstage. The boards echo with great performances, from the Barrymores acting family to Christopher Plummer playing John Barrymore in 1997 to unknowns creating a success in the musical smash *Rent*. The

■ The Ethel Barrymore Theater opened in 1928.

best way to savor Broadway is to buy a ticket and go. You might find yourself in a Moorish palace inside the **Al Hirschfeld Theater** (*302 W. 45th St.*) or amid plasterwork seemingly from the Renaissance at the Shubert or gazing at a French garden dance above the proscenium arch of the **Cort** (*138 W. 48th St.*), whose exterior, by the way, was based on Marie-Antoinette's Petit Trianon at

Broadway Theater Information
☎ 888/276-2392
nyc.com/broadway

New Amsterdam

✉ 214 W. 42nd St.

☎ 866/870–2717 (Ticketmaster) for show tickets

🚇 Subway: A, C, E, N, R, S, 1, 2, 3, 7 to Times Sq.

newamsterdam
theatre.com

Café Carlyle

✉ The Carlyle Hotel, 35 E. 76th St.

☎ 212/744–1600

thecarlyle.com

Versailles. You can also tour some theaters, such as the sumptuously renovated **New Amsterdam,** which one reviewer called "walking into a dream."

Preservation

A decision made in the 1980s to give most of Times Square's legitimate theaters the status of historic landmarks was an important step in saving them. Unfortunately, five venerable theaters, the Bijou, the Astor, and the original Helen Hayes among them, had already been destroyed by this time. Preservationists turned their attention to the nine 42nd Street theaters west of Times Square, decayed almost to the point of ruin or converted to "grind houses," showing pornographic movies

INSIDER TIP:

Many visitors head for Broadway when dusk falls, but cabarets such as the Café Carlyle—where Broadway performers come to spread their wings— offer a more intimate experience.

–DAISANN McLANE
National Geographic writer

and "adult" fare. Disney's 1995 commitment of eight million dollars to restore the New Amsterdam changed the area's fate. Now the nonprofit Times Square Business Improvement District guides the plan that is rescuing the theaters and revitalizing the area.

The stunning renovation of the New Amsterdam set the standard to follow. The original theater was the height of opulence, with promenades and a roof garden. From 1913 to 1927, the Ziegfeld Follies were produced here. Today the theater has been returned to use in all its art nouveau splendor: *Aladdin,* on stage since 2014, offers theater the whole family can enjoy.

So stand in line at TKTS (see p. 111) at Duffy Square, mingle with the crowds to get your discount seats (cash only), and feel the excitement build. As the lights go down and the curtain rises, let Broadway theater sweep you off your feet. ■

EXPERIENCE: Laugh Out Loud at a Comedy Club

So this guy walks into a comedy club ...

New York City attracts all kinds of aspiring comics, and a wide pool of talent can be found at clubs around town, from national headliners to comedy show writers to local up-and-comers. A Midtown favorite is **Carolines** (*1626 Broadway, tel 212/757–4100, carolines.com*). Clubs such as **Gotham Comedy Club** (*208 West 23rd St., bet. 7th & 8th Aves., tel 212/367–9000, gothamcomedyclub.com*) in Chelsea and the **Comedy Cellar** (*117 MacDougal St., tel 212/254–3480, comedycellar.com*) in Greenwich Village are always good for a laugh. Fans of improv should check out the **Upright Citizens Brigade Theatre** in Chelsea (see Travelwise p. 265).

You've been great, good night!

EXPERIENCE: Witness a Manhattan "Solstice"

New Yorkers like to think of their city as the center of the world, if not the entire universe. But twice a year you can join the citizens of Manhattan as they get a geographical reminder that they are mere Earthlings, like the rest of us, spinning around our mother star, the sun. This occurs around the time of the summer and winter solstices, when the solar system aligns with the street grid of Manhattan and anyone standing on one of its cross streets above 14th Street can peer westward in summer to catch the sun setting directly in line with the skyscrapers, or eastward in winter as it rises.

For 22 days on either side of the summer solstice (around June 21) New Yorkers are treated to the spectacle of the setting sun's golden glow filling the canyons between the towers (weather permitting).

In winter, the reverse phenomenon occurs, and you can watch the sun rise spectacularly by standing on the western side of the island and watching the new day's light climb the eastern end of the cross streets. This occurs either side of the winter solstice (around December 21).

This seemingly cosmic drama, dubbed "Manhattanhenge" by locals, is actually a happy happenstance of light and town planning. The City Commissioners' Plan of 1811 laid out the streets of Manhattan in accord with the island's natural axis, and, in fact, the street plan, and consequently the grid of skyscrapers, is turned 29 degrees north from true east-west, so the sunsets and sunrises each align twice a year, on dates around the summer solstice and winter solstice. The American Museum of Natural History explains the phenomenon, and posts the best dates to catch the solar show (*amnh.org/our-research/*

Looking west across the island, the Chrysler Building and the New York Times Building salute the Manhattan sunset.

INSIDER TIP:

The Tudor City Bridge on 42nd Street offers one of the best views of Manhattanhenge for the pedestrian.

—JUSTIN KAVANAGH
National Geographic International Editions editor

---

hayden-planetarium/resources/ manhattanhenge).

As Midtown has towered ever upward since the Commissioners' grid webbed the island, Manhattan has transmogrified into a vast metropolis of man-made canyons, walled by skyscrapers (see

pp. 122–123). The clusters of towers in Midtown and in lower Manhattan are indicative of what is underground here: strong layers of Manhattan Schist near the surface. A spine of this rock, suitable for laying the strong foundations needed to support skyscrapers, runs from north to south of the island. This strata of schist dips well below the surface around Washington Square; hence the lack of tall buildings between Midtown and Lower Manhattan.

To see Manhattanhenge you just have to follow the sequence of streets towards the north from 14th Street, since below that, as we said, the streets aren't perfectly parallel and don't form the characteristic urban grid. Either end of 42nd Street offers a great vantage point, depending on the solstice, or in summer venture out to Long Island City to see the entire skyline.

Bring a camera, and join the natives who gather giddily to gaze in wonder: The sun's collusion with the monoliths of Manhattan is a spectacle to behold. For tours that include Manhattanhenge try: *bikethebigapple.com/manhattanhenge.php* and *meetup.com /nynightndayevents/events.*

ROCKEFELLER CENTER

Rockefeller Center—with its walkways, sunken plaza, gardens, outdoor sculpture, and art deco buildings—has been copied but never surpassed. Bounded by Fifth and Sixth Avenues (Avenue of the Americas) and 48th and 51st Streets, this 19-building city within a city is arguably the most successful urban development ever.

Rockefeller Center
Map p. 106

As a visitor, a good place to start is **Radio City Music Hall,** where the high-kicking, 36-member dance team, the Rockettes, still performs

◾ The lighting of the immense Rockefeller Center tree is a highlight of the New York holiday season.

Christmas and Easter shows and where top singers perform throughout the year. Behind the scenes one-hour **Stage Door Tours** are offered daily (*9.30 a.m.–3 p.m., tickets required*).

The music hall stands at the edge of the original 14 buildings that comprised the center when it opened in 1940; five buildings west of Sixth Avenue were added after 1945. For a detailed guide to the complex, go to the **Comcast Building** at 30 Rockefeller Plaza. Headquarters for NBC is here, and outside (*bet. W. 49th & 50th Sts.*), the morning *Today Show* with Savannah Guthrie and Hoda Kotb broadcasts live. Watch it through the glass-enclosed set. In the center of the complex is a flag-lined sunken plaza. Here you can skate outdoors in winter, or in summer dine at Rock Center Café, which takes over the rink.

Past the rink is the sloping Promenade, where a holiday light display complements the lighting of an immense Christmas tree in 30 Rockefeller Plaza, the focus every holiday season. Sit by the floral displays and sculpture in the Channel Gardens and then wander onto Fifth Avenue.

The elegant **Rainbow Room** on the 65th floor of 30 Rockefeller Plaza is treasured for its revolving floor, cocktails, and spectacular views. Here you can dance to a live Big Band orchestra or enjoy the spirited crowd at Bar SixtyFive. In good or bad weather you can explore the many shops and eateries in the complex's underground concourse.

John D. Rockefeller developed Rockefeller Center, a site originally intended as a home for the Metropolitan Opera, but

EXPERIENCE: See NY From the Top of the Rock

For a 360-degree view of New York, climb 70 stories to the **Top of the Rock Observation Center** (*30 Rockefeller Plaza*). Designed to evoke the decks of art deco ocean liners, the Observation Center reopened in 2005 after being closed for nearly 20 years. In 2014, U2 helped launch *The Tonight Show Starring Jimmy Fallon* there. The streamlined design features non-reflective safety glass on the 67th and 69th floors and an open-air 70th floor. A glass-topped elevator ride, video exhibits, and a Swarovski-crystal chandelier add to the experience. Buy tickets online (*topoftherocknyc.com/ticket-menu*, $$$$), at the box office (*W. 50th St., bet. 5th & 6th Aves.*), or by phone (*tel* 877/NYC–ROCK).

INSIDER TIP:

If you are in the city at the end of January or beginning of February, don't miss the annual Chinese New Year show at Radio City Music Hall. The dancing, costumes, and music are out of this world.

—JARED PEARMAN
National Geographic contributor

when the stock market crashed, the Met reneged. In late 1929 Rockefeller announced a plan for a commercial complex to house the new radio and television industry.

When the Radio Corporation of America (RCA) moved into the building, the entire complex became known as Radio City, a name that soon gave way to Rockefeller Center. The name

of the adjacent Radio City Music Hall stuck. It remains, with 6,200 seats, the country's largest theater, and it is a link with a time when RCA, RKO, and NBC were primary tenants. Rockefeller Center now houses publishing and communications organizations.

Not part of the complex but nearby are two historic streets. "Swing Street," 52nd Street between Fifth and Sixth Avenues, was the world center of jazz in the 1930s.

All that remains of that era is the brownstone housing the swank **21 Club** restaurant (*21 W. 52nd St., tel 212/582-7200*). Still vital as a district is "Diamond Row," along 47th Street; the diamond cutters who formed it were European Jews fleeing Nazism. ∎

Rainbow Room

- ✉ 30 Rockefeller Plaza, 65th floor
- ☎ 212/632–5100
- 💲 $$$$
- 🚇 Subway: B, D, F to 47th–50th Sts.–Rockefeller Center

rainbowroom.com

Radio City Music Hall

- ✉ 1260 6th Ave.
- ☎ 212/247–4777
- 💲 Tours: $$$$
- 🚇 Subway: B, D, F to 47th–50th Sts.–Rockefeller Center

msg.com/radio-city-music-hall

SKYSCRAPERS WALKING TOUR

This zigzag tour passes buildings pivotal in the city's architectural history. It begins just north of Grand Central Station with the baroque-towered Helmsley Building, which straddles Park Avenue, crosses Park Avenue a number of times, and ends with the art deco Fuller Building on Madison Avenue.

The General Electric Building, also known as 570 Lexington Avenue.

Built in 1929 as the New York Central Building—to house the railroad company—the **Helmsley Building** ❶ (*230 Park Ave., bet. E. 45th & E. 46th Sts.*) is stunning inside, and its white-towered outline is impressive. Sadly, in 1963 the Pan Am (now Met Life) Building went up, blocking some views of it. Continue north three blocks, to 301 Park Avenue, to see the famed art deco **Waldorf-Astoria Hotel.** Its twin 625-foot (190 m) towers are residences for the rich and famous. It's currently being renovated but you can imagine its luxurious lobby, decorated with bronze and mahogany and marble columns. Turn left (west) on East 50th Street, crossing Park Avenue, and look back for a better perspective on the Met Life's overshadowing of the Helmsley. Such architectural incongruity is a common theme in Midtown Manhattan. Go right at Madison Avenue to the **Villard Houses** (*Nos. 451–455*), part of the **Lotte**

> **NOT TO BE MISSED:**
>
> General Electric Building
> • Seagram Building • Citigroup Center • Sony Building
> • Fuller Building

New York Palace (see Travelwise p. 247; formerly the Helmsley Palace Hotel). Built for railroad tycoon Henry Villard, beginning in 1883, the Villard Houses are six brownstones joined to look like a Renaissance palace. It was saved from demolition in the 1980s by incorporating the east wing into the Palace Hotel lobby. You can stop for tea beneath the gilded ceiling in the Villard Restaurant.

Take a right at 51st Street and a right at Park Avenue for **St. Bartholomew's Church** ❷. This 1919 Byzantine-style Episcopal church

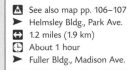

- See also map pp. 106–107
- ▶ Helmsley Bldg., Park Ave.
- ↔ 1.2 miles (1.9 km)
- About 1 hour
- ▶ Fuller Bldg., Madison Ave.

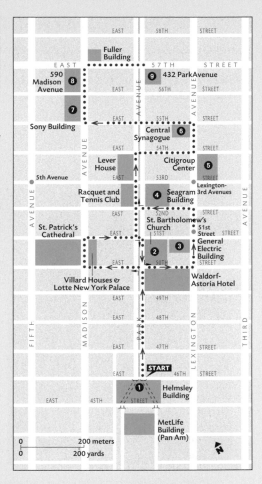

exemplifies the city's movement north; the congregation was formerly located on Madison Avenue and East 44th Street. The Stanford White porch, with carvings by Phillip Martiny and Daniel Chester French, came from the earlier church. Go left (east) on East 50th Street to Lexington Avenue; turn left. The art deco **General Electric Building** ③ (*570 Lexington Ave.*), built in 1931 as the RCA Victor Building, was sheathed in brick and terra-cotta to complement St. Bartholomew's.

Go left at East 52nd Street and right to 370 Park Avenue, the **Racquet and Tennis Club,** built in 1918. This members-only male bastion is a copy of an Italian palazzo. Across the street is the 1958 bronze-glass-and-steel **Seagram Building** ④ (*375 Park Ave.*), by German-born architect Mies van der Rohe. A block north at 390 Park Avenue, the landmark 1952 **Lever House** was the city's first glass slab office building. Turn right at East 54th Street to **Citigroup Center** ⑤ (1977) on Lexington between 53rd and 54th Streets. Its chisel-shaped top is a modern reference point on the skyline. Inside are stores and St. Peter's Lutheran Church. Go left on Lexington Avenue, and on the corner of 55th Street is the city's oldest continuously used synagogue, the onion-domed **Central Synagogue** ⑥ (*123 E. 55th St., tel 212/838–5122, free tours Weds. 12:45 p.m.*), dating from 1872.

Turn left onto E. 55th Street and after two blocks, turn right. **The Sony Building** ⑦ (1984), designed by Philip Johnson (*550*

Madison Ave.), in grey-pink granite crowned with a colossal gable, is considered to be the first post-modern skyscraper. It was declared a historical landmark in 2018. Farther along, the green granite 1983 **IBM Building** ⑧ (*590 Madison Ave.*) has an atrium for refreshment amid soothing bamboo trees and a sculpture garden. Last stop is the art deco **Fuller Building** ⑨ (*41 E. 57th St. at Madison Ave.*), built in 1929. Note the Elie Nadelman sculpture, "Construction Workers," above the entrance. Inside are galleries, including Howard Greenberg on the 14th floor.

ST. PATRICK'S CATHEDRAL

St. Patrick's is massive: At 332 feet long and 174 feet wide (101 m x 53 m), it is among the world's largest cathedrals. Offering quiet refuge in busy Midtown, it is in constant use for weddings and other events, while its entrance steps are the ideal platform from which to watch the endless parade of pedestrians.

St. Patrick's Gothic spires vie with Fifth Avenue's high-rises.

St. Patrick's Cathedral

Map p. 106

5th Ave. & 50th St.

212/753–2261

Subway: B, D, F to 47th–50th Sts.–Rockefeller Center; E to 5th Ave./53rd St.

saintpatricks cathedral.org

Its architecture is timeless; James Renwick, Jr., modeled it on the Gothic cathedral in Cologne, Germany, also borrowing elements from other cathedrals in Europe. The spires were finished in 1888; at 332 feet tall (101 m), they towered above the city until the 1930s, when skyscrapers began to appear. Renwick's original east front was replaced in 1906 by the Lady Chapel, designed by Charles T. Mathews. The three sets of bronze doors on Fifth Avenue are a 1949 addition. Elizabeth Ann Seton, the first American-born saint, is among the saints of New York depicted on the central doors; inside is a shrine to her, along with a bronze statue.

Go inside—visitors are expected to respectfully wander to view the interior. The central nave can seat 2,500 people. It is 108 feet high (33 m) and 48 feet wide (14.6 m). Be sure to visit the **Lady Chapel** honoring the Blessed Virgin, where there is a marble Pietà (1906) by William O. Partridge. Unlike most Gothic cathedrals, there are no flying buttresses, but above the altar is a 57-foot (17 m) bronze baldachin. Note, too, the entryway, especially magnificent when light streams in through the 26-foot-wide (8 m) **Rose Window** above the **Great Organ** over the **Great Bronze Doors.**

Archbishop John Hughes announced plans for the church in 1858. His successor, Archbishop John McCloskey, opened the church on May 25, 1879. The $1.9 million cathedral is dedicated to the patron saint of Ireland. ∎

FIFTH AVENUE TODAY

Midtown Fifth Avenue bears little resemblance today to its residential past as Millionaires' Row. Still, there are signs of that history among all that is new. Architecturally, the stretch covered here features Grand Army Plaza, St. Patrick's Cathedral, Rockefeller Center, and other historic buildings.

FAO Schwarz recently reopened its doors inside Rockefeller Center. It's the perfect place to shop for a book or an Eloise doll: The six-year-old fictional character of Kay Thompson's series. Now, little girls flock to **American Girl Place** (609 5th Ave., tel 202/371-2220) for doll grooming, studio photographs, and maybe a spot of brunch.

INSIDER TIP:

Look for the pig of St. Patrick's, a small, playful gargoylesque detail on the exterior of the Lady Chapel. It's on the corner of Madison Avenue and 51st Street.

–WILL KATINSKY
National Geographic contributor

Tiffany & Co. (727 5th Ave.) originated on lower Broadway, but the glitter of gems remains the same, so take a look inside.

At the bronze-colored **Trump Tower** (725 5th Ave., tel 212/832-2000) there's shopping and a waterfall. On opposite corners at 55th Street are two fine hotels, the **Peninsula New York,** a 1905 beaux arts landmark, and the 1904

St. Regis, built by John Jacob Astor. In 1917 **Cartier** (653 5th Ave.) converted two turn-of-the-20th-century mansions into its jewelry emporium, while high-fashion **Versace** occupies a house built in 1902–1905 by George W. Vanderbilt (647 5th Ave.). **Saks Fifth Avenue** (611 5th Ave.) opened in 1924 in this Renaissance-style building. The 1927 **Fred F. French Building** (551 5th Ave.), with its multicolored faience, is a classic example of setback architecture. ∎

EXPERIENCE: Walk in a Window Wonderland

The Rockefeller Center Christmas tree isn't the only thing that sparkles for the holidays. Between mid-November and New Year's, Manhattan's large department stores unveil beautifully decorated windows, from classic to avant-garde. Take a walking tour (approximately 90 minutes), starting at **Macy's** (34th St. & Broadway); go east to Fifth Avenue, turn left, and head north for **Lord & Taylor**'s windows at 38th Street. Continue north to 48th Street for the **Saks Fifth Avenue** display. View the elaborate dioramas at **Bergdorf Goodman** (Fifth Ave. at 57th St.), then walk east to Madison Avenue and up to 60th Street for **Barneys'** windows. Then head east on 60th Street to **Bloomingdale's** at Lexington Avenue.

MUSEUM OF MODERN ART

When the Museum of Modern Art (MoMA) closed for reconstruction in 2002, it was attracting more than 1.6 million visitors annually. The museum's 2005 transformation into what the *New York Times* called "one of the most exquisite works of architecture to rise in this city in at least a generation" heightened enthusiasm worldwide for this already favorite cultural destination. Now, with further expansion planned, MoMA is about to become even bigger.

■ Monet's triptych "Water Lilies" graces MoMA's main gallery at the renovated museum.

From Cézanne to Chuck Close, from the earliest daguerreotypes to interactive video and electronic displays, MoMA has it all—as well as spaces and galleries designed to match the type and scale of works displayed.

From its beginnings in 1929, the museum's guiding principle has been to move beyond the narrow definition of art, which includes painting, sculpture, and drawing, to embrace all the visual fields. MoMA was a pioneer in the fields of architecture and graphic, industrial, and textile designs. It collected and exhibited photographs long before other major museums and was early to collect and preserve significant films. Since then its holdings have steadily increased, and its

physical structure has been redefined and renovated to keep pace. This has included adding a variety of dining options: two cafés and The Modern, the museum's fine-dining restaurant and bar, with a patio on the garden. For shopping, visitors can choose among a wide range of items in all prices at two shops. The **MoMA Design & Book Store** across from the museum specializes in objects licensed from the collection, from jewelry and scarves to glassware.

The Collection

MoMA's permanent collection includes 150,000 paintings, sculptures, drawings, prints, photographs, design objects, and architectural drawings and models. There are some 22,000 films, videos, and media works; 300,000 books, periodicals, and artists' books; 2,500 linear feet (762 m) of historical documentation in the MoMA Archives; and a photographic archive of tens of thousands of photographs.

Museum Highlights

The new MoMA that opened in 2005 has nearly doubled in size and added 40,000 square feet (3,716 sq m) in exhibition space. It can now present the most extensive display of its collection ever, including many previously unexhibited works. On view are selections from each of the museum's six curatorial departments: Film and Media;

INSIDER TIP:

Use your cell phone to connect to MoMA's Wi-Fi server, download apps, and listen to commentary on the artworks and exhibitions. Go to *moma.org /explore/mobile.*

–MATT HANNAFIN
National Geographic contributor

Prints and Illustrated Books; Architecture and Design; Drawings; Photography; and Painting and Sculpture. Among them are some of the museum's best loved works, including Vincent van Gogh's "The Starry Night" and Pablo Picasso's "Les Demoiselles d'Avignon."

Film & Media: Works are shown in two areas of the museum. The two movie theaters on the lower level have daily programs selected from the museum's 20,000 moving-image works. These cover more than a century, from the days of Thomas Edison to the present. The Media Gallery on the second floor has both installations and electronic media.

Prints & Illustrated Books: These are on the second floor (along with the Contemporary Galleries, Media Gallery, special exhibitions, and Café 2), drawn from a collection of more than 50,000 prints and illustrated books from the 1880s to the present. Among highlights are the Edvard Munch print "Madonna" (1895–1902) and a 1913 illustrated book combining art by Sonia Delauney-Terks and poetry by Cendrars.

Architecture & Design: With exhibits on the third floor, this diverse collection provides an extensive overview of modernism. The architecture collection documents buildings and contains more than 60 models and 1,000 drawings, plus the large **Ludwig Mies van der Rohe Archive.** The design collection has more than 3,000 objects, ranging from appliances, furniture, and classic cars to textiles, silicon chips, typography, and posters: Rody Grauman's "85 Lamps Lighting Fixture" (1992), Christopher Dresser's fanciful red-and-black "Watering

Museum of Modern Art (MoMA)

🅰 Map p. 106

✉ 11 W. 53rd St., bet. 5th & 6th Aves.

☎ 212/708–9685

🕐 Closed Tues., Thanksgiving Day, & Christmas Day

💲 $$$. Advance admission tickets are available online at moma. org or from Ticketmaster at 212/220–0505 or ticketweb. com

🚇 Subway: E to 5th Ave./53rd. St.; B, D, F to 47th–50th St.–Rockefeller Center

moma.org

NOTE: Lines for admission and the checkroom are often long, so travel light for your museum visit. All items larger than 11 x 14 inches (28 x 38 x 13 cm) must be held in the checkroom. Some luggage may not be accepted.

MoMA Design & Book Store

✉ 44 W. 53 St.

☎ 212/708–9700

🚇 Subway: E to 5th Ave./53rd. St.; B, D, F to 47th–50th St.–Rockefeller Center

momastore.org

Can" (painted tin-iron, circa 1896), and Ludwig Mies van der Rohe's perspective drawing for a 1921 crystal tower, "Friedrich-strasse Skyscraper" brilliantly illustrate the synthesis of architecture and design.

Photography: MoMA's collection of more than 25,000 photographs, from 1840 to the present, is one of the world's most important. The museum

Stieglitz, Man Ray, Imogen Cunningham, Manuel Alvarez Bravo, Diane Arbus, and more. In the contemporary arena, a landmark acquisition was the purchase of Cindy Sherman's black-and-white "Untitled Film Stills" series; Andreas Gursky's one-man show (1999) and Lee Friedlander's 2005 retrospective drew large crowds. MoMA's annual curated exhibit "New Photography" can be counted

■ **One of Sol LeWitt's "Wall Drawings." The American artist has created more than 1,000 unique but similarly titled pieces since his career began in the 1960s.**

began collecting in 1930. In 1955, Edward Steichen, then chairman, curated the seminal "Family of Man" exhibit, raising awareness of photography as an art form. MoMA's third-floor galleries contain works from William Henry Fox Talbot and others at the dawn of the medium, as well as later celebrated photographers Julia Margaret Cameron, Alfred

on for outstanding new talent, such as Sam Taylor-Wood in the 1998–1999 show: Using a rotating camera that records close to 360 degrees in five seconds, she created large-scale color panoramas blending aspects of motion and still photographs.

Painting & Sculpture: Works from this collection, shown on floors four and five, are likely to elicit the greatest collective response, for so many of them are iconic, often-published masterworks—only here you see the real thing. Containing more than 3,500 works from the late 19th century to the present, MoMA's modern painting and sculpture collection is the world's largest and most inclusive. Perhaps you will be fortunate enough to see its earliest work, Paul Cézanne's Post-Impressionist painting "The Bather" (circa 1885). Contemporary artists in the collection include James Rosenquist, Susan Rothenberg, Cai Guo-Quiang, Chris Ofili, Richard Serra, and others.

To enter more deeply into the world of painting, choose some works for comparison. Paul Gauguin's depiction of a Polynesian goddess in "The Seed of the Areoi" (oil on burlap, 1892); Frida Kahlo's "Self-Portrait with Cropped Hair" (oil on canvas, 1940); and Andy Warhol's rendition of a goddess of popular culture, "Gold Marilyn Monroe" (silkscreen ink on synthetic polymer paint on canvas, 1962) can spark fascinating discussions on the painterly canonization of women. Comparing two sculptures, Marcel Duchamp's "Bicycle Wheel" (1951) and Chris Burden's "Medusa's Head" (1990), raises fundamental questions about artmaking and influence. Both sculptures use altered common objects and rely on a conceptual premise and absurdist visual surprise. "Medusa's Head" does not feature twine or snakes

Art on Paper

The third floor holds selections from the collection's nearly 10,000 works on paper, including those done in pencil, ink, and charcoal, plus watercolors, collages, gouaches, and mixed-media pieces. Highlights include works by such artists as Georges-Pierre Seurat, Paul Klee, Egon Schiele, and Dieter Roth. Joan Miró's "The Beautiful Bird Revealing the Unknown to a Pair of Lovers" (1941) is an obsessively meticulous drawing with a nature theme, from his Constellation series. In contrast is a classic Georgia O'Keeffe work (and a bequest of the artist): "An Orchid" (1941), a fluid, sensual, green-and-white composition.

or a predictable component for the hair but, instead, model railroad tracks and seven scale model trains. And Duchamp's "Bicycle Wheel," his first Readymade, is not simply a bicycle wheel mounted upside down on a kitchen stool.

Floors four and five are replete with other equally wondrous works, of Claude Monet, Pablo Picasso, Piet Mondrian, Jackson Pollack, Alexander Calder, Joseph Cornell, and Eva Hesse, to name just a few.

You may prefer to find your favorite work and stay with it for a time. Allow at least one piece to work its magic on you. Perennial favorites are Henri

Picasso's "Les Demoiselles d'Avignon" (1907) is among the thousands of works on display at MoMA.

Rousseau's "The Sleeping Gypsy" (1897), Henri Matisse's "Dance 1" (1909), Vincent van Gogh's "The Starry Night" (1889), and Alberto Giacometti's "The Palace at 4 a.m." (1932).

On the fifth floor, you can stop in at the Terrace 5 Café and, season permitting, look down on the garden as you sip your drink or cocktail on the terrace. Café 2, located on the second floor, is another option for refreshments.

Back on the first floor, the garden and its many sculptures are still there for your return, and so is Auguste Rodin's "Monument to Balzac" (1898, cast 1954), presiding spirit of the lobby.

The extension of the structure that is currently underway will add 30% more display space to the ground floor and to the 2nd, 4th, and 5th floors. As you leave, pick up brochures (with material on the research resources and study centers), plus schedules and flyers on the many workshops, lectures, films, and special events. You may also consider planning a trip to MoMA's affiliate, PS1, devoted to the advancement of contemporary art. It is housed in a 100-year-old Romanesque Revival school building in Long Island City, where it has mounted many provocative visual arts exhibits over the past quarter century (see sidebar p. 226). ■

History of MoMA

The idea for the museum was conceived in the winter of 1928–1929 when Abby Rockefeller, the wife of John D. Rockefeller, Jr., and Lillie P. Bliss met in Cairo, Egypt. They decided that the United States must have a museum devoted to modern art and sculpture, works other museums refused to exhibit. Mary Quinn Sullivan became the third partner in the enterprise. The "ladies," as they were called, enlisted the aid of A. Conger Goodyear, a museum trustee and collector, and art historian Paul J. Sachs. Soon the museum opened in a small gallery on the 12th floor of the Heckscher Building (*750 5th Ave. at 57th St.*) with a brilliant 27-year-old art scholar, Alfred H. Barr, Jr., as director. Barr shaped the museum during its early years and insisted on expanding the museum's horizons to include all the visual arts.

In 1932 the museum moved into a town house at its current location on West 53rd Street. In 1936, MoMA commissioned architect Edward Durell Stone and Philip Goodwin, to design a new building on the 53rd Street site. The new museum, which opened in 1939, was fronted by a sheath of glass and marble and was one of the country's first examples of the international style. The museum doubled in size in 1984, with additions by architect Cesar Pelli. It owes its current state to the 2005 reconstruction, but remains a work in progress, with an expansion project that includes the demolition of the adjoining building that was once the home of the Folk Art Museum, on W. 53rd Street.

More Midtown North Sites

There are many art venues to choose from in Midtown Manhattan, so why not take a chance and have a wander through **Christies** (*20 Rockefeller Plz., 48th St & 49th St, tel 212/636–2000, christies.com, closed Sat.–Sun.*) or **Sotheby's** (*1334 York Ave, tel 212/606–7000, sothebys.com*) to see what private collectors are selling these days, and for how much. It's a free fix of art, sculpture, and design that you may never see displayed in public again.

Carnegie Hall

Tchaikovsky was among the first to conduct in this premier performance space, which opened in 1891. Since then, every major figure in classical music as well as the celebrated in jazz, pop, and rock have performed here. Even if you cannot take in a concert, stopping in at the **Rose Museum** (*tel 212/903-9629*) on the second floor places you inside Andrew Carnegie's famed concert hall. The museum holds fascinating material, music, and even instruments, such as Benny Goodman's clarinet and Toscanini's baton. When Lincoln Center opened in 1962, Carnegie Hall was scheduled for demolition. It was saved by the efforts of violinist Isaac Stern. *carnegiehall.org* ✉ 154 W. 57th St. at 7th Ave. ☎ 212/247–7800 🚇 Subway: N, Q, R to 57th St./7th Ave.

International Center of Photography (ICP)

This unique institution is the largest photography museum-school in the world and the only museum in New York dedicated solely to photography. Here changing exhibitions are installed, many drawn from the museum's 100,000 original prints spanning the history of photography. Across the street is the new state-of-the-art school facility.

The museum entrance opens onto a large airy space with a museum shop. Ahead the spacious gallery area begins, continuing downstairs.

An elevator or a wide stairwell reaches the second floor, where there are more galleries. At least three shows are usually on display. A museum café on the lower floor offers light fare.

Recent exhibits included "Henri Cartier-Bresson: The Decisive Moment" and "Edmund Clark: The Day the Music Died." Retrospectives have showcased artists such as Imogen Cunningham, Man Ray, Annie Leibowitz, David Hockney, and many more.

Cornell Capa, the former *Life* magazine photographer who founded the ICP in 1974, did so to present and preserve all aspects of photography—from photojournalism to the avant-garde, from master photographers to emerging talents. ICP also sponsors monthly lectures and symposia and approximately 400 courses a year, taught by leading photographers. *icp.org* ✉ 1133 Ave. of the Americas at 43rd St. ☎ 212/857–0000 or 800/688–8171 (mail order) 🕐 Closed Mon. 💲 $$ 🚇 Subway: B, D, F to 42nd St.

Intrepid Sea-Air-Space Museum

This unique museum of naval aviation history is moored at a Hudson River dock. The *Intrepid* is a decommissioned aircraft carrier that fought in World War II and the Korean and Vietnam Wars. After two years of refurbishment, the *Intrepid* reopened in 2008. The recently reopened Space Shuttle Pavilion showcases the space shuttle *Enterprise,* the prototype NASA orbiter that made the trip to New York from Washington, D.C., and survived damage from Hurricane Sandy. *intrepidmuseum.org* ✉ Pier 86, One Intrepid Sq., W. 46th St. & 12th Ave. 💲 $$$ ☎ 212/245–0072 🚇 Subway: A, C, E to 42nd St.

Japan Society Gallery

In addition to its own small collection of 20th-century woodblock prints by Shiko Munakata, the gallery exhibits art from other institutions. The society opened the gallery here in 1971. Its small lobby garden, with a pool and bamboo trees, provides a peaceful retreat from the hustle and bustle of Midtown Manhattan. *japansociety.org /gallery*  333 E. 47th St. ☎ 212/832–1155 🕐 Closed Mon. 💲 $$ 🚇 Subway: E to Lexington Ave./53rd St.; 6 to 51st St.

Museum of Arts & Design

This appealing museum features works that blur the line between craft and art—from decorative arts to traditional crafts. In 2008, the museum moved into its new Columbus Circle location, where a facade was added of terra-cotta and glass panels that create an iridescent effect. Cuts in the original walls of the building allow lights in to illuminate exhibitions in a spacious gallery area. Visitors can also get a behind-the-scenes look at artists at work at the Open Studios (6th floor). *madmuseum. org* ✉ 2 Columbus Circle ☎ 212/299–7777 💲 $$ 🕐 Closed Mon. 🚇 Subway: A, B, C, D, 1 to 59th St.–Columbus Circle; N, Q, R, to 57th St./7th Ave.

■ Beyond a carpet of tulips stands the grande dame of New York hotels, the Plaza.

The Paley Center for Media

Along with exhibits, vintage props, screening rooms, and memorabilia, this venue provides listening stations, computers for accessing your favorite television or radio episode (the collection contains more than 140,000 programs and advertisements), and workshops for both children and adults. Worth watching for are the excellent programs year-round in the on-site theaters, many with celebrity guests. Guests of the programs open to the public include John Goodman and actors from today's most popular television series. *paleycenter.org* ✉ 25 W. 52nd St. ☎ 212/621–6600 🕐 Closed Mon.–Tues. 💲 $$ 🚇 Subway: E to 5th Ave./53rd St.; B, D, F to 47th–50th Sts.–Rockefeller Center

Plaza Hotel

Gracing Grand Army Plaza is the Plaza Hotel, a French-style château of immense proportions, designed in 1907 by Henry J. Hardenbergh and reopened in 2008 after a two-year renovation. The Plaza has long been a celebrity magnet—F. Scott Fitzgerald lived here, Marilyn Monroe visited, and *North by Northwest, Breakfast at Tiffany's,* and other screen classics were filmed on-site. Drinks in the Palm Court or dinner in the Rose Club offer the ambience of old New York (see Travelwise p. 246). *theplazany .com* ✉ 768 Fifth Ave. at Central Park South 🚇 Subway: N, R to 5th Ave./59th St.; F to 57th St.; 4, 5, 6 to 57th St.

Turtle Bay Historic District

This delightful enclave of brownstones near the UN (see p. 111) has been home to literati and luminaries, from Max Perkins and E. B. White to Katharine Hepburn and Stephen Sondheim. White's *The Second Tree from the Corner* immortalizes a tree in Turtle Bay Gardens, a large communal garden in the Italianate style, built in the 1920s. *turtlebay-nyc. org* ✉ 224 E. 47th St., bet. 2nd & 3rd Aves. ☎ Turtle Bay Association: 212/751–5465

Elegant avenues and tranquil side streets where great fortunes, great architecture, and great art find one another

UPPER EAST SIDE

■ The spiderweb-like interior dome of the Guggenheim Museum

UPPER EAST SIDE

The Financial District may be the place money is made in New York, but the Upper East Side is where it lives. From 59th Street north to 96th, Park Avenue and Fifth Avenue bracket a district of high-rise apartment houses and low-rise side-street brownstones that exist in a totally different reality from the rest of America, a reality not only of general wealth and privilege but of old-monied New York society.

Once there, you can savor life as the upper crust lives it. A visit to the Metropolitan Museum of Art can be enhanced by taking tea at the classic Carlyle Hotel on Madison Avenue. Many of Fifth Avenue's museums are in what were once millionaires' mansions. Or go to the galleries, where the rich indulge their mostly conservative tastes. One of the most prestigious, the Hirschl & Adler Galleries (*730 5th Ave, tel 212/535–8810, hirschlandadler.com*) is housed in a landmark residence.

But the Upper East Side is not all upper-class extravagance and ostentation. The avenues farther east—Lexington, Third, Second, and beyond—are today home to the middle class as well as the rich and the upwardly mobile. Here the restaurants and bars tend toward the young and hip, though literati hangouts like The Writing Room (formerly Elaine's restaurant; *1703 2nd Ave., bet. 88th & 89th Sts., tel 212/335–0075, thewritingroomnyc.com*) still thrive here too.

In 2017, work was completed on the first phase of the Second Avenue Subway project, which, for the moment, has extended the Q line north along Second Avenue from the Lexington Avenue/63rd Street station. Three new stations have been built as far as 96th Street. The goal of the project is to connect the entire section from East Harlem (*125th St.*) to Lower Manhattan (*Hanover Square*).

Spanish Harlem

North of 96th Street, the Upper East Side turns into Spanish Harlem. These lively, overcrowded, and often impoverished streets have very little in common with the elegant avenues and side streets farther south. The neighborhood was largely Italian until Puerto Ricans and other Latin Americans began settling there after World War II. Museum Row's northernmost museum, El Museo del Barrio, embodies the culture of the district and connects it to the wider currents of Latino communities throughout the United States.

Historic Districts

The historic buildings of the Upper East Side are preserved in several districts. Among the hundreds of important buildings are early apartment houses, such as 998 Fifth Avenue, a massive Italian Renaissance-style palazzo. Designed by McKim, Mead & White in 1912, it became, in form and function, the ideal to which other apartment houses aspired. ∎

NOT TO BE MISSED:

EAST DRIVE

5th Avenue

GRAND ARMY PLAZA

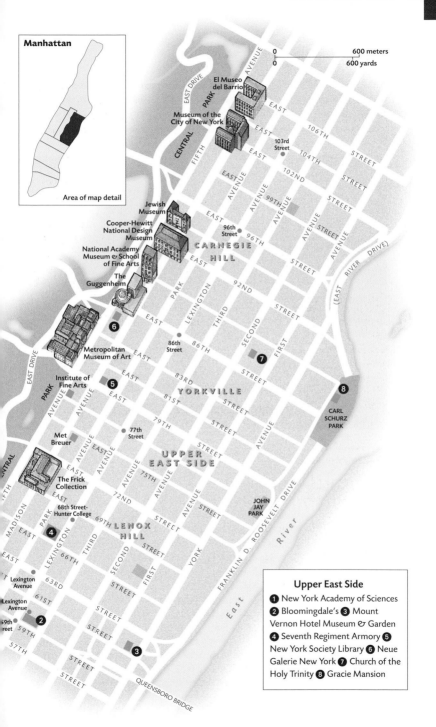

Manhattan

Area of map detail

EL Museo del Barrio

Museum of the City of New York

Jewish Museum

Cooper-Hewitt National Design Museum

National Academy Museum & School of Fine Arts

The Guggenheim

CARNEGIE HILL

Metropolitan Museum of Art

Institute of Fine Arts

YORKVILLE

Met Breuer

UPPER EAST SIDE

The Frick Collection

68th Street-Hunter College

LENOX HILL

JOHN JAY PARK

CARL SCHURZ PARK

CENTRAL PARK

EAST RIVER DRIVE

(EAST RIVER DRIVE)

FRANKLIN D. ROOSEVELT DRIVE

East River

QUEENSBORO BRIDGE

0 — 600 meters
0 — 600 yards

Upper East Side
❶ New York Academy of Sciences
❷ Bloomingdale's ❸ Mount Vernon Hotel Museum & Garden
❹ Seventh Regiment Armory ❺ New York Society Library ❻ Neue Galerie New York ❼ Church of the Holy Trinity ❽ Gracie Mansion

FRICK COLLECTION

A visit to the Frick Collection is a trip back to the Gilded Age, when millionaires competed to build mansions along elegant Fifth Avenue and fill them with art treasures. Housed in the former residence of industrialist Henry Clay Frick (1849–1919), the collection has welcomed visitors from around the world since its celebrated opening as a museum and library in 1935.

■ The Frick's largest room, the skylit West Gallery, combines old masters and the ambience of a classic New York mansion.

Frick Collection

- ⓜ Map p. 135
- ✉ 1 E. 70th St.
- ☎ 212/288-0700
- ⌚ Closed Mon.
- 💲 $$$$
- 🚇 Subway: 6 to 68th St.–Hunter College

frick.org

NOTE: Children under ten are not admitted, and those under 16 must be accompanied by an adult.

In contrast to the monumental character of some of the city's museums, the Frick is just the right size for a serene immersion in the arts in a refined setting. A free acoustical guide (in six languages) and a brochure with a floor plan guide you through the collection's 19 rooms. A small shop is outside the Reception Hall, and across from it is the entrance to a downstairs gallery for changing exhibits.

The main collection is on the first floor. The **Boucher Room** just off the East Vestibule is unforgettable, adorned with a series of decorative panels entitled "The Arts and Sciences," depicting cherublike children engaged in various adult activities. Created by François Boucher (1750–1752), the artworks once graced **Mrs. Frick's sitting room** upstairs. Portraiture by William Hogarth and Sir Joshua Reynolds and others lines the walls of the **Dining Room,** which also holds the fine "Mall in St. James Park" (1783) social landscape by Thomas Gainsborough.

The highlight of the **Fragonard Room** is the lighthearted 18th-century series of paintings, "The Progress of Love," by Jean-Honoré Fragonard. The austere **Living Hall** is dominated by "Portrait of a Man in a Red Cap" by Titian (ca 1465–1470), "St. Jerome" by El Greco (1590–1600), and "St. Francis in the Desert" by Giovanni Bellini (1480). Beyond is the wood-paneled **Library,** filled with works by British artists, including Gainsborough, John Constable, and Joseph Mallord William Turner.

A portrait by Jean-Auguste-Dominique Ingres, "Comtesse d'Haussonville" (1845) in the **North Hall** is among the most popular. Dutch artist Johannes Vermeer's "Officer and Laughing Girl" (ca 1655–1660) and "Girl Interrupted at Her Music" (1658–1659) hang in the **South Hall.** Adjacent to the halls is the Garden Court; save this for last.

Visitors take a breath as they enter the **West Gallery;** it is long, high, and skylit, very unlike what has preceded. A gallery of this sort characterized 19th-century upper-class homes. Here is a formidable grouping not to be missed: Rembrandt's portrait of himself as an older gentleman (1658) plus important works by Paolo Veronese, Sir Anthony Van Dyck, Jean-Baptiste-Camille Corot, Diego Velázquez, and more.

The **Enamel Room** at one end is intimate, replete with French Limoges enamels, including the exquisite "Seven Sorrows of the Virgin" (1500–1550). The **Oval Room,** formerly Frick's office, has large portraits by Van Dyck

and Gainsborough and a life-size Jean-Antoine Houdon sculpture of "Diana the Huntress." The **East Gallery** contains a pair of James McNeill Whistlers and works by Edouard Manet and Francisco Goya.

Proceed to the enclosed **Garden Court,** with a pool, greenery, benches, portrait busts, and a charming bronze angel by Jean Barbet, with the year 1475 engraved on its left wing. In this soothing place you may reflect upon all you have seen.

Frick Family Legacy

Frick, a self-made man, was criticized at an early age as being "a little too enthusiastic about pictures." Starting in coal mines, he was a millionaire by age 30. He moved to New York in 1900. Philanthropically inclined, he built his mansion with the idea of eventually turning it into a museum open to the public. In 1920, Frick's daughter opened the **Frick Art Reference Library,** with 750,000 photographs and 174,000 books and catalogs. ∎

Frick Art Reference Library

✉ 10 E. 71st St.
☎ 212/547-0641
🕐 Closed Sun. year-round; Sat. Jun.–Jul; Mon., Fri., & Sat. in Aug.
🚇 Subway: 6 to 68th St.–Hunter College

frick.org/visit/library

METROPOLITAN MUSEUM OF ART

New York's Metropolitan Museum of Art is the largest museum in the Western Hemisphere. Its collection, more than two million items, is not only broad but deep, with holdings so large that some collections might be considered museums unto themselves. The best way to approach it is to understand the museum's arrangement and select a limited number of areas to see during your visit. Those who do not usually come away feeling overwhelmed.

■ The Great Hall of the Met, where visitors can orient themselves before plunging into the seemingly endless collections

The museum itself is a very large structure. Study it from the Fifth Avenue side before you go in. Large hanging banners announce important temporary exhibits. You might decide to see just one of these, but if you want to explore the collection in more detail, it helps to have a general idea of how the building is laid out.

Think of the museum as a rectangle with a stairway in the middle that divides right and left. Then divide each side into front and back. Look at the twin columns flanking the entrance. On the front right side of those columns is the Egyptian Collection (and the Temple of Dendur), and on the back side, the American Wing (which continues in the same position onto the second floor). To the front left side of the columns you will find Greek and Roman art. On the back left side is the Lila Acheson Wallace Wing with 20th- and 21st-century art. In between are the arts of Africa, Oceania, and the Americas.

Once you enter and pay your admission, if you walk up the grand staircase immediately in front of you, you will be on the second floor in what many consider to be the heart of this museum, its superior collection

More Reasons to Visit the Met

In addition to lectures, concerts, and films, the Met holds a reference facility and print study rooms. The **Uris Center** on the ground floor has its own library and classrooms and publishes educational books and films. The museum also offers an array of shopping options. **The Met Store** (*tel 800/468-7386, store.met museum.org*) on the first floor has separate boutique shops and features not just books and reproductions covering the history of world art, but also fine jewelry, clothing, children's toys and games, recordings, three-dimensional reproductions, and more. It is a unique source of gifts for all occasions, with a mail-order catalog as well, plus ancillary city shops, including one at Rockefeller Center (*15 W. 49th St.*). Food options include the **Cantor Rooftop Garden Bar** (*open Apr.–Oct.*) and the ground-floor cafeteria. But there is no truer New York pastime than buying food from a vendor outside the Met and sitting on the steps overlooking Fifth Avenue.

of European painting, sculpture, and decorative arts. There you will find masterpieces by Botticelli, Brueghel, Rembrandt, Vermeer, Degas, and Rodin, plus the Petrie Sculpture Court, a delightful and contemplative place to relax Although things will feel more complicated once you enter the museum, if you can keep in mind the rough locations of these five areas (Egyptian; American; Greek and Roman; Africa, Oceania, and the Americas; and modern art) on the first floor, and, at the top of the stairs on the second floor, European paintings, you can be assured of finding your bearings, and once you are in each area, finding your way back out.

Planning What to See

When you enter, pick up a floor plan (see p. 140). If you do not want to go on your own, there are guides and recorded tours to take you through almost every part of the museum. A relaxing way to enjoy the ambience, architecture, and sheer beauty of the interior is to visit after 5

p.m. on Friday or Saturday. Then you can have drinks at the Balcony Bar while in the Great Hall a string quartet performs classical music. Many people are drawn by masterpieces in the permanent exhibition. However, the temporary exhibits are just as important. *Armenia!*, for example, from 2018–2019, highlighted the artistic and cultural achievements of the Armenian population over a period of fourteen centuries.

History

In 1866 John Jay, a diplomat, lawyer, and grandson of America's first chief justice, told a group of American businessmen visiting Paris that the time had come "for the American people to lay the foundation for a national institution and gallery of art." His words so stirred them that, on their return, they put poet and newspaper editor William Cullen Bryant at the head of a committee charged with founding the Metropolitan Museum of Art.

Metropolitan Museum of Art

- Map p. 135
- 1000 5th Ave. at E. 82nd St.
- 212/535-7710
- $$ ticket includes admission to the Cloisters (see pp. 195–197) and Met Breuer (see p. 149).
- Subway: 4, 5, 6 to 86th St.

metmuseum.org

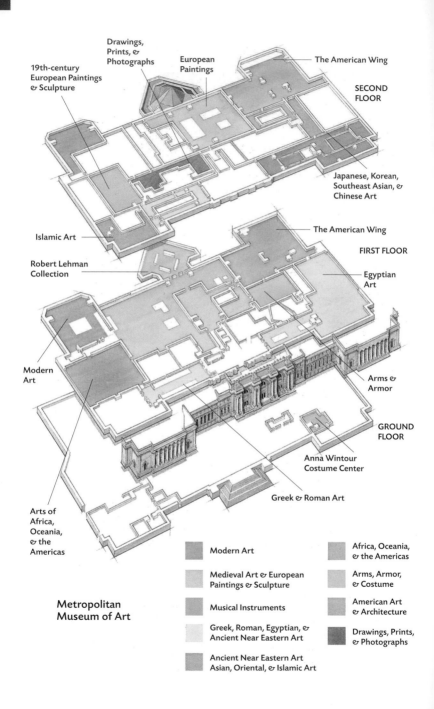

Drawings,
Prints, &
Photographs

European
Paintings

The American Wing

SECOND
FLOOR

19th-century
European Paintings
& Sculpture

Japanese, Korean,
Southeast Asian, &
Chinese Art

Islamic Art

The American Wing

FIRST FLOOR

Robert Lehman
Collection

Egyptian
Art

Modern
Art

Arms &
Armor

GROUND
FLOOR

Anna Wintour
Costume Center

Greek & Roman Art

Arts of
Africa,
Oceania,
& the
Americas

Modern Art

Medieval Art & European
Paintings & Sculpture

Musical Instruments

Greek, Roman, Egyptian, &
Ancient Near Eastern Art

Ancient Near Eastern Art
Asian, Oriental, & Islamic Art

Africa, Oceania,
& the Americas

Arms, Armor,
& Costume

American Art
& Architecture

Drawings, Prints,
& Photographs

Metropolitan
Museum of Art

In 1870 the museum opened in temporary quarters. The next year it acquired a collection of 174 European paintings and hired Calvert Vaux and Jacob Wrey Mould to design its first building. This small, redbrick high Gothic building had a steel-and-glass roof and was situated at the edge of Central Park at 82nd Street and Fifth Avenue, the very spot that Vaux and his partner Frederick Law Olmsted, in their "Greensward plan" for Central Park (see pp. 168–169), had set aside for a museum. The front entrance of the museum originally faced Central Park.

As the Metropolitan grew, the Vaux-Mould building was literally swallowed up by new wings and additions. The signature Fifth Avenue facade, with its neoclassical features, and Great Hall, was designed by Richard Morris Hunt and executed by his son between 1902 and 1926. McKim, Mead & White added the north and

■ Portrait of George Washington by Gilbert Stuart (1755–1828)

south wings in 1911 and 1913. A comprehensive architectural plan for the museum was executed between 1971 and 1991 by the firm Kevin Roche John Dinkeloo & Associates, who designed the ground floor's Lehman Pavilion, the Sackler Wing for the Temple of Dendur, and the Michael C. Rockefeller Wing to house the arts of Africa, Oceania, and the Americas. The museum's new American Wing (1980) was built around the

EXPERIENCE: The Little Apple–New York for Kids

The **Met** has a special page on its website devoted to its many children's and family exhibits and workshops (*metmuseum.org/learn/kids-and-families*). In addition to the city's museums and shows, Central Park (see pp. 167–172) offers great entertainment for children: the **Carousel** and **Central Park Zoo** (*near 64th St.*) are open year-round; puppeteers bring magic tales to life at the **Swedish Cottage Marionette Theater** (*79th St. & West Dr., cityparksfoundation.org*); while **Trump Rink** (*63rd St., wollmanskating rink.com*) is an ice-skating venue in winter and a mini-amusement park in summer. The 7.8-foot-tall (2.4 m) Statue of Liberty built

from Legos, in front of the **Lego Store** (*200 5th Ave., tel. 212/255–3217, stores.lego.com*), will inspire young builders, while doll lovers will enjoy a visit to **American Girl Place** (*609 5th Ave., tel. 212/371–2220, americangirl. com*). Visit **Books of Wonder** (*18 W. 18th St., booksof wonder.com*), the city's oldest, largest independent children's bookstore, or **Dinosaur Hill** (*306 E. 9th St., tel 212/473–5850, dino saurhill.com*) for handmade toys. Gamers head to the **Compleat Strategist** (*11 E. 33rd St., tel 212/685–3880, thecompleatstrat egist.com*). And comics lovers should go to, where else, **Forbidden Planet** (*832 Broadway, tel 212/473–1576, fpnyc.com*).

■ The Temple of Dendur, a gift from Egypt to the U.S., stands alone as it once did on the Nile.

old and provides generous new space for the Americana collection, by then the largest in the country. The Lila Acheson Wallace Wing housing modern art was added in 1987. Renovations are constantly under way. In 2009, the museum was in the midst of modernizing the Islamic Galleries and American Wing, and the Costume Institute was renamed the Anna Wintour Costume Center after a 2014 renovation.

Building the Collection

In 1883 the museum purchased a large collection of architectural casts. At the time, the museum assumed, wrongly, that important European masterpieces would never become available for purchase, so "casts and reproductions" were considered

important parts of the collection. For years, according to a 1917 guide, "models, on a scale of one-twentieth of the original, of the Parthenon, the Pantheon, Notre-Dame, and the Hypostyle Hall of Karnac" greeted visitors in the Great Hall.

In 1887 an extraordinary loan of 37 European paintings from railroad financier Henry Gurdon Marquand instantly gave the museum national status. New works included Vermeer's "Young Woman With a Water Jug," still a treasure of the collection, as well as paintings by Van Dyck, Rembrandt, Franz Hals, Petrus Christus, Turner, and Gainsborough. In 1913 a bequest from Benjamin Altman, the department store owner, which included almost 500 Chinese porcelains and several

Rembrandts, came with several strings attached, one being that the paintings hang "in a single line, not one above the other," as was then the custom in museums.

After financier J. P. Morgan died in 1913, his son gave 40 percent of his huge collection to the Met. Other important acquisitions included, in 1929, the collection of French Impressionists assembled by Louisine Havemeyer. It took the museum decades to develop an interest in American art. In 1930 it rejected Gertrude Vanderbilt Whitney's offer of 500 modern American paintings so quickly that her agent did not have time to add that the offer included a new wing to house them.

Overview: Ground Floor

Many visitors might overlook the **Anna Wintour Costume Center** because of its location, but if your interest is fashion, this is a must-see. Noted for its imaginative exhibits, the institute began independently in 1937 as the Museum of Costume Art and became part of the Met in 1946. In 2009, a new partnership with the Brooklyn Museum transferred that institution's renowned costume collection—possibly the world's foremost holdings of American fashion from the late 19th to mid-20th centuries—to the Met, bringing its total holdings to about 100,000, dating from the 15th century to the present and representing both traditional garb and high fashion from every corner of the world.

Overview: First Floor

The founders of the Metropolitan believed that American painting, decorative arts, and furniture had no place in a serious museum. That attitude began to change after the museum's first exhibit of American furniture and silver in 1909 proved immensely popular. American arts and crafts became a separate department in 1922, and the **American Wing** opened in 1924. In 1980, it was renovated and expanded: It now occupies galleries on two floors and is a world unto itself

---

INSIDER TIP:

With natural light flooding in from floor- to-ceiling windows, and the majesty of the glowing sandstone, the Temple of Dendur is a great place to take a breather from the density of New York.

–JENNIFER EMMETT
National Geographic editor

---

where one can easily spend an entire day. The collection here is indeed varied, with everything from an unsurpassed assemblage of American paintings to a rare Honus Wagner baseball card to a room from the Frank Lloyd Wright Prairie House in Minnesota. Period rooms are organized chronologically, beginning with the earliest colonial ones on the third floor. A major reconstruction of the wing took place in 2009–2010.

Highlights include the wing's focal point, the glass-covered **Charles Engelhard Court** on the first floor, which features fountains, Central Park views, an 1824 bank facade from Wall Street, and stained glass by Louis Comfort Tiffany. In the courtyard, flooded with natural light, the work of well-known sculptors, including Gutzon

■ **The Arms and Armor Collection has long been a favorite.**

Borglum (of Mount Rushmore fame), is displayed on a rotating basis. There are many significant American paintings, including those of the Hudson River school, Winslow Homer, Childe Hassam, and Mary Cassatt. Try to see the largest painting in the Metropolitan, John Vanderlyn's "Panorama of the Palace and Gardens of Versailles" (1818–1819). On the second floor in the new wing there are portraits of George

Washington by Charles Willson Peale and Gilbert Stuart. Emanuel Leutze's popular "Washington Crossing the Delaware" (1851) is also here.

Located in a first-floor wing donated by Nelson Rockefeller, in memory of his son, Michael, who died on an expedition in New Guinea, is the **Arts of Africa, Oceania, and the Americas.** It incorporates some 3,300 works from Rockefeller's Museum of Primitive Art, located in Midtown Manhattan from 1957 to 1975. Don't miss the sculptures of the Buli Master, one of the first African artists of international renown.

The Egyptian Collection: Any tour of the museum would devote considerable attention to the extensive Egyptian Collection, even if it did not have its counterpart next door: the exquisite three-room **Temple of Dendur** (ca 23–10 B.C.). Since 1978, the temple has rested in isolated splendor in its own hangar-size gallery in the **Sackler Wing.** The temple was originally commissioned by the Roman emperor Augustus as a tribute to the Nile god, Osiris. The gateway leading to the temple is adorned with reliefs showing Augustus honoring local gods. What is most fascinating is how the temple came to rest in New York City. When it was threatened due to construction of the Aswan High Dam, it was given to the United States, transported block by block, and then reassembled.

The Egyptian Collection, located in adjacent galleries, features objects and artifacts spanning more than three and a half millennia, from ca 3000 B.C. to A.D. 641. The collection is organized chronologically. The tomb of Perneb (ca 2440 B.C.), a reconstruction of the mastaba, or tomb, in which an official of the Old Kingdom was buried, is very impressive, with vivid reliefs of servants preparing food. Also of note are the statues from the funerary temple of Queen Hatshepsut (ca 1473–1458 B.C.), including one in which she wears masculine garb. Finally, see the remarkably detailed models of daily life in the 11th Dynasty (ca 2046–1995 B.C.).

The European Collections:

Near the stairs you will find the department of **European Sculpture and Decorative Arts,** which surrounds the department of medieval art. Its galleries include works from the Renaissance to the early 20th century. Be sure to visit the **European Sculpture Court.** Noteworthy is Auguste Rodin's "The Burghers of Calais" (1885–1895), depicting citizens who saved Calais from English reprisals. The **Jack and Belle Linsky Galleries,** a collection of furniture, bronzes, exquisitely detailed objects, and paintings includes Fra Bartolomeo's "Portrait of a Man" (after 1497).

This department also encompasses the **Robert Lehman Collection,** which came to the museum with the stipulation that the art be displayed in rooms re-created from the donor's home. Thus it is that one of the country's most outstanding private art collections came to reside in a

modern glass pyramid-shaped pavilion, the **Robert Lehman Wing,** at the center of the museum's western facade. Among the seven re-created rooms, the **Grand Gallery** includes works by Corot, Monet, and van Gogh, but the collection covers works by old masters to 20th century art. Among the highlights are Gauguin's "Tahitian Woman Bath-

Arms & Armor

Located on the first floor to the right of the staircase and past European and Decorative Arts, the Arms and Armor Collection has, for decades, been one of the first sought out by young boys. Especially popular here is the Equestrian Court, whose armored knights on horseback evoke the world of King Arthur and the Knights of the Round Table. The Japanese armor is highlighted by fierce face masks worn in battle. American arms include a Kentucky rifle and a Colt revolver.

ing" (1891) and El Greco's "St. Jerome as a Cardinal" (ca 1600–1610). The 15th-century Italian masterpieces in the exquisite Red Velvet Room include Giovanni de Paolo's "Expulsion from Paradise" (ca 1445) and Botticelli's "Annunciation" (ca 1490).

By the turn of the 19th century, the Metropolitan had acquired considerable **Greek and Roman Art,** including Cypriot statues

The Magic of the Met's Musical Instruments

Musicians and music lovers should turn right at the top of the stairs on the second floor, to the collection of rare and fascinating musical instruments. Dating from prehistory to the present, the instruments are from Europe, the Americas, Asia, and Africa. Among the distinguished objects here is the oldest surviving piano (1720) by Bartolomeo Cristofori, inventor of the instrument; Andres Segovia's guitars; and Native American pipes. Visitors can hear the sounds of instruments on audio guide. Mrs. Mary Crosby Brown's donation, in 1889, of 270 instruments is at the heart of the collection. Like other donors, she continued to collect and donate to the museum; by 1906 there were 3,500 instruments; today there are more than 5,000.

and artifacts donated by Louis Palma di Cesnola, director of the museum from 1879 to 1904, and the Roman and Etruscan glass from Henry Gurdon Marquand. Don't miss the Boscoreale frescoes, from a villa buried under volcanic ash by the eruption of Vesuvius in 79 A.D.; the Kouros (700 B.C.), the earliest Greek marble statue in the museum; and the Euphronios vase (ca 515 B.C.), depicting detailed scenes from the Trojan War.

Originally based on the collection made by J. P. Morgan, the **Medieval Art** galleries, on the first floor behind the staircase, span 12 centuries, from 300 to 1500. Included are early Christian art, the Romanesque Chapel, medieval tapestries, paintings, and sculpture, plus the **Medieval Treasury,** containing items of gold and other precious metals. Of particular importance are the Antioch Chalice, a sixth-century liturgical cup; the 15th-century "Annunciation" tapestry from Arras, France; and the glazed terracotta altarpiece by Andrea Della Robbia depicting the Assumption. Those interested in this period will also want to visit the Metropolitan's museum devoted to

medieval art in a medieval setting, the Cloisters (see pp. 195–197).

Housed in the first-floor **Lila Acheson Wallace Wing** (1987), named for a founder of *Reader's Digest,* the **Modern Art** department is strong in an area the museum once spurned—modern American paintings. The wing housing it is worth a visit for its own sake, for its glass curtain walls and roof garden. This department began with Alfred Stieglitz's collection of modern painting, sculpture, and drawings that his widow, Georgia O'Keeffe, gave to the museum in 1949. Highlights include Jackson Pollock's "Autumn Rhythm (Number 30)" (1950); Mark Rothko's "No. 13 (White, Red on Yellow)" (1958); and Jasper Johns's "White Flag" (1955). Henri Matisse's "Nasturtiums with the Painting 'Dance'" (1912) was one of the first works shown by the artist in the U.S. as part of the 1913 Armory Show.

Overview: Second Floor

In addition to the collections below, this floor also includes the remaining exhibits of the **American Wing.**

Spanning 6000 B.C. to the seventh century A.D., the **Ancient**

Near Eastern Art galleries include Assyrian art, Mesopotamian art, pre-Islamic antiquities from Iran, and Achaemenid, Parthian, and Sasanian art. Be sure to see the gypsum statue of a bearded Sumerian worshipper (ca 2750–2600 B.C.) and the small, headless "Seated Female" sculpture, the oldest of the collection's notable pieces, dating to sixth- or seventh-millennium B.C. Mesopotamia or Syria.

A highlight of the **Chinese Art** galleries is Dong Yuan's "The Riverbank," a monumental tenth-century hanging scroll landscape. Also, visit the **Astor Court Garden,** a 16th-century-style garden for meditation. It was constructed for the museum in 1979 by Chinese craftspeople using ancient techniques and tools.

The **Drawings, Prints, & Photographs** collection holds some extraordinary works, including drawings by Michelangelo and

Matisse, prints by Rembrandt, and photographs collected by Alfred Stieglitz. Visit the **Howard Gilman Gallery,** inaugurated in 1997. Three changing exhibits yearly include photographs from the private 5,000-piece collection of the late Howard Gilman.

The 30 galleries devoted to **European Paintings** form an especially rich part of the museum, spanning five centuries. Two of the galleries are devoted to Italian Renaissance painting (Mantegna, Botticelli, Della Robbia) and Dutch painting (Rembrandt, Hals, Vermeer, Ruisdael). These works came from the Benjamin Altman Collection, bequeathed to the museum in 1913 by the department store millionaire. The masterpieces in this gift made the Metropolitan one of the world's leading museums. The galleries are arranged by school: 18th-century Venetian painting (Tiepolo); 15th-century Italian

"The Harvesters" (1565) by Pieter Brueghel the Elder is one of a series representing the seasons.

painting (Filippo Lippi, Ghirlandaio, Signorelli, Perugino); 17th-century Dutch portraits (Rembrandt, Hals); English portraits (Reynolds, Gainsborough, Lawrence); and so forth. A highlight here is Rembrandt's "Aristotle With a Bust of Homer" (1653), purchased by the museum in 1961 for a record sum at the time of $2.3 million.

Extensive **Far Eastern Art** galleries wind through the second floor and encompass some 60,000 objects from the second millennium B.C. to the 20th century, including paintings, prints, calligraphy, sculptures, lacquers, textiles, metalwork, and ceramics from Japan, China, South Asia, the Himalayan kingdoms (Nepal, Tibet), and Southeast Asia (Thailand, Indonesia, Cambodia, Myanmar, and Vietnam). Well worth seeing are the collection of Chinese ceramics, which dates back to China's historical beginnings, the Shang dynasty (17th–11th centuries B.C.); the collection of large Chinese Buddhist sculptures; a 5th-century Standing Buddha from northern India; and the **Khmer Courtyard,** featuring the Angkor period (9th–13th centuries).

The **Greek and Roman Art** galleries continue onto the second floor. They include a fine collection of Greek vases.

One of the jewels of the Metropolitan is the **Islamic Art** collection. This starts with works from the reign of the four caliphs in A.D. 632, extends into the 19th century, and stretches geographically from Spain east to Southeast Asia. Highlights include a re-created early 18th-century Ottoman

reception room from Damascus, Safavid-period rugs from Iran, and Mughal-period miniature paintings form India. After extensive renovation and enlargement, the New Galleries for the Art of the Arab Lands, Turkey, Iran, Central Asia, and Later South Asia reopened in 2011, to much popular acclaim.

The sweeping display of **Japanese Art** in familiar settings is spread out over ten galleries. Chronological and thematic displays include some exquisitely detailed tapestries and ceremonial costumes and a re-creation of a *shoin,* or study.

The **19th-century European Painting and Sculpture** collection is one of the greatest of its kind in the world. The collection is displayed in galleries that reflect the spirit of the period. Two galleries are named for the collection's great benefactors, Louisine and H. O. Havemeyer. Mrs. Havemayer's interest in European Impressionist and Post-Impressionist paintings began with her friendship with the American painter Mary Cassatt. The museum's holdings include many works by such well-known artists as Courbet, Corot, Degas, Manet, Monet, Cézanne, Seurat, van Gogh, and Rodin. There are also areas devoted to neoclassicism, Romanticism, the Barbizon school, French still lifes, pastels, and salon painting. The paintings are displayed in a loose chronological order, starting with neoclassicists David and Ingres and ending with such late 19th and early 20th-century work as Pissarro's "Garden of the Tuileries" (1899) and Henri Rousseau's "The Repast of the Lion" (1907). ■

MET BREUER

The modernist building, constructed in 1966 by the Hungarian architect, Marcel Breuer was the home of the Whitney Museum of American Art for decades, before the museum moved to the Meatpacking District. Since 2016, it has been home to the separate branch of the Metropolitan Museum, which presents temporary exhibits of modern and contemporary art as well as works from the museum's permanent collection.

The museum, located at the intersection of Madison Avenue and 75th Street, looks like an immense, upside-down ziggurat, a monolith of granite, cement, and glass.

For fifty years, it was the home of the Whitney Museum of American Art, which has moved to the Meatpacking District, near High Line Park, to a new building designed by Renzo Piano. When the Breuer Building became a separate branch of the Metropolitan Museum of Art (The Met) in 2016, its interior was renovated by Beyer Blinder Belle Architects & Planners, who maintained many of its original features including cement walls, stone floors, and bronze fixtures. Guests are greeted by a modern LED-light illumination system in the lobby, an update of the famous round lights, designed by Breuer himself. The five floors of the museum offer a rich program of cultural events and artistic performances as well as displaying the Met's 20th- and 21st-century collections.

The pride and joy of the collection are the masterpieces of early American modernism and abstract expressionism.

Works on display in the museum include those of Alfred Stieglitz, Arthur Dove, Marsden

■ The outside of the Metropolitan Museum of Modern Art, the Met Breuer, on the Upper East Side

Hartley, Georgia O'Keeffe, and John Marin.

One of the most important recent exhibits displayed the works of Klimt, Schiele, and Picasso belonging to the Scofield Thayer collection.

By the end of 2020, the Met intends to vacate the Breuer Building, giving the Frick Collection a home during its overhaul, and revive its plans for David Chipperfield's extension to its Fifth Avenue location. ■

Met Breuer
- ⓜ Map p. 135
- ✉ 945 Madison Ave.
- ☎ 212/731–1675
- 🕐 Closed Mon.
- 💲 $$
- 🚇 Subway: 6 to 77th St.

metmuseum.org/ breuer

THE GUGGENHEIM

The Solomon R. Guggenheim Museum is the only building in New York by Frank Lloyd Wright, possibly America's greatest architect ever. Today, half a century after Wright's concrete spiral opened on Fifth Avenue, it remains the very symbol of modernism, its profile inseparable from the Guggenheim name. In 2008, the museum completed a major three-year restoration and features a light projection, created by artist Jenny Holzer, displayed on the building's facade.

■ The Guggenheim's spiral ramp offers easy access to the collection. The snail, the concrete tornado, and the inverted cupcake are just three of the nicknames the building has acquired.

Solomon R. Guggenheim Museum

🅰 Map p. 135
✉ 1071 5th Ave. at E. 89th St.
☎ 212/423–3500
🕐 Closed Thurs.
💲 $$
🚇 Subway: 4, 5, 6 to 86th St.

guggenheim.org

NOTE: Admittance is "pay what you wish" on Saturdays from 5 p.m. to 7.45 p.m.

The Guggenheim, as it is called, grew out of the private collection of millionaire Solomon R. Guggenheim. He began collecting old masters but expanded into modern art under the influence of Hilla Rebay von Ehrenwiesen, a European artist and baroness, opening the Museum of Non-Objective Painting in 1939. In 1943 it was Rebay who selected and hired Wright as the architect for a new museum. In a letter that must have appealed to his considerable ego, she wrote: "I need a fighter, a lover of space, an originator, a tester

and a wise man ... I want a temple of spirit, a monument!" Non-objective painting, as Rebay defined it, "represents no object or subject known to us on earth. It is simply a beautiful organization arranged in rhythmic order of colors and forms to be enjoyed for beauty's sake."

Wright responded that he was "eager to build to objectify the non-objective point of view." That was 1943. Over the next 16 years Wright submitted six sets of plans and 749 drawings. Wright informed his clients that he was striving for "one extended expansive well-proportioned floor space from bottom to top ... gloriously lit from above." Guggenheim died in 1949 but left two million dollars to build the museum. In 1956 construction began. The museum opened to the public in October 1959. Wright had died six months before, on April 9.

Today's Collection & Temporary Exhibits

The present collection covers the history of modern art, including European art of the first half of the 20th century as well as late 19th-century and postwar European and American art. Acquisitions in film, photography, multimedia, and high-technology art keep the collection up to date. Over the past two and a half decades, the museum has produced more than 300 special temporary exhibitions, ranging from retrospectives of American and international artists (including Louise Bourgeois, Richard Prince, and Robert Rauschenberg); historical surveys focused on 20th-century art; exhibitions focused on different countries' or regions' artistic heritage (such as 1996's "Africa: The Art of a Continent" and 2006's "Spanish Painting from El Greco to Picasso"); and exhibitions devoted to design and architecture, including a retrospective of designs by Frank Gehry (the architect responsible for the Guggenheim's remarkable museum building in Bilbao, Spain) and another detailing "The Art of the Motorcycle," for which the Rotunda and galleries displayed 80 great motorcycle designs, stretching back to 1884. Among

the most recent exhibits are "One Hand Clapping," oils on canvas and virtual reality simulators that narrate the effects of globalism on our understanding of the future.

The Rotunda & the Ramp

Immediately upon entering from Fifth Avenue you confront the daring design. To the left is the museum store, but ahead is the Great Rotunda, spiraling upward 92 feet (28 m) to the domed skylight. A grand ramp circles the Rotunda all the way up, providing the bulk of the museum's exhibition space.

INSIDER TIP:

An architectural gem, the Guggenheim and its spiraling galleries are a compelling way to view art. Look also into the educational programs that accompany the cutting-edge exhibits.

–CORNELIA SECKEL
Publisher, **ART TIMES**
Literary Journal

Walk all the way to the top (the cantilevered ramp that circles the interior through five levels is a quarter of a mile/0.4 km long), or use the elevators. Wright expected visitors to start at the top and work their way down. You don't have to, though: An elevator allows access to each level of the gradually pitched ramp, letting off on a mercifully non-sloping gallery.

Exploring the Collection

Exhibits frequently change, and not all of the permanent collection is on display at any given time. You can navigate the sites of all the temporary and permanent exhibits online (*guggenheim.org/new-york/visit/plan-your-visit/map*). You can also always locate some examples of works by key

Guggenheims Across the World

The Guggenheim's mission of bringing modern art to the world doesn't end on Fifth Avenue. Four adjunct museums, with feature exhibitions as well as permanent collections, are located in Venice, Italy; Berlin, Germany; Bilbao, Spain; and Abu Dhabi, U.A.E. In addition, several new spaces are currently being planned around the world, and the museum regularly lends artwork to tour other museums.

artists. The museum's collection includes more than 200 works by Wassily Kandinsky, some of which are always on display (on a rotating basis) at the museum's dedicated **Kandinsky Gallery.** It also has works by Brancusi, Calder, Delaunay, Klee, Miró, Nevelson, and Mondrian, to name but a few. Favorites include Chagall's "Paris Through the Window" (1913), Léger's "Great Parade" (1954), Modigliani's "Nude"

(1917), and Picasso's "Woman Ironing" (1904).

The **Thannhauser tower galleries** (named for Justin K. Thannhauser, a dealer and collector who donated 75 Impressionist and Post-Impressionist works) display both the permanent collection and contemporary changing exhibits. Levels 2, 5, and 7 contain larger works, while level 4 is low-ceilinged and holds drawings and smaller paintings, plus the **Robert Mapplethorpe Gallery** for photography. There are also four video viewing rooms and a fifth-floor sculpture terrace.

On ramp 3 are the **Guggenheim Family Galleries.** In 1963, Solomon's niece, Peggy Guggenheim, a gallery owner, collector, and, briefly, wife of Max Ernst, gave the museum works representing surrealism, cubism, and abstract expressionism.

Many of the special exhibits draw large crowds and often forge new artistic or curatorial ground. In 2008, the exhibition "Imageless: The Scientific Study and Experimental Treatment of an Ad Reinhart Black Painting" took as its subject the art of conservation and forensics as they related to a single painting, Ad Reinhart's important but heavily damaged *Black Painting* (1960–1966), a monochromatic work of minimalism. Going back further, the reopening celebration after the museum's 1992 restoration included a building-wide installation by light artist Dan Flavin, centered on a 12-sided column of light that ascended from the base of the Rotunda to its similarly 12-sided skylight. ∎

EXPERIENCE: Indulge Yourself With Afternoon Tea

Whether a traditional high tea with scones, a casual American tea, or a Japanese-style tea is your cuppa of choice, you'll find a wide variety of tea venues in Manhattan. Say when ...

Treat yourself to a traditional high tea on the Upper East Side, at the **Carlyle's Tea Gallery** (35 E. 76th St., tel 212/744–1600), inspired by the sultan's dining room at the Topkapi Palace in Istanbul, or at the **Bosie Tea Parlor** (1293 10 Morton St., tel 212/352–9900), near Bleeker Street in Greenwich Village, where you can find a selection of 100 kinds of tea and an array of French pastries.

Other excellent alternatives include **Harney &**

English high tea, set with finger sandwiches, scones, and pastries

INSIDER TIP:

Take an afternoon stop at Tea and Sympathy [108 Greenwich Ave.] in Greenwich Village for a true taste of Britain—it's excellent for scones with clotted cream. The playful waitstaff is a hoot, too.

–GARRETT BROWN
National Geographic contributor

Sons (433 Broome St., tel 212/933–4853), tea producers since 1983, and Lady Mendl's Tea Salon, which serves an opulent tea at the Inn at Irving Place, in an elegant Victorian brownstone.

All three **Alice's Tea Cup**

locations (102 W. 73rd St., tel 212/799–3006, for all locations see alicesteacup. com) offer full tea service with generous scones daily in an Alice-in-Wonderland-themed atmosphere. Meanwhile, the **Palm Court** at the Plaza Hotel (tel 212/546–5300; see p. 132) serves English, French, and Russian tea daily in an extravagant palm tree setting.

You can recover your Zen Midtown at **Radiance**

Tea House & Books (158 W. 55th St., tel 212/217–0442), or head to the East Village to **Cha-An** (230 E. 9th St., tel 212/228–8030), another fine Japanese teahouse. If you want the real Japanese tea ceremony, try contacting **Globus Washitsu** (889 Broadway, bet. 19th & 20th Sts., nycwashitsu.com, e-mail: info@tea-whisk.com), a private tatami room near Union Square, which requires guests take an hour-long introductory class.

COOPER HEWITT SMITHSONIAN DESIGN MUSEUM

The museum's collection of some quarter of a million objects constitutes a history of design from the sixth century B.C. up to the present day. And a visit to its home, the former Andrew Carnegie mansion, provides a window into New York's Gilded Age. Built between 1899 and 1902, Carnegie chose the site—far north of where his peers were living at the time—for the space it allowed for an expansive garden and lawn, a Manhattan rarity then and now.

■ Extensive grounds surround the Carnegie mansion, now home to the Cooper-Hewitt.

Cooper Hewitt Smithsonian Design Museum

- 🅰 Map p. 135
- ✉ 2 E. 91st St.
- ☎ 212/849-2950
- 💲 $$
- 🚇 Subway: 4, 5, 6 to 86th or 96th St.

cooperhewitt.org

Founded in 1897 as the Cooper Union Museum for the Arts of Decoration, the Cooper-Hewitt has occupied its present quarters only since 1976. Though the museum was undertaken as a resource for decorators, architects, and other professionals, its appeal today is wide-ranging, and its eclectic collection remarkable. Thematic exhibits on urban architecture and graphic design change constantly, weaving material from the collection's four main areas: product design

and decorative arts; drawings, prints, and graphic design; textiles; and wall coverings. With a small exhibition area on the ground floor, the primary galleries are on the street-level first floor and second floor. The library and archives on the third floor are open by appointment. An appointment is also needed to visit the Design Resource Center.

The entrance opens on the first-floor **Great Hall.** Other first-floor rooms, now used as galleries, include the **Music Room,** with a bagpipe motif in the ceiling; the **Garden Vestibule,** with leaded Tiffany windows; the formal **Dining Room,** where guests included such luminaries of the day as Booker T. Washington, Mark Twain, and Marie Curie; and the **Breakfast Room,** overlooking the garden and leading to the skylit conservatory.

The museum is at its most enjoyable when it pays serious attention to everyday objects— buttons, watches, razors, wallpaper, cameras, computers—almost anything imaginable. Exhibits can zero in on usually unexamined elements of everyday life: the lowly doghouse, for instance—as rendered by leading architects. One

2011 exhibit was "Tangible Earth," the world's first digital interactive globe, conceived by Shinichi Takemura to raise awareness of global environmental issues. "Design for Life," staged on the museum's centennial in 1997, illustrated the range of the collections. The 300 offerings included 1930s wallpaper, a 1936 cocktail shaker shaped like a penguin, a scale model of the Marmon 16—a sedan designed in 1930 to compete with the Cadillac—and a Tiffany goblet made for Andrew Carnegie in 1907.

Interior Decoration Started Here

Sarah and Eleanor Hewitt, founders of the museum, were, like other wealthy young women of the time, well traveled. Impressed by the Musée des Arts Decoratifs in Paris and London's Victoria and Albert Museum, they set out to emulate them in their museum.

New York is the undisputed center of American interior design. It owes that status to the Hewitt sisters and others working to develop the field at the turn of the century. The Hewitts believed that by educating the wealthy and the decorators who worked for them, taste would filter down to the masses. Author Edith Wharton echoed the Hewitt philosophy in her influential *The Decoration of Houses:* "When the rich man demands good architecture his neighbors will get it too ... Every carefully studied detail, exacted by those who can afford to indulge their taste, will in time find its way to the carpenter-built cottage" (1897).

In 1905, Elsie de Wolfe, the country's first professional interior decorator, began catering to the wealthy. That same year, Frank Alvah Parsons introduced interior decoration courses at his art school—today the Parsons School of Design. In 1913 Wanamaker's opened the first interior decorating department in a store. Three

Carnegie's Home

Andrew Carnegie's house itself is extraordinary, so plan to spend time looking at the interior as well as the collection. On entering the first-floor Great Hall, note the wood paneling throughout. Carnegie's use of Scottish oak reflects his love of his homeland. Always interested in new technology and design, Carnegie had his home equipped with the first domestic electric elevator and state-of-the-art air-conditioning and heating systems. On the west side of the hall is a gallery that was formerly his study. The low doorway is a clue to Carnegie's height; he was only about 5'2" (1.57 m). Closed for extensive renovation, the mansion reopened in 2014.

years later architect Augustus Sherrill Winton founded the New York School of Interior Decoration (today Design), now a thriving institution at 155 East 56th Street. By the 1970s, "interior design" was the preferred term. ∎

JEWISH MUSEUM

Housed in a French Gothic château-style mansion, this esteemed institution is an important repository of Jewish culture and art. Through exhibits ranging from contemporary art to rare ethnographic material, and programs designed to engage all ages, Jews and non-Jews alike, it illuminates the remarkable scope and diversity of Jewish culture. The museum's collection holds some 30,000 items, from coins and medals to ceremonial objects, paintings, and archaeological treasures, capturing four thousand years of history.

■ A Czech Torah scroll at the Jewish Museum

Jewish Museum

- 🅰 Map p. 135
- ✉ 1109 5th Ave. at 92nd St.
- ☎ 212/423–3200
- 🕒 Closed Weds.
- 💲 $$
- 🚇 Subway: 4, 5, 6 to 86th or 96th St.

thejewishmuseum .org

The first and second floors of the museum are devoted to special temporary exhibits, which may be historical or contemporary in nature and which often attract very large crowds. Special exhibitions run the gamut—from art inspired by the Holocaust to portraits of famous Jews by Andy Warhol. One 2014 exhibition, "Chagall: Love, War, and Exile," displayed works created by Marc Chagall in the years prior to, during, and after World War II.

If it's your first time at the museum, don't miss the permanent exhibit "Scenes from the Collection," which is divided into 7 sections. The exhibit is on the third floor and its approximately 600 items range from archaeological finds to contemporary art.

One of the most remarkable exhibits at the museum includes the reconstruction of an antique synagogue, a hall dedicated to the Sabbath with an audio installation and a collection of silver menorahs.

Among the more spectacular artifacts are two venerable Torah arks, one from 18th-century Bavaria and one from Urbino, Italy, circa 1500. You can also view selected television and radio programs from the museum's archives or visit the delightful interactive **Children's Gallery.**

Founded in 1904, the Jewish Museum is operated by the Jewish Theological Seminary. For 40 years its collection was housed in the seminary's library. It moved in 1947 to its present home, a 1908 mansion designed by architect C. H. P. Gilbert for Polish-born businessman and philanthropist Felix M. Warburg, and donated by his widow.

That same year, the museum acquired the **Benjamin and Rose Mintze Collection,** 500 items from Poland—kiddush cups, Torah crowns and mantles, and Hanukkah lamps. ■

EXPERIENCE: Discover Gotham City in Neo-Modernist Architecture

New York is known for its architecture, but after the 1950s—which produced Lever House, the Seagram Building, and other modern landmarks (see p. 123)—the city went into an architectural funk, broken only by the building of the World Trade Center in 1970–1972. Strangely, or perhaps touchingly, the twin towers' destruction in 2001 seems to have unleashed a new architectural golden age in the city.

To get a feel for the new buildings, you have to see them from the sidewalk, turning a corner for that first exhilarating shock of the new. Start with the best: the geometric, 46-story **Hearst Tower** (*8th Ave. & 57th St.*). Designed by Norman Foster, it is an ultramodern structure of interlocking stainless-steel triangles that zig and zag as they rise. At the base of the building is the recycled six-story shell of the 1928 Hearst building, which provides both design counterpoint and metaphor: When it opened in 2006, the tower was one of the first in New York to incorporate extensive "green" technology. Step inside to enjoy "Icefall," a three-story waterfall that flows over 595 glass blocks and is fed with rainwater collected from the roof. Above this is "Riverlines," a massive mural by Richard Long using mud from the Hudson River and England's Avon River.

Two blocks north, at 2 Columbus Circle, the **Museum of Arts & Design** (see p. 132) is another New York recycling story. Built as the short-lived Huntington Hartford Gallery (1964–1969), its original windowless facade was half Venetian palazzo and half marble tea

cozy. It was rebuilt to its ultramodern form between 2002 and 2008. Note its curving, iridescent skin, made up of 22,000 pale, glazed ceramic tiles.

Travelers stepping onto 8th Avenue from the Port Authority Bus Terminal now look up in awe at Renzo Piano's **New York Times Building** (*620 8th Ave, bet.

The Hearst Tower: Manhattan's first "green" high-rise building

41st & 42nd Sts.). Opened in 2007, this tower rises 52 stories high, with a "second-skin" curtain wall extending higher. This curtain, glazed with low emissivity glass, maximizes natural light, while

186,000 ceramic rods form a screen to block direct sunlight.

Opposite Bryant Park, the 54-story **Bank of America Tower** (2009; *42nd St. & 6th Ave.*) is crystalline in form, its facets suggesting different shapes from different angles.

At 11th Avenue and 19th Street, Frank Gehry's ten-story **IAC Building** was completed in 2007. Visible from the High Line (see pp. 92–93), the design is apt for its Hudson River-side location, with an organic shape flowing like waves or windblown sails, and a milky white glass "skin."

On the Lower East Side, at Bowery and Prince Streets, the seven-story **New Museum** (see p. 69) looks like an off-kilter stack of white, mesh-clad gift boxes.

Frank Gehry's 76-story **8 Spruce Street** (originally Beekman Tower) is located south of City Hall. This may be the perfect contemporary fusion of old New York and new: Its steel skin—crinkled and undulating in trademark Gehry style—overlays a skyscraper that is classic Gotham. Just two blocks from the old World Trade Center site, this edifice may be the ultimate affirmation that New York architecture is back: modern but classic, strange but true.

MUSEUM OF THE CITY OF NEW YORK

In 1923 New York City decided that, like other great cities, it must have a museum to document its history. The result is the Museum of the City of New York (MCNY), a treasure-house of some 1.5 million objects from the city's storied past, from Dutch colonial times to the present, which it displays in a rich schedule of ongoing and temporary exhibits that explore New York's past, present, and future and celebrate its diversity and culture.

The sumptuous late 19th-century bedroom of John D. Rockefeller, Sr.

Museum of the City of New York

- Map p. 135
- 1220 5th Ave. at 103rd St.
- 212/534-1672
- $$
- Subway: 6 to 103rd St.; 2, 3 to Central Park North–110th St.

mcny.org

This is a fascinating place where you can find such seemingly unrelated displays as the charred timbers of a 17th-century merchantman that burned off the shores of the island of Manhattan; furniture of New York cabinet-maker Duncan Phyfe; and Gypsy Rose Lee's "chaste G-string with her name embroidered in blue silk by her own hand." There is also an outstanding collection of Currier & Ives prints as well as a photo archive that includes the **Jacob Riis Collection,**

documenting life in New York's most impoverished areas during the late 19th century. In total, the museum's collection is divided into seven curatorial areas: the Furniture and Decorative Art Collection; Prints, Drawings, and Photographs; Manuscripts and Ephemera; the New York Theater and Broadway Collection; the Toy Collection; New York Fashion, Costumes, and Textiles; and New York Paintings and Sculpture.

If you're lucky, perhaps you'll catch some of the museum's

treasures that are not often displayed, including vintage Barbie dolls or a lock of George Washington's hair.

A series of recent renovations have made the museum's presentations more dynamic, favoring a range of temporary exhibits with wide-ranging themes.

The permanent exhibit, "New York at Its Core," narrates the city's 400 years of development using 450 historical objects, including photos, prints, paintings, videos, and interactive digital displays.

The museum's lifeblood are the temporary exhibits; they bring into focus the countless threads that weave the history and the culture of New York. In 2008 and 2009, the museum launched exhibitions on the golden age of New York baseball, the city's transformation under masterplanner Robert Moses, and the decay of the South Bronx in the 1970s and 1980s. "Paris/New York" explored the artistic relationship between the two cities during the 1925–1940 period, while "Growing and Greening New York" explored the challenges in redesigning New York and New York life to promote sustainability.

"Through a Different Lens: Stanley Kubrick Photographs" is one of the more recent exhibitions, with 129 of the famous director's shots and 12,000 negatives from his five years as a photographer for *Look* Magazine.

"Germ City: Microbes and the Metropolis" is organized in collaboration with the New York Academy of Medicine and Wellcome. It's a completely different kind of show, dedicated to the interaction between humans and infectious diseases in the urban context of New York.

Another significant temporary exhibit is **"Rebel Women,"** which uses photos, clothing, prints, and paintings from the museum's collection to tell the story of independent, revolutionary women. From different social classes, races, and ideologies, these women challenged New York's middle-class conventions during the Victorian era and inspired the subsequent 20th-century feminist movement. The concept of the female's role as the keeper of virtue, limited to a domestic position, was already deteriorating but it would take a lot more time for American society to mature.

On a lighter note, "City as Canvas" was a first-time exhibition of works from the expansive streetart collection of Martin Wong, an East Village artist and collector of graffiti art. ∎

Toy Stories

The always popular "New York Toy Stories" exhibit, on the museum's third floor, features a collection of dollhouses and doll furniture from 1769 to the present. Especially captivating is the dollhouse created by Carrie Stettheimer in the 1920s. Its interior includes an art gallery with miniatures of paintings by Marcel Duchamp and other artists of the first New York avant-garde.

MORE STOPS ALONG FIFTH AVENUE

While the Met and the Guggenheim may well be the first sites you visit along upper Fifth Avenue, there are several other important museums and cultural centers that deserve your attention. In one afternoon you can explore the art and culture of Germany, Austria, Latin America, the Caribbean, Ireland, Africa, and the Ukraine—all in one 30-block stretch.

■ "The (S) Files 007," a modern sculpture at Museo del Barrio

Neue Galerie New York

🅐 Map p. 135

✉ 1048 5th Ave. (enter on 86th St.)

☎ 212/994–9493

🕐 Closed Tues.–Wed.

💲 $$

🚇 Subway: 4, 5, 6 to 86th St.

neuegalerie.org

NOTE: Children under 12 not admitted; those 13–16 must be accompanied by an adult.

Neue Galerie New York

For a museum with a European flavor, visit this diamond of Fifth Avenue's Museum Mile. Housed in a splendid 1914 beaux arts limestone mansion built for industrialist William Starr Miller and later occupied by Mrs. Cornelius Vanderbilt III, the Neue Galerie New York is devoted to early 20th-century German and Austrian art and design. Its works represent the pinnacle of the modernist German Expressionism and Bauhaus movements in Vienna and Berlin between 1900 and 1938, before a Nazi ban on experimental art.

The transformation of one of Fifth Avenue's most opulent landmark residences into a museum began with the dream of two collectors. Ronald Lauder, philanthropist and businessman son of cosmetics magnate Estée Lauder, and art dealer Serge Sabarsky envisioned a museum that would exhibit the best examples of the German and Austrian art they loved. Sabarsky purchased the building for the Neue Galerie in 1994. After Sabarsky's death in 1996, Lauder bought the building and made their dream a reality. The name Neue Galerie ("new gallery" in German) links the museum to the modernist wave of European galleries in the early 20th century, especially Vienna's Neue Galerie, founded in 1923.

The collection is made up of more than 800 works from the Sabarsky Foundation, 500 from the Lauder family, and some 100 purchased by the museum. Included are 100 paintings and graphic works by Gustav Klimt and Egon Schiele, the largest holding of works by these artists outside Vienna. In 2018, there was also an exhibit organized for the 100th anniversary of their deaths. Klimt's famous 1907 portrait of Adele Bloch-Bauer is the undisputed highlight.

Visiting the Gallery: On the first floor are a bookstore, a design center selling many items exclusive to the museum, and the Viennese-style Café Sabarsky, with authentic Austrian meals and superb pastries and coffee.

On the second floor, you'll find galleries containing paintings and drawings from late 19th-century Vienna, like Klimt's "Dancer" (1916–1918) in oil and numerous Schiele self-portraits. Oskar Kokoschka, Max Beckmann, and Emil Nolde are also represented.

The third-floor galleries feature German movements and artists, from Vassily Kandinsky and Paul Klee to Laszlo Moholy-Nagy and Ludwig Mies van der Rohe.

Decorative arts from the Wiener Werkstätte and Bauhaus design movements, including sleek furniture, decorative jewelry, ceiling fixtures, and flatware, are also on display. Lectures, music, films, and cabaret performances are offered.

El Museo del Barrio

El Museo del Barrio, at the north end of Museum Row, is the city's only major museum dedicated to the art and culture of Latin America and the Caribbean. It is one of the country's premier Latino cultural institutions.

Founded in 1969, the museum grew out of the social movements of the 1960s, when local Puerto Rican artists began protesting their lack of representation in downtown museums. In 1994, the museum broadened its mission to present and preserve the art and culture of all Latin American communities throughout the United States. Its permanent collection contains more than 8,000 objects from all over Latin America

and the Caribbean, including pre-Columbian ceramics and vessels from the Taino culture of Puerto Rico and the Dominican Republic (cultural homelands to so many New Yorkers); Mexican masks and *santos* (carved saints); and paintings, sculptures, graphic works, and photographs by artists of Latin American descent. After a one-year closure for a renovation that completely modified the

---

INSIDER TIP:

The Neue Galerie is a gem that houses a fine collection of early 20th-century Austrian and German art, a great gift shop, and a café that people flock to—sometimes without even looking at the art.

—DORIS BERGMAN
Producer, NY1 New

---

structure, the museum is reopening with a retrospective exhibit dedicated to the Argentinian artist, Liliana Porter, and an urban photography exhibit. The museum is housed in the 1915 Heckscher Building, which features a school, a Latin music conservatory, and El Museo's Heckscher Theater, where the museum and other cultural groups present films, musical performances, plays, and Latino cultural celebrations such as the Day of the Dead, Carnaval, and Three Kings Day. Public programs also include independent film and video screenings, neighborhood

**El Museo
del Barrio**

🅰 Map p. 135

✉ 1230 5th Ave.
at 104th St.

☎ 212/831-7272

🕐 Closed Mon.–
Tues.

💲 $

🚇 Subway: 6 to
103rd St.

elmuseo.org

American Irish Historical Society (AIHS)

- ✉ 991 5th Ave. at E. 80th St.
- ☎ 212/288–2263
- 🕐 Closed Sat.–Sun.
- 🚇 Subway: 4, 5, 6 to 86th St.

aihs.org

Goethe Institut– New York

- ✉ 30 Irving Pl.
- ☎ 212/439–8700
- 🕐 Closed Sat.–Sun.
- 🚇 Subway: 4, 5, 6 to 86th St.

goethe.de

New Africa Center

- ✉ 1280 5th Ave. at 110th St.
- 🚇 Subway: 6 to 110th St.

theafricacenter.org

Ukrainian Institute of America

- ✉ 2 E. 79th St.
- ☎ 212/288–8660
- 🕐 Closed Mon.
- 💲 Donation suggested
- 🚇 Subway: 6 to 77th St.

ukrainian institute.org

tours, dance groups, poetry readings, and an annual *coquito* (Puerto Rican eggnog) tasting.

One recent memorable show was "Nexus: New York 1900–1945, Encounters in the Modern Metropolis," which examined how avant-garde artists from Latin America and the United States influenced one another in the early 20th century, while mixing in New York's vibrant art scene.

American Irish Historical Society (AIHS)

Open to members and their guests, this society sponsors concerts, readings, and lectures throughout the year. Its library is the most complete private collection of Irish and Irish-American history and literature in the country.

Goethe Institut– New York

Founded in 1957, Goethe Institut–New York is run by the Goethe Institut in Munich for the purpose of promoting German language study and cultural exchange. With three locations in New York, the Goethe Institute has a library/information service and sponsors frequent lectures and exhibits.

A popular recent attraction was Rimini Protokoll's "Call Cutta in a Box," an interactive play in which ticketholders chat with a call center in Calcutta, India.

INSIDER TIP:

For a "well off Broadway" experience, go to Brandy's Piano Bar [235 E 84th St, tel 212/744–4949], where performers and waitstaff get everyone in the mood to belt out their favorite show tunes. All together now ...

–BRET BARASCH
Onward Publishing New York, EVP

New Africa Center

Museum Mile was extended all the way to the top of Central Park with the New Africa Center (formerly the Museum for African Art), which opened its new home in 2015. Founded in 1984, this museum has produced more than 60 shows and traveling exhibits exploring aspects of Africa's cultural and artistic heritage—from ancient traditions to retrospectives of individual artists to shows exploring folk and mural arts.

Ukrainian Institute of America

Housed in a French Renaissance mansion, the institute has a large collection of paintings, sculpture, textiles, and more. It presents lectures, conferences, exhibits, films, and classical music. A Ukrainian, William Dzus, founded the institute in 1948 and helped fund the building's purchase in 1955. ∎

IN & AROUND THE UPPER EAST SIDE

The Upper East Side has such an abundance of landmark buildings that you can spot eye-pleasing architecture everywhere, much of it from a more gracious past. You can also indulge in extravagant shopping, or find a place for quiet repose.

You can find elegant designer clothing at stores along Madison Avenue in the 60s, or wander in **Bloomingdale's** flagship store reigning over an entire city block. For classic river views, try strolling along the East River between 53rd and 59th Streets. That enclave, called Sutton Place, includes two public parks at 53rd and 57th Streets.

A four-minute bird's-eye view of the city can be had by taking the **Roosevelt Island Tramway** to the East River island of the same name and back (*60th St. & 2nd Ave., tel 212/832–4555, rioc.ny.gov/302/Tram, $*). Also on the East River, **Rockefeller University** (*1230 York Ave., rockefeller.edu*) is a world-renowned research institute for medicine and the physical sciences.

Mount Vernon Hotel Museum & Garden

This quiet site may seem out of place, but from 1826 to 1833, as an elegant country day retreat, it welcomed the city's burgeoning upper middle class. The museum illuminates early 19th-century hotel life. Originally the land was part of a 23-acre (9.3 ha) plot purchased in 1795 by Col. Stephen Smith and his wife, Abigail Adams (daughter of President John Adams), who christened the site Mount Vernon after President Washington's

■ The 19th-century Mount Vernon Hotel Museum

home. Finances forced them to sell before they could build, but the name remained. An enterprising merchant opened the first Mount Vernon Hotel on the site in 1808. Fire destroyed the building in 1826, but another hotel followed when the next owner converted the surviving stone carriage house into a much finer day resort. This building was sold after 1833 for a private residence.

In the 1930s the Colonial Dames of America rescued the building. Its reinterpretation was completed in 2000, and its furnished rooms reflect its heyday. Men caroused in the Tavern Room or retreated to the more sedate Gentleman's Parlor. Women enjoyed singing and needlework in the richly decorated Ladies' Double Parlors. This is a rare architectural time capsule, replete with artifacts and a sense of times past. ■

Bloomingdale's

- ✉ 1000 3rd Ave. at 59th St.
- ☎ 212/705–2000
- 🚇 Subway: N, R, Q, 4, 5, 6 to Lexington Ave./ 59th St.

bloomingdales.com

Mount Vernon Hotel Museum & Garden

- 🗺 Map p. 135
- ✉ 421 E. 61st St., bet. 1st & York Aves.
- ☎ 212/838–6878
- 🕐 Closed Mon.
- 💲 $$
- 🚇 Subway: N, R, Q, 4, 5, 6 to Lexington Ave./ 59th St.

mvhm.org

SILK STOCKING DISTRICT

Zip code 10021 is one of the wealthiest U.S. postal codes in the United States. Covering the area from East 61st to East 80th Streets between Fifth Avenue and the East River, it has at its heart the so-called silk stocking district. This is where the institutions of wealth, power, and social standing are located—find in these blocks the city's fanciest clubs, the best private schools, and architecturally distinguished churches and synagogues.

■ The Union Club, founded in 1836, is New York's oldest social club.

At the hub (but south of the geographic center) of the silk stocking district is the fortresslike 1880 **Seventh Regiment Armory** (*643 Park Ave., bet. E. 66th & 67th Sts., tel 212/616-3930, armoryonpark.org*), a 19th-century architectural treasure. When socially prominent New Yorkers formed the unit in 1847, it was known as the Silk Stocking Regiment. The men designed their own uniforms and raised the money to build the armory. Following extensive renovation, the building now hosts art exhibitions, lectures, and unconventional performances in its magnificent 19th-century interior, with designs by Louis

Comfort Tiffany, Stanford White, and other great names. The magnificent 54,000-square-foot (5,016 sq m) Drill Hall is one of the largest unobstructed interior spaces in the city.

From the armory it's only a few steps to the haunts of the elite. Literally in the armory's shadow, the **Cosmopolitan Club** (*122 E. 66th St., off Park Ave., closed to public*) is a refuge for professionals. Its counterpart for society women, the **Colony Club** (*564 Park Ave. at E. 62nd St., closed to public*), founded in 1903, is located in a 1916 building designed by Delano & Aldrich. The **Lotos Club** (*5 E. 66th St., off 5th Ave., closed to public*), the city's oldest literary society, is in a 1900 house. It was designed by Richard Howland Hunt at the request of Mrs. Elliott F. Shepard, daughter of William H. Vanderbilt, as a wedding gift for her daughter.

The **Union Club** (*101 E. 69th St. at Park Ave., closed to public*), founded in 1836, is only two blocks away in 1933 quarters designed by Delano & Aldrich. The nearby **Metropolitan Club** (*1 E. 60th St. at 5th Ave., closed to public*) was founded by Union Club members disgruntled when their friends and relatives were turned down for membership. The Metropolitan is housed in an 1893 building designed by Stanford White, who also did, in 1906, the **Harmonie Club** (*4 E. 60th St., closed to public*), founded by German Jews in 1852.

The spiritual needs of the silk stocking district are met by a variety of churches and synagogues. Within view of the armory, the neo-Gothic **Central Presbyterian Church**

The elegant Upper East Side

INSIDER TIP:

For a certain brand of romantic, 169 East 71st Street, between Lexington and Third Avenues, is a major landmark. It's where Truman Capote's Holly Golightly, played on-screen by Audrey Hepburn, lived in *Breakfast at Tiffany's.*

—MATT HANNAFIN
National Geographic contributor

(*Park Ave. & E. 64th St., tel 212/838–0808*), built from 1920 to 1922, was originally the Baptist church where John D. Rockefeller worshipped. Socially prominent Episcopalians can still expect to be christened, confirmed, married, and eulogized at **St. James Episcopal Church** (*865 Madison Ave. at E. 71st St., tel 212/774–4200*). This neo-Gothic church (1884) was rebuilt in 1924 by architect Ralph Adams Cram.

Roman Catholics and Jews, once excluded from the seat of power, are today well represented in the silk stocking district. The 1929 **Temple Emanu-El** (*5th Ave. at E. 65th St., tel 212/744–1400*), a combination of Western and Byzantine architectural styles, was the first reformed congregation in the city. It is one of the largest synagogues in the world, seating 2,500—more than St. Patrick's Cathedral.

Well-scrubbed schoolchildren, accompanied by nannies or governesses, go to prestigious and academically rigorous institutions such as **Dalton, Chapin, Spence,** and **Brearley;** there is also John Kennedy, Jr.'s alma mater, **St. David's** (*12–16 E. 89th St.*), in a row of neo-Georgian town houses designed in 1919 by Delano & Aldrich.

Clubs, cathedrals, and schools aside, the silk stocking district is also notable for beautiful homes, from the apartment buildings of Park Avenue to the elegant townhomes that line the cross streets. Two contenders for the title of "best block on the Upper East Side" are East 95th Street between Park and Lexington Ave., full of elegant, low-rise 19th-century town houses, and East 70th Street between Park and Lexington Ave., whose 19th-century homes are set unusually far back, giving the street a wide, airy feel.

More Places to Visit in the Upper East Side

Asia Society

This organization and repository of Asian art is housed in a 1981 red granite building designed by Edward Larrabee Barnes. Its permanent collection of Asian art and crafts is based on one compiled by John D. Rockefeller III, who founded the society in 1956 to promote understanding of Asian art and culture. *asiasociety.org* ✉ 725 Park Ave. at 70th St. ☎ 212/288–6400 🕒 Closed Mon. 💲 $$ 🚇 Subway: 6 to 68th St.-Hunter College

■ Once a country estate, Gracie Mansion today functions as the mayor's official residence.

Episcopal Church of the Holy Trinity, Yorkville

This complex of French Renaissance-style structures was built in 1896–1899 to serve the quickly growing immigrant population of Yorkville. This once mainly German-Hungarian district runs from East 77th to 96th Streets. There is an interesting stretch along Second Avenue in the mid-80s with traditional German shops and delicatessens. ✉ 316–322 E. 88th St. ☎ 212/289–4100 🚇 Subway: 4, 5, 6 to 86th St.

Gracie Mansion, the Mayoral Home

This well-preserved federal house was built in 1799 by shipping merchant Archibald

Gracie on the site of a Revolutionary fort. In 1924, the house became the first home of the Museum of the City of New York. In 1942 it became the mayor's official residence, and in recent years it has been used as accommodation for visiting officials and dignitaries. Guided tours include the mayor's study, featuring Childe Hassam lithographs of New York street scenes and a permanent exhibit on the history of the house. Gracie Mansion is located in **Carl Schurz Park,** an uncrowded, ten-acre (4 ha), riverside tract with wonderful views of the East River and Roosevelt Island. ✉ 88th St. & East End Ave. ☎ 212/570–4751 🕒 Open Mon. only; reservations required 💲 $$ 🚇 Subway: 4, 5, 6 to 86th St.

New York Society Library

The city's oldest library, founded in 1754, is housed in a landmark town house (1917). Its ground floor is open to the public, although only members can borrow books. *nysoclib.org* ✉ 53 E. 79th St. at Madison Ave. ☎ 212/288–6900 🚇 Subway: 6 to 77th St.

Society of Illustrators: Museum of American Illustration

This unusual museum exhibits commercial illustration, an art form not usually displayed. Housed in an 1875 carriage house, the society, founded in 1901 to promote the art of commercial illustration, had as early members such notables as Charles Dana Gibson, William Glackens, Norman Rockwell, and Frederic Remington. The museum's collection consists of some 1,500 original works from 1838 to the present. There is an extensive bookstore. *societyillustrators.org* ✉ 128 E. 63rd St., bet. Park & Lexington Aves. ☎ 212/838–2560 🕒 Closed Sun.–Mon. 💲 Donation suggested 🚇 Subway: N, R, Q, 4, 5, 6 to Lexington Ave./59th St.; F to Lexington Ave./63rd St.

More than 800 acres (323 ha) of lush lawns, trees, and meandering paths smack-dab in the middle of Manhattan

CENTRAL PARK

The Mall in Central Park, lined with American elms

CENTRAL PARK

Few of the 20 million people a year who use the park realize that its gates—at least its 18 original ones—have names, although only three are inscribed: the Inventors', Mariners', and Engineers' Gates. Unknowingly, you may be entering through the Artists' Gate (Central Park South and Sixth Avenue) or, at the opposite, northern end, the Warriors' Gate, or at some other titled entrance.

Central Park, the first large public park in America, is a product of vision, revision, and compromise. Its inspiration was the great parks of London and Paris. Wealthy New Yorkers believed that a park in New York would add to the city's cachet, give them a place to drive their carriages, and provide the working classes with healthful recreation. Although the park has gone through periods of neglect and deterioration during its century and a half history, it has consistently played an important role in city life.

When you visit Central Park today, you will see it at its spanking best. Improvements, undertaken at the initiative of the Central Park Conservancy, a private group that contributes substantially to the park's fund-raising efforts, have included reseeding the Great Lawn, restoring the park's five man-made lakes to the designers' original vision, and restoring the Swedish Cottage, a model schoolhouse that was shipped from Sweden for the 1876 Philadelphia Centennial Exposition and now is home to a marionette theater for kids.

Greensward Plan: An Urban Vision

Central Park's naturalistic landscaping hides its mostly man-made origins. The area, now 843 acres (341 ha), was filled with shanties and small farms when the state legislature, in 1853, authorized the city to seize a 700-acre (283 ha) parcel.

Four years later, the Central Park Commission held a contest to determine the design of the park. The winning entry, a "Greensward plan," based on romantic landscaping notions then popular in England, was submitted by Frederick Law Olmsted, who would oversee its construction as the park's superintendent, and his partner, Calvert Vaux. The plan stressed variety and contrast: open meadows, dense woods, and formal areas such as the Mall. The park's "one great purpose," Olmsted wrote, is "to supply to the hundreds of thousands of tired workers, who have no opportunity to spend their summers in the country, a specimen of God's handiwork."

It took some 20,000 laborers 20 years to construct Central Park, which

---

NOT TO BE MISSED:

Sunbathing on the expansive lawn of Sheep Meadow   170

The peaceful Mall promenade   170

Photogenic Bethesda Fountain and Terrace   170–171

Renting a boat and paddling around the Lake   170–171

The romantic Bow Bridge   171

Bird-watching along the narrow paths of the Ramble   171

Jogging around the Jacqueline Kennedy Onassis Reservoir   172

Visiting the Conservatory Garden   172

WE
SID

PARK
WE

CENTRAL
PARK

Tavern on
the Green

WEST DRIVE

HECKSCHE
SOFTBALL
FIELDS

59th Street-
Columbus Circle

COLUMBUS
CIRCLE

CENTRAL PARK
SOUTH

opened in stages, beginning in December 1858. In that time, they removed three million cubic yards (2.3 million m³) of soil, blasted the rocky outcroppings to create the picturesque rifts the Olmsted-Vaux plan called for, planted four or five million trees and 816 varieties of other plants, drained marshlands, and dug the reservoir that is today named for Jacqueline Kennedy Onassis and circumscribed by a popular 1.6-mile (2.5 km) jogging path.

There have been encroachments on the park's open space: wings added to the Metropolitan Museum of Art, the Tavern on the Green

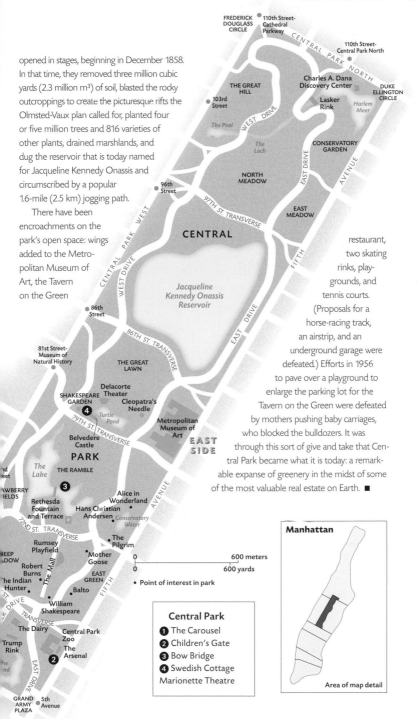

restaurant, two skating rinks, playgrounds, and tennis courts. (Proposals for a horse-racing track, an airstrip, and an underground garage were defeated.) Efforts in 1956 to pave over a playground to enlarge the parking lot for the Tavern on the Green were defeated by mothers pushing baby carriages, who blocked the bulldozers. It was through this sort of give and take that Central Park became what it is today: a remarkable expanse of greenery in the midst of some of the most valuable real estate on Earth. ■

FREDERICK DOUGLASS CIRCLE
110th Street-Cathedral Parkway
CENTRAL PARK NORTH
110th Street-Central Park North
Charles A. Dana Discovery Center
DUKE ELLINGTON CIRCLE
THE GREAT HILL
103rd Street
Lasker Rink
Harlem Meer
WEST DRIVE
The Pool
The Loch
CONSERVATORY GARDEN
EAST DRIVE
AVENUE
96th Street
NORTH MEADOW
97TH ST. TRANSVERSE
EAST MEADOW
CENTRAL PARK WEST
CENTRAL
WEST DRIVE
FIFTH
Jacqueline Kennedy Onassis Reservoir
86th Street
EAST DRIVE
86TH ST. TRANSVERSE
81st Street-Museum of Natural History
THE GREAT LAWN
Delacorte Theater
Cleopatra's Needle
SHAKESPEARE GARDEN
❹
Turtle Pond
79TH ST. TRANSVERSE
Metropolitan Museum of Art
EAST SIDE
Belvedere Castle
PARK
The Lake
THE RAMBLE
AVENUE
❸
Alice in Wonderland
STRAWBERRY FIELDS
Bethesda Fountain and Terrace
Hans Christian Andersen
Conservatory Water
72ND ST. TRANSVERSE
The Pilgrim
SHEEP MEADOW
Rumsey Playfield
Mother Goose
The Mall
Robert Burns
EAST GREEN
The Indian Hunter
FIFTH
Balto
William Shakespeare
WEST DRIVE
The Dairy
Central Park Zoo
TRANSVERSE
Trump Rink
The Arsenal
❷
EAST DRIVE
GRAND ARMY PLAZA
5th Avenue

0 —— 600 meters
0 —— 600 yards
• Point of interest in park

Central Park
❶ The Carousel
❷ Children's Gate
❸ Bow Bridge
❹ Swedish Cottage Marionette Theatre

Manhattan

Area of map detail

AROUND CENTRAL PARK

Where to start? The major attractions are south of 86th Street, so you might begin with a group of attractions near the Children's Gate (64th Street and Fifth Avenue) and work your way north. Descend the stairs off Fifth Avenue to the Arsenal, a redbrick fortress built in 1848 to house armaments, now the Parks Department headquarters.

■ Central Park was not at all "central" when created, but it has since been hemmed in by the city.

Central Park

◪ Map pp. 168–169

Visitor Information

✉ Central Park Information, The Dairy, 65th St.

☎ 212/794-6564

centralparknyc.org

Central Park Zoo

◪ Map p. 169

✉ 5th Ave. at E. 64th St.

☎ 212/439-6500

🅢 $$

🚌 Bus: M1–M5; Subway: N, R to 5th Ave./59th St.; 6 to 68th St.–Hunter College

centralparkzoo.com

The walkway around the building will take you to the **Central Park Zoo,** which offers its 130 resident species natural settings instead of cages. Feeding time for the sea lions (at 11.30 a.m., 2 p.m., and 4 p.m.) is a favorite with children, as is the adjacent **Tisch Children's Zoo.** West of the zoo is the **Dairy,** an 1870 building designed by Calvert Vaux, now a park information center. Contact the Dairy about free walking tours, offered by the Central Park Conservancy.

Beyond is the **Chess and Checkers House** (secure chess pieces at the Dairy with a deposit) and the **Carousel,** the latter a Coney Island transplant and, at

$2 a ride, one of the park's most popular attractions. Footpaths in the park meander, but there are signs, and local visitors can help with directions as well.

Northwest of the Dairy, the **Sheep Meadow** is a huge expanse of lawn. Next to it on the east is the **Mall** (*bet. 66th & 72nd Sts.*), a formal promenade lined with American elms, which includes the sculpture-lined Literary Walk at its southern end. At the northern end are steps to the **Bethesda Fountain and Terrace** (*at 72nd St.*). This two-level architectural space centers on the sculptured fountain "Angel of the Waters," by Emma Stebbins. It overlooks the serpentine 18-acre (7.2 ha) body of water known as

INSIDER TIP:

A walk in Central Park is just a perfect day in New York. For an expert guided tour, check out *centralpark.com/tours/walking.* Tour subjects are Art & Architecture, Movies & TV Sites, Hidden Secrets, and Holiday Sights.

—TOM O'NEILL
National Geographic writer

the **Lake.** Boats and bikes can be rented at the **Loeb Boathouse** on the Lake's eastern end (*74th St.*), and there is a delightful open-air bar/café. Closer to Fifth Avenue (*at 74th St.*) is **Conservatory Water,** known as the Model Boat Pond, for the remote-controlled boats raced here. There's also an ice-cream café.

About a quarter mile (0.4 km) west of Bethesda Fountain and Terrace, just off the park entrance at Central Park West and 72nd Street, **Strawberry Fields** honors the musician John Lennon, who in 1980 was killed in front of his home at the Dakota Apartments, just across the avenue on Central Park West. His widow, Yoko Ono, funded the 2.5-acre (1 ha), tear-shaped garden, which is named for Lennon's song "Strawberry Fields Forever." Naples, Italy, donated the central sidewalk mosaic, with the word "Imagine" at the center.

Throughout the summer, free events—from concerts to opera to readings, all with professional performers—happen daily at **Central Park SummerStage** (*tel 212/360-2777, cityparksfoundation.org/summerstage*) at Rumsey Playfield (*near the Mall*). For the action-minded, there are free Rollerblading clinics at the West 72nd Street park entrance, on weekends from April through October.

The cast-iron **Bow Bridge** (*mid-park around 74th St.*) across the Lake leads to the **Ramble,** a 37-acre (15 ha), hilly maze of paths and foliage, a favorite with bird-watchers. Near the park's West Drive (*around 79th St.*) is the **Swedish Cottage Marionette Theatre.** Next door, the **Shakespeare Garden,** established in

Carousel
- Map p. 169
- E. 64th St.
- 212/439-6900 ext. 12
- Nov. to Mar.: call ahead
- $

Loeb Boathouse
- 212/517-2233
- $$$ for boat rentals (plus deposit), $$-$$$ for bike rentals (plus deposit)

Swedish Cottage Marionette Theatre
- Near West Dr.
- 212/988-9093
- Summer only; closed Sun.–Mon.
- $$ (reservations required)

Delacorte Theater
- Map p. 169
- 212/539-8750
- Summer only
- Free, but tickets required

publictheater.org

EXPERIENCE: Giddyup Uptown: Equine Pursuits in Central Park

While it's true that few New Yorkers would be caught dead riding in a carriage around Central Park, it's also true that the park was made to be seen by horse—either by carriage on its roadways or horseback on its 6-mile (9.6 km) bridle path. Year-round, you can find carriages for hire along Central Park South between Fifth and Sixth Avenues. They charge $50 for the first 20 minutes and $20 for each additional 10 minutes. Riders can also take guided rides on the bridle path through **Horseback Riding NYC** (*W. 67th St. tel 845/386-3388, www.centralparkhorsebackrides.com*), which charges $125 per hour, by appointment only, spring, summer, and fall.

■ Once upon a time in Central Park: Children love to climb onto the lap of the Hans Christian Andersen statue.

Henry Luce Nature Observatory

⊠ Belvedere Castle
☎ 212/772–0210
🕒 Closed Mon.

Charles A. Dana Discovery Center

⊠ Northern shore, Harlem Meer
☎ 212/860–1370

Trump Rink

⊠ E. 63rd St.
☎ 212/439–6900
💲 $$

wollmanskatingrink
.com

1916 on the 300th anniversary of the Bard's death, contains many of the plants mentioned in his works. **Shakespeare in the Park** produces Shakespeare plays, and others, performed in summer at the open-air **Delacorte Theater.**

On Turtle Pond (formerly Belvedere Lake), picturesque **Belvedere Castle** nestles into the rock outcropping. The castle houses the **Henry Luce Nature Observatory.** The Wood and Water Discovery Room is at the center of the observatory's children's programs. **The Great Lawn** (*mid-park from 79th to 85th Sts.*) is where the Metropolitan Opera and the

New York Philharmonic perform free summer concerts. It is behind the Metropolitan Museum of Art, where **Cleopatra's Needle,** the park's most prominent landmark, is also located. This 65-foot-tall (20 m) granite obelisk, dating from about 1475 B.C., was Egypt's gift to the U.S. in 1885.

The park north of here is wilder and less densely peopled. One major exception is the jogging path around the 106-acre (43 ha) **Jacqueline Kennedy Onassis Reservoir.** The **Conservatory Garden** (*5th Ave. at 105th St.*) is entered via the Vanderbilt Gate that once graced the Vanderbilt mansion on Fifth Avenue.

At the northern end of the park is the 11-acre (4.4 ha) Harlem Meer, where the **Charles A. Dana Discovery Center** offers nature programs for children and families. For a wintertime activity, try ice-skating at **Lasker Rink** (*bet. 106th & 108th Sts., tel 212/492–3856*), which in summer is a pool. Even more popular is **Trump Rink,** down at the park's southern end. In winter, it attracts more than 4,000 ice-skaters every day. ■

Discover Sculpture in the Park

The first statue in Central Park, a bronze bust of German dramatist and philosopher Friedrich Schiller, was placed in the Ramble in 1859. Other literary figures, like Robert Burns and Sir Walter Scott, are represented on the Mall's southern end along Literary Walk. The only American is Fitz-Greene Halleck, a member of the literary Knickerbocker Group. Sculptor John Quincy Adams Ward did the bronze statue of William Shakespeare, the realistic "Indian Hunter" (1886), located southwest of the Mall, and "The Pilgrim" (1884) on the 72nd Street transverse, just south of Conservatory Lake. Here, children climb over the bronze grouping "Alice in Wonderland" (1959), by Jose de Creeft, and sit on the lap of Hans Christian Andersen (1956), rendered in bronze by Georg John Lober.

A lively neighborhood with a rich heritage in the arts, spread out between two of the city's best parks

UPPER WEST SIDE

The New York City Ballet and other performing arts troupes call Lincoln Center home.

UPPER WEST SIDE

Bordered on the west by Riverside Park and the Hudson River and on the east by Central Park, this popular residential neighborhood extends from West 59th Street north to 110th Street. Busy thoroughfares lined with shops and historic buildings cross quiet side streets with handsome brownstones. In this community the arts, commerce, and residential life peacefully coexist.

The Upper West Side has attractions that draw visitors, but not so many as to overwhelm its neighborhood appeal.

The multifaceted Time Warner Center at Columbus Circle provides a fitting gateway to treasures farther on. The American Museum of Natural History is one of the great museums of its kind in the world. The New-York Historical Society is another wonderful institution families will enjoy. Lincoln Center is the country's foremost performing arts center, a must for those interested in live orchestral or chamber music, ballet, theater, or opera. The surrounding area is filled with cafés, restaurants, and delightful small stores, where you will find yourself among many residents and thus see how many New Yorkers live.

NOT TO BE MISSED:

The Dakota Led the Way for Settlement

The major factors in developing the Upper West Side were access and transportation. Before the elevated line along Columbus Avenue was completed in 1879, the area was filled with shanties and squatters, many of them displaced by the development of Central Park. Still, the construction of the Dakota Apartments in 1884 in such an out-of-the-way wasteland was considered a rash and daring move—hence its name.

But others followed: In 1884 Isidor Straus, a merchant who would eventually take over R. H. Macy's, moved to 105th Street and West End Avenue to be near Riverside Park; Union general William Tecumseh Sherman moved into a house on West 71st Street in 1886. The arrival of the subway in 1904 prolonged the boom, which lasted into the late 1920s and early 1930s, years that saw the construction of the huge twin-towered apartment hotels on Central Park West.

Developers hoped that the Upper West Side would attract the city's social and business elite. Instead it tended to draw New Yorkers engaged in the arts or publishing or advertising and similar fields. One prestigious address, the Ansonia Hotel (1904), had as residents such diverse individuals as baseball star Babe Ruth, novelist Theodore Dreiser, composer Igor Stravinsky, impresario Florenz Ziegfeld, and tenor Enrico Caruso.

The Upper West Side still attracts celebrities for its many amenities, the nearness of the park, the historical integrity of its buildings, and the fact that many other stars live here as well. ∎

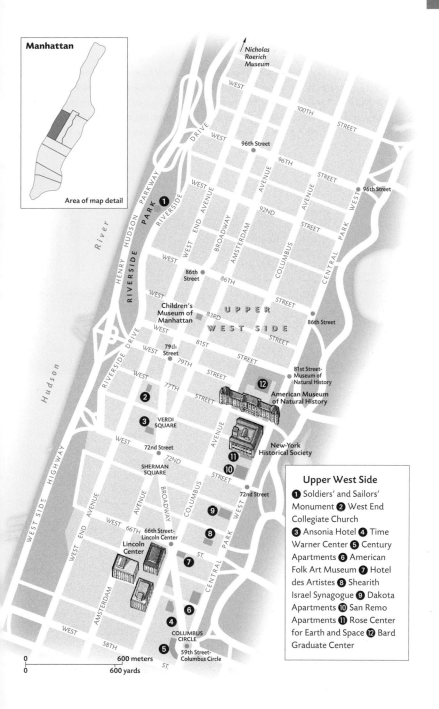

Manhattan

Area of map detail

Nicholas Roerich Museum

WEST 100TH STREET

96th Street

WEST 96TH STREET

96th Street

HENRY HUDSON PARKWAY

RIVERSIDE PARK

RIVERSIDE DRIVE

WEST END AVENUE

BROADWAY

AMSTERDAM AVENUE

COLUMBUS AVENUE

CENTRAL PARK WEST

River

Hudson

WEST 92ND STREET

❶

WEST 86TH STREET

86th Street

Children's Museum of Manhattan

UPPER WEST SIDE

83RD STREET

86th Street

WEST 81ST STREET

79th Street

81st Street-Museum of Natural History

WEST 79TH STREET

WEST 77TH STREET

❷

❶²

American Museum of Natural History

VERDI SQUARE

❸

72nd Street

New-York Historical Society

❶❶

SHERMAN SQUARE

WEST 72ND STREET

❶⁰

72nd Street

CENTRAL PARK WEST

❾

WEST 66TH STREET

66th Street-Lincoln Center

❽

Lincoln Center

BROADWAY

COLUMBUS AVENUE

AMSTERDAM AVENUE

WEST END AVENUE

WEST SIDE HIGHWAY

❼

❻

❹

WEST 58TH STREET

COLUMBUS CIRCLE

❺

59th Street-Columbus Circle

0   600 meters
0   600 yards

Upper West Side

❶ Soldiers' and Sailors' Monument ❷ West End Collegiate Church ❸ Ansonia Hotel ❹ Time Warner Center ❺ Century Apartments ❻ American Folk Art Museum ❼ Hotel des Artistes ❽ Shearith Israel Synagogue ❾ Dakota Apartments ❿ San Remo Apartments ⓫ Rose Center for Earth and Space ⓬ Bard Graduate Center

LINCOLN CENTER

The Lincoln Center for the Performing Arts, the country's largest performing arts center, celebrated its fiftieth anniversary in May 2009 amid redevelopment of its 16.3-acre (6.6 ha) complex in the Lincoln Square neighborhood. The major renovation included the expansion and revitalization of Alice Tully Hall, the School of the American Ballet, and The Juilliard School. The Film Society of Lincoln Center also expanded with the new Elinor Bunin Munroe Film Center.

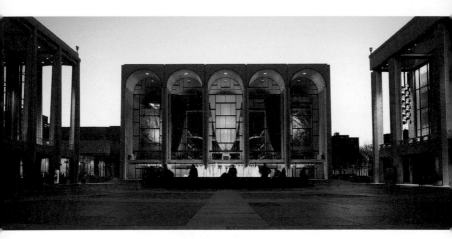

At dusk, Lincoln Center glows with soft lighting.

Some five million people a year attend performances at Lincoln Center. In addition to regular concerts and performances by the Metropolitan and New York City Operas, the New York Philharmonic, and the American Ballet Theater, Lincoln Center is noted for featured events such as concerts at Alice Tully Hall, the summer Lincoln Center Festival, and the Mostly Mozart Festival. As a public space, Lincoln Center serves and pleases even those who have never been inside its theaters, with summer nights at the fountain, and outdoor dances in the spacious plaza.

In 1987, on the bicentenary of Mozart's death, the center's various concert stages were used to perform all of the composer's works in more than 500 concerts. Plays and musicals are staged at the Vivian Beaumont Theater.

New York Public Library of the Performing Arts

One of the New York Public Library's great collections—on music, dance, and theater—opened in Lincoln Center in 1965. The research library, open to the public (*tel 212/870–1605, closed Sun. & Mon.*), has more than 350,000 books, records, tapes, CDs, videos, music scores, and materials suitable for children. Researchers can use the collections on the third floor. Four galleries hold rotating exhibits.

The **Dance Collection,** the world's largest archive on the subject, has more than 30,000 books as well as manuscripts, costume and set designs, and taped interviews with leaders in the field. It includes the Jerome Robbins Archive of Recorded Moving Image, a collection of videos and films of dance performances.

The **Music Division** comprises the Rodgers & Hammerstein Archives of Recorded Sound—approximately half a million recordings and videos—and the American Collection of jazz, pop, and imprints of colonial music. The **Billy Rose Theater Collection** includes thousands of clippings, programs, posters, and photos on theater, film, radio and TV, vaudeville, the circus, and magic. The **Theatre on Film and Tape Archives** has more than 1,600 films and videos of live performances.

Sculptures

Lincoln Center has several modern sculptures, notably Henry Moore's "Reclining Figure" (1965), a 30-foot-long (9.1 m), bronze abstract sculpture in two segments located in the reflecting pool. Moore hoped that "it will give contrast to the architecture, which, like all architecture, is rather geometric and static." Alexander Calder's spiderlike "Le Guichet" (1963), a 14-foot-high (4.2 m) assemblage consisting of a large steel plate attached to four legs, is located in front of the library of the performing arts. In the park across from Lincoln Center is a bronze bust by Milton Hebald of Richard Tucker, the Metropolitan Opera's leading tenor from 1945 until his death in 1975.

Lincoln Center for the Performing Arts

🗺 Map p. 175

✉ 10 Lincoln Center Plaza, Broadway at 65th St.

☎ 212/721–6500. Information & schedules: 212/546–2656. Lincoln Center tour: 212/875–5350. Metropolitan Opera House backstage tours: 212/769–7028 (operaed.org; reservation required).

🚇 Subway: 1 to 66th St.–Lincoln Center

lincolncenter.org

EXPERIENCE:
Step Out at Manhattan's Outdoor Dance Parties

Perhaps the city's best known outdoor dance party, **Midsummer Night Swing** (*midsummernightswing.org*) at Lincoln Center happens each July with live bands performing swing, salsa, disco, and tango. Instead of buying tickets for access to the dance floor, many just dance outside the perimeter for free. In summer, free tango dancing (*newyorktango.com*) can be found in Central Park at the Shakespeare Statue (*enter the park at 65th St.*). Both salsa and tango dancing are offered seasonally in the back of **Chelsea Market** (*chelseamarket.com*). Finally, try attending a dance studio open house. Once a month, **Dance Manhattan** (*tel 212/807–0802, dance-manhattan.com*) hosts a free night of dance, including a dance showcase performance.

Juilliard School

✉ 60 Lincoln
Center Plaza,
155 W. 65th St.,
bet. Broadway &
Amsterdam Ave.

☎ 212/799–5000

juilliard.edu

Construction

Robert Moses, New York's mid-20th-century master planner and builder, conceived of Lincoln Center as an urban renewal project. Construction, its costs largely underwritten by the Rockefeller family, caused the demolition of several West Side landmarks and the dislocation of the tenement dwellers who had inhabited the neighborhood for years. High-rise housing for 10,000 people

Juilliard School

The Juilliard School is one of the world's foremost performing arts conservatories. Founded in 1905, it moved to its current location in 1968. It houses Alice Tully Hall, home to the Chamber Music Society of Lincoln Center, which offers concerts and educational programs throughout the year. The 2009 addition of the Irene Diamond Building added rehearsal studios, offices, a music technology center, and a writing and communication center.

was built along West End Avenue, but the construction of Lincoln Center irrevocably changed the area from a working-class to a middle-class neighborhood. Ironically, just before they were demolished, the tenements had one last moment of artistic glory—as the street setting for the film version of the musical *West Side Story* (1961).

The first building in the complex was the $19.7 million concert hall designed by Max Abramovitz, which opened on September 23, 1962. Philharmonic Hall, as it was called then, was plagued from the beginning with acoustical problems, which were finally solved in 1976 after several major readjustments. The auditorium, seating more than 2,700 people, was renamed **Avery Fisher Hall** in 1973, after the philanthropic manufacturer of high-fidelity equipment, who donated ten million dollars to Lincoln Center. Some of the funds went toward the acoustics.

Architect Wallace K. Harrison designed the **Metropolitan Opera House,** the largest (nearly 4,000 seats) and most costly ($46.9 million) hall in the complex. Philip Johnson was the architect of the third largest building, the 1964 **David H. Koch Theater** (previously the New York State Theater). It, too, had poor acoustics, a problem that was remedied in 1982. These three principal buildings, wrote architectural critic Ada Louise Huxtable, "are lushly decorated, conservative structures that the public finds pleasing and most professionals consider a failure of nerve, imagination and talent."

The **Lincoln Center Theater,** a building housing both the Vivian Beaumont and the Mitzi E. Newhouse Theaters, and the New York Public Library of the Performing Arts was completed in 1965 in an unusual collaboration between architects: Eero Saarinen & Associates did the theater, while Skidmore, Owings & Merrill designed the library. ■

TIME WARNER CENTER

Spreading outward and upward on 3.4 acres (1.3 ha), Time Warner Center at Columbus Circle rises at the convergence of five major corridors: Central Park West, Central Park South, Broadway, 58th Street, and 60th Street. No single complex since Rockefeller Center has offered such unrivaled possibilities for entertainment, dining, shopping, lodging, and public enjoyment. It is at once a New York landmark and a cultural heart of the city.

Since its 2004 opening, the center has drawn tourists and residents equally. Its lobbies are enhanced by performance events and displays, while Whole Foods on the lower level is a delight unto itself. Among the 40 shops are family favorites, such as H&M and J. Crew, and designer/boutique stores, from

■ The Time Warner Center towers over Columbus Circle.

INSIDER TIP:

Grab food from Whole Foods at Columbus Circle and enter Central Park across the street. Enjoy a picnic and a ride on the old-fashioned carousel. It will bring back sweet childhood memories.

—MARIAN PORGES
Senior producer, NBC News

J. W. Cooper for homemade boots and Montmartre for women's fashions, to Armani Exchange and Williams-Sonoma. Also on-site are the Equinox Fitness Club, a bank, and restaurants helmed by world-acclaimed chefs, from Masa and Porter House, to Thomas Keller's Per Se.

The center's most unique offering is its **"Jazz at Lincoln Center"** (Artistic Director Wynton Marsalis), which produces nearly 3,000 events annually here at Frederick P. Rose Hall—the first education, performance, and broadcast facility devoted to jazz—and around the world. **Dizzy's Club Coca-Cola** has jazz, drinks, great views, and a late-night menu plus "After Hours" sets. For other spectacular views seek out the sky-high public spaces of the Mandarin Oriental Hotel New York (enter on 60th St.). ■

Time Warner Center

🄰 Map p. 175

✉ 10 Columbus Circle; Jazz at Lincoln Center box office: Cnr. of 60th St. & Broadway

☎ Dizzy's Club Coca-Cola: 212/258-9595

🚇 Subway: A, B, C, D, 1 to 59th St.–Columbus Circle

shopsatcolumbus circle.com

WALK FROM PARK TO PARK

The Upper West Side once boasted some of New York's finest hotels and most desirable residences. This walking tour visits those bygone days, beginning with grand old buildings at Central Park West and West 70th Street. It ends on the relaxing greenery of Riverside Park, with its view of the Hudson River and the Palisades and spaces for jogging, baseball, cross-country skiing, or just taking it easy.

Begin at the **Shearith Israel Synagogue ❶** (*8 W. 70th St. at Central Park W., tel 212/873–0300*), a Spanish and Portuguese synagogue built in the classical revival style in 1897 by the oldest Jewish congregation in New York. The Sephardic Jews arrived from Brazil in 1654. One block north, at 115 Central Park West, the **Majestic Apartments** were built by Irwin S. Chanin in 1930–1931. It is one of four twin-towered apartment buildings facing the park. The dark Gothic building across the road is the **Dakota Apartments,** where John Lennon lived in the 1970s, before being shot at the arched entrance in 1980. To pay respects, visit the **Strawberry Fields ❷** (see p. 171) near the 72nd Street entrance to Central Park.

Exit the park and head west on West 71st Street. The area between Central Park West and Columbus Avenue has a fine range of 1890s brownstones with high stoops and balustrades. The Roman Catholic **Church of the Blessed Sacrament ❸** (*152 W. 71st St., bet. Columbus Ave. & Broadway*) is a neo-Gothic landmark designed in 1917 by Gustave Steinback. At No. 171, the beaux arts **Dorilton,** topped by a two-and-a-half story mansard roof, is now a landmark apartment building. Yet when it opened in 1902, a critic wrote that "the sight of it makes strong men swear and weak women shrink affrighted," and it was mocked for the same multiplicity of details for which it is lauded today.

The square nearby, at the intersection of Amsterdam Avenue and Broadway at West 73rd Street, is **Verdi Square ❹**, named for a statue of Giuseppe Verdi unveiled in 1906, five years after the Italian composer's death. The statue sits on a cylindrical pedestal; figures of four of his

> **NOT TO BE MISSED:**
>
> **Strawberry Fields • Church of the Blessed Sacrament • Soldiers' and Sailors' Monument**

characters surround the base—Falstaff, Aida, Otello, and Leonora. An ornate **subway kiosk,** designed in 1904, graces the island across the intersection. At 2100 Broadway, the **former Central Savings Bank** building (1928) is an imposing backdrop for the Verdi statue.

From Broadway to Riverside Drive

Proceed north (uptown) along Broadway, where you can browse for books and CDs among the street stalls. The beaux arts **Ansonia Hotel,** at No. 2109 (*bet. W. 73rd & 74th Sts.*), is one of New York's most acclaimed apartment buildings. The Broadway ground floor now houses mainly retail space; the entrance is around the corner on West 73rd Street. Architect Paul E. M. Duboy gave this ornamented building its Parisian flair. Solid construction for fireproofing made its apartments soundproof, which pleased its tenants and guests, including Igor Stravinsky, Enrico Caruso, and Babe Ruth.

Turn left on West 77th Street to No. 250. The beaux arts **Hotel Belleclaire** (1901) is the first known design of architect Emery Roth, Sr. Continue on West 77th Street to West End Avenue. The **West End Collegiate Church ❺** (*368 West End Ave.*) is an 1893 Dutch Renaissance structure marked by stepped gables. It is a direct descendant of New Amsterdam's first church (a Dutch Reformed church built in 1628); No. 312 was for

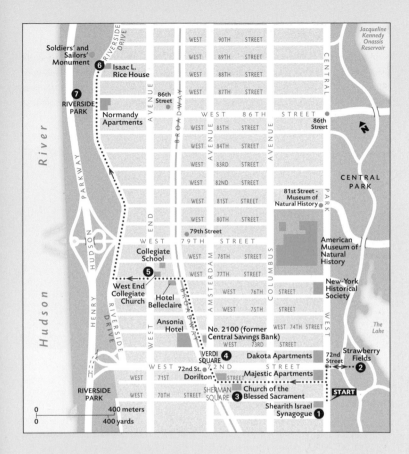

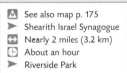

many years home to jazz legend Miles Davis. Walk west, to Riverside Drive, and turn right to an area lined with stunning homes, with a historic district of 1890s row houses between West 80th and 81st Streets. Those by architect Clarence F. True are Nos. 103, 104, 105, and 107–109.

At 140 Riverside Drive (the entrance is around the corner on West 86th Street), the 19-story **Normandy Apartments** by Emery Roth combine art deco touches with details borrowed from the Italian Renaissance. One of two freestanding mansions remaining on Riverside Drive, the **Isaac L. Rice House 6**, at the intersection of 89th Street, was designed by Herts and Tallent, theatrical designers. The 100-foot-tall (30.5 m)

⛰	See also map p. 175
➤	Shearith Israel Synagogue
↔	Nearly 2 miles (3.2 km)
⏱	About an hour
➤	Riverside Park

Soldiers' and Sailors' Monument, honoring the Civil War dead, is opposite in **Riverside Park 7**.

Both Riverside Drive and Riverside Park are designated scenic landmarks. The land was set aside in 1865 to enhance real estate values and, in 1873, Frederick Law Olmsted designed the park. Sloping down toward the Hudson, it's a perfect place to relax after your long walk.

NEW-YORK HISTORICAL SOCIETY

Founded in 1804, the New-York Historical Society is the oldest museum in the city and the second oldest in the country. The society's name proudly retains the hyphen in New-York that was in use when the society was founded. Its holdings include the country's largest collection of Tiffany lamps, John James Audubon's original watercolors for his *Birds of America*, millions of books and manuscripts, as well as a special 9/11 archive.

The granite-faced exterior of the society's austere neoclassical home

New-York Historical Society

- Map p. 175
- 170 Central Park West, bet. 76th & 77th Sts.
- 212/873–3400
- Closed Mon., library closed Sun.–Mon.
- $$
- Subway: B, C to 81st St.– Museum of Natural History

nyhistory.org

The museum moved to its present neoclassical building in 1908. The entrance on West 77th Street leads into an elegant hall, with several galleries and a gift shop. Recent exhibits of note have included "Harry Potter: A History of Magic," in celebration of the first book's 20th anniversary.

There are more galleries on the next three floors. The second floor holds the **Department of Prints, Photographs, and Architectural Collections.** Also here is **Dexter Hall,** with 19th-century masterpieces from the society's permanent collection. Among the artists represented are Thomas Cole and John Trumbull. The **Henry Luce Center,** on the fourth floor, is an innovative display of nearly 40,000 objects covering 400 years of American history. The Luce Center holds rare materials, such as the original Audubon watercolors.

More Highlights

The **Luman Reed Gallery,** named for a 19th-century collector and patron of the arts, is a re-creation of the picture gallery at Reed's 13 Greenwich Street residence, where he lived in the 1830s. Reed believed that art was important to the development of the nation and commissioned Thomas Cole, the founder of the Hudson River school of landscape painting, to create a five-part allegory. "The Course of Empire" is the focal point of the gallery here, but it also holds Dutch, Flemish, German, and Italian paintings and engravings.

The **9/11 Collections** are particularly affecting. After the attack on the World Trade Center, the New-York Historical Society compiled, catalogued, and exhibited historical evidence. Staff members gathered artifacts at the site and thousands of 9/11-related objects from sources including the Fresh Kills Landfill, police and fire departments, the 24-hour relief centers at St. Paul's Chapel, and Nino Vendome's Canal Street restaurant.

Finally, the society's library is well worth visiting, and no appointment is needed. Its scope is immense, with 600,000 volumes and more than a million manuscripts, including the first printing of Lincoln's Second Inaugural Address. An outstanding collection of 18th-century newspapers includes the city's earliest, the *New-York Gazette* (1725–1744) and John Peter Zenger's *New-York Weekly Journal.*

Specialized Collections

The silver collection, with objects from the colonial through Victorian periods, includes work by New York silversmith Myer Myers and flatware that belonged to such important families as the Roosevelts and the Schuylers. The **Neustadt Collection** of Tiffany lamps was compiled by a New York physician in the latter half of the 20th century. The **Bella C. Landauer Collection of Business and Advertising Ephemera,** with more than one million items, is open by appointment only.

History

The society has its roots in a collection of "everything and from whatever clime," assembled by John Pintard, one of its founders, and briefly displayed in City Hall in 1791. The historical society is also an art museum, the only one in New York until the Metropolitan Museum of Art opened in 1870. In 1858 the society received the collection of Luman Reed, a wealthy grocer; when he died in 1836, friends arranged for his art collection to be displayed to the public—an enterprise they called the New York Gallery of Fine Arts—in the Rotunda in City Hall Park. When the Rotunda closed, the collection was given to the Historical Society. ■

EXPERIENCE: Live the High Life—Great New York Views

No city does a room with a view like New York. On the Upper West Side, the **Press Lounge** (*653 11th Ave., tel 877/843–8869*) is a stunning rooftop bar at the Ink 48 Hotel. It's so far west that you can see the Manhattan skyline ... from Manhattan. For a dramatic trip into the fictitious, try the rooftop at the "McKittrick Hotel" in Chelsea for interactive performances atop the **Gallow Green Rooftop** (*mckittrickhotel.com/gallow-green*). **Gaonnuri** (see Travelwise p. 242), a superb Korean restaurant hidden in an office building, is another secret Manhattan spot with great views. To look across to Brooklyn, dine at **Riverpark** (see Travelwise pp. 244). To enjoy the Manhattan skyline from afar, try the elegant **River Café** under the Brooklyn Bridge (see Travelwise p. 255).

For the ultimate view of New York and its boroughs, visit the **Observation Deck** on the 102nd floor of One World Trade Center (Freedom Tower, see p. 63).

AMERICAN MUSEUM OF NATURAL HISTORY

With its huge skeletons of dinosaurs and dioramas of cavemen, the American Museum of Natural History is a great place to take children. But, make no mistake, it is not a museum primarily for them. It is a complex scientific and educational institution and one of the largest and most important museums in the world. Sprawled out over four square blocks, the museum owns nearly 40 million specimens (including 96 percent of all known species of birds).

The reproduction of a *Barosaurus* dominates the Theodore Roosevelt Rotunda on the second floor of the museum.

Visitors—more than three million a year—must decide what and how much to see in the museum's maze of buildings. There are guided tours of certain exhibits, but many people solve the problem by heading straight for something they know. Often this is the dinosaurs; the reproduction of the 55-foot (16.8 m) *Barosaurus* in the second-floor Rotunda stops people in their tracks, and many more dinosaurs await on the fourth floor. Some visitors head for the North American Indian exhibits, or the **Milstein Hall of Ocean Life,** with its giant blue whale immersed in a virtual ocean, or the **Hall of Biodiversity,** featuring an African rain forest: Both are on the first floor, but there is much from which to choose.

The first floor of the museum includes halls and exhibit spaces devoted to birds, invertebrates, North American mammals, fish, forests, and the environment of New York State. The **Hall of the Northwest Coast Indians** has two imposing lines of totem poles running down the center of the room. A 34-ton (30.8 metric tons) piece of a meteorite discovered in 1894 in Greenland

and excavated by explorer Robert Peary is a highlight of the **Arthur Ross Hall of Meteorites.** The **Hall of Gems** includes the 563-carat "Star of India" sapphire that J. P. Morgan donated to the museum in 1900.

The second-floor **Whitney Hall of Oceanic Birds** is named after Harry Payne Whitney, who supported the museum's ornithological research and collecting expeditions in the 1920s and 1930s.

On the third floor is the **Margaret Mead Hall of Pacific Peoples,** reflecting the studies of anthropologist Margaret Mead, who worked in the museum's Anthropology Department until

Evolution of Vertebrates," a video presentation narrated by Meryl Streep, shown in the 200-seat theater. The **Hall of Saurischian Dinosaurs** (those that could walk upright) includes mounted skeletons of *Tyrannosaurus rex* and *Apatosaurus,* the latter sporting a longer tail after a recent reinstallation. The **Hall of Ornithischian Dinosaurs** includes the armored *Stegosaurus,* discovered in Wyoming, and *Styracosaurus,* with a spiked neck and nose. Two halls in the **Lila Acheson Wallace Wing of Mammals and Their Extinct Relatives** showcase 250 fossils, including mastodons, saber-toothed cats, and giant sloths. Highlights are a baby mammoth and a 12-million-year-old

American Museum of Natural History

🅰 Map p. 175

✉ Central Park West at 79th St.

☎ 212/769–5100 or 212/769–5200 (reservation for special events)

💲 Donation ($$-$$$ online, to avoid queues)

🚇 Subway: B, C to 81st St.– Museum of Natural History; 1 to 79th St.

amnh.org

NOTE:
The museum has a useful interactive floor plan on its website: *amnh.org/plan-your-visit/interactive-floor-plan.*

Liftoff at the Rose Center for Earth and Space

The Rose Center, part of the American Museum of Natural History, is one of New York's most recent architectural icons; here you can experience a multisensorial approach to the universe. Its heart is a gleaming glass cube enveloping the four-million-pound (1.8 million kg) **Hayden Sphere.** In the **Hayden Planetarium,** visitors experience outer space via the world's largest and most powerful virtual reality simulator. Other areas include the **Hall of Planet Earth** (HoPE), the **Hall of the Universe,** the **Scales of the Universe,** and the dynamic **Cosmic Pathway,** a spiraling ramp that ushers visitors down through 13 billion years of cosmic evolution.

her death in 1978. Other halls on the floor include ones devoted to reptiles and amphibians, eastern Woodland and Plains Indians, primates, and North American birds.

Six halls on the grandly restored fourth floor follow 500 million years of the evolution of vertebrates—animals with backbones. The **Miriam and Ira D. Wallach Orientation Center** and the **Hall of Vertebrate Origins** introduce the story. Start by viewing "The

horse, *Protohippus.* The refurbished 3,100-square-foot (2,880 sq m) Audubon Gallery reopened to the public (in 2007) for the first time in decades, showcasing original paintings and lithographs by John James Audubon and sons. Throughout the museum are opportunities for shopping, dining, and entertainment: including the Dino Store, the Cosmic Shop, the Main Shop, the IMAX theater, the Museum Food Court, the Starlight Café, and more.

Rose Center for Earth and Space

✉ Central Park West at 81st St.

☎ 212/769–5100 or 212/769–5200 (reservation for Hayden Planetarium)

🚇 Subway: B, C to 81st St.– Museum of Natural History

The equestrian statue at the museum's main entrance is by James Earle Fraser and shows a vigorous Theodore Roosevelt, flanked by two guides, one African, the other Native American.

The museum strives to exhibit its specimens in the most educational and compelling manner. Thus, the **Spitzer Hall of Human Origins** (*first floor*) contains dioramas of our hominid ancestors in action that capture the drama inherent in the story of man. Similarly, the dioramas in the **Akeley Memorial Hall of African Mammals** (*second floor*) are startlingly realistic in their detail. Many demonstrations, talks, and special events—such as the popular "Butterfly Conservatory" (an annual event) and "Meet the Scientist Day"—are designed for children. This grand institution always surprises and delivers more than one could possibly expect.

INSIDER TIP:
Once a year, in early summer, the American Museum of Natural History holds an ID Day: Experts will examine and analyze any natural artifacts you've had for years or found recently.

—PETER GWIN
National Geographic writer

The museum has begun its 300 million dollar expansion, which should be completed before the end of 2020. The Richard Gilder Center for Science, Education, and Innovation will add 135,000 square feet (12,500 sq m) of display space and laboratories to the structure. The innovative exterior design was inspired by recycling. ■

EXPERIENCE: Debating the Ultimate Bagel

If you've never had an authentic New York City bagel before, make sure to sample this quintessential New York breakfast from at least one of the establishments below—then feel free to join the everlasting debate as to who makes the best, whether a bagel should be toasted or not (if fresh and warm, no need to toast, we say), or whether a bagel should be eaten plain or with a schmear of cream cheese and salmon (freshly sliced Nova, of course). In recent years, oversize doughy bagels have made their appearance with increasing frequency, but these do not compare to the dense and chewy traditional bagels that are smaller, more compact, and more flavorful, with a hint of crunch to the exterior.

To enjoy Manhattan bagels like a real New Yorker (or to take some home and store in the freezer for extended eating), try a weeklong bagel-a-day sampling, including stops at **Absolute Bagels** (*2788 Broadway, near 107th St., tel 212/932–2052*); **Bagel Oasis** (*183–12 Horace Harding Expressway, Fresh Meadows, Queens, tel 718/359–9245*); **Brown Bagels** (*132 W. 31st St., Midtown, tel 212/971–0002*); **Chelsea Bagel & Café** (*139 W 14th St, tel 212/980–1010*); **Ess-a-Bagel** (*831 Third Ave. at 50th St. & 51st St., Midtown, tel 212/980–1010*); **H&H Bagels** (*1551 2nd Ave at 80th St. & 81st St., tel 212/734–7441*); and **Murray's Bagels** (*500 Sixth Ave. at 13th St., tel 212/462–2830*).

MORE PLACES TO VISIT IN THE UPPER WEST SIDE

Central Park West, a grand counterpart to the millionaires' mansions of the Upper East Side, is graced by the dramatic silhouettes of multi-towered apartment buildings. These monumental structures are especially concentrated between West 62nd and West 91st Streets. In the same area, several smaller and specialized Upper West Side museums might well be of interest.

American Folk Art Museum

Self-taught folk artists have spent lifetimes building castles out of old bottles or creating remarkable paintings, sculptures, or other fine artworks. The American Folk Art Museum has amassed more than 7,000 works that span a period from the 18th century to today and include compelling portraits and fascinating quilts. The most remarkable are on display at the museum halls in the Upper West Side. Recent exhibitions include "Charting the Divine Plan: The Art of Orra White Hitchcock (1796–1863)."

Bard Graduate Center Gallery

At this interesting, intimate gallery, located inside the art faculty of the Bard Graduate Center, visitors can see pioneering exhibits of decorative arts, design history, and material culture. Organized with the assistance of eminent researchers, curators, and institutions from all over the world, the exhibitions display a vast range of objects including some on loan from public and private collections, many of which have never been seen before in New York.

■ The Dakota Apartments were built in 1884.

Central Park West

Several of the impressive buildings along Central Park West were either built or commissioned by the Irwin Chanin Company. Chanin first encountered art deco at the 1925 Paris Exposition and, on his return, introduced the style in his New York buildings, including the 1931 **Century Apartments** (*25 Central Park W. at 62nd to 63rd Sts.*). The **New York Society for Ethical Culture** (*2 W. 64th St., tel 212/874–5210*) is an austere art nouveau building

American Folk Art Museum

🅰 Map p. 175

✉ 2 Lincoln Sq., bet. 65th & 66th Sts.

☎ 212/595–9533

🕐 Closed Mon.

🚇 Subway: 1 to 66th St.–Lincoln Center

folkartmuseum.org

■ **The eclectic interior of the Nicholas Roerich Museum**

Bard Graduate Center Gallery

- Map p. 175
- 18 W 86th St.
- 212/501–3023
- Closed Mon.; free entrance Wed.
- Subway: 1, 2 to 86th St.

bgc.bard.edu/gallery

Children's Museum of Manhattan

- Map p. 175
- 212 W. 83rd St.
- 212/721–1234
- Closed Mon.
- $$
- B, C to 81st St.–Museum of Natural History; 1 to 86th St.

cmom.org

Nicholas Roerich Museum

- Map p. 175
- 319 W. 107th St. at Riverside Dr.
- 212/864–7752
- Closed Mon. & a.m. daily
- Subway: 1 to Cathedral Parkway–110th St.

roerich.org

of 1910. This humanist religious organization was instrumental in the founding of the ACLU and the NAACP. The heavily ornamental art deco brick building at 55 Central Park West (*cnr. of 66th St.*) was the setting for the 1984 film *Ghostbusters.*

At 1 West 67th Street, the **Hotel des Artistes** opened in 1918. Residents of the kitchenless apartments ordered their meals from the ground-floor **Café des Artistes.** Although the apartments now have kitchens, the café remained one of the city's most popular restaurants until it finally closed in 2009. Architect Henry J. Hardenbergh's **Dakota Apartments** (*1 W. 72nd St.*) were completed in 1884. The German Renaissance-style structure was named after the Dakota Territory, in response to criticism of the building's then remote location. Its many celebrity occupants have included actress Lauren Bacall, singer Roberta Flack, and Yoko Ono and John Lennon, who was shot out front in 1980. The **San Remo** (1930), between 74th and 75th

Streets, features neoclassical trim and circular Roman towers. Past the beaux arts New-York Historical Society (see pp. 182–183) and the American Museum of Natural History (see pp. 184–186), the **Beresford** (*211 Central Park W. at 81st St.*) has three baroque towers. In the 1950s, resident Alan Jay Lerner wrote the lyrics for *My Fair Lady* here. The 1931 **Eldorado** (*300 Central Park W., bet. 90th & 91st Sts.*) has art deco trim. Novelist Sinclair Lewis lived here in the 1940s in what he described as a "gaudy flat, a cross between Elizabeth Arden's Beauty Salon and the horse-stables at the Ringling Circus Winter Quarters."

Children's Museum of Manhattan

Near Broadway, the five floors of this fun museum are devoted to educational activities and hands-on exhibits for children and include a room of children's books and a television studio.

Nicholas Roerich Museum

Farther uptown, this museum is dedicated to Russian-born Nicholas Roerich (1874–1947), a mystic, philosopher, stage designer, painter, and writer. He was nominated for a Nobel Peace Prize for his proposal (ratified in the U.S. as the Roerich Pact in 1935) that important cultural, scientific, and religious sites be protected by treaty in wartime as in peacetime. The museum contains about 200 of his paintings, examples of his writings, and art from his collection. ■

A medieval cloister, a renowned university, an immense cathedral, and a melting pot of different races and ethnic groups

THE HEIGHTS & HARLEM

■ An arcade at The Cloisters in Fort Tryon Park

| THE HEIGHTS & HARLEM

As the island of Manhattan narrows at its northern end, it also rises in an undulating and disorderly sequence of rocky outcroppings, escarpments, ridges, plateaus, and bluffs until it reaches its greatest elevation—267.75 feet (81.61 m)— near where Fort Washington once stood. Here, during the Revolution, American troops made a last stand against the British before being driven from the island.

Northern Manhattan is made up of several historic neighborhoods. At the northernmost tip is ethnically diverse Inwood, where, some believe, Peter Minuit "bought" the island from the Indians. To the south is Washington Heights, today home to immigrants from the Dominican Republic. Here the streets teem with life, convenience stores are called bodegas, and Spanish is the preferred language.

Farther south is Hamilton Heights, home to Ecuadoreans, Chinese, Dominicans, and African Americans, among others. Within Hamilton Heights is Sugar Hill (*W. 145th St. to W. 155th St., bet. Amsterdam & Edgecombe Aves.*), a well-to-do neighborhood that was the epicenter of the Harlem Renaissance. And between 125th and 110th Streets is Morningside Heights, where Columbia University—nearly 22,500 students

enrolled in its 17 schools—and its women's affiliate, Barnard College, are at the heart of a lively neighborhood.

The eastern section of northern Manhattan is Harlem, world-famous in the 1920s as a vital center of African-American culture. Harlem was Jewish, German, and Irish until 1905, when an African-American realtor, Philip A. Payton, rented apartments to African Americans in a building on West 133rd Street. Today, the demographics are shifting and national chains are investing in this prime marketplace. As you exit the subway at 125th Street, a Starbucks awaits, along with the famed Apollo Theater.

When northern Manhattan was truly the hinterlands, Manhattanites such as Alexander Hamilton and John James Audubon owned large tracts of land there. On the northern edge of Harlem is onetime Coogan's Bluff, a turn-of-the-19th-century neighborhood on the Harlem River between 155th and 160th Streets. Here the revered Polo Grounds once stood, home of the New York Giants from the 1890s until the baseball team moved to San Francisco in 1957.

Fort Tryon Park, with its splendid view of the Hudson River, is the location of The Cloisters Museum, the best assemblage of medieval art and architectural elements in America. Near Columbia in Morningside Heights is the Cathedral Church of St. John the Divine, the largest Gothic cathedral in the world. In Riverside Park, the General Grant National Memorial is the final resting place of the 18th U.S. president.

Audubon Terrace is an enclave of buildings housing cultural institutions, such as the American Academy and Institute of Arts and Letters, an honor society of 250 writers,

NOT TO BE MISSED:

Visiting the world's largest Gothic cathedral, St. John the Divine 192

Strolling Columbia University's classical quad 193

The grandeur of Grant's Tomb 194

The medieval art and quiet gardens at The Cloisters 195–197

Exploring 125th Street, Harlem's main drag 198–199, 202

Taking in a show at the Apollo 199

Dining at Red Rooster, one of Harlem's hippest soul-food restaurants 199

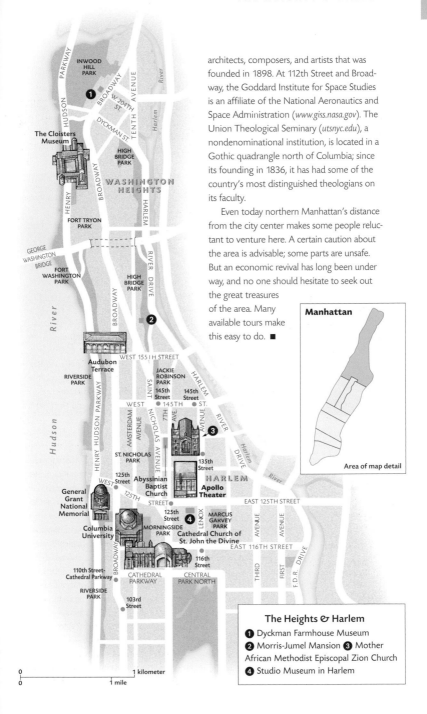

architects, composers, and artists that was founded in 1898. At 112th Street and Broadway, the Goddard Institute for Space Studies is an affiliate of the National Aeronautics and Space Administration (*www.giss.nasa.gov*). The Union Theological Seminary (*utsnyc.edu*), a nondenominational institution, is located in a Gothic quadrangle north of Columbia; since its founding in 1836, it has had some of the country's most distinguished theologians on its faculty.

Even today northern Manhattan's distance from the city center makes some people reluctant to venture here. A certain caution about the area is advisable; some parts are unsafe. But an economic revival has long been under way, and no one should hesitate to seek out the great treasures of the area. Many available tours make this easy to do. ■

Manhattan

Area of map detail

INWOOD HILL PARK

The Cloisters Museum

HIGH BRIDGE PARK

WASHINGTON HEIGHTS

FORT TRYON PARK

GEORGE WASHINGTON BRIDGE

FORT WASHINGTON PARK

HIGH BRIDGE PARK

River

Hudson

Audubon Terrace

WEST 155TH STREET

RIVERSIDE PARK

JACKIE ROBINSON PARK

145th Street   145th Street

WEST   145TH   ST.

ST. NICHOLAS PARK

125th Street

General Grant National Memorial

Abyssinian Baptist Church

125TH STREET

HARLEM

Apollo Theater

EAST 125TH STREET

125th Street

Columbia University

MORNINGSIDE PARK

MARCUS GARVEY PARK

Cathedral Church of St. John the Divine

EAST 116TH STREET

116th Street

110th Street-Cathedral Parkway

CATHEDRAL PARKWAY

CENTRAL PARK NORTH

RIVERSIDE PARK

103rd Street

0   1 kilometer
0   1 mile

The Heights & Harlem
❶ Dyckman Farmhouse Museum
❷ Morris-Jumel Mansion ❸ Mother African Methodist Episcopal Zion Church
❹ Studio Museum in Harlem

CATHEDRAL CHURCH OF ST. JOHN THE DIVINE

Because it has taken more than a century (and counting) to build, the Cathedral Church of St. John the Divine in Morningside Heights has had, for many years, the distinction of being both a landmark of New York's cultural and religious landscape and a work in progress.

■ Greg Wyatt's Peace Fountain, next to the cathedral, dramatizes the struggle between good and evil.

Cathedral Church of St. John the Divine

🄰 Map p. 191

✉ 1047 Amsterdam Ave. at W. 112th St.

☎ 212/316–7540

💲 Donation

🚇 Subway: 1 to Cathedral Parkway—110th St.

stjohndivine.org

The cornerstone was laid on St. John's Day, December 27, 1892. The construction of the choir and crossing was begun in the Byzantine-Romanesque style. In 1911, architect Ralph Adam Crams took over; his nave and west front were in French Gothic style. Building ceased during World War II, resuming in 1979. Although damaged by fire in 2001, the cathedral continues to evolve and extend its mission of social activism.

The Episcopal bishop at the time construction began was Henry Codman Potter, who believed the cathedral should serve all creeds, nations, and levels of society. St. John's today lives up to this philosophy, engaging in community service and work among the poor. Church outreach activities include concerts, art exhibits, lectures, theater, and holiday offerings. The main attraction, however, remains the incredible structure itself. You can marvel at the beauteous interior—the nave alone is 248 feet (75.5 m) long and 124 feet (38 m) high; more than 10,000 pieces of glass are in the 40-foot-diameter (12 m) Great Rose Window. ■

COLUMBIA UNIVERSITY

As a leading light of the Ivy League, Columbia University, located in upper Manhattan's Morningside Heights, is both an integral part of New York City and its history and an educational entity set apart from it.

The university's location in the heart of the Morningside Heights neighborhood means that this is no ivory tower, isolated from the citizenry. While there is a large distinct quad, there are also many places in its seven-block campus (between Amsterdam Avenue and Broadway) where you can pass between the university grounds and the city streets without knowing it. The **Wallach Art Gallery** in Lenfest Center of the Arts has changing exhibits on art history and visual arts. The adjacent streets offer many coffee-houses, ethnic restaurants, and bookshops.

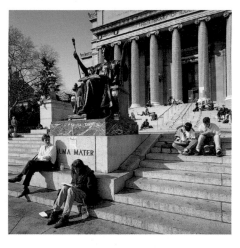

Daniel Chester French's 1903 "Alma Mater" graces the steps of Columbia University's Low Library.

From Downtown to Uptown

Chartered in 1754, Columbia first met in the schoolhouse of Trinity Church in Lower Manhattan. Colonial-era graduates included Alexander Hamilton and DeWitt Clinton. It moved to Madison Avenue and 49th Street in 1857. This tract of land on Fifth Avenue between 47th and 51st Streets eventually became home to Rockefeller Center. The university moved to its Morningside Heights campus in 1897.

At its heart was domed **Low Library,** modeled on the Roman Pantheon. It is named for Seth Low, donor of the library, and

Columbia's president from 1890 to 1901. He moved the university to Morningside Heights, added the School of Nursing and the Teachers' College, and strengthened ties with Barnard, Columbia's affiliated women's college. In 1934, Low Library was turned into administrative offices. However, it remains—together with Daniel Chester French's huge bronze statue, "Alma Mater" (1903), at the foot of the library's steps—a symbol of a great university.

Among other campus buildings, **St. Paul's Chapel** on the main quad, and McKim, Mead & White's 1927 **Casa Italiana** on Amsterdam Avenue, stand out. ■

Columbia University
- Map p. 191
- Broadway & W. 116th St.
- 212/854–1754 or 212/854–4900 (visitor center & tours)
- Subway: 1 to 116th St.– Columbia University

columbia.edu

Wallach Art Gallery
- 212/854–6800
- Closed Mon.– Tues. & a.m. daily

wallach.columbia.edu

GENERAL GRANT NATIONAL MEMORIAL

Grant's Tomb, the largest mausoleum in the United States, was until World War I one of the most popular sights in New York City. A former president of the United States, a native of the Midwest, and a victorious commander of Union forces in the Civil War, Ulysses S. Grant (1822–1885) moved to New York in 1884.

General Grant National Memorial

Map p. 191

Riverside Dr. & W. 122nd St.

646/670-7251

Subway: 1 to 116th St.–Columbia University

nps.gov/gegr

■ The tomb of Ulysses S. Grant, the only U.S. president buried in New York City, overlooks the Hudson River.

Grant was immensely popular when he died. One million people observed his funeral procession in 1885. Mayor William R. Grace donated the land for the tomb, and the Grant Memorial Association raised $600,000 to build it. President Benjamin Harrison laid the cornerstone in 1892.

Architect John H. Duncan's 150-foot-tall (45 m) granite tomb consists of a domed rotunda ringed by Ionic columns atop a square base. Over the entrance, carved figures representing Victory and Peace flank a plaque inscribed with Grant's famous words, "Let Us Have Peace."

The interior of the tomb, a cruciform in Carrara marble, is based on Napoleon's Tomb in Paris. Grant's military victories and Robert E. Lee's surrender at Appomattox are the subjects of mosaics above the windows. A double staircase leads down to the crypt where Grant and his wife, Julia Dent Grant, are interred. Bronze busts along the wall depict Grant's generals, among them William Tecumseh Sherman and Philip Sheridan. The tomb was taken over by the National Park Service in 1959 and restored in 1997.

Ulysses S. Grant died on July 23, 1885, at the age of 63. ■

THE CLOISTERS MUSEUM & NEARBY

At the far north of Manhattan, nestled on a cliff within flower-planted Fort Tryon Park, stands The Cloisters, devoted to art and architecture of the Middle Ages. Many people find a visit to be a uniquely contemplative experience. The surrounding area hosts an eclectic array of historic and cultural sites.

The Cloisters

The Cloisters opened to the public in 1938 as a branch museum of the Metropolitan Museum of Art. The arcades of four different medieval cloisters have been integrated to create a sympathetic context for the exhibition of sculpture, tapestry, stained glass, metalwork, paintings, and manuscripts. "Cloister" denotes a covered walkway surrounding a large open courtyard with access to other monastic buildings. In similar manner, the museum's cloisters are passageways to galleries.

The nucleus of the collection, including large sections of the medieval buildings, was gathered by American sculptor George Grey Barnard (1863–1938) while he was living in France. In 1925, John D. Rockefeller, Jr., purchased the collection for the Metropolitan Museum of Art. He also provided the building and its Fort Tryon setting and donated works from his own collection.

Four Cloisters: The main level, where one enters, contains a number of gallery areas enclosing two cloisters. The capitals of the 12th-century **Cuxa Cloister** have robust Romanesque carvings of double-bodied animals with a single head, a design that fits corners well. In the **St. Guilhem Cloister,** built about A.D. 804 by a peer of Charlemagne's court, drill holes in a honeycomb pattern embellish the capitals. On the lower level, **Trie Cloister** is from a 16th-century convent

---

---

destroyed by Huguenots. And encompassing a medieval herb garden, the **Bonnefont Cloister** is from the late 13th or early 14th century. Its naturalistic floral decorations were a reaction to grotesque Romanesque carvings.

The museum is organized in roughly chronological manner,

The Cloisters Museum

- Map p. 191
- Fort Tryon Park, W. 190th St. at Fort Washington Ave.
- 212/923–3700
- Closed Mon.
- $$ (see pp. 138–139)
- Subway: A to 190th St.

metmuseum.org/cloisters

Heather Garden at Fort Tryon Park

- Map p. 191
- W. 190th St., just inside the gateway of Margaret Corbin Circle

forttryonparktrust.org

■ The plantings at The Cloisters' garden were inspired by the museum's famed Unicorn Tapestries.

**Dyckman
Farmhouse
Museum**

🅰 Map p. 191

✉ 4881 Broadway
at W. 204th St.

☎ 212/304–9422

🕐 Open Thur.–Sat.

💲 Donation

🚇 Subway: A
to Inwood–
207th St.

**dyckmanfarmhouse
.org**

beginning with art from the Romanesque period, continuing through the Gothic era, and ending with the flowering of medieval art around 1520. Although every space contains superb art, especially popular on the main floor are the 15th-century stained-glass panels in the **Boppard Room;** the idealized funerary monument in the **Gothic Chapel** of a crusader knight portrayed as young man, eyes open and hands joined in prayer; and the **Unicorn Tapestries Room,** where six woven tapestries (circa 16th century, Brussels) tell an allegorical story of the Incarnation of Christ. Downstairs, the **Treasury** displays small objects, such as a 12th-century walrus ivory cross, while the **Glass Gallery** contains glass, sculpture, and tapestries.

You will also want to visit the excellent gift shop and bookstore, try out the café, and take advantage of the spectacular views of the Hudson River from the grounds. Be forewarned: Some bus tours leave you at the base of the hill, so expect a walk.

Dyckman Farmhouse Museum

Just northeast of The Cloisters is the Dyckman Farmhouse Museum, a Dutch colonial house with gambrel roof and overhanging eaves. Until 1871 it belonged to the Dyckman family, owners of Manhattan's largest farm in colonial times (some 300 acres/121 ha surrounding the house). The house was rebuilt in 1783 after the British destroyed it before evacuating the city. Early in the 20th century two Dyckman descendants repurchased the house, furnished it in period style, and then donated it to the city. Manhattan's only remaining farmhouse, it opened as a museum in 1916. There is a formal garden in the rear.

Audubon Terrace

A couple of miles south of The Cloisters, Audubon Terrace is a distinguished beaux arts complex that was built, beginning in 1904, on farmland that once belonged to painter and naturalist John James Audubon. Railroad magnate Archer Milton Huntington developed the site as a museum complex, with Spanish Renaissance buildings around a long plaza adorned with monumental statuary. Today these house the American Academy of Arts and Letters, the Hispanic Society of America (which Huntington founded in 1904), and Boricua College, founded in 1974 to meet the needs of Puerto Rican and other Hispanic students.

Also on the site, entered only via 156th Street, is the exquisite **Church of Our Lady of Esperanza.** Señora Doña Manuela de Laverrerie de Barril, wife of the Spanish consul-general in New York, founded it as a church for Spanish-speaking people. After her untimely death, Huntington saw the church through to completion in 1911. In 1912, Spain's King Alfonso XIII donated the stained-glass windows, skylight, and lamp.

The **American Academy of Arts and Letters,** an organization of artists and writers, limited to 250 living members, is housed in two buildings designed by McKim, Mead & White, and Cass Gilbert. These house the North and South Galleries, where annual exhibitions in March and May are open to the public. Original members included Henry Adams, William and Henry James, Theodore Roosevelt, Augustus Saint-Gaudens, John La Farge, and Mark Twain.

The Ghosts of the Morris-Jumel Mansion

Near Audubon Terrace, the Morris-Jumel Mansion was built in 1765 by a British military officer, Roger Morris. It served as George Washington's headquarters for a month in 1776 before the British took it over. A French merchant, Stephen Jumel, and his American wife, Eliza Bowen, restored it in 1810. After Jumel's death, Bowen, a former prostitute, was married briefly to Aaron Burr, formerly vice president, who divorced her. The house, a museum since 1904, is noted for its Palladian portico, an octagon room, and Georgian interiors ... and its ghosts. Strange phenomena have been attributed to the ghosts of the Jumels and of Burr.

The museum and reference library of **Hispanic Society of America** with more than 200,000 books and manuscripts are an outstanding resource for the study of the arts and cultures of Spain, Portugal, and Latin America. ■

Audubon Terrace
- Map p. 191
- Broadway bet. 155th & 156th Sts.
- Subway: 1 to 157th St.

Church of Our Lady of Esperanza
- 624 W. 156th St.
- 212/283–4340

American Academy of Arts and Letters
- 633 W. 155th St.
- 212/368–5900
- artsandletters.org

Hispanic Society of America
- 613 W. 155th St.
- 212/926–2234
- Closed for renovation, only by reservation.
- hispanicsociety.org

Morris-Jumel Mansion
- Map p. 191
- 65 Jumel Terrace
- 212/923–8008
- Closed Mon.
- $
- Subway: C to 163rd St.– Amsterdam Ave.
- morrisjumel.org

IN & AROUND HARLEM

Stretching from 110th to 168th Street, Harlem is one of the city's most vibrant neighborhoods. Historically significant as home to the African-American cultural awakening known as the Harlem Renaissance, and later as home to the famed Apollo Theater, Harlem has been undergoing a second renaissance over the past decade, in commerce, culture, property redevelopment, and tourism.

■ 125th Street is a thriving corridor in the heart of Harlem.

Abyssinian Baptist Church

🅰 Map p. 191

✉ 132 Odell Clark Pl. W. at 138th St.

☎ 212/862–7474

🚇 Subway: B, C, 2, 3 to 135th St.

abyssinian.org

NOTE: Harlem Heritage Tours & Cultural Center *(104 Malcolm X Boulevard, tel 212/280–7888, harlemheritage.com)* runs daily tours ($$$$) of Harlem. Reservations are required.

The **St. Nicholas Historic District,** a late 19th-century development of four block fronts along West 138th and 139th Streets between Adam Clayton Powell Jr. and Frederick Douglas Boulevards, is the work of three prominent architects—James Brown Lord, Bruce Price, and Stanford White. During the 1920s the development, known as Striver's Row, was home to many prominent blacks, including surgeon Louis T. Wright, architect Vertner Tandy, and bandleader Fletcher Henderson.

Close by is the **Abyssinian Baptist Church,** known for its prominent minister, Adam Clayton

Powell, Jr. (1908–1972), the first black congressman from New York City. Founded in 1808, its church building dates from 1923. **Mother African Methodist Episcopal Zion Church** (*140 W. 137th St.*) is the oldest black congregation in New York (1796). George W. Foster, Jr., one of the country's first black architects, designed the neo-Gothic building, completed in 1925. Foster collaborated with Vertner Tandy on the 1911 neo-Gothic **St. Philip's Episcopal Church** (*204 W. 134th St.*).

Hamilton Heights Historic District, on Harlem's western edge, includes the fine collection of row houses known as Sugar Hill (*W. 145th to W. 155th Sts., bet. Amsterdam & Edgecombe Aves.*), built in 1886–1906 on land once belonging to Alexander Hamilton. To the south is the **North Campus of City College** (*Convent Ave. bet. W. 138th & W. 140th Sts.*), a collection of Gothic buildings constructed in the early 20th century.

The **Mount Morris Park Historic District** (*W. 118th to 124th Sts., bet. Fifth Ave. & Adam Clayton Powell Jr. Blvd.*) contains a number of landmark churches and some of the city's finest brownstones. The neighborhood takes its name from the park in its center (renamed Marcus Garvey Park in 1973, after the black nationalist leader), which has the city's only remaining fire watchtower. The 1888 **St. Martin's Episcopal Church & Rectory** has been called the finest Romanesque Revival religious complex in the city; it also possesses the smaller (42 bells) of the city's two carillons (the other is at Riverside Church in Morningside Heights).

New businesses and revitalization efforts are enriching Harlem's main east–west thoroughfare, 125th Street (Martin Luther King Boulevard). Upscale stores, multiplex cinemas, and a rejuvenated **Apollo Theater** attract droves of visitors. Built in 1914, the Apollo began featuring black entertainers, such as Bill "Bojangles" Robinson, in the 1930s.

Also on 125th Street—at Adam Clayton Powell Jr. Boulevard (Seventh Avenue)—**Hotel Theresa,** known in its heyday as the Waldorf of Harlem, still stands, although it is now an office building called Theresa Towers. Built in 1913 when 125th Street was a white area, the Theresa did not admit blacks until 1940; by *(continued on p. 202)*

(continued on p. 202)

St. Martin's Episcopal Church & Rectory
- Map p. 191
- 230 Lenox Ave.
- 212/534–4531
- Subway: 2, 3 to 125th St.

Apollo Theater
- Map p. 191
- 253 W. 125th St.
- Tours: 212/531–5337 ($$$); tickets: 212/307–7171 (Ticketmaster)
- Subway: A, B, C to 125th St.
- apollotheater.org

EXPERIENCE: Enjoy the Best of Harlem Today

There's always a lot to do in Harlem, and what you do there ain't nobody's business but your own; but it helps to know some of the main attractions and coolest activities:

• One of New York's best nights out is still Amateur Night at the Apollo. Contact the **Apollo Theater** (see above) to catch the show that has attracted dreamers since Ella Fitzgerald won the contest in 1934.

• Lift your spirit on Sunday by attending **Canaan Baptist Church** (*132 W. 116th St., tel 212/866–0301, cbccnyc.org*). Powerful preaching and uplifting, joyous gospel singing make for a thrilling morning.

• Try **Dinosaur BBQ** (*700 W 125th St, tel 212/694–1777*) by the Hudson River for huge portions and good live music.

• Take a **Harlem is Home Tour** (*tel 917/583–4109 or 212/658–9160, harlemonestop.com*) through Sugar Hill, once home to boxer Joe Louis and author Ralph Ellison. Other historical, cultural, and gospel music tours are available.

• For some of the best down-home southern cooking, you can't beat **Miss Maude's Spoonbread Too** restaurant (*547 Lenox Ave., tel 212/690–3100,*

spoonbreadinc.com/miss_maudes.htm), known for its fried chicken. The restaurant's inexpensive meals begin with a basket of hot corn bread and are served with your choice of sides. Visit a second location, **Miss Mamie's Spoonbread Too** (*366 W. 110th St., tel 212/865–6744, spoonbreadinc.com/miss_mamies.htm*). Owner Norma Jean Darden also caters the best Harlem events.

• **Minton's Playhouse** (*206 W. 118th St., tel 212/243–2222, mintonsharlem.com, closed Mon.–Tues.*) is the latest incarnation of one of Harlem's oldest music clubs, where bebop was born, and Dizzy Gillespie, Charlie Parker, Miles Davis, and Thelonious Monk were "discovered."

• **Red Rooster** (*310 Lenox Ave., tel 212/792–9001, redroosterharlem.com*) is chef Marcus "Joar" Samuelson's new hot spot and an instant hit in Harlem for its great soul food and celebrity clientele.

• View the work of artists of African descent at the **Studio Museum** (see sidebar p. 202), which also offers a wide range of public programs, events, and workshops.

THE HARLEM RENAISSANCE

The cultural flowering of black New York, a period known as the Harlem Renaissance, took place in the liberating years of the 1920s. The black artists, writers, and musicians who gathered in Harlem shared the belief that black culture had the power to improve the status of their race. It was also the first time that black intellectuals looked to Africa, folk culture, and black heroes as a source of racial pride.

Harlem's Cotton Club in its heyday

The roots of the renaissance have been traced back to *The Souls of Black Folk* (1903) by W. E. B. Du Bois. In it he wrote: "The problem of the twentieth century is the problem of the color-line." Later, Du Bois was editor of *The Crisis: A Record of the Darker Races,* a magazine published in 1910 by the National Association for the Advancement of Colored People (NAACP). In its pages, he encouraged blacks to relate to their common African heritage—a philosophy known as Pan-Africanism. Du Bois pinned his hopes on what he called the "New Negro" and the

"Talented Tenth," the privileged group that "rises and pulls all that are worthy of saving up to their vantage ground."

An all-black musical revue, *Shuffle Along,* which opened on Broadway in 1921, giving, in the words of African-American poet Langston Hughes (1902–1967), "a scintillating sendoff to that Negro Vogue in Manhattan," is often cited as the beginning of the Harlem Renaissance. Although the production, which starred Florence Mills, was not much more than a sophisticated minstrel show, it paved the way for other black shows on Broadway, and whites flocked to

Harlem to hear the likes of Fletcher Henderson, Cab Calloway, and Duke Ellington at the Cotton Club and other nightspots.

It was in literature that the spirit of the Harlem Renaissance was best expressed. An early work was "If We Must Die," a sonnet written in 1919 by Claude McKay, a Jamaican immigrant who has been called the Harlem Renaissance's first celebrity. A response to violence against blacks, the poem ended: "Like men we'll face the murderous, cowardly pack / Pressed to the wall, dying, but fighting back!" Other literary highlights included the mid-decade publication of poetry by Countee Cullen and Langston Hughes.

In 1924, Charles Johnson, an African-American sociologist and editor-in-chief of *Opportunity: a Journal of Negro Life,* organized a dinner to introduce Harlem writers to the white publishing establishment. As a result of

■ **Duke Ellington (1899–1974)**

INSIDER TIP:

For a taste of 1920s Harlem, take the "Harlem Renaissance Multimedia Walking Tour" through Harlem Heritage Tours (see p. 198). Over two hours, a lifelong resident of Harlem will show you the sights, complemented with photos and music, that played a part in the historic movement.

—CHARLES E. COBB, JR.
National Geographic writer

the dinner, the editors of a white magazine, *Survey Graphic,* invited Alain Locke, a Phi Beta Kappa graduate of Harvard (1907) and the first African-American Rhodes Scholar, to put together a special issue on "the progressive spirit of contemporary Negro life." The issue became a landmark book, *The New Negro.*

In 1926 white author Carl Van Vechten

(a "Negrotarian," as whites attracted to Harlem were called) published a best-selling novel about Harlem. His book increased interest in Harlem among whites, although it was controversial among blacks.

Visual artists are probably the least remembered from the decade, with the exception of photographer James VanDerZee, who documented the movement and whose work is well represented at the Studio Museum in Harlem (see sidebar p. 202). Illustrator Aaron Douglas did covers for the journal *Opportunity.* Painter William H. Johnson specialized in primitive-style paintings of religious themes. Augusta Savage was the Harlem Renaissance's best-known sculptor and ran the Savage Studio of Arts and Crafts, which reached out to younger artists.

The crash of 1929 and the ensuing Depression effectively killed the Harlem Renaissance. During the 1930s, unemployment in Harlem was five times that of the rest of the city. Looking back on that time, most participants realized that cultural ferment in Harlem had failed to benefit blacks as a whole.

As Langston Hughes put it: "The ordinary Negroes hadn't heard of the Negro Renaissance. And if they had, it hadn't raised their wages any."

Schomburg Center for Research in Black Culture

- ✉ 515 Malcolm X Blvd. (aka Lenox Ave.) at 135th St.
- ☎ 917/275–6975
- 🕐 Closed Sun.
- 🚇 Subway: 2, 3 to 135th St.

schomburg.org

Studio Museum 127 (Studio Museum in Harlem)

- 🗺 Map p. 191
- ✉ 429 W. 127th St. (temporary location)
- ☎ 212/864–4500
- 🕐 Open p.m. Thur.–Sun.
- 🚇 Subway: 2, 3 to 125th St.

studiomuseum.org

Studio Museum in Harlem

Founded in 1967 to provide studio space for Harlem artists, the Studio Museum is a leading museum of black culture.

The museum's permanent collection includes paintings by Romare Bearden, Jacob Lawrence, and Faith Ringgold, and photography by James VanDerZee and Gordon Parks.

In the late 1970s the Studio Museum merged with the James VanDerZee Institute. The museum sponsors lectures, workshops, artists-in-residence programs, and films. It also has a shop selling books and African crafts.

1946, it was celebrated as "social headquarters for Negro America." Heavyweight champion Joe Louis and musicians Duke Ellington, Lena Horne, and Paul Robeson were among its many celebrity guests. From 1948 to 1953, the hotel was the childhood home of late Secretary of Commerce Ron Brown, whose father was manager. By the mid-1950s the Theresa's popularity was beginning to decline. In the early 1960s the hotel housed Malcolm X's Organization of Afro-American Unity.

Though Harlem's main street changes and evolves in pace with the rest of the city, its authenticity remains—in historic sites, sidewalk vendors, and proprietor-run shops, clubs, and restaurants.

Schomburg Center for Research in Black Culture

Named for Arthur A. Schomburg (1874–1938), a black Puerto Rican bibliophile, collector, and scholar, the center is one of the best research facilities in the world for the study of the black experience. Among more than five million items in the collection are 150,000 books, 400 black newspapers, and 1,000 periodicals. Rare books include early editions of the poetry of Phyllis Wheatley, an American slave, and Richard Wright's *Native Son,* in the original manuscript. Its facilities include a theater, art galleries, and bookstore/gift shop.

The center's collection is based on material Schomburg compiled after moving to New York from Puerto Rico in 1891. In 1911 he cofounded the Negro Society for Historical Research. In 1926, the Carnegie Foundation purchased his collection for $10,000. Today it is described as "the most extensive collection of African-American history and culture in America" (5,000 books, 3,000 manuscripts, 2,000 etchings, and thousands of pamphlets). The foundation donated it to the New York Public Library. Shortly afterward, the library moved it to Harlem to the 135th Street Branch Division of Negro Literature, where Schomburg served as curator. The branch library was housed in a 1905 building where renaissance writers often met. In 1980, the collection was moved to an adjacent building; the original building was redone as gallery space for exhibits. ■

Rich ethnic communities, museums, parks, charming historic districts, and—a New York rarity—wide-open spaces

THE OUTER BOROUGHS

The Brooklyn Bridge: A dramatic exit from Manhattan across the East River

THE OUTER BOROUGHS

Gone are the days when a visit to the outer boroughs was a maybe on the list of things to do in New York. Today your top ten destinations will likely include at least one borough. There is something for everyone, from Brooklyn's Prospect Park to the "Artloop" of museums in Queens to the pastas of Arthur Avenue, the Little Italy of the Bronx.

Leading the list of Bronx attractions is the family-friendly Bronx Zoo and the impressive New York Botanical Garden.

Brooklyn also has outstanding cultural institutions. The Brooklyn Academy of Music, known as BAM, is a preeminent performing arts center. The Brooklyn Museum is an institution that would be the pride of any city.

Some people believe Staten Island is the city's undiscovered treasure. It offers unique museums and colonial-era buildings.

Its immigrant populations give Queens a vital, ethnic flavor. But it is the influx of cultural organizations that has caused a spike in tourism. MoMA PS1 Contemporary Art Center broke new ground when it opened its vast exhibit space in 1997, and in 2000 when

NOT TO BE MISSED:

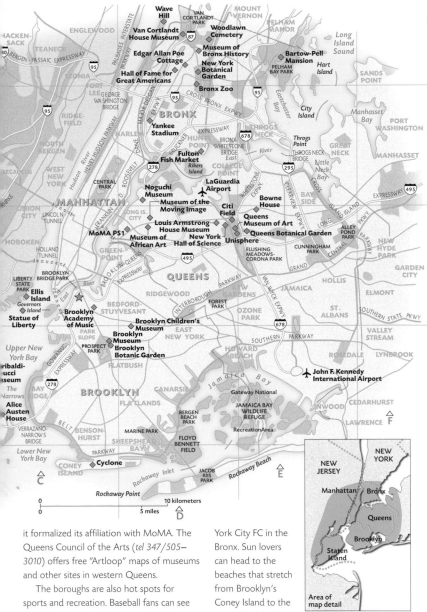

it formalized its affiliation with MoMA. The Queens Council of the Arts (*tel 347/505–3010*) offers free "Artloop" maps of museums and other sites in western Queens.

The boroughs are also hot spots for sports and recreation. Baseball fans can see the Yankees up in the Bronx and the Mets at Queens' Citi Field. Queens also hosts the tennis U.S. Open each summer. Soccer fans can watch the new MLS team New York City FC in the Bronx. Sun lovers can head to the beaches that stretch from Brooklyn's Coney Island to the Long Island Rockaways. Brooklyn and Staten Island both boast excellent nature preserves, including Jamaica Bay Wildlife Refuge. ■

IN & AROUND BROOKLYN

One of New York's most diverse and hippest areas, Brooklyn is now stealing Manhattan's thunder with its many interesting neighborhoods, cultural gems, lively music scene, and unexpected oases. Start with a visit to fashionable Park Slope—a quick subway ride from Lower Manhattan—and work your way east to Prospect Park and its nearby museums and gardens.

■ Victory in a chariot drawn by four horses surmounts the triumphal arch at Grand Army Plaza

St. John's Episcopal Church
✉ 139 St. John's Pl., Brooklyn
☎ 718/783–3928

Grace United Methodist Church
✉ 33 7th Ave., Brooklyn
☎ 718/230–3473

Memorial Presbyterian Church
✉ 186 St. John's Place, Brooklyn
☎ 718/638–5541

Park Slope Historic District

The residential Park Slope Historic District retains better than anywhere else the look and feel of late 19th-century New York. The neighborhood developed in its urban form during the late 19th century, when Prospect Park was in its first decades of bloom and the new Brooklyn Bridge was facilitating an easier commute to Manhattan. By 1890, the Slope had become the richest neighborhood in the United States, its streets sprouting mansions and two- and three-story row houses that have been the very definition of New York style ever since.

The area of greatest interest runs south from Flatbush Avenue, covering the blocks between Prospect Park West and Seventh Avenue. At 25 Eighth Avenue and Lincoln Place, the **Montauk Club** (1889–1891; *closed to the public*) is an old-style men's club whose terra-cotta detailing mixes Venetian palazzo style with sculptural representations of the Montauk Indians. At St. John's Place and Seventh Avenue await three exceptional Gothic-style churches: **St. John's Episcopal Church** (1889), **Grace United Methodist Church** (1883), and **Memorial Presbyterian Church** (1883). The blocks of Seventh Avenue running south of here compose one of the neighborhood's main shopping and restaurant thoroughfares.

Throughout the area, literally thousands of period row houses draw the eye, though some are more significant than others. On **Carroll Street** between Eighth Avenue and Prospect Park West, Nos. 838, 842, and 846 (all dating from 1887) were designed by C. P. H. Gilbert, an in-demand architect among New York's wealthiest families in the late 19th century. Other

INSIDER TIP:

INSIDER TIP:

At the northern reaches of Park Slope, Brooklyn Bridge Park is the Manhattan skyline's optimum photo op stop. The rocky shoreline and grassy knoll give you ample room to contemplate the perfect angle.

—JOHNNA RIZZO
National Geographic writer

examples of his work can be found on neighboring **Montgomery Place** and **Garfield Place,** two of the city's—and the country's—most gorgeous blocks. **Prospect Park West** was known in the 1880s and 1890s as the Gold Coast; its park-facing mansions were also built by New York's elite.

Prospect Park & Environs

Landscape architects Frederick Law Olmsted and Calvert Vaux thought that Prospect Park (1866–1868), abutting Park Slope to the east, was their best effort; today many agree. Unlike Central Park, which is confined in a rectangular box, Prospect Park's 526-acre (212 ha) area is irregularly shaped, a configuration that makes it seem more a natural part of the urban landscape.

A short distance from the Brooklyn Public Library is the northern entrance to the park, **Grand Army Plaza.** Designed as a relatively quiet, peaceful entree,

the plaza was gradually built up after its 1867 opening, gaining its 80-foot (24 m) memorial arch in 1892. Erected to honor the Union dead from the Civil War, the arch is topped by a bronze group done by sculptor Frederick W. MacMonnies at the turn of the 19th century. Traffic around the plaza is awful, but renovations being considered might improve the situation.

By the park entrance is a detailed standing park map for orientation. First, you enter the enormous 75-acre (30 ha) **Long Meadow,** usually filled with clusters of people barbecuing, playing catch, sunning, playing guitars, and relaxing. From here, the park unfolds in a succession of open spaces alternating with intimate ones—**Prospect Lake,** a 60-acre (24 ha), stream-fed pool surrounded by meadows, and the

(continued on p. 210)

Brooklyn Bridge Park

📍 Map p. 205 C3

✉ Plymouth St. bet. Main & Washington Sts., Brooklyn

🚇 Subway: A, C to High St.; F to York St.; 2, 3 to Clark St.

nycgovparks.org/ parks/brooklyn bridgepark

Prospect Park

📍 Map p. 205 C2

✉ Boathouse Visitor Center, Lincoln Rd. entrance, Brooklyn

☎ 718/965–8951 Forthcoming events: 718/965–8999

🚇 Subway: 2, 3 to Grand Army Plaza

prospectpark.org

EXPERIENCE: Hear NY Harmonics at Bargemusic

Why hear chamber music at a staid old concert hall when you can hear it aboard a 116-year-old steel barge that once hauled coffee around New York Harbor? In 1976, violinist Olga Bloom converted the 100-foot (30.5 m) vessel into a floating concert hall, and today her organization presents more than 200 concerts a year in a room paneled with hardwoods from an old Staten Island ferry. There's seating for 170 people, and performers play in front of a huge window offering views of Manhattan. **Bargemusic** (*tel 718/624–4924, bargemusic .org*) is moored at the Fulton Ferry Landing, at the end of Old Fulton Street near the Brooklyn Bridge. Tickets cost $35–$45.

BROOKLYN HEIGHTS WALK

Brooklyn Heights was developed in the 18th century as the city's first suburb and is now its first historic district. Many streets in this well-kept neighborhood are named for early landowners. Go there to escape busy Manhattan, to enjoy spectacular views of the city from the Brooklyn Heights Promenade, and to absorb the atmosphere of 19th-century privilege and contentment its tranquil streets exude.

Take the subway to **Borough Hall** ❶ (*209 Joralemon St.; subway lines A, C, F, 2, 3, 4, & 5 stop here*), a highly regarded marble Greek Revival building constructed between 1845 and 1848 as the Brooklyn City Hall and renamed Borough Hall after the 1898 consolidation with Manhattan and the other boroughs. From the Hall, continue west on Joralemon Street to No. 170. The colleges of Oxford and Cambridge were the model for Minard Lafever's Gothic Revival **Packer Collegiate Institute** (1856), among the city's oldest private schools.

Turn right onto Henry Street and head north toward Remsen Street. **Our Lady of Lebanon Cathedral** ❷ dates from 1846 and was designed in the Romanesque Revival style

---

INSIDER TIP:

For the quintessential New York experience—and great views—walk the Brooklyn Bridge. When it opened in 1883, the bridge's towers were the tallest structures in New York. Start in Brooklyn Heights at Cadman Plaza and Middagh Street, just west of the first stop in Brooklyn on the A and C trains, cross into the park, and follow signs to the footpath.

—PATRICIA SHAW
National Geographic contributor

NOT TO BE MISSED:

Our Lady of Lebanon Cathedral
• Brooklyn Historical Society • Brooklyn Heights Promenade • Montague Street

---

by Richard Upjohn, the architect responsible for Wall Street's Trinity Church (see p. 57). Its ornate bronze doors were salvaged from the great French ocean liner *Normandie*. Continue on Henry Street and turn right onto Montague. At the corner of Clinton Street, **St. Ann's and the Holy Trinity Episcopal Church** ❸ (*tel 718/875–6960*) is another work by Minard Lafever. When built in 1844–1847, it was the largest church in Brooklyn. The red sandstone exterior and the stained-glass windows by William and John Bolton have been restored, and there are free organ concerts every Wednesday at 1 p.m. between September and June.

Turn left on Clinton Street and left again on Pierrepont Street to No. 128, the **Brooklyn Historical Society** ❹ (*tel 718/222–4111, brooklynhistory.org, closed Mon.–Tues.*), where many unusual Brooklyn artifacts are exhibited. The Renaissance-style exterior has terra-cotta ornamentation, and its interior is a designated landmark. Built between 1842 and 1844 at Pierrepont Street and Monroe Place, the **First Unitarian Congregational Society** ❺ (*tel 718/624–5466, fuub.org*) is widely considered to be one of Lafever's masterpieces.

Continue on Pierrepont to Willow Street and turn right. This pleasant street has fine examples of residential architecture. Look up at

 See also map
pp. 204–205

► Borough Hall

⟷ 2 miles (3.2 km)

🕐 2 hours

► Plymouth Church
of the Pilgrims

Nos. 108, 110, and 112 on the west side, whose bay windows, dormers, towers, and doorways make them examples of the 1880s shingle style. Across the street, an earlier stable at 151 and 155–159 Willow Street was, according to legend, linked to a tunnel used for the Underground Railroad.

Turn left on Clark, and then right, which places you on **Brooklyn Heights Promenade ⑥**, a parklike, cantilevered walkway completed in 1950 above the Brooklyn Queens Expressway. Running between Remsen and Orange Streets, it offers incomparable views of the harbor, the Brooklyn Bridge, Lower Manhattan, and the Statue of Liberty.

With the water on your left, pass Pineapple Street, turning right onto Orange Street, left on Willow Street, and then right to **24 Middagh Street ⑦**. The beautifully proportioned, federal-style, clapboard house at the corner of Willow Street is the former Eugene Boisselet residence. It is one of Brooklyn Height's oldest houses, dating from at least 1824, though some sources track it back to 1815.

Continue to Hicks Street and turn right, then left on Orange Street. Between Hicks and Henry Streets, the famous Plymouth Church, now **Plymouth Church of the Pilgrims ⑧** (*tel 718/624–4743, plymouth church.org*), is a simple, barnlike brick structure designed by Joseph C. Wells and completed in 1849. The parish house and connecting arcade at 75 Hicks Street are 1913 additions.

From 1847 to 1887, Henry Ward Beecher (brother of Harriet Beecher Stowe, the author of *Uncle Tom's Cabin*) was the church's pastor. Beecher was a spellbinding preacher and an ardent abolitionist. To demonstrate the horrors of the slave trade, he once auctioned off a slave girl from the pulpit and then used the proceeds to buy her freedom, a scene recalled in sculpture in the garden. Beecher was later accused of improper relations with a married woman. Although he was exonerated, the scandal proved damaging to his career.

You're now well positioned to explore more of Brooklyn: Turn right at the corner of Henry, and head to **Montague Street,** the commercial heart of the Heights with many fine shops and restaurants. If your exertions have left you hungry or thirsty, **Brooklyn Heights Wine Bar** (*50 Henry St., 718/855–5595, brooklynheightswinebar.com*) makes an excellent resting point for the weary walker.

Brooklyn Museum

- Map p. 205 C2
- 200 Eastern Pkwy, Brooklyn
- 718/638–5000
- Closed Mon.– Tues.; "First Saturdays" have free evening admission (except Sep.) & special events
- $$$
- Subway: 2, 3 to Eastern Parkway

brooklynmuseum.org

quiet **Ravine,** with Brooklyn's only remaining stand of native forest. As the 19th century progressed, more formal elements were added to the park, such as gates, pavilions, and the Corinthian templelike **Croquet Shelter** at Parkside Avenue on the park's southern end near Prospect Lake.

One of the favorite park attractions is the **Prospect Park Carousel,** a reminder of the days when Brooklyn was a center of carousel manufacturing, from 1875 to 1918. Nearby, located in an 18th-century structure, **Lefferts Historic House** (*452 Flatbush Ave. at Ocean Ave, tel 718/789–2822, closed Mon.–Wed. & a.m. daily*) offers period rooms, workshops, and crafts demonstrations. A popular children's destination is the 12-acre (5 ha) **Prospect Park Zoo** (*450 Flatbush Ave., tel 718/399–7339*).

Throughout the year, the park is used by joggers, skaters, and hikers, plus there are

sponsored festivals and performing arts events; many are held at the **Prospect Park Bandshell** (*Prospect Park W. at 9th St., tel 718/965–8999*).

Olmstead and Vaux designed **Eastern Parkway,** a boulevard and designated landmark running east from Grand Army Plaza. Follow it about half a mile (0.8 km) to the **Brooklyn Museum.**

Brooklyn Museum

Housed in a 19th-century beaux arts landmark, the Brooklyn Museum is New York's second-largest museum. Its permanent collection holds more than one million objects, from ancient masterpieces to contemporary works. Exhibits change often.

Contemporized front grounds blend handsomely with the museum's original architecture and statuary, while a sweeping entryway opens onto an information area, coat check, and gift shop.

■ George Caleb Bingham's "Shooting for the Beef" (1850)

Farther along is the **Blum Gallery,** which houses changing exhibits. Also on this floor are a café and, outdoors, the **Steinberg Family Sculpture Garden,** with a Coney Island lion from Steeplechase Park

---

INSIDER TIP:

The First Saturdays program at the Brooklyn Museum is a great way to unwind from the week. From 5 p.m. to 11 p.m., the museum offers live music and free exhibits.

—BETSY ROACH
TV & Film licensing director,
National Geographic

---

and a monumental 19th-century replica of the Statue of Liberty.

Museum Highlights: On the first floor, visitors can wander among the **Arts of Africa** and view Rodin sculpture. In 1923 the Brooklyn Museum was the first to exhibit African objects as art— one masterpiece here is the brass figure of a horn blower, made for a 16th-century Nigerian king of Benin. On the second floor are the **Asian and Islamic collections.** The grouping of later Persian art from the Qajar period (1779–1924) is one of the finest outside Iran.

The third floor holds the fine Egyptian collection (see below). European paintings are also here, including works by 19th-century French artists—Cézanne, Degas, Matisse, and others—splendidly installed in a skylit court. On the fourth floor, **The Elizabeth A. Sackler Center for Feminist Art** is centered on Judy Chicago's iconic "The Dinner Party," a triangular table whose porcelain place settings represent 39 historically significant women.

Luce Center for American Art: This area, on the fifth floor, was established by a $10 million grant from the Henry Luce Foundation. Here the innovative **Visible Storage/Study Center** lets the public view some 2,500 objects from the museum's collection of American painting and sculpture, as well as material from the Decorative Arts, Native American, and Print, Drawing, and Photography collections. The Luce Center's second component is the installation **"American Identities."** Taking up several themed galleries, it draws from the museum's 2,500 oil paintings, sculptures, watercolors, and pastels from 1720 to the late 20th century. Contemporary photographs and short period films enrich each exhibit. The scope is immense, from objects such as a basket made by the last Brooklyn Canarsie Indian and a 1930s RCA Victor portable phonograph to paintings by Winslow Homer, Thomas Eakins, and Georgia O'Keeffe. Edward Hicks's "The Peaceable Kingdom" is also here.

Egyptian Collection: Covering four millennia, this world-famous collection is based on the bequest of Charles Edwin Wilbour (1833–1896).

**Brooklyn
Children's
Museum**

🅰 Map p. 205 D2

✉ 145 Brooklyn
Ave., Brooklyn

☎ 718/735–4400

🕐 Closed Mon.

💲 $$

🚇 Subway: 3 to
Kingston Ave.

brooklynkids.org

A journalist turned Egyptologist, Wilbour conducted extensive excavations in the Nile Valley. His widow gave his library and collection to the museum, and in 1932 their children provided an endowment to establish the museum's Department of Egyptology. The Egyptian Collection tells the story of Egyptian art through more than 1,200 objects—sculpture, relief, paintings, pottery, and papyri—from Egypt's earliest known origins (ca 3500 B.C.) until the period of Roman rule (30 B.C.–A.D. 395). This spectacular long-term

installation is replete with treasures, including one of Wilbour's more famous finds: a plaque depicting King Akhenaten, who became pharaoh in 1352 B.C., and his wife Nefertiti. Be sure to see the material from the reign of King Tutankhamun (ca 1336–1327 B.C.); the extraordinary "Coffin for an Ibis," made for a mummified bird believed to be a manifestation of the god Thoth; and 30 limestone blocks with finely carved reliefs, some still in progress, from the tomb of Nespeqashuty (664–610 B.C.).

Development of the Museum:
Walt Whitman was among the early directors of the Brooklyn Apprentices Library, founded in 1823 to aid youths "in becoming useful and respectable members of society." The library grew to become the Brooklyn Institute of Arts and Sciences—later renamed the Brooklyn Museum.

In 1893 architects McKim, Mead & White won the public competition to design a new building. Their ambitious plan would have made the Brooklyn Museum the world's largest, surpassing the Louvre, but only the west wing and one court were ever finished.

Today, modernization is ongoing. The front entrance (2005), with its stepped glass pavilion, creates an exhilarating gateway, while the adjacent public plaza offers pleasant seating amidst dramatic water features. Even the nearby subway entrance was re-oriented and its interior renovated.

Another World: Brooklyn Children's Museum

Located about a mile and a quarter (2 km) northeast of the Brooklyn Museum, this was the world's first children's museum, founded in 1899.

In 2008 it doubled in size and became New York's first green-certified museum. You can't miss it: It's the yellow, L-shaped wedge at the corner of St. Marks and Brooklyn Avenues. Inside, galleries feature hands-on activities and role-playing opportunities, as well as a permanent collection of some 30,000 objects, from dolls to fossils. One permanent exhibit, called "World Brooklyn," features a child-size Brooklyn cityscape, complete with kid-size shops and theaters.

Brooklyn Botanic Garden

Directly next to the Brooklyn Museum lies the Brooklyn Botanic Garden. From the aromatic Fragrance Garden to the winding Japanese Garden, it is a triumph of the garden designer's art. With a seemingly endless succession of formal and informal landscapes and different specialized areas, the garden seems much larger than its mere 52 acres (21 ha).

The Brooklyn Institute of Arts and Sciences founded the Botanic Garden in 1910. Architects McKim, Mead & White designed the **Victorian Palm House** and administration building, and landscape architect Harold Caparn laid out the grounds.

Important additions in 1914 were the **children's garden,** where schoolchildren are able to learn techniques of vegetable and flower gardening, and the **Japanese Hill-and-Pond Garden,** north of the main entrance. Designed by a Japanese artist living in New York, the garden borders a pond overlooked by a shrine to the Shinto god of the harvest. Nearby is the rectangular **Cherry Esplanade,** planted with double rows of Kwanzan cherry trees, a gift from Japan. Cherry blossom season in May draws large crowds.

The 1988 **Steinhardt Conservatory** houses the Bonsai Museum, with more than 750 species of bonsai, and an exhibit called the "Trail of Evolution," illustrating four billion years of plant development. The conservatory also includes the Aquatic

■ **More than 200 cherry trees draw crowds of admirers every spring to the Brooklyn Botanic Garden.**

House, with displays of water lilies and other water plants. On the lower level, visit the Conservatory Gallery, with changing art exhibits.

Coney Island

At the very southern end of Brooklyn, Coney Island is one of those places that's more vibrant in the collective imagination than in real life. Though it's a bona fide New York neighborhood, with some 51,000 mostly Russian, African-American, and Hispanic residents, the island is most famous for its amusement parks, which flourished in the early 20th century, went into a steady decline after World War II, then gained a "faded grandeur" cachet in the late 1980s and 1990s. Today its fate is up in the air as city agencies and private developers wrestle with "revitalization" plans, made ever more urgent by the damage caused by Hurricane Sandy. But changes—big ones—are afoot.

Brooklyn Botanic Garden

🅰 Map p. 205 C2

✉ 990 Washington Ave., Brooklyn

☎ 718/623–7200

🕐 Closed Mon.

💲 $$; free entrance Fri. a.m. Mar.–Nov. & weekdays Dec.–Feb.

🚇 Subway: B, Q to Prospect Park (no B on weekends); 2, 3 to Eastern Parkway; 4 to Franklin Ave.

bbg.org

Coney Island

🅰 Map p. 205 C1

🚇 Subway: D to Coney Island/Stillwell Ave.

New York Aquarium

✉ Surf Ave. &
   W. 8th St.,
   Brooklyn

☎ 718/265—3474

nyaquarium.com

Coney Island is an hour-long subway ride from Manhattan. On Stillwell Avenue, the original **Nathan's Famous** hot dog stand has been dispensing dogs and soda since 1916, with a short interruption due to Sandy. Three attractions have landmark status. The legendary **Cyclone,** a gravity-ride, wooden track roller coaster, was built in 1927. The **Wonder Wheel,** a 150-foot-high (45 m) Ferris wheel, opened in 1920. The **Parachute Jump,** near the Coney Island Boardwalk, came to Coney Island from the New York World's Fair of 1939—1940. Although long closed, the steel tower recently got a $2 million LED lighting upgrade. The **New York Aquarium** is right off the Boardwalk. Keep walking east on the Boardwalk and you'll end up in **Brighton Beach,** an enclave of Russian and Ukrainian immigrants, with many cafés, restaurants, and shops where you will hear only Russian spoken.

Coney Island's Three Parks: Coney Island was actually three amusement parks. George Tilyou opened Steeplechase Park at West 17th Street in 1897; here patrons raced on mechanical horses attached to iron rails or held on to a fast-spinning wooden disk called the Human Roulette Wheel. Luna Park (1903) was a fantasyland of minaret towers, its buildings outlined by more than a million lightbulbs. The third park, Dreamland, quieter and more tasteful, had reproductions of the Tower of Seville and Venetian canals. Fire ended it in 1911. Luna Park burned in 1944, and Steeplechase Park closed in 1964. ■

EXPERIENCE: Brooklyn—A Night Out

Brooklyn is where hip New Yorkers go to party these days. The **Music Hall of Williamsburg** (66 N. 6th St., tel 718/486—5400, musichallofwilliamsburg.com) is like its Manhattan sibling, the Bowery, but larger and more upscale; it's got three floors, with a bar on each. The club books some of the biggest touring indie acts from a variety of genres, including rock, hip-hop, and electronic. Even though it's relatively new, the **Knitting Factory** (361 Metropolitan Ave., tel. 347/529—6696, bk.knittingfactory.com) is a real indie institution in New York. Neither too elegant nor too underground, this concert venue proposes some of the best new artists in circulation, as well as stand-up comedy with Will Miles, Clark Jones, and Kenny DeForest. If you're looking for a true temple to the underground, go to **Saint Vitus** (1120 Manhattan Ave., saintvitusbar.com) where the volume and the energy levels of genuine punk, rock, and metal are always at the maximum. The bar's unique, intimate shows have starred such famous bands as Nirvana, The Descendants, Neurosis, Megadeth, Anthrax, Refused, Babes in Toyland, and Sick of it All.

The peculiarly lit rooms at the vintage, labyrinth-like **Brooklyn Night Bazar** (150 Greenpoint Ave, bkbazaar. com) offer a variety of experiences that include karaoke, films, flea markets, and, above all, live music, famous DJs, and emerging indie artists. **The House of Yes** (2 Wyckoff Ave., houseofyes.org) proposes disco, funk, soul, R&B, and electronic music. Don't miss their themed events with circus acrobats, full moon parties, and 1990s revival nights.

IN & AROUND STATEN ISLAND

The ferry crossing from Manhattan to Staten Island will take you to the St. George Ferry Terminal. From there, you can explore the area on foot or take a bus from the terminal to the nearby attractions: the Snug Harbor Cultural Center, the Alice Austen House, and the zoo. Then, enjoy the amazing view of the Upper Bay from the 295-foot-tall (190 m) New York Wheel, which was one of the biggest Ferris wheels in the United States when it was built.

The Staten Island Ferry's 5-mile (8 km), 25-minute ride provides unforgettable views.

The Ferry Terminal & Northern Staten Island

Leaving the terminal on Richmond Terrace, you'll find **Borough Hall,** which has historical exhibits. On the island's northern end inside Snug Herbor Campus, the **Staten Island Museum** (*1000 Richmond Terrace, closed Mon.–Tues., tel 718/727–1135, statenislandmuseum.org*) has more than two million items, including 55,000 photos and a fine collection of 19th-century painting, sculpture, and decorative arts.

Located in the impressive Greek Revival buildings, the **Snug Harbor Cultural Center & Botanical Garden** was founded in 1831 as a retirement home for sailors. Located in the 19th century reproduction of a Greek temple is the **Newhouse Center for Contemporary Art** (*tel. 718/425–3511, snug-harbor.org/visual-arts, closed Jan.–Feb. and Mon.–Wed., $*), a collective art gallery. Other attractions you can visit in the area include the **Staten Island Children's Museum** (*tel 718/273–2060, closed Mon., $$*), with interactive exhibits, and the **Staten Island Botanical Garden** (*tel 718/448–2500, snug-harbor.org/botanical-garden, closed Sat.–Sun. $*).

Farther inland, the 8-acre

Snug Harbor Cultural Center & Botanical Garden

- Map p. 204 B2
- 1000 Richmond Terrace, Staten Island
- 718/448–2500
- Closed Mon.
- Free ($ for some attractions)
- Bus: S40 from the ferry terminal

snug-harbor.org

Staten Island Zoo

🏛 Map p. 204 B2

✉ 614 Broadway, Staten Island

☎ 718/442–3100

💲 $ (free Wed. after 2 p.m.)

statenislandzoo.org

Alice Austen House

🏛 Map p. 204 C2

✉ 2 Hylan Blvd., Staten Island

☎ 718/816–4506

🕐 Closed Mon. (Jan.–Feb. only by reservation)

💲 $ donation

🚌 Bus: S51 from ferry terminal

aliceausten.org

(3.2 ha) **Staten Island Zoo,** founded in 1936, is known for its Serpentarium with its many North American rattlesnakes.

Alice Austen House

South of the ferry terminal on the eastern shore of the island stands the onetime home of Alice Austen (1866–1952), one of America's finest early women photographers. Now a museum dedicated to Austen's life and work, the house was originally built as a cottage in the early 18th century. Austen's grandfather purchased it in 1844 and remodeled it in the Gothic Revival style. A visit here provides an opportunity not only to view some of Austen's work, but to savor the lifestyle of Staten Island's middle class at the turn of the 19th century, when travel was as much by water as by foot—hence the waterfront location of the better homes.

Much of Austen's extant work consists of scenes from her pleasant surroundings and lifestyle—picnics, the interiors of friends' homes, motor racing, and parties. One sequence done for a woman's "how-to" book on bicycling illustrated the art of mounting, pedaling, and dismounting in a long skirt. More daring, and difficult to achieve, given the cumbersome equipment she used, was her street photography. Austen ventured into the midst of New York City to photograph such subjects as immigrants arriving at the Battery and at the Quarantine Station on Staten Island. Her work on the Lower East Side includes the well-known 1896 photograph of an egg peddler on Hester Street. In this body of work, Austen has been cited alongside photographers Jacob Riis and Lewis Hine, who focused on social issues of the time.

An inheritance from her father enabled Austen to live comfortably for most of her life, until losses in the 1929 stock market crash forced her to mortgage the house, which she lost in 1945. By the time a researcher for *Life* magazine came across some of her photographs in 1951, she was an indigent resident at the Staten Island Farm Colony. *Life* did an article on her that gave her the funds to spend the last six months of her life in a private nursing home. The article also spurred the Staten Island Historical Society to acquire what remained of

EXPERIENCE: The Staten Island Ferry & New Routes

The **Staten Island Ferry** is one of New York's most iconic rides, linking the southern tip of Manhattan to the borough of Staten Island, 5.2 miles (8.3 km) to the south. It's a vital lifeline for Staten Islanders, but it also gives visitors a chance to experience the grandeur of New York Harbor completely free of charge. Go to the Whitehall Terminal, 1 Whitehall Street at South Street, and get aboard as soon as the big doors open to the best views of the Statue of Liberty, Ellis Island, and the Manhattan skyline. Crossings take 25 minutes, with departures every 15 to 30 minutes. In addition to the connections to Staten Island and Governors Island, the NYC Ferry (*ferry.nyc*) now has four new routes that connect Manhattan to South Brooklyn, Long Island City, Astoria, Rockaway in Queens, and Soundview in the Bronx. The price of the ticket is the same as that of a subway ticket.

The 1696 Voorlezer House at Staten Island's Historic Richmond Town

her work. The Friends of Alice Austen House are gradually restoring the residence, which was declared a city landmark in 1971. Today the Alice Austen House preserves her home, her place in the history of American photography, and, most importantly, her work, a fascinating female perspective on the New York of a century ago.

Historic Richmond Town

About 5 miles (8 km) inland and southwest of the Alice Austen House, Historic Richmond Town is proof that New York City has everything—even a restored rural village. Here you can browse through a late 19th-century general store (in the Stephens-Black House) or watch craftsmen make wood-splint baskets in the Basketmaker's House (1810) or throw pots in the basement of the Guyon-Lake-Tysen House, an

exquisite Dutch Colonial–style house built about 1740 (with later additions).

The site has some of the oldest restored buildings in the city. The wood-and-stone Britton Cottage (ca 1670) predates the founding of the settlement in 1690. The house was moved to Richmond Town in 1967. Because Richmond Town was located at the center of the island, it became the seat of government about 1730.

Eleven of the 27 buildings are original to the site, including the circa 1696 Voorlezer House—also the oldest surviving elementary school in the country. The settlers, members of the Dutch Reformed Church, built the house for their lay reader, or *voorlezer*, who was also the schoolteacher. In 1855, the congregation built the Parsonage for the Dutch Reformed minister, but by then their church was in decline.

**Historic
Richmond Town**

🅰 Map p. 204 B1

✉ 441 Clarke Ave.,
   Staten Island

☎ 718/351–1611

🕐 Closed Mon.–
   Tues.; free
   entrance Fri.

💲 $

🚌 Bus: S74 from
   ferry terminal

**historicrichmond
town.org**

Garibaldi-Meucci Museum

- Map p. 204 B2
- 420 Tompkins Ave., Staten Island
- 718/442–1608
- Closed Sun.–Tues.
- $
- Bus: S52, S78 to Tompkins Ave.

garibaldimeucci museum.org

Conference House

- Map p. 204 A1
- 298 Satterlee St., Staten Island
- 718/984–6046
- Closed Jan.–Mar. (call for details), & Mon.–Thurs.
- $
- Bus: S78 to Craig Ave., walk one block south into the park

conferencehouse.org

Jacques Marchais Museum of Tibetan Art

- Map p. 204 B1
- 338 Lighthouse Ave., Staten Island
- 718/987–3500
- Closed Mon.–Tues. (in Jan. only Sat.)
- Donation
- Bus: S74 to Lighthouse Ave.

tibetanmuseum.org

Pierre Billiou House

- Map p. 204 B1
- 1476 Richmond Rd., Dongan Hills, Staten Island
- 718/351–1611
- By appointment, call caretaker

The Greek Revival Third County Courthouse (1837) is now the visitor center and the first stop on a tour of the restoration to see craftsmen and costumed staff re-enacting life in the 17th century. The historical museum is also located in a government building: the Richmond County Clerk's and Surrogate's Office (1848). The museum's permanent exhibit examines the economy and history of the island.

More Sites on Staten Island

Garibaldi-Meucci Museum: Inland from the Alice Austen House, this circa 1840 farmhouse is known for its two

---

Tour the Conference House

One of the oldest houses in the city, the two-and-a-half-story Billopp House, named for Christopher Billopp, who built it in about 1680, is located in a park on the southern tip of Staten Island. Its current name refers to an unsuccessful peace conference that took place in the early days of the American Revolution—on September 11, 1776—between American patriots Benjamin Franklin, John Adams, and Edward Rutledge and British Vice Admiral Lord Richard Howe. The house is open for guided tours and the grounds are a pleasant spot to picnic.

---

famous residents. One of them, Antonio Meucci (1808–1889), was an Italian-born immigrant with a plausible claim to having invented the telephone several years before Alexander Graham Bell; the other was the Italian hero Giuseppe Garibaldi (1807–1882). Meucci moved to Staten Island in 1850. His attempts to take out a patent on his invention failed because of his poverty and poor English. When Garibaldi fled to New York after the defeat of the republican forces in Italy, Meucci took him in. Garibaldi lived there for almost a year until finally returned to Italy in 1853 to resume his political struggle. Throughout the house are exhibits on the men's lives, including a prototype of Meucci's telephone and his death mask.

Jacques Marchais Museum of Tibetan Art: Not far from the Richmond Town restoration, built in the style of Tibetan monasteries, this museum houses the art collection of a Madison Avenue art dealer, Edna Coblentz, who devoted her life to studying and collecting Tibetan art.

Pierre Billiou House (Billiou-Stillwell-Perine House): This is the oldest building surviving on Staten Island and one of the oldest house museums, having been opened to the public in 1919. The original stone farmhouse was built in the 1660s; additions extended the house in every direction over the next century and a half. ■

IN & AROUND THE BRONX

Named an "All-American City" in 1997, the Bronx is best known as home of the Bronx Bombers, the New York Yankees. However, it has other grand attractions that are equally worth exploring. Ever popular attractions include the Bronx Zoo and the New York Botanical Garden, but a tour with the Bronx County Historical Society (*tel 718/881–8900*) offers a more intimate experience and a variety of choices.

The Enid A. Haupt Conservatory is an architectural highlight of the New York Botanical Garden.

Sites in Central Bronx

New York Botanical Garden:

Unlikely as it may seem, New York City is a mecca for garden lovers. All four outlying boroughs have outstanding botanic gardens, but anyone here on a garden tour must make the New York Botanical Garden in the Bronx a priority. Established in 1891, the garden offers 250 acres (101 ha) of gardens, forest, and scenic landscapes, including the **Peggy Rockefeller Rose Garden.** The rose garden is based on plans drawn by the well-known garden designer Beatrix Farrand in 1916. At

the 12-acre (5 ha) **Everett Children's Adventure Garden** (opened 1998), children can look for frogs in a pond, explore the "kids only" meadow path, and examine their finds through a laboratory microscope. A comprehensive, 20-year, garden-wide renaissance has renovated landscapes and gardens and added a visitor center, two cafés, a new herbarium, a plant research laboratory, and propagation greenhouses.

The Botanical Garden is distinguished architecturally by the **Enid A. Haupt Conservatory** (1902), based on London's

New York Botanical Garden

- Map p. 205 D5
- 2900 Southern Blvd., Bronx
- 718/817–8700
- Closed Mon.
- $$–$$$ (free Sat. 9 a.m.–10 a.m. & all day Wed.)
- Subway & bus: B, D, or 4 to Bedford park Blvd. (subway); Bx26 to Mosholu Gate entrance (bus); Train: Metro–North from Grand Central Terminal

nybg.org

Bronx Zoo

🅰 Map p. 205 D5

✉ Fordham Rd.
  & Bronx River
  Pkwy., Bronx

☎ 718/367–1010

💲 $$$ (free Wed.)

🚇 Subway: 2 to
  Pelham Parkway;
  Bus: BxM11
  from Madison
  Ave. (bet. 26th
  St. & 99th St.);
  Train: Metro
  North from
  Grand Central
  Terminal

bronxzoo.com

Crystal Palace of 1851. Its Palms of the Americas Gallery, 100 feet (30.5 m) in diameter, is located under the 90-foot-high (27.5 m) glass dome, and there are ten other glass galleries. One wing includes a misty tropical rain forest that can be viewed from various heights on an elevated catwalk as part of the ongoing exhibit "A World of Plants." Every year, the garden hosts seasonal exhibitions, including perennial favorites such as the **Holiday Train Show** (late Nov.–early Jan.) and the **Orchid Show** (late Feb.–early April).

Bronx Zoo: Whatever name you choose to call it—Bronx Zoo (official), New York Zoological Park (earlier), or Wildlife Conservation Society (parent organization)—it is, for viewing wild animals in natural surroundings, unsurpassed in the country. Situated on 265 acres (107 ha), with

some 4,500 animals representing more than 500 species, it is the country's largest urban zoo.

From JungleWorld to African Plains to World of Reptiles, you can visit habitats of all seven continents, each filled with native animals. What the zoo has been most famous for since its inception in 1899, however, is its innovative approaches to zookeeping. The use of natural settings surrounded by moats rather than cages, and a dedicated breeding center for endangered species are two such innovations. The designs of both **Himalayan Highlands** (1986) for snow leopards and the **Congo Gorilla Forest** (1999), a 6.5-acre (2.6 ha) African rain forest habitat with 20-plus lowland gorillas, incorporate habitats in which the animals can roam, explore, and play.

Tiger Mountain features endangered Siberian tigers in re-created environs where visitors can observe the big cats' natural behavior (including swimming underwater). The indoor **Butterfly Garden,** filled with more than 1,000 butterflies (including the Monarch), is especially magical.

In the heart of the park, the **Sea Lion Pool** offers feedings twice daily. Around the pool, the gorgeous beaux arts buildings of Astor Court comprise the zoo's original campus, built at the turn of the 19th century. One of its buildings, the 1903 Lion House, was renovated to host **Madagascar!,** an exhibit featuring lemurs, hissing cockroaches, and other oddities from the east African island.

EXPERIENCE: *Salute!*
Dine in the Real Little Italy

While Manhattan's Little Italy long ago transformed from authentic to theme park, the Bronx's **Arthur Avenue** is still the real thing—and it's all about the food. **Zero Otto Nove** (*2357 Arthur Ave., tel. 718/220–1027, 089bronx.com*) is the area's best restaurant, with an old Italian ambience and daily specials. **Pasquales Rigoletto** (*2311 Arthur Ave., tel 718/365–6644*) is for people-watching: It's big, the food is big, and the people who eat there are big, loud, and very Italian. **Egidio Pastry Shop** (*622 E. 187th St. at Hughes Ave., one block E of Arthur Ave., tel 718/295–6077*) serves great cappuccino and cannolis. Arthur Avenue is about five blocks from the Bronx Zoo.

■ The Bronx Zoo's Tiger Mountain re-creates a corner of the Amur Valley, located between China and Russia, for Siberian tigers.

Wave Hill Vistas

The two historic mansions on this 28-acre (11.3 ha) estate were built in the mid-19th and early 20th centuries. Theodore Roosevelt, Mark Twain, and Arturo Toscanini lived here at different times. Today, Wave Hill is a cultural center, but most visitors come to tour the stunning gardens with a view overlooking the Hudson River and New Jersey Palisades.

Bronx Community College:

The campus boasts two architectural treasures designed by Stanford White: **Gould Memorial Library** (1887–1899) and the **Hall of Fame for Great Americans** (*University Ave. & W. 181st St., tel 718/289–5910*). The latter, a 630-foot-long (192 m) neoclassical colonnade, holds portrait busts of 98 famous Americans, from Eli Whitney to Franklin D. Roosevelt.

Edgar Allan Poe Cottage:

Shortly after he moved to the Bronx in 1846, Edgar Allan Poe described his home as "a snug little cottage." He wrote *Ulalume* and *The Bells* here. The house became a museum in 1917. Three downstairs rooms have been restored to the period Poe lived here; upstairs is an exhibit on his life and an audiovisual presentation.

Sites in Northern Bronx

Museum of Bronx History:

This museum (*3266 Bainbridge Ave., open Sat. & Sun., tel 718/881–8900*) offers unique artifacts relating to the borough's past and a research library. It is housed in the circa 1758 Valentine-Varian House.

Woodlawn Cemetery: Among

the 300,000 interred in the 400 acres (161 ha) of the pastoral

Wave Hill
- Map p. 205 D5
- W. 249th St. & Independence St., Bronx
- 718/549–3200
- Closed Mon.
- $ (free Tues., Sat. a.m., & seasonally)
- Subway: A to Inwood–207th St., then No. 7 bus northbound

wavehill.org

Edgar Allan Poe Cottage
- Map p. 205 D5
- E. Kingsbridge Rd. & Grand Concourse, Bronx
- 718/881–8900
- Closed Mon.–Fri.
- $
- Subway: D, 4 to Kingsbridge Rd.

Van Cortlandt House Museum

 Map p. 205 D5

✉ Van Cortlandt Park, W. 246th St. & Broadway, Bronx

☎ 718/543–3344

🕐 Closed Mon.

💲 $

🚇 Subway: 1 to 242nd St.

vancortlandt house.org

Bartow-Pell Mansion

🗺 Map p. 205 E5

✉ 895 Shore Rd. N., Pelham Bay Park, Bronx

☎ 718/885–1461

🕐 Closed Mon.– Tues., Thurs.–Fri.

💲 $

bartowpellmansion museum.org

Seastreak Ferries

✉ Pickups at various New York City and New Jersey locations

seastreak.com

1863 Woodlawn Cemetery (*Jerome Ave. at Webster Ave. & E. 233rd St., tel 718/920–0500*) are Herman Melville, Miles Davis, and F. W. Woolworth, in an Egyptian Revival mausoleum.

Van Cortlandt House Museum: Built in 1748, this elegant Georgian-style manor house was briefly used by George Washington during the Revolution. Today it is filled with antiques that span the history of this remarkable family, which lived in the house until 1889. Included are a painted cupboard made in the Hudson Valley in the early 18th century and a Gilbert Stuart portrait of John Jacob Astor, who was related to the Van Cortlandts by marriage.

Elsewhere in the Bronx

Bartow-Pell Mansion: Thomas Pell purchased land on Long Island Sound from Indians in 1654, but this mansion was not built until 1842. Ten rooms of the classical revival mansion are filled with period furniture, much of it on loan from city museums. The spiral staircase has been attributed to Minard Lafever, a friend of the family. The city purchased the house and the stone carriage house (1840) in 1888; it opened as a museum in 1946.

City Island: A century-old bridge connects the mainland to two-mile-long (3.2 km) City Island, a picturesque fishing village rich in nautical history. Its blend of boatyards, seafood restaurants, galleries, and antique

shops overlooks Eastchester Bay and Long Island Sound—to some it resembles a New England fishing village. Boatmakers here have built five America's Cup winners. Don't miss the quaint Victorian architecture along Schofield Street.

Yankee Stadium: In April 2009, after more than eight decades in "the house that Ruth built," the New York Yankees moved across the street. The new Yankee Stadium (*bordered by 161st & 164th Sts. & Jerome & River Aves., tel 718/293–6000 or 212/307–1212 Ticketmaster*) was designed to resemble the pre-renovated exterior of

---

INSIDER TIP:

A Yankee home game is a must, and a great way to get there is via a Seastreak ferry. The pre-game atmosphere onboard is electric.

—ALLY THOMPSON
National Geographic contributor

---

the original 1923 stadium and maintains its field dimensions, but the new stadium includes modern amenities and more comfortable seating. Monument park, a tribute of monuments and plaques honoring some of the past Yankees players and managers, was relocated from the old stadium. Currently, the stadium also hosts MLS team New York City FC. ∎

IN & AROUND QUEENS

Think of cultural diversity and a wealth of attractions when you envision Queens. Known since Dutch colonial times as a place of religious freedom, it still draws new immigrant populations, giving the number 7 subway line its identity as the International Express. New York's second-largest Chinatown and a growing Asian influence, a Little India, the Greek neighborhood of Astoria, and terrific options for eating and shopping: These are just a few reasons to sample Queens.

Sites in Eastern Queens

Flushing Meadows-Corona Park: In addition to a thriving arts scene, Queens offers many unique places great for families. Thanks to its hosting of two World's Fairs, in 1939–1940 and 1964–1965, the Flushing Meadows–Corona Park area is today the site of many of the borough's leading attractions. With 1,255 acres (507 ha), it is the city's second largest park. Several fair structures remain, most prominently the **Unisphere,** the largest globe in the world, built by U.S. Steel as the symbol of the 1964–1965 World's Fair.

The Unisphere, a colossal legacy of the 1964–1965 World's Fair

Another refurbished structure, the New York City Building (used for fairs in both 1939–1940 and 1964–65), is now the **Queens Museum** (*tel 718/592–9700, queensmuseum. org, closed Mon.–Tues.*). It houses contemporary art and the world's largest architectural scale model, a 9,335-square-foot (867 sq m) panorama of New York City.

Also in the park, the 1964–1965 World's Fair Space Center was converted into the **New York Hall of Science** (*tel 718/699–0005, nysci.org*) in 1986. It features more than 450 interactive displays on physics, biology, and technology, including one titled "Infinite Potentials," 40 works of art inspired by stem cells, which capture the future of research and therapeutic possibilities.

Even Shea Stadium, former home of the New York Mets, was a project related to the 1964–1965 fair. Shea was demolished in 2008, and the Mets' new home, **Citi Field,** opened in April 2009 in what was the Shea parking lot.

Near Citi Field: East of the park, the 1661 **Bowne House** (*37–01 Bowne St. at 37th Ave., Wed. 1 p.m.–4 p.m. & by*

reservation, tel 718/359–0528, bownehouse.org) is the oldest in Queens; it was built by John Bowne, a convert to Quakerism, whom Peter Stuyvesant arrested in 1662 for holding Quaker meetings in the house. By ordering Stuyvesant to free him, the Dutch West India Company established the principle of

718/939–0647, queenshistorical society.org), which exhibits memorabilia from the residents, including its second owner, Joseph King, Doughty's son-in-law. There is a Victorian parlor and changing exhibits on Queens history.

The 38 acres (15 ha) of the **Queens Botanical Gardens** (43–50 Main St., tel 718/886–3800,

▪ Nearly a century of multimedia memorabilia and technology are presented at MMI.

Louis Armstrong House Museum

Map p. 205 D5

34–56 107th St., Corona, Queens

718/478–8274

Closed Mon.

louisarmstronghouse.org

religious tolerance in the colony (see p. 23). Nine generations of Bownes occupied the house through 1945, when it became a museum.

Close by, the **Friends Meeting House** (tel 718/358–9636) was built by Bowne and other Quakers in 1694. It has been used for Quaker services almost continuously since. Another Quaker, Charles Doughty, built the nearby Kingsland Homestead about 1785. It is now the **Queens Historical Society** (143–135 37th Ave., tel

queensbotanical.org, closed Mon.) in Flushing include the 4,000-plant rose garden donated by Oregon-based Jackson and Perkins, which started in Queens. There is also a Wedding Garden for marriage ceremony photographs, and a Constructed Wetlands Garden, where recycled gray water is used to foster wetland plant communities.

Louis Armstrong House Museum: In a working-class neighborhood in Corona, Queens, the Louis Armstrong

House Museum offers an intimate look into the life of the world's legendary jazz giant. With his wife, Lucille, "Satchmo" lived here from 1943 until his death in 1971.

Sites in Western Queens

Museum of the Moving Image: The Museum of the Moving Image (MMI) is America's only museum devoted exclusively to the study of film, television, and digital media and their impact on American culture and society. It's located in one of 13 buildings that comprise the 14-acre (5.6 ha) studio where production first began in the Silent Era and, after a hiatus, is now back in full swing. The museum houses more than 130,000 moving-image artifacts—a dazzling array covering art, history, techniques, and technology, from which it draws for exhibits, screenings, and other programs.

Famous Players–Lasky (later Paramount Pictures) was the first to film at Astoria Studios, in 1920.

The property transferred to the U.S. Army in 1942, which used it for its own productions until 1971. Falling into disrepair, the studio was saved by the Astoria Motion Picture and Television Foundation in 1977; it obtained landmark status soon after. In 1982, wanting to return the studio to its feature-film production abilities, the city awarded its redevelopment to George Kaufman, who renamed it Kaufman Astoria Studios. A major museum expansion was recently completed, which nearly doubled its size, including the addition of a new extension, a garden for outdoor events, new galleries, and several cutting-edge moving image displays.

Nostalgia buffs will gravitate to the stunning memorabilia, from a chariot from *Ben-Hur,* to the Yoda puppets from *The Empire Strikes Back,* to razzle-dazzle costumes from the movie *Chicago.* Interactive programs let you become part of moviemaking: Graft your voice onto famous film scenes or insert sound effects into film clips.

The new gallery dedicated to the Muppets creator, Jim Henson, opened in 2017 with approximately 300 puppets, sets, and costumes donated by the Henson family. Vintage serials play in the whimsical re-creation of a 1920s Egyptian Revival–style movie palace.

Retrospectives, screenings, and special events are offered year-round in the museum's theater.

The Noguchi Museum:

Need a break from New York's restless energy? Take a trip to this converted factory building, where

Museum of the Moving Image
- Map p. 205 D5
- 35th Ave. at 36th St., Queens
- 718/777–6888
- Closed Mon.–Tues.; free entrance Fri. 4 p.m.–8 p.m.
- $$
- Subway: R (R, G weekends) to Steinway St.; N to 36th Ave.

movingimage.us

The Noguchi Museum
- Map p. 205 D4
- 32–37 Vernon Blvd. at 33rd Rd.
- 718/204–7088
- Closed Mon.–Tues.; free entrance on the first Fri. of every month.
- $$
- Subway: N to Broadway in Queens

noguchi.org

MoMA PS1 Contemporary Art Center

🅐 Map p. 205 D3

✉ 22–25 Jackson Ave. at intersection of 46th Ave., Long Island City, Queens

📞 718/784–2084

🕐 Closed Tues.– Wed.

💲 $ donation

🚇 Subway: E to Court Sq./23rd St., G, 7 to Court Sq.

momaps1.org

Socrates Sculpture Park

✉ 32–01 Vernon Blvd. at Broadway, Long Island City, Queens

📞 718/956–1819

🚇 Subway: N to Broadway in Queens

socratessculpture park.org

works by world-renowned sculptor Isamu Noguchi (1904–1988) are displayed in a space the artist designed himself. Outside, the building encircles a garden containing major granite and basalt sculptures, their abstract forms both elemental and refined. Inside, 13 galleries display works in stone, bronze, and wood, plus dance sets for choreographer Martha Grimes, models for public artworks, and space devoted to Noguchi's interior design work and Akari light sculptures, iconic lamps whose modern design was influenced by traditional Japanese paper lanterns. Special temporary exhibitions illuminate various aspects of Noguchi's work, its historical context, and its impact on younger artists.

Noguchi was born in Los Angeles. His father was a Japanese poet and his mother

MoMA PS1 Contemporary Art Center

Leading the Queens art scene, MoMA PS1 is located in what was an abandoned public school (P.S. 1). It was founded in 1971 as the Institute for Art and Urban Resources Inc. Reopened in 1997 after a three-year renovation, it became a Museum of Modern Art affiliate in 2000. With 125,000 square feet (11,612 sq m) of exhibit space, it is the world's largest museum for contemporary art.

INSIDER TIP:

Take the E or F train to Roosevelt Avenue and explore Indian/ Pakistani/Bangladeshi 74th Street before heading east on Mexican/ Colombian/Ecuadorean Roosevelt Avenue. You won't experience such diversity (and street food) anywhere else.

—SETH KUGEL
Former New York Times travel writer

an American writer. He moved to New York in 1923 to study medicine but turned instead to art. In 1968 the Whitney Museum mounted a retrospective of his work. The permanent Noguchi Museum grew from the artist's studio, which he established beside the museum in the 1960s.

Socrates Sculpture Park:
Catty-corner from the Noguchi Museum, right on the river, is the Socrates Sculpture Park. The four-acre (1.6 ha) site was an abandoned riverside landfill until local artists began transforming it in 1986. Today it's part park, part museum, part studio, with artists creating and displaying large-scale works on site. In summer, the park offers children's art classes and a film festival. There are wonderful views of the Manhattan skyline and a completely relaxed, do-it-yourself vibe. ■

Sandy beaches, wineries, historic sites, innovative museums, and scenery of wondrous beauty, all a short hop from NYC

EXCURSIONS

■ Bear Mountain Bridge in the Hudson River Valley

EXCURSIONS

Sooner or later, even those who thrive on New York's intensity feel the need to get away from the city that never sleeps. For anyone so inclined, there are many outstanding choices within shouting distance of the city. There are beaches, mountains, rivers, lakes, and, because much early history occurred in the region, an abundance of historic sites.

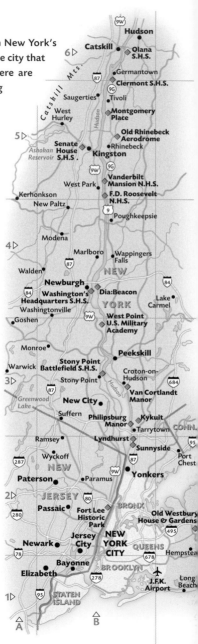

Getting out of the city is another matter. There are subways, buses, trains, and rental cars from which to choose. Your own vehicle may be the most difficult. Train travel can be pleasant, though crowds can make traveling during commuter hours stressful. Buses can be fast—once they get out of Manhattan.

This chapter covers the Hudson River Valley and Long Island, two regions rich in attractions and quite different in topography, scenery, and character. The Hudson River Valley was home to Rip Van Winkle, Washington Irving's famous character; Long Island lives eternally in literature as the land of F. Scott Fitzgerald's Gatsby. The robber barons of the Gilded Age constructed their ostentatious mansions and gardens on the exclusive North Shore of Long Island. In colonial times, patroons built their magnificent estates along the Hudson. The descendants of Cornelius Vanderbilt constructed houses in both places.

Hudson River Valley

In 1807 inventor Robert Fulton built a steam-powered boat, the *Clermont*. Its inaugural run—along the Hudson River, from New York to Albany in 32 hours—signaled the first profitable venture in steam navigation. But it was the 1825 opening of the Erie Canal, from Albany to Buffalo, that made the Hudson River even more important commercially to Manhattan, as a link between the city and the Great Lakes via the canal. More than Long Island, the Hudson River Valley has retained its historic flavor, with stretches as unspoiled as they were in the early 19th century.

Long Island

One hundred and twenty miles long (193 km) and 23 miles across (27 km) at its widest, Long Island is mostly flat. Its North Shore is graced by picturesque harbors and inlets. On its southern side, the Atlantic rolls into its beaches and barrier islands. Farms once covered the island; today they are

found only on its eastern end. During the American Revolution, General Howe drove off Washington and his troops in the Battle of Long Island, August 26–31, 1776, and the island remained in British hands for the rest of the war. Industries that rose there—whaling, shipbuilding, and shipping—are completely gone, the waters now used more for sport than for commerce.

America's newly rich industrialists began building their mansions on the North Shore at the turn of the 20th century. During the roaring 1920s, Long Island was a playground for the wealthy. F. Scott Fitzgerald captured the era in *The Great Gatsby*. After World War II, developers turned large tracts into housing developments and malls. Today, populous western Long Island blends seamlessly into New York City. But there are places where you can step back in time—into a horticultural paradise of the very rich at Old Westbury Gardens, or the simple farming life of Old Bethpage Village. You can also tour Long Island wine country, which over the past three decades has grown from a single winery to more than 50. ■

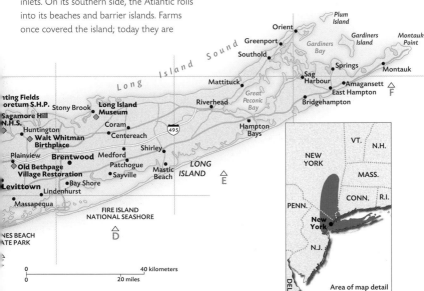

HUDSON RIVER VALLEY

This visit to the Hudson River Valley proceeds north along the west bank, crosses the river at Catskill, and returns down the east side. Although it covers only 200 miles (322 km) or so, it would take several days to thoroughly see and do everything along the way. However, any combination of sites would make an interesting trip. Travelers wanting a shorter journey can use any of the several bridges across the Hudson River to return to New York.

■ Antique artillery pieces guard the Hudson River on heights overlooking West Point.

Stony Point Battlefield State Historic Site (SHS)

🅰 Map p. 228 B3

✉ Park Road off US 9W

☎ 845/786–2521

West Point

🅰 Map p. 228 B3

Visitor Information

✉ Building 2110, West Point

☎ 845/938–2638 or 845/446–4724

usma.edu
westpointtours.com

West of the Hudson

Start in New Jersey at **Fort Lee Historic Park** (*Hudson Terrace, Palisades Interstate Park, njpalisades.org/fortlee.html*), south of the George Washington Bridge. In November 1776, from this vantage point, George Washington watched Fort Washington in northern Manhattan fall to the British. Proceeding north, enter New York State and detour to the **Stony Point Battlefield State Historic Site (SHS).** Here, Gen. Anthony Wayne routed the British on July 16, 1779. From the small museum you can take a battlefield tour.

Continue on US 9W to **West Point,** where the U.S. Military Academy overlooks a spectacular bend in the Hudson River. Try to visit in the spring or fall when the cadets parade. West Point has trained Army officers since 1802. Before it was a school, West Point was a fortification, designed and built in 1778 by Tadeusz Kosciuszko, a Polish officer who fought in the Revolution for the Americans. Most famous American generals graduated from West Point, but not all excelled. Ulysses S. Grant finished in the bottom half of his class; Dwight Eisenhower was a mediocre student.

INSIDER TIP:

For one of the best views of the Hudson Valley and terrific hiking among some interesting rock formations try the trails at Mohonk Mountain House in New Paltz.

—JESSICA NAPOLI
National Geographic contributor

West Point Museum has an extensive collection of weapons, military art, uniforms, and dioramas explaining historic battles. The **Old Cadet Chapel** (1836) is in the post cemetery. Bertram Grosvenor Goodhue designed the 1910 **Cadet Chapel** in the neo-Gothic style.

After leaving West Point on US 9W, stop in Newburgh at **Washington's Headquarters SHS,** the Hasbrouck House. There is also a museum of Revolutionary War artifacts on the grounds.

The next stop going north is the town of **New Paltz,** founded by French Huguenots in 1677. Seven stone houses (1692–1717) remain on Huguenot Street. Tours are conducted Tuesday through Sunday from the Historical Society (*88 Huguenot Street, closed Wed., tel 845/255–1660, huguenotstreet.org, tours $$*).

From New Paltz continue north on I-87 to **Kingston,** the Revolutionary War capital of New York. The first state constitution was adopted in 1777 at the **Senate House SHS** (*296 Fair St., tel 845/338–2786*). Maps of walking tours through Kingston's Stockade

Historic District are available at the Heritage Area Visitor Center (*20 Broadway, tel 845/331–7517*).

The Waterfront on the Rondout, just south of the Center, is ideal for lunch, offering great dining options looking onto the Hudson River, next to TR Gallo Waterfront Park (see Travelwise p. 256).

For a memorable overnight stay 13 miles (21 km) north, call well in advance to Saugerties Lighthouse, an 1869 landmark that once guided vessels on the Hudson and now operates as a two-room B&B (see Travelwise p. 256).

East of the Hudson

Leaving Kingston, cross the Hudson at Catskill on the Rip Van Winkle Bridge. Take N.Y. 9G south a mile (1.6 km) to **Olana SHS,** a villa overlooking the Hudson. Its owner, painter Frederic Church (1826–1900), designed it in a style he called "personal Persian."

Mohonk Mountain House

✉ 1000 Mountain Rest Rd., New Paltz

☎ 845/883–3798

mohonk.com

Washington's Headquarters State Historic Site (SHS)

🅰 Map p. 228 B4

✉ Liberty & Washington Sts., Newburgh

☎ 845/562–1195

💲 $

Olana State Historic Site (SHS)

🅰 Map p. 228 B6

✉ N.Y. 9G, Hudson

☎ 518/828–0135

🕑 Open Jun.–Nov.

💲 $

olana.org

EXPERIENCE: Unwinding at Pacem in Terris

In Warwick, New York, 50 miles (80 km) northwest of Manhattan, Pacem in Terris (*96 Covered Bridge Rd., tel 845/986–4329, frederickfranck.org, paceminterris@frontier net.net, closed Mon.–Fri. & Nov.–April*) is the home and sculpture garden of Dutch artist, writer, and humanitarian Frederick Franck (1909–2006). The garden comprises six meditative acres (2.4 ha) on the banks of the Wawayanda River—walk along paths lined with sculptures in metal, wood, stone, and glass. The entire property reflects the themes that informed Franck's life and work: peace, spiritualism, humanity, and the inhumanity of war and neglect.

EXPERIENCE: Savor Slow Food in New York

A visit to **Stone Barns Center for Food and Agriculture** (*630 Bedford Rd., Pocantico Hills, tel 914/366–6200*), just outside Sleepy Hollow, is an enriching experience of an organic farm. The farm, on 80 acres (32 ha) that once belonged to the Rockefeller Estate, promotes local food through sustainable and community-supported agriculture. Rotational grazing allows livestock to be reared in a natural way, while sustaining the land's ecological balance. The farm's

200 varieties of vegetables include rarities such as celtuce, suiho, hakurei turnips, New England Eight-Row Flint seed corn, and finale fennel. You can sample these in exquisite dishes at the adjacent restaurant, **Blue Hill at Stone Barns** (*tel 914/366–9606*), where guests are served the "Farmer's Feast," a five-course tasting of the week's harvest. **Blue Hill** (see Travelwise pp. 241–242) in New York City also offers this feast of artisanal cuisine and wines.

Clermont State Historic Site (SHS)

- 🗺 Map p. 228 B6
- ✉ 87 Clermont Ave., Germantown
- ☎ 518/537–6622
- 🕐 See website for seasonal hours
- 💲 $

friendsofclermont. org

Montgomery Place

- 🗺 Map p. 228 B5
- ✉ N of Kingston Rhinecliff Bridge
- ☎ 845/758–5461
- 🕐 Closed Mon.
- 💲 $$

Dia:Beacon

- 🗺 Map p. 228 B4
- ✉ 3 Beekman St., Beacon, NY
- ☎ 845/440–0100
- 🕐 Closed Tues.– Wed.; Thur. Jan.–Mar.
- 💲 $$
- 🚆 Train: Metro North's Hudson Line from Grand Central Terminal

diaart.org

Continue south on N.Y. 9G to the **Clermont SHS** in Germantown. This was the home of Robert R. Livingston, a member of the Continental Congress and Chancellor of New York who administered the first presidential oath of office to George Washington. The house (named after the boat of his business partner, Robert Fulton) was burned by the British in 1777 and later rebuilt. Just off N.Y. 9G, in Annandale-on-Hudson, is **Montgomery Place.** This mansion was built in 1805 for Janet Montgomery, the widow of Gen. Richard Montgomery.

For a great family outing, visit **Old Rhinebeck Aerodrome** (*9 Norton Rd., Red Hook, closed Nov.–Apr., tel 845/752–3200, oldrhinebeck.org*) for air shows, biplane rides, and a museum of vintage planes, cars, and motorcycles.

North of Poughkeepsie on N.Y. 9 is the lavish **Vanderbilt Mansion National Historic Site (NHS)** (*Map p. 228 B5, 119 Vanderbilt Park Rd., Hyde Park, tel 845/229–7770, nps.gov/vama, call for hours, $$*) built for Frederick

W. Vanderbilt in 1899. Continuing south, US 9 brings you to the **Home of Franklin D. Roosevelt NHS** (*114 Estates Lane, Hyde Park, tel 845/229–5320, nps.gov/hofr*) in Hyde Park, an 1826 house that remains much as it was when Roosevelt died in 1945. Roosevelt and his wife, Eleanor, are buried in the rose garden. Also on the grounds is the Franklin D. Roosevelt Museum and Library. Two miles (3.2 km) east is the **Eleanor Roosevelt NHS** (*54 ValKill Park Rd., Hyde Park., tel 800/229–9422, nps.gov/elro*). After her husband died, Eleanor lived in the cottage, Val-Kill, until her death in 1962. **The Culinary Institute of America** (*tel 845/452–9600, ciachef .edu*) is also located in Hyde Park. Reservations are needed for its four excellent student-run restaurants.

Farther south, in Beacon, lies the art museum **Dia:Beacon, Riggio Galleries.** Built in 1929 as a Nabisco box factory, it offers a vast exhibition space lit by skylights. Filling that space is Dia's permanent collection, a treasure trove of works by art luminaries from the 1960s to the present, including Andy Warhol, Sol LeWitt, Gerhard Richter, and Donald Judd. ∎

LONG ISLAND

Long Island is for many people the undiscovered island. It consists of four counties: Brooklyn and Queens (boroughs of New York City) and Nassau and Suffolk. Millionaires' estates dot the North Shore, while the Hamptons have become celebrity central in the summer.

Having promised his English bride that he would create an estate for her similar to her childhood home, John Jay Phipps, son of Andrew Carnegie's business partner, built **Old Westbury House & Gardens,** a 105-acre (42.5 ha) manor house and estate, in 1906. The landscaped gardens that surround the mansion include a two-acre (0.8 ha), brick Walled Garden with flower borders in bloom from spring to fall. In May the 2,000 tulips are the attraction; in June it's the arrangement of 300 giant pink and blue delphiniums.

The 409-acre (165 ha) **Planting Fields Arboretum State Historic Park** was once the estate of English-born William Coe, an insurance executive who completed his Elizabethan-style manor house in 1921. The gardens contain more than 600 species of plants, including an ever growing collection of rhododendrons and azaleas, and more than 300 camellias grown in a conservatory.

After he graduated from Harvard, Theodore Roosevelt helped to design **Sagamore Hill National Historic Site (NHS)** (*20 Sagamore Hill Rd., Oyster Bay, by guided tour only, house closed Mon.–Tues., tel 516/922–4788, nps. gov/sahi*). He used this rambling 23-room mansion as his summer White House while he was

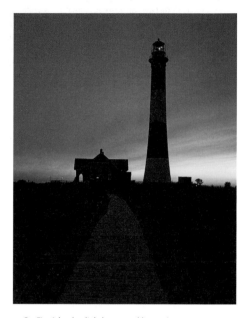

On Fire Island, a lighthouse and keeper's cottage

president—and here he indulged himself in "hard work and the joy of life." The interior, decorated with hunting trophies and mementoes of his travels, reflects his vigorous lifestyle. In 1938 his son built the Old Orchard House next door, now a museum with exhibits on Roosevelt.

In the early 19th century, Long Island was agricultural, and the 50 buildings in the **Old Bethpage Village Restoration** re-create a village of this era. The Powell Farmhouse is on its original site, but the other buildings, including

Old Westbury House & Gardens

- Map p. 228 C2
- 71 Old Westbury Rd., Old Westbury
- 516/333-0048
- Closed Jan.–Mar.

oldwestburygardens .org

Planting Fields Arboretum State Historic Park

- Map p. 229 C2
- 1395 Planting Fields Rd., Oyster Bay
- 516/922-9200

plantingfields.org

Old Bethpage Village Restoration

- 🅰 Map p. 229 C2
- ✉ 1303 Round Swamp Rd., Old Bethpage
- ☎ 516/572–8400
- 🕐 Closed Mon.– Tues. & Jan.– Mar.

Walt Whitman Birthplace

- 🅰 Map p. 229 C2
- ✉ 246 Old Walt Whitman Rd., South Huntington
- ☎ 631/427–5240
- 🕐 Closed Mon.– Tues. Sep.–Jun.

waltwhitman.org

a church, country store, tavern, and houses, were moved here from elsewhere on Long Island. The restoration is also a working farm with volunteers in period costume demonstrating agricultural techniques and crafts.

Walt Whitman (1819–1892) spent the first four years of his life in the farmhouse that is now the **Walt Whitman Birthplace.** The life of America's greatest poet is illuminated by 19th-century furnishings in the restored home and museum with 130 Whitman portraits, Whitman's voice on tape, manuscripts, and artifacts.

Founded in 1939, the **Long Island Museum** (*1200 N.Y. 25A, Stony Brook, tel 516/751–0066,*

---

longislandmuseum.org, closed Mon.– Weds.) is a historical complex noted for its Carriage Museum. There are more than 200 horse-drawn carriages, including a 23-foot-long (7 m) painted omnibus. The **Art Museum** owns many works by genre painter William Sydney Mount, born nearby in 1807, who did scenes of rural Long Island. Mount's 1725 family home is on the museum grounds.

The South Shore on the Atlantic is known for its remarkable barrier beaches: **Fire Island National Seashore** (*tel 631/687–4750, nps.gov/fiis*) and the 2,413-acre (976 ha) **Jones Beach State Park** (*tel 516/785–1600*), with undeveloped areas for nature lovers and an outdoor concert stadium.

The Hamptons and Montauk, on Long Island's eastern tip, are synonymous with celebrity sightings and wealth. After rubbing shoulders, visit the **Pollock-Krasner House** (*830 Springs Fireplace Rd., tel 631/324–4929*) in the Hamptons town of Springs, where Jackson Pollock lived and painted between 1946 and 1956. ∎

TRAVELWISE

TAXI! The ever busy New York taxicab

TRAVELWISE

PLANNING YOUR TRIP

New York City's **Visitor Information Centers** (tel 212/484–1200, nycgo.com) offer useful information at the following sites:

NYC Information Center Midtown (810 Seventh Ave., bet. W. 52nd & W. 53rd, tel 212/484–1222)

NYC Information Center at Macy's Herald Square (151 W. 34th St., bet. Seventh Ave. & Broadway, tel 212/494–3827)

NYC Information Center, Times Square Plaza (tra Seventh Ave., Broadway, W 44th St e 45th Street, tel 212/484–1222)

Also see theater and entertainment hotlines listed in the entertainment section (pp. 262–265). For a personalized introduction to a neighborhood, contact **Big Apple Greeter** (tel 212/669–8159, bigapplegreeter.org). This non-profit will match knowledgeable New Yorkers with visitors. Reserve two–three weeks in advance.

Weather

It's hard to visit New York without spending time outdoors and exploring indoor sites, so dress in layers year-round. On average, temperatures from December to February range from 23°F to 40°F (-5°–4°C). Expect spring showers March to May, but with temperatures between 48°F and 68°F (9°–20°C). June through September temperatures usually range between 60°F and 95°F (15.5°–35°C), peaking in July and August, which tend to be hot and humid; thunderstorms can break any afternoon. By October and November, the city cools to 38°F to 63°F (3°–17°C).

Useful Websites

new.mta.info Metropolitan Transit Authority, for schedules and maps of city subways and buses. **nymag.com** New York magazine, for food/entertainment listings.

Major Events & Festivals

JANUARY

Winter Antiques Show, Seventh Regiment Armory, tel 718/292–7392, thewintershow.org

Restaurant Week, all around town, nycgo.com/restaurant-week

FEBRUARY

Chinatown Lunar New Year Parade, betterchinatown.com

Westminster Kennel Club Dog Show, Madison Square Garden, westminsterkennelclub.org

MARCH

St. Patrick's Day Parade, 5th Ave.

Macy's Flower Show, Macy's Herald Square, 151 W. 34th St., tel 212/695–4400

APRIL

Tribeca Film Festival, tel 219/941–2400, tribecafilm.com (see sidebar p. 71)

Baseball season, Yankee Stadium, tel 877/469–9849, mlb.com/yankees; Mets Citi Field, tel 718/507–8499, mlb.com/mets

New York International Auto Show, Jacob Javits Center, tel 800/282–3336, autoshowny.com

MAY

Bike New York, Five Borough Bike Tour, tel 212/870–2080 ext. 111, bikeny.org

Fleet Week, West Side piers, militarynews.com

Ninth Avenue International Food Festival, from 42nd to 57th Streets, tel 212/581–7029, ninthavenuefoodfestival.com

Washington Square Outdoor Art Exhibition, tel 212/982–6256, wsoae.org

JUNE

Museum Mile Festival, Fifth Ave. from 82nd to 105th Sts., tel 212/606–2296, museummilefestival.org

Gay Pride March, Fifth Ave. bet. 52nd St. & the Village, tel 212/807–7433, nycpride.org

Coney Island Mermaid Parade, coneyisland.com/programs/mermaid-parade

JULY

4th of July, fireworks over the East River, tel 212/494–4495

Lincoln Center Festival, lincolncenter.org

AUGUST

Lincoln Center Out of Doors, tel 212/875–5456, lincolncenter.org/out-of-doors

U.S. Open Tennis, Flushing Meadows Park, Queens, tel 800/990–8782, usopen.org

SEPTEMBER

West Indian-American Day Carnival, Eastern Pkwy., Brooklyn, tel 718/467–1797, wiadcacarnival.org

New York Film Festival, Lincoln Center, tel 212/875–5610, filmlinc.org

OCTOBER

BAM Next Wave Festival, Brooklyn Academy of Music, tel 718/636–4100, bam.org

Blessing of the Animals, Cathedral of St. John the Divine, tel 212/316–7540, stjohndivine.org

Greenwich Village Halloween Parade, 6th Ave., Spring St.–21st St., halloween-nyc.com

NOVEMBER

New York City Marathon, tel 855/569–6977, www.nyrr.org

Radio City Christmas Spectacular, tel 866/858–0007, www.rockettes.com

Macy's Thanksgiving Day Parade, from W. 77th St. & Central Park W. to 34th St. & Broadway, tel

212/494–4495, macys.com/social/parade

DECEMBER

Tree Lighting, Rockefeller Center, tel 212/332–6868, rockefeller center.com

Miracle on Madison, Madison Ave., madisonavenuebid.org/miracle-on-madison/

New Year's Eve, Times Square, tel 212/768–1560, timessquare nyc.org

GETTING AROUND
From the Airports

Air-Ride *(tel 800/247–7433)* provides recorded information on transportation to and from airports.

Buses

Newark Airport Express *(tel 908/354–3330, newarkairportexpress. com)* from Newark Airport and Grand Central, Bryant Park, and Port Authority.

NYC Express Bus *(tel 718–777–5111, nycairporter.com)* has regular buses to/from JFK, LaGuardia, and Newark airports to/from Grand Central Terminal, Times Square, and Port Authority Bus Terminal.

SuperShuttle *(tel 800/258–3826, supershuttle.com)* runs to JFK and LaGuardia to/from most hotels.

Car services

Try to book 24 hours in advance. **Carmel,** tel 866/666–6666, carmellimo.com; **Airlink** (hotel pickup), tel 212/812–9000 goairlinkshuttle.com.

Taxis to JFK: Fixed rate of $52 to Manhattan, excluding tolls and tip; **taxis to LaGuardia:** By the meter, $25–$30; **taxis to Newark:** Dispatcher-determined flat rate of $50–$70, excluding tolls and tip.

Mass Transit

Information: tel 212/878–7000, new.mta.info

Buses & Subways

These cover most of the city and cost $2.50 per ride (half price for seniors and disabled, free for children under 3'8"), including a transfer. Subways are a good choice for long distances and during rush hour. Buses can be slow. You'll find free subway maps at all stations and bus maps on the buses.

Lost & Found, tel 212/712–4500

MetroCards are on sale in news-stands in subway stations. With the pay-per-ride system, the price of your ticket is deducted from your card when you take the subway or bus, while weekly or monthly passes can be used for an unlimited number of trips. Subway/bus transfers made within two hours of your original boarding are included in the price of each trip. Subways require MetroCards; buses take Metro-Cards or exact change ($2.50).

Taxis Take only yellow cabs with the medallion numbers on the roof and the rates on the door. The base fare is $2.50, then 50 cents for every additional fifth-mile (4 blocks) or every minute in stopped or slow traffic. There's also a $1 peak-hour surcharge and a 50-cent night surcharge. There is no charge for other passengers or luggage. Tips expected are 15 percent.

NY Water Taxi *(nywatertaxi.com)* runs ferries around Manhattan and to the outer boroughs.

PRACTICAL ADVICE

New York now ranks among the safest large U.S. cities. That said, keep the following in mind:

• Don't give your bags to anyone in an airport or train/bus station other than authorized personnel.

• Only take official yellow taxis from the airport. Their rates are set by the city, unlike those of the "gypsy cab" operators.

• Carry your wallet in a place you can be constantly mindful of (not a back pocket), and be sure all bags are securely closed.

• Many panhandlers you'll see on the streets and subways are practiced professionals. Just say "no."

• Have a clear idea of where you're going in the outer boroughs. The streets aren't laid out as logically as in Manhattan, most are named rather than numbered, it's almost impossible to hail a taxi, and subways aren't as easy to find. At night, some areas can get desolate.

• While city parks aren't necessarily dangerous at night, tune your awareness up a notch. Use common sense when it comes to particularly dark or empty sections.

• When on the subway at night, ride the more crowded center cars.

• Be aware of those around you when using ATMs, and don't count your money on the street.

TRAVELERS WITH DISABILITIES

Airport Travelers' Aid, tel 718/656–4870.

Asser Levy Playground *(E. 23rd at Asser Levy Pl., near the East River, tel 212/447–2023, nycgovparks.org/parks/asserlevy)* has a playground for disabled children and a free outdoor pool.

Big Apple Greeter is a clearing-house for information for disabled travelers and offers tours led by volunteers; see p. 236.

Lighthouse International *(250 W. 64th St., tel 800/284–4422, lighthouseguild.org)* has Braille maps and events by and for the visually impaired.

EMERGENCIES

Any emergencies, tel 911.

• **Crime Victims Hotline,** tel 212/577–7777.

• **Poison Control Center,** tel 800/222–1222.

• **Medical emergencies:** Go to the nearest emergency room (call 411 for the nearest hospital) or call 911 for an ambulance.

HOTELS & RESTAURANTS

The selection and price range of places to sleep in the city that never does is remarkably varied, with options for every taste and budget. In fact, there are probably more bargains to be had in New York than in any other city—with low-cost options including cozy B&B's and small older hotels in some of the most interesting neighborhoods. Or you can spend a few days in an inexpensive place and then splurge on the kind of metropolitan luxury one only finds in the world's major cities. When it comes to food, one can eat well in a historic Lower East Side deli, an ornate Chinese banquet hall, or a cozy French bistro that seats only 12; or savor delectable fare by a world-class chef in an extravagant room high above Manhattan. While roaming the streets sightseeing or shopping, there is nothing more satisfying than sampling the offerings of sidewalk vendors or noshing the entire length of an avenue during one of the city's many food festivals. New Yorkers are endlessly inventive about new places to eat and drink: In 2013, one enterprising artist even opened an illicit, invite-only speakeasy bar in a Chelsea water tower.

Hotels

Once you determine your total room budget, decide what neighborhood or area appeals to you and then research in depth. From Lower Manhattan to the Upper East and West Sides and beyond, the city teems with shopping, sightseeing, and cultural and historic attractions. If you are drawn more to Broadway or other West Side attractions, then a place in the Times Square or Lincoln Center area may be best. Taxis are usually available, but a ride from the West Village to the Upper East Side, for example, can be quite expensive and also—depending on traffic—slow. Be sure to calculate transportation into both your time and money budgets. If you have limited time in the city, choosing a hotel by location is imperative, to avoid spending half your trip in subways or stuck in traffic. For disabled access, it is recommended you check with the hotel to establish the extent of their facilities. Also verify parking or access to parking spaces. All hotels are air-conditioned.

Restaurants

New York may well be the world's best-fed city. The variety of restaurants—from the hautest French to the simplest Asian, and absolutely everything in between—is unsurpassed. You can find great meals at reasonable prices all over town, but you can also spend a king's ransom if you start hitting the top-shelf restaurants. Often, the challenge is getting a reservation.

Included in the listings below are restaurant closings, though you should always check times when making a reservation, which is recommended when possible. Verify access for those with disabilities; facilities vary, depending on how old the restaurant is as well as its size. If you can't get through to a place by phone, it is likely to be so popular that reservations are impossible to come by. Prices at lunch can be expected to be lower than at dinner at the more upscale establishments, and many of these restaurants offer a special prix fixe menu that can be a real bargain. All restaurants are air-conditioned unless otherwise noted and all are nonsmoking.

Organization

Hotels and restaurants listed here have been grouped first according to neighborhood, then listed alphabetically by price range.

Abbreviations:
L = lunch
D = dinner
Credit card abbreviations: AE (American Express); DC (Diner's Club); MC (Mastercard); V (Visa).

▶ **LOWER MANHATTAN**

Hotels

🏨 **HOTEL ON RIVINGTON**
🍽 **$$$$$**
107 RIVINGTON ST.
(BET. LUDLOW & ESSEX STS.)
TEL 212/475–2600
hotelonrivington.com
This gleaming 21-story glass tower in the historic Lower East Side offers terrific city views from the floor-to-ceiling glass windows in every room. Cutting-edge designers injected creativity into all aspects of the hotel's chic look. Many rooms have balconies, and unusual amenities include Japanese soaking tubs and in-room spa services. For food, drink, and socializing, try **S'Zen**, the bar on the second floor.
📷 94 rooms, 16 suites
🚇 F to Delancey, J to Essex St.
💳 All major cards

🏨 **MILLENNIUM HILTON**
$$$$$
55 CHURCH ST.
TEL 212/693–2001
hiltonhotels.it
Top-end Financial District destination. High-tech style with a fax in each room, and some beautiful views of New York Harbor. Lower rates available weekends.

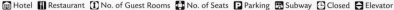
🏨 Hotel 🍽 Restaurant 📷 No. of Guest Rooms 🪑 No. of Seats 🅿 Parking 🚇 Subway 🕐 Closed 🛗 Elevator

PRICES

HOTELS

An indication of the cost of double room in the high season is given by **$** signs.

$$$$$	Over $325
$$$$	$260-$325
$$$	$200–$260
$$	$140–$200
$	Under $140

RESTAURANTS

An indication of the cost of three-course meal without drinks is given by **$** signs.

$$$$$	Over $80
$$$$	$50–$80
$$$	$35–$50
$$	$20–$35
$	Under $20

🏨 569 🚇 1 to Cortlandt St.;
A to Chambers St. 🏊 🏋
🃏 All major cards

🏨 SOHO GRAND
$$$$$
310 W. BROADWAY
(BET. GRAND & CANAL STS.)
TEL 212/965–3000
sohogrand.com
Striking design and a fashionable, pet-friendly destination for those who enjoy the downtown vantage point. Endless interesting stores and galleries are within walking distance.
🏨 353 + 4 suites 🚇 A, C, E to
Canal St. 🃏 🃏 All major cards

🏨🍴 HOLIDAY INN WALL ST.
$$
51 NASSAU ST.
TEL 212/227–3007
hiwallstreethotel.com
A small, clean, affordable alternative in the "very heart of it" that puts you a short walk from Wall Street and the 9/11 Memorial. The **Federal Café** offers hearty American fare all day. Check the website regularly for seasonal deals.
🏨 113 🚇 J, 2, 3 to Fulton St.
🃏 🃏 All major cards

Restaurants

🍴 ECCO
$$$$
124 CHAMBERS ST. (BET.
CHURCH ST. & W. BROADWAY)
TEL 212/227–7074
eccorestaurantny.com
Savory Italian cooking well worth the steep price. Try the veal scaloppine with artichokes, penne *arrabiata,* or assorted grilled fish.
🍴 75 🚇 A, C, 1, 2, 3 to
Chambers St. 🕐 Closed L Sat. &
all day Sun. 🃏 All major cards

🍴 NOBU
$$$$
195 BROADWAY
TEL 212/219–0500
noburestaurants.com
A deservedly popular Nobu Matsuhisa–Drew Nieporent venture with exciting Japanese cuisine and dramatic design. Specialties include black cod with miso and *tiradito,* and there's a huge raw bar.
🍴 100 🚇 1 to Franklin St.
🃏 All major cards

🍴 ODEON
$$$$
145 W. BROADWAY
(AT THOMAS ST.)
TEL 212/233–0507
theodeonrestaurant.com
Hip downtown eatery with reliable French and American food, good late-night scene. Recommended dishes are steak au poivre, steak frites, and other classic bistro fare.
🍴 140 🚇 1 to Chambers St.
🃏 All major cards

🍴 BALTHAZAR
$$$
80 SPRING ST. (AT CROSBY ST.)
TEL 212/965–1414
balthazarny.com
A beautiful SoHo brasserie with matching menu, upbeat tempo, breakfast, lunch, and dinner, late nights and weekend brunch. The oysters and cold seafood platter are particularly impressive.
🍴 160 🚇 6 to Spring St.
🃏 All major cards

🍴 BISTRO LES AMIS
$$$
180 SPRING ST (BET. THOMPSON & SULLIVAN STS.)
TEL 212/226–8645
bistrolesamis.com
Bistro standards like coq au vin, steaks, and seafood, plus great people-watching through the lace curtained windows.
🍴 60 🚇 C, E to Spring St.
🃏 All major cards

🍴 BLUE RIBBON
$$$
97 SULLIVAN ST.
(BET. PRINCE & SPRING STS.)
TEL 212/274–0404
blueribbonrestaurants.com
Minimalist brasserie with excellent raw bar (ask for Alonso's sauce) and eclectic menu. They even have fondue and *pupu* platters. Evenings only.
🍴 45 🚇 C, E to Spring St.
🃏 All major cards

🍴 DELMONICO'S
$$$
56 BEAVER ST.
(NEAR WILLIAM ST.)
TEL 212/509–1144
delmonicosny.com
A classic dating from 1827, birthplace of eggs Benedict and lobster Newburg.
🍴 140 🚇 2, 3, 4, 5 to Wall St.
🕐 Closed Sat. L & Sun.
🃏 All major cards

🍴 RAOUL'S
$$$
180 PRINCE ST. (BET. SULLIVAN & THOMPSON STS.)
TEL 212/966–3518
raouls.com
Always happening, lively French bistro/bar, garden in season, good late at night. The steak au poivre and foie gras terrine are recommended.
🍴 200 🚇 C, E to Spring St.,
1 to Houston St. 🕐 Closed L
🃏 All major cards

🃏 Nonsmoking   🃏 Air-Conditioning   🃏 Indoor Pool   🃏 Outdoor Pool   🃏 Health Club   🃏 Credit Cards

SAMMY'S ROUMANIAN STEAKHOUSE

$$$

157 CHRYSTIE ST.

TEL 212/673–0330

www.sammysromanian.com

Unbelievable only-in-New York option for a schmaltz-laden Jewish meal in an old-fashioned Lower East Side location. Go for the classics: brisket, chopped liver, along with a bottle of vodka in an ice block. Or try the tenderloin steaks, then make your own egg creams with U-bet syrup and seltzer right at your table.

110 F to 2nd Ave., D to Grand Street Closed L & major Jewish holidays All major cards

THE ALLEY CAT

$$$

10 THEATRE ALLEY

(TRA BROADWAY E NASSAU ST.)

TEL 212/461–4300

thebeekman.com

This speakeasy is located in what was once a 20th-century engine room inside the Hotel Beekman. Designed to look like the backstage of a theater, the bar offers snacks and drinks inspired by Japanese izakayas, and a food menu created by the chef, Tom Colicchio.

50 2, 3 to Fulton St., 4, 5, 6 to Brooklyn Bridge All major cards

TRINITY PLACE

$$$

115 BROADWAY

(S SIDE OF ZUCCOTTI PARK)

TEL 212/964–0939

trinityplacenyc.com

This atmospheric bar and backroom restaurant in a converted bank vault is abuzz every weekday with the Wall Street crowd. The dining room has the feel of a modern-day speakeasy. Irish chef Donal Crosbie offers classics such as beef & Guinness pie and a great Kobe burger, and don't leave without trying the sticky toffee pudding.

140 R to Cortlandt St.; 2, 3, 4, 5 to Wall St. Closed Sat.–Sun. All major cards

EDI & THE WOLF

$$

102 AVE. C (CNR. E 7TH ST.)

TEL 212/598–1040

ediandthewolf.com

Named for two Michelin-starred chefs, this rustic restaurant inspired by the taverns of the Austrian quarter offers traditional Austrian cuisine and a rich, thoughtful list of European wines.

60 M9 Avenue C & East 7th Street Closed L Mon.–Fri. All major cards

GREAT NEW YORK NOODLE TOWN

$$

28 BOWERY (AT BAYARD ST.)

TEL 212/349–0923

greatnynoodletown.com

No-frills Chinatown setting serves great dishes until 4 a.m.: salt-baked seafood, duck with flowering chives, noodles with ginger scallion sauce.

60 N, R, 6 to Canal St. Cash only

JOE'S SHANGHAI

$$

9 PELL ST.

(BET. BOWERY & MOTT STS.)

TEL 212/233–8888

joeshanghairestaurants.com

Often a wait but worth it for broth-filled crab or pork dumplings and a large selection of other Shanghai savories. The eggplant with garlic sauce and bean curd wrapped in spinach are very good.

85 N, R, 6 to Canal St. Cash only

PASTEUR GRILL AND NOODLES

$$

85 BAXTER ST.

TEL 212/608–3656

pasteurgrillnoodles.com

This small but very popular locale serves a variety of delicious Vietnamese dishes, including spring rolls and hot noodle soups.

55–60 N, R, 6 to Canal St. All major cards

BO KY

$

80 BAYARD ST. (BET. MOTT & MULBERRY STS.)

TEL 212/406–2292

bokynyc.com

Dozens of inexpensive Vietnamese soups served in a plain Chinatown setting with communal tables. The favorite is curried chicken, and they do a decent roast duck.

100 6 to Canal St. Cash only

BUBBY'S

$

120 HUDSON ST.

(AT N. MOORE ST.)

TEL 212/219–0666

bubbys.com

Casual, popular spot for comfort food and homemade baked goods at all three meals, plus weekend brunch.

120 1 to Franklin St. Closed Sun. DC, MC, V

SOMETHING SPECIAL

COWGIRL HALL OF FAME

$

519 HUDSON ST.

TEL 212/633–1133

cowgirlnyc.com

A theme restaurant that rings absolutely authentic, with Western decor, lots of wood, antlers, barbed wire, cowboy trappings, and a re-created 1950s-era motel room where you wait to be seated. Definitely casual and for those with hearty appetites. Good for families, too: There is a special children's menu, and a small gift shop sells collectibles.

283 1 to Christopher St. AE, MC, V

 Hotel Restaurant No. of Guest Rooms No. of Seats Parking Subway Closed Elevator

🍴 DOJO
$

14 W. 4TH ST. (AT MERCER ST.)
TEL 212/505–8934
dojorestaurant.com
Classic, inexpensive NYU student spot serving Asian, Asian-inspired, vegetarian, and other dishes from a large menu.
🚇 N, R to 8th St.–NYU
💳 Cash only

🍴 JING FONG
$

20 ELIZABETH ST.
(BET. BAYARD & CANAL STS.)
TEL 212/964–5256
jingfongny.com
Overwhelming and unforgettable dim sum paradise in the late morning/lunchtime hours. Don't miss the Chinese chive dumplings and the taro leaf–wrapped packages of sticky rice, chicken, and sausage. Huge and bustling.
🪑 1,000 🚇 6 to Canal St.
💳 AE, MC, V

🍴 KATZ'S DELICATESSEN
$

205 E. HOUSTON ST.
(AT LUDLOW ST.)
TEL 212/254–2246
katzsdelicatessen.com
Classic Lower East Side destination for hot dogs, the best pastrami, corned beef, pickles, and Dr. Brown's soda.
🪑 340 🚇 F to 2nd Ave.
💳 AE, MC, V

🍴 LOMBARDI'S
$

32 SPRING ST.
(BET. MOTT & MULBERRY STS.)
TEL 212/941–7994
firstpizza.com
Allegedly the originator of New York pizza, still serving on the same street. As good as ever.
🪑 100 🚇 6 to Spring St.
💳 Cash only

🍴 NHA TRANG
$

87 BAXTER ST.
TEL 212/233–5948
nhatrangnyc.com
No-nonsense setting for Vietnamese fare. Try pork chops and hot and sour shrimp soup, then sweet Vietnamese coffee.
🪑 80 🚇 6 to Canal St.
💳 MC, V

🍴 WO HOP
$

17 MOTT ST. (BET. MOSCO ST. & CHATHAM SQ.)
TEL 212/962–8617
wohopnyc.com
A Chinatown classic. Go to the kitchen area in the basement for noodle nirvana.
🪑 50 🚇 4, 6 to Spring St.
💳 Cash only

▶ THE VILLAGES

Hotels

🏨 HOTEL GANSEVOORT
🍴 $$$$$

18 9TH AVE. (BET. LITTLE W. 12TH & 13TH STS.)
TEL 212/206–6700
hotelgansevoort.com
This 186-room hotel in the chic Meatpacking District offers spectacular views of the city and the Hudson River from its room balconies and 45-foot (14 m) heated rooftop pool. Very large spa. **The Chester** restaurant, with spectacular decor, has backlit colored glass throughout.
🛏 186 🚇 A, C, E, L to 14th St.
💳 All major cards

🏨 THE STANDARD
🍴 EAST VILLAGE
$$$$$

25 COOPER SQ.
(BOWERY & 5TH ST.)
TEL 212/475–5700
standardhotels.com/
east-village
Chic hotel whose curved, glassy, 21-story tower was built around an 1845 tenement building. Stylish rooms blend a minimalist aesthetic with natural woods for comfort, plus views from floor-to-ceiling windows. **Café Standard** offers American cuisine and cocktails from breakfast till late.
🛏 145 🚇 6 to Astor Pl.
💳 All major cards

🏨 THE BOWERY HOTEL
$$$$

335 BOWERY
TEL 212/505–9100
theboweryhotel.com
Luxury and comfort characterize this hotel, located 5 minutes on foot from Bleeker Street Station. On the ground floor, Gemma, an Italian trattoria, serves seasonal and traditional dishes and Italian wines. The hotel has an outdoor terrace, a fitness center, free bicycles, and a film library.
🛏 135 rooms 🚇 4, 6, B, D, F, M Broadway-Lafayette Bleecker Street 💳 All major cards

🏨 WASHINGTON SQUARE HOTEL
$$

103 WAVERLY PLACE
(AT MACDOUGAL ST.)
TEL 212/777–9515 OR
800/222–0418
wshotel.com
European-style hotel in the heart of Greenwich Village, just off the park. Recently renovated, century-old hotel with well-furnished rooms and a pleasant restaurant.
🛏 180 🚇 A, B, C, D, E, F to W. 4th St. 🎽 💳 All major cards

Restaurants

SOMETHING SPECIAL

🍴 BLUE HILL
$$$$$

75 WASHINGTON PL.
TEL 212/539–1776
bluehillfarm.com
Dan Barber's "farm-to-fork" and "dock-to-dish" restaurant is located in a landmark

Greenwich Village "speakeasy," just off Washington Square Park. The menu showcases local food and a wine list with artisanal producers. Ingredients come from nearby farms, including Stone Barns Center for Food and Agriculture (see sidebar p. 232). Choose from the menu or opt for the "Farmer's Feast," a fabulous five-course tasting of creatively presented dishes from the week's harvest. A night of sheer pleasure for the palate; you'll only wish you had longer to savor all the flavors.

🛏 71 🚇 A, B, C, D, E, F to W. 4th St. 🕐 Closed L ⊘ All major cards

🍴 ONE IF BY LAND, TWO IF BY SEA
$$$$$
17 BARROW ST.
TEL 212/255–8649
oneifbyland.com
Located in a 1786 landmark stone carriage house once the home of Aaron Burr, this elegant restaurant overlooks a private garden with festive lights. Inside, candles, live piano music, flowers, and four fireplaces create an ambience perfect for a romantic meal or a large celebration. Menu favorites are Beef Wellington and contemporary interpretations of classic dishes. And, if you are one of the lucky, you may dine there on a night when Burr's ghost, victorious after his duel with Alexander Hamilton, appears.

🛏 150 🚇 A, B, C, D, E, F to W. 4th St. ⊘ All major cards

🍴 BABBO
$$$$
110 WAVERLY PL.
TEL 212/777–0303
babbonyc.com
Mario Batali's excellent, adventurous Italian restaurant features game,

traditional Italian dishes, and pasta tasting menus. Getting reservations can be challenging.

🛏 126 🚇 A, B, C, D, E, F to W. 4th St. 🕐 Closed L ⊘ All major cards

SOMETHING SPECIAL

🍴 GOTHAM BAR & GRILL
$$$$
12 E. 12TH ST. (BET. 5TH AVE. & UNIVERSITY PLACE)
TEL 212/620–4020
gothambarandgrill.com
In this spacious multilevel Gramercy-area eatery, the architecture, as well as the food, stands out: One reviewer called this award-winning, postmodern warehouse conversion "an awesome dining temple." Chef Alfred Portale serves up specialties such as grilled rack of lamb and seared yellowfin tuna, and signature Gotham chocolate cake.

🛏 150 🚇 4, 5, 6 to Union Sq. 🕐 Closed Sat. & Sun. L ⊘ All major cards

🍴 JAMES BEARD HOUSE
$$$$
167 W. 12TH ST.
(BET. 6TH & 7TH AVES.)
TEL 212/675–4984
jamesbeard.org
Gastronomic Carnegie Hall featuring the world's best chefs, a different one nightly. Call for calendar. Advance reservations only.

🛏 90 🚇 1, 2, 3 to 14th St. ⊘ All major cards

🍴 MINETTA TAVERN
$$$$
113 MCDOUGAL ST.
TEL 212/475–3850
minettatavernny.com
This casual bistro, loved by personalities such as Ernest Hemingway, Ezra Pound, and Dylan Thomas, serves tasty steaks and excellent cocktails.

🛏 150 🚇 A, B, C, D, E, F to W. 4th St. 🕐 Closed L Mon.–Tues. ⊘ All major cards

🍴 GAONNURI
$$$
1250 BROADWAY, (PENTHOUSE, 39TH FL.)
TEL 212/971–9045
gaonnurinyc.com
One of Midtown's best-kept secrets, this top-floor oasis offers authentic Korean cuisine, superb views of the city, and excellent cocktails. Gaonnuri translates as "center of the world." Its owner insists it's the highest Korean restaurant on Earth.

🛏 120 🚇 B, D, F, N, Q, R to 34th St. 🕐 Closed Sun. L ⊘ All major cards

🍴 TOLOACHE
$$$
205 THOMPSON ST, (BLEEKER STREET)
TEL 212/420-0600
toloachenyc.com
A Mexican bistro, it belongs to a chain of restaurants known for the originality of its food and for its margaritas. It offers more than a dozen kinds of chili made with natural ingredients.

🛏 100 🚇 1, 2 to Houston St. 🕐 Closed Sat. & Sun. L ⊘ All major cards

🍴 CARACAS AREPA BAR
$$
3½ EAST 7TH ST. (AT 1ST AVE)
TEL 212/529–2314
caracasarepabar.com
Dine-in or take-out Venezuelan corn cakes with savory fillings in an intimate setting.

🚇 L to 1st Ave., F to 2nd Ave. ⊘ All major cards

🍴 JAPONICA
$$
100 UNIVERSITY PL.
TEL 212/243–7752
japonicanyc.com
Sushi and Japanese fare;

popular for lunch and dinner. 🔲 84 🔲 4, 5, 6 to Union Sq. 💳 AE, MC, V

🍴 MANCORA
$$
97 1ST AVE.
(AT 6TH ST.)
TEL 212/253–1011
mancoranyc.com
Peruvian dishes from ceviche to beef and chicken.
🔲 6 to Bleecker St.
💳 MC, V

🍴 TEA & SYMPATHY
$$
108 GREENWICH AVE.
(BET. 12TH & 13TH STS.)
TEL 212/807–8329
teaandsympathynewyork.com
Tiny storefront serving delicious, hearty British fare, like steak-and-Guinness pie, and bangers and mash. Traditional high tea offered. Takeout available; small shop next door.
🔲 22 🔲 A, C, E to 14th St.
💳 MC, V

🍴 CORNER BISTRO
$
331 W. 4TH ST.
(AT 14TH ST.)
TEL 212/242–9502
cornerbistrony.com
Bar for burgers and fries on paper plates. Get the Bistro burger, with cheese, bacon, lettuce, and tomato, all for $8.75.
🔲 34 🔲 A, C, E to 14th St.
💳 Cash only

🍴 PATISSERIE CLAUDE
$
187 W 4TH ST.
TEL 212/255–5911
The warm, buttery smell wafting from this tiny café tells you all you need to know: Stop in for *une café* and melt-in-your-mouth quiche or pastries while walking in the Village.
🔲 10 🔲 1 to Christopher St.
💳 All major cards

🍴 POMMES FRITES
$
123 2ND AVE.
(BET. 7TH ST. & ST. MARKS PL.)
TEL 212/674–1234
pommesfritesnyc.com
Not quite a meal, but a nice, big snack of Belgian-style fries in a paper cone. Try the *especial* sauce for dipping and the malt vinegar.
🔲 3 tables 🔲 6 to Astor Place
💳 Cash only

🍴 VESELKA
$
144 2ND AVE.
(AT 9TH ST.)
TEL 212/228–9682
veselka.com
Casual neighborhood hangout with Ukrainian specialties, especially soups, and timeless murals. Open 24 hours. Try buckwheat pancakes or challah French toast.
🔲 60 🔲 6 to Astor Place
💳 All major cards

▶ MIDTOWN SOUTH

Hotels

🏨 INN AT IRVING PLACE
$$$$$
56 IRVING PLACE
(BET. 17TH & 18TH STS.)
TEL 212/533–4600 OR
800/685–1447
innatirving.com
Romantic, Victorian-style hotel in two 1834 town houses, with four-poster beds. Try high tea at Lady Mendl's Tea Salon (on the premises).
🛏 12 suites 🔲 4, 5, 6 to Union Sq. 💳 All major cards

🏨 ST. GILES THE TUSCANY
$$$$
120 E. 39TH ST.
TEL 212/686–1600
tuscany.stgilesnewyork.com
Stylish Midtown sanctuary

with wonderful amenities and large rooms with Italian marble bathrooms.
🛏 124 🔲 4, 5, 6 to Grand Central 🎾
💳 All major cards

SOMETHING SPECIAL

🏨 🍴 THE STANDARD HIGH LINE
$$$$
848 WASHINGTON ST.
(AT 13TH ST.)
TEL 212/645–4646
standardhotels.com/high-line
It's all about the views at this André Balazs hotel, which literally straddles the new High Line Park in the hip Meatpacking District, just one block from the Hudson River. Its streamlined rooms are 20th-century modern and all are angled to maximize the views. The Standard Plaza and the Standard Grill offer a good selection of indoor and outdoor dining. Hotel bikes are available to rent.
🛏 338 🔲 A, C, E to 14th St.
💳 All major cards

🏨 FREEHAND NEW YORK
$$$
23 LEXINGTON AVENUE (BET.
E 23RD & E 24TH STS.)
TEL 212/475–1920
freehandhotels.com/
new-york
The Freehand Hotel in the Flatiron District is part of a chain of hotels inspired by the design of European hostels. It's housed in the former George Washington Hotel, home to writers, musicians, and internationally famous artists. It was designed by Roman and Williams and features custom commissioned artwork by the students of Bard College. The atmosphere is welcoming and functional, with a variety of room sizes and types that range from king rooms to bunk

---

🅂 Nonsmoking 🅰 Air-Conditioning 🏊 Indoor Pool 🏊 Outdoor Pool 🎾 Health Club 💳 Credit Cards

rooms. Since 2018, it has been home to three bars with original culinary concepts.

🛈 395 🚇 4, 5, 6 to 23rd St.
📺 🅦 All major cards

🏨 HOTEL METRO
$$$

45 W. 35TH ST.
(BET. 5TH & 6TH AVES.)
TEL 212/947–2500
hotelmetronyc.com
Stylish, art deco rooms and a roof terrace with views of the Empire State Building.

🛈 181 🚇 1, 2, 3 to 34th St.
📺 🅦 All major cards

🏨 THE EVELYN
$$–$$$

7 E. 27TH ST.
(BET. 5TH & MADISON AVES.)
TEL 212/545–8000
theevelyn.com
This hundred-year-old hotel set in what used to be Tin Pan Alley, home to successful singer/songwriters in the 1930s and 40s, appeals to creative, budget conscious travelers. Culture and pop art are still the inspiring muses here.

🛈 140 🚇 N, R, 6 to 28th St.
🅦 AE, MC, V

Restaurants

🍽 ELEVEN MADISON PARK
$$$$

11 MADISON AVE.
(BETWEEN 24TH & 25TH STS.)
TEL 212/889–0905
elevenmadisonpark.com
After four months of interior renovation, this three Michelin starred restaurant reopened in 2017. The dining room features the artwork of Rita Ackerman, which you can admire as you enjoy chef Daniel Humm's tasting menu.

🍴 80 🚇 4, 5, 6, Q, R to 23rd St. 🕐 Closed Mon.–Thur. L 🅦 All major cards

🍽 GRAMERCY TAVERN
$$$$

42 E. 20TH ST. (BET. BROADWAY & PARK AVE. S.)
TEL 212/477–0777
gramercytavern.com
Well-executed, contemporary cuisine, fine wines, clubby atmosphere, with Tavern Room as a more casual option. Under chef Michael Anthony, the menu has turned more rustic. Try the sturgeon with brussels sprouts and chestnuts.

🍴 140 + 40 tavern area 🚇 6 to 23rd St. 🅦 All major cards

🍽 I TRULLI (& ENOTECA)
$$$$

124 E. 27TH ST. (BET. LEXINGTON AVE. & PARK AVE. S.)
TEL 212/481–7372
itrulli.com
The foods and wines of Italy's Apulia region, with excellent homemade pastas, especially *bavette a funghi,* rotisserie chicken, and wood-roasted fish. Next-door Enoteca is a wine bar serving casual food.

🍴 150 🚇 6 to 28th St.
🕐 Closed Sat. & Sun. L
🅦 All major cards

🍽 OLD HOMESTEAD STEAK HOUSE
$$$$

56 9TH AVE
TEL 212/242–9040
theoldhomesteadsteakhouse.com
A timeless classic in the heart of the trendy Meatpacking District, Old Homestead has been here since 1868. Greg and Marc Sherry's restaurant is legendary for its prime aged Texas-size slabs of beef-sirloin, porterhouse, or filet mignon.

🍴 225 🚇 A, C, E to 14th St.
🅦 All major cards

🍽 PERIYALI
$$$$

35 W. 20TH ST.
TEL 212/463–7890
periyali.com
Established destination for

PRICES

HOTELS
An indication of the cost of double room in the high season is given by **$** signs.

$$$$$	Over $325
$$$$	$260–$325
$$$	$200–$260
$$	$140–$200
$	Under $140

RESTAURANTS
An indication of the cost of three-course meal without drinks is given by **$** signs.

$$$$$	Over $80
$$$$	$50–$80
$$$	$35–$50
$$	$20–$35
$	Under $20

home-style Greek food, with exquisitely simple fish and authentic dishes. Try *pikantikes salates* to start, then grilled octopus or lamb.

🍴 100 🚇 F to 23rd St.
🕐 Closed Sat. L
🅦 All major cards

🍽 RIVERPARK
$$$$

450 E 29TH ST.
TEL 212/729–9790
riverparknyc.com
Fine dining with fine views of the East River. Chef Sisha Ortúzar showcases the restaurant's on-site urban farm. Riverpark's modern American menus change daily, highlighting seasonal ingredients from local farms, green markets, and Riverpark Farm.

🍴 65 + 72 terrace 🚇 6 to 28th St. 🅦 All major cards

🍽 UNION SQUARE CAFÉ
$$$$

21 E. 16TH ST. (BET. 5TH AVE. & UNION SQ. W.)
TEL 212/243-4020
unionsquarecafe.com
Award-winning and eternally successful formula of chef

🏨 Hotel 🍽 Restaurant 🛈 No. of Guest Rooms 🍴 No. of Seats 🅿 Parking 🚇 Subway 🕐 Closed 🛗 Elevator

Carmen Quagliata's eclectic, well-executed cuisine, great wines, and attentive service. Signature dishes include fried calamari with spicy anchovy sauce and filet mignon of tuna.

🚇 125 🚇 4, 5, 6 to Union Sq. 🏧 All major cards

HANGAWI
$$$
12 E. 32ND ST.
(BET. 5TH & MADISON AVES.)
TEL 212/213-0077
hangawirestaurant.com
An otherworldly Korean vegetarian experience. Dishes are prepared with unusual but memorable roots and greens.

🚇 60 🚇 N, R to 34th St.; 6 to 33rd St 🏧 All major cards

THE RED CAT
$$$
227 10TH AVE.
(BET. 23RD & 24TH STS.)
TEL 212/242-1308
redcatrestaurants.com
This warm and welcoming bistro has radishes and salt at the bar and offers hearty and delicious dishes like pierogi, double-cut pork chops, and crispy green beans.

🚇 80 🚇 C, E, 1, 9 to 23rd St. 🏧 All major cards

HILL COUNTRY
$$–$$$
30 W. 26TH ST.
(BET. 6TH AVE. & BROADWAY)
TEL 212/255-4544
hillcountryny.com
Texas BBQ and live music, with brisket, sausage, ribs, and more. Served on butcher paper. May be the city's best fried chicken.

🚇 N, R to 28th St. 🏧 All major cards

BOTTINO
$$
246 10TH AVE. (AT 24TH ST.)
TEL 212/206-6766
bottinonyc.com
This chic art-world favorite, nestled among Chelsea's

galleries and near the new High Line Park, serves upscale Italian fare lubricated by much wine.

🚇 C, E to 23rd St. 🕐 Open for L Tues.–Sat. only

EATALY
$$
200 5TH AVE.
(BET. 23RD & 24TH ST.)
TEL 212/229-2560
eataly.com
The high-quality Italian food market, part of Oscar Farinetti's famous chain, also has four restaurants that serve Italy's gastronomic delights.

🚇 E, W to 23rd St. Try also new restaurant in Downtown, 4 World Trade Center, Floor 3, 101 Liberty Street 🚇 1 to WTC Cortlandt

ELMO
$$
156 7TH AVE.
(BET. 19TH & 20TH STS.)
TEL 212/337-8000
elmorestaurant.com
Fashionistas flock to Elmo, which has raised comfort food to an art. Favorites include butternut squash soup with scallions, chicken pot pie, and the special Elmo burger.

🚇 110 🚇 C, E to 23rd St. 🏧 All major cards

EMPIRE DINER
$–$$
210 10TH AVE.
TEL 212/335-2277
empire-diner.com
One of the great New York diners, with an arte-moderne exterior that has made it a star of movies, TV shows, and a Tom Waits album cover. Amanda Freitag recently revived this retro favorite, along with its famous patty melt and thick-cut fries, and coffee strong enough to stand up for itself.

🚇 50 🚇 C, E to 23rd St. 🏧 All major cards

PETE'S TAVERN
$–$$
129 E 18TH ST.
TEL 212/473-7676
petestavern.com
One of the city's oldest eateries (1864). Great place for value lunch on the prix fixe menu. The Penne à la vodka, the half spring chicken, or any of the classic burgers, such as O. Henry's Roma Burger, will satisfy the weary walker or shopper, but it's not only about the food. You'll also be charmed by the old photos, stories, and newspaper articles about William Sydney Porter, better known as O. Henry, who was a regular customer here.

🚇 4, 5, 6 to Union Sq. 🏧 All major cards

EISENBERG'S SANDWICH SHOP
$
174 5TH AVE.
(BET. 22ND & 23RD STS.)
TEL 212/675-5096
eisenbergsnyc.com
Landmark Jewish diner in Chelsea. Great Reubens and tuna salad on rye.

🚇 34 🚇 N, R to 23rd St. 🏧 Cash only

THE GREY DOG CHELSEA
$
242 W. 16TH ST.
(BET. SEVENTH AVE. & 8TH AVE.)
TEL 212/229-2345
thegreydog.com
Of the various locations in Manhattan, we suggest the one in Chelsea that has a comfortable, relaxing bar with American fare where you can have a snack or even lunch or dinner.

🚇 40 🚇 A, C, E, L to 14th St. 🏧 All major cards

TIA POL
$
205 10TH AVE. (OFF 22ND ST.)
TEL 212/675-8805
tiapol.com

🚭 Nonsmoking 🅰 Air-Conditioning 🏊 Indoor Pool 🏊 Outdoor Pool 🏋 Health Club 🏧 Credit Cards

The brick walls enclose some of the highest rated tapas and traditional Basque dishes in New York City, with outstanding croquettes, excellent cod dishes, and nightly specials.

🛏 40 🚇 C, E to 23rd St. 🃏 All major cards

▶ **MIDTOWN NORTH**

Hotels

🏨 **ALGONQUIN**
$$$$$
59 W. 44TH ST.
(BET. 5TH & 6TH AVES.)
TEL 212/840–6800
algonquinhotel.com
New York's literary landmark since the 1920s, a real fixture. Charming, traditional Victorian rooms with modern services, nice lobby for cocktails, nice locale.

🛈 175 🚇 B, D, F to 42nd St. 🃏 All major cards

🏨 **FOUR SEASONS**
$$$$$
57 E. 57TH ST.
(BET. PARK & MADISON AVES.)
TEL 212/758–5700
fourseasons.com
This 52-story art deco–style monument designed by I. M. Pei and completed in 1993 has received top ratings and boasts the largest rooms in the city, with accompanying big views. Expect modernistic furniture, giant Florentine marble bathrooms, and elaborate bedside push-button systems.

🛈 370 🚇 N, Q, R, 4, 5, 6 to Lexington Ave./59th St. 🃏 🃏 All major cards

🏨 **HOTEL ELYSÉE**
$$$$$
60 E. 54TH ST.
(BET. MADISON & PARK AVES.)
TEL 212/753–1066
elyseehotel.com
Built in the 1920s, this

delightful hotel offers jazz-age decor, charming rooms with antiques, a small roof terrace, evening wine and cheese, and a free pass to NY Sports Club.

🛈 88 + 11 suites 🚇 E to Lexington Ave.; 6 to 51st St. 🃏 🃏 All major cards

🏨 **JW MARRIOTT ESSEX HOUSE HOTEL**
$$$$$
160 CENTRAL PARK S.
(BET. 6TH & 7TH AVES.)
TEL 212/247–0300 OR
888/645–5697
marriott.com
Now part of Marriott, Essex House completed a $90 million refurbishment that conserved its dramatic art deco setting and added high-tech, environmentally friendly features to the hotel's stunning views of Central Park.

🛈 516 + 81 suites 🚇 A, B, C, D, 1 to Columbus Circle–59th St.; N, Q, R to 57th St./7th Ave. 🃏 🃏 All major cards

🏨 **PENINSULA**
$$$$$
700 5TH AVE. (AT 55TH ST.)
TEL 212/956–2888 OR
800/262–9467
peninsula.com
Turn-of-the-20th-century beaux arts landmark, with views down Fifth Avenue. Art nouveau furnishings and oversize beds and bathrooms. More luxurious trappings at the rooftop spa and Salon de Ning, excellent for summer-time cocktails and city views.

🛈 250 🚇 E to 5th Ave./53rd St.; F to 57th St. 🃏 🃏 All major cards

🏨 **PLAZA HOTEL**
$$$$$
CENTRAL PARK SOUTH
768 5TH AVE. (AT 59TH ST.)
TEL 212/759–3000
fairmont.com/
the-plaza-new-york
In 2005, this city icon

underwent a $400 million makeover in which 523 of its rooms were converted into 152 ultra-expensive condos. Luckily, there are still 282 hotel rooms and suites, including the suite where the beloved children's book character Eloise has "lived" since 1955. The Grand Ballroom, Palm Court (with Tiffany Ceiling), Oak Room, and Oak Bar were all retained in the building's transformation, and some basic historic features were restored. Strolling the exterior grounds at the corner of Central Park is a must.

🛈 282 🚇 N, R to 5th Ave./59th St. 🃏 🃏 All major cards

🏨 **ROYALTON**
$$$$$
44 W. 44TH ST.
(BET. 5TH & 6TH AVES.)
TEL 212/869–4400
royaltonhotel.com
Phillipe Starck interiors with high-tech modern lobby, restaurant, bar, and lovely rooms with slate fireplaces and round bathtubs.

🛈 137 + 31 suites 🚇 1, 2, 3, 7 to Times Sq. 🃏 🃏 All major cards

🏨 **ST. REGIS**
🍴 **$$$$$**
2 E. 55TH ST.
(BET. 5TH & MADISON AVES.)
TEL 212/753–4500
stregisnewyork.com
Elaborately restored 1904 beaux arts gem, with elegant yet accessible public rooms and the finest service and amenities. Enjoy the riches of **Lespinasse**, one of New York's top restaurants, and of the great King Cole Bar, dominated by the engaging Maxfield Parrish mural of the king himself.

🛈 322 🚇 E to 5th Ave./53rd St.; N, R to 5th Ave./59th St. 🃏 🃏 All major cards

---

 Hotel   Restaurant   No. of Guest Rooms  No. of Seats   Parking   Subway   Closed ⬛ Elevator

THE RITZ–CARLTON NEW YORK, CENTRAL PARK

$$$$$

50 CENTRAL PARK S.
(AT 6TH AVE.)
TEL 212/308–9100 OR
ritzcarlton.com

Formerly the St. Moritz, this 33-story luxury hotel offers glamour, a great location (with some of the city's best views), special value in complimentary Bentley service within Midtown, butlers, and fabulous lounges. **Auden Bistro & Bar** restaurant serves excellent culinary experience.

🚻 261 🚇 F to 57th St.
🚫 All major cards

THE SHOREHAM

$$$$$

33 W. 55TH ST.
TEL 866/950–8893
shorehamhotel.com

Attractive art deco interior with aluminum furniture and many nice touches.

🚻 47 + 37 suites 🚇 E to 5th Ave./53rd St.; N, Q, R to 57th St./7th Ave. 🚫 All major cards

WALDORF-ASTORIA & WALDORF TOWERS

$$$$–$$$$$

301 PARK AVE.
(AT 50TH ST.)
TEL 212/355–3000
waldorfastoriacollection.com

The great Waldorf-Astoria is one of the quintessential New York hotels. The art deco lobby is magnificent, and the exclusive, elaborately appointed Waldorf Towers (floors 28–42) provide quarters for visiting presidents, among others.

🚻 1,410 🚇 E to Lexington Ave./53rd St.; 6 to 51st St. 🏥 🚫 All major cards

CASABLANCA HOTEL

$$$$

147 W. 43RD ST.
(BET. 6TH AVE. & BROADWAY)
TEL 212/869–1212 OR
888/922–7225
casablancahotel.com

They're serious about the name, with Moroccan touches mixing with modern, a guest lounge called Rick's Cafe, and a vaguely North African outdoor courtyard. Rooms are well outfitted.

🚻 40 + 8 suites 🚇 1, 2, 3, 7 to Times Sq.–42nd St. 🏥
🚫 All major cards

LOTTE NEW YORK PALACE

$$$$

455 MADISON AVE.
TEL 212/888–7000
lottenypalace.com

This unmistakable site, located in what was once the iconic Villard Mansion, designed in 1882 by Stanford White, has maintained all of its original opulence despite a series of renovations. Its elegant 55-story tower dominates St. Patrick's Cathedral. One of the best places to eat in the area is in the Villard Restaurant, located in the hotel's courtyard.

🚻 600 🚇 E to 5th Ave./53rd St.; B, D, F to 47th–50th St.–Rockefeller Center 🏥
🚫 All major cards

SOMETHING SPECIAL

MILLENNIUM HILTON NEW YORK ONE UN PLAZA

$$$$

1 UNITED NATIONS PLAZA 44TH
TEL 212/758–1234 OR
866/866–8086
millenniumhotels.com

Staying here puts you in the midst of global drama, as diplomats and staff rush to the UN or their offices on the first 27 floors of the UN Plaza. The award-winning modern building rises high above the East Side. Hotel rooms—all with stunning views—start at the 28th floor. Artworks from New York City and various nations are found throughout the hotel. You will want to use the excellent sports facilities, including indoor tennis courts, a pool, and an on-site reflexologist. Shuttle services for city sites and the airports.

🚻 428 🚇 4, 5, 6, 7 to 42nd St.
🏊 🏥 🚫 All major cards

THE MANSFIELD

$$$$

12 W. 44TH ST.
(BET. 5TH & 6TH AVES.)
TEL 212/277–8700 OR
800/255–5167
mansfieldhotel.com

Former bachelors' residence combining chess by the fireplace with pillowtop mattresses, a modern gym, and romantic late 19th-century ambience. Welcoming library with concerts and cappuccino.

🚻 103 + 26 suites 🚇 B, D, F to 42nd St.; 1, 2, 3, 7 to Times Sq. 🏥 🚫 All major cards

THE PARAMOUNT

$$$$

235 W. 46TH ST.
(BET. BROADWAY & 8TH AVE.)
TEL 212/764–5500
nycparamount.com

Phillipe Starck–designed lobby and playful, attractive decor in the heart of the theater district.

🚻 601 + 12 suites 🚇 1, 2, 3, 7 to 42nd St.–Times Sq. 🏥
🚫 All major cards

ROGER SMITH

$$–$$$

501 LEXINGTON AVE.
TEL 212/755–1400
rogersmith.com

Casual 1929 boutique hotel has a strong arts orientation, with an in-house gallery and performance space. Continental breakfast is included.

🚻 130 🚇 E to Lexington

Ave./53rd St.; 6 to 51st St.
All major cards

Restaurants

🍴 AQUAVIT
$$$$$
65 E. 55TH ST.
(BET. MADISON & PARK)
TEL 212/307–7311
aquavit.org
Fancy and fine Scandinavian
fare. House specialties are
gravlax, baked salmon, and
Swedish meatballs.
🍽 180 🚇 E to 5th Ave./
53rd St. 🕐 Closed Sat. L &
Sun. All major cards

🍴 AUREOLE
$$$$$
135 W. 42ND ST.
(BET. MADISON & PARK AVES.)
TEL 212/319–1660
charliepalmer.com/
properties/aureole
Charlie Palmer's famous
contemporary American cuisine is a fine dining experience.
Chef Marcus Gleadow-Ware's
menu offers delights including
New Zealand king salmon
gravlax, Thai spiced Maine
lobster, and beef pot-au-feu,
a hearty beef and vegetable
bouillon. The seasonal prix fixe
menu is recommended.
🍽 37 🚇 B to 42nd St.
🕐 Closed Sat. L & Sun.
All major cards

🍴 FELIDIA
$$$$$
243 E. 58TH ST.
(BET. 2ND & 3RD AVES.)
TEL 212/758–1479
felidia-nyc.com
Supreme Northern Italian cuisine by Lidia Bastianich. Wonderful pasta and risottos, and
the specialties of Trieste.
🍽 90 🚇 N, Q, R, 4, 5, 6
to Lexington Ave./59th St.
🕐 Closed Sat. & Sun. L
All major cards

🍴 FOUR SEASONS
$$$$$
42 E 49TH ST.
TEL 212/754–9494
fourseasonsrestaurant.com
Timeless design by Philip
Johnson with the most
professional service and
American cuisine. Try the
crab cakes or steak tartare.
🍽 100 🚇 6 to 51st St.; E, F to
Lexington Ave. 🕐 Closed Sun.
& Sat. L All major cards

🍴 LA GRENOUILLE
$$$$$
3 E. 52ND ST.
(BET. 5TH & MADISON AVES.)
TEL 212/752–1495
la-grenouille.com
Haute French cuisine in
flower-filled splendor.
🍽 80 🚇 E to 5th Ave./53rd
St. 🕐 Closed Sun.–Mon.
All major cards

🍴 LE BERNARDIN
$$$$$
155 W. 51ST ST.
(BET. 6TH & 7TH AVES.)
TEL 212/554–1515
le-bernardin.com
Outstanding French
seafood cuisine and elegant,
nearly flawless service.
Outstanding black bass
ceviche, tuna tartare, prix
fixe menus.
🍽 38 tables 🚇 1 to 50th St.
🕐 Closed Sat. L & all day Sun.
All major cards

🍴 NOBU 57
$$$$$
40 W. 57TH ST.
(BET. 5TH & 6TH AVES.)
TEL 212/757–3000
noburestaurants.com
This bi-level spin-off offers
Nobu Japanese-fusion favorites such as sweet miso black
cod, plus new delights. Reservations are recommended.
🍽 200 🚇 F to 57th St.;
N, R to 5th Ave/59th St.
All major cards

🍴 PER SE
$$$$$
10 COLUMBUS CIRCLE

TEL 212/823-9335
perseny.com
This temple for Thomas Keller's
Napa Valley cuisine is in the
vein of his famous California
French Laundry. The ambience
is a little austere, but the food
has critics raving. The menu
changes daily, with a set of five-
and nine-course tasting menus.
Views over Central Park are
lovely. Book far, far ahead.
🚇 A, B, C, D, 1 to 59th St.–
Columbus Circle 🕐 Closed
Mon.–Thurs. L
All major cards

🍴 "21"
$$$$
21 W. 52ND ST.
(BET. 5TH & 6TH AVES.)
TEL 212/582–7200
21club.com
A New York institution since
1930, with both inventive
and classic American cuisine,
famous dishes of chicken
hash and burgers, and great
Bloody Marys.
🍽 150 🚇 B, D, F to 47th–
50th Sts.–Rockefeller Center
🕐 Closed Sun.
All major cards

SOMETHING SPECIAL

🍴 DADONG
$$$$
3 BRYANT PARK
(TRA 41TH ST. E 42TH ST.)
TEL 212/355–9600
dadongny.com
The Dadong franchise has 16
locations in China and has been
awarded a number of Michelin
stars. This is its first international
location, inaugurated in 2017.
Located near Bryant Park, it
occupies the 2nd and 3rd floors
of the Cube Building, with a
comfortable cocktail bar, an
original style dining room, and
a garden. The refined Chinese
menu includes a roast duck that
you don't want to miss.
🍽 440 🚇 B, D, F, M to 42nd
St./Bryant Pk. 🕐 Closed Sun.
All major cards

🏨 Hotel 🍴 Restaurant 🛏 No. of Guest Rooms 🍽 No. of Seats 🅿 Parking 🚇 Subway 🕐 Closed 🛗 Elevator

🍴 OCEANA
$$$$
120 W. 49TH ST.
(BET. MADISON & PARK AVES.)
TEL 212/759–5941
oceanarestaurant.com
Chef Neil Gallagher does wonders with seafood. House specialties include lobster salad.
🚻 100 🚇 B, D, F to 47th–50th Sts.–Rockefeller Center ⏰ Closed Sat. & Sun. L 💳 All major cards

🍴 RÔTISSERIE GEORGETTE
$$$$
14 E 60TH ST.
TEL 212/390–8060
rotisserieg.com
Simply prepared meat is the specialty at this refined French restaurant near Central Park but the menu also includes vegetarian and fish-based dishes. The special poulet rôti, or roasted chicken, is a must. The simplicity of the cuisine and the raw materials used guarantee that there are no traces of gluten in their dishes.
🚻 100 🚇 N, Q, R to 5th Ave. & 60th St. ⏰ Closed Sat. L 💳 All major cards

🍴 SMITH & WOLLENSKY
$$$$
797 3RD AVE. (AT 49TH ST.)
TEL 212/753–1530
smithandwollenskynyc.com
One of the city's finest steakhouses.
🚻 300 🚇 6 to 51st St. ⏰ Closed Sat. & Sun. L 💳 All major cards

🍴 SUSHI–ANN
$$$$
38 E. 51ST ST.
(BET. MADISON & PARK AVES.)
TEL 212/755–1780
sushiann.net
Fabulous sushi and sashimi. Put yourself in the hands of the chef if you can afford it.
🚻 80 🚇 6 to 51st St. ⏰ Closed Sat. L & all day Sun.

💳 All major cards

🍴 THE AVIARY NYC
$$$$
80 COLUMBUS CIRCLE
TEL 212/805–8800
theaviarynyc.com
This Chicago concept restaurant opened on the 35th floor of the Mandarin Oriental in 2017. It offers spectacular views of Central Park and the Manhattan skyline and is the way to get into the speakeasy, The Office. The restaurant proposes an interactive experience and truly original cocktails, including the "Cloche Encounters of the 46 Kind," served in a glass vessel, closed in a plastic bag filled with floating substances.
🚻 90 🚇 A, B, C, D, 1, 2 to 59th St./Columbus Circle 💳 All major cards

🍴 BECCO
$$$
355 W. 46TH ST.
(BET. 8TH & 9TH AVES.)
TEL 212/397–7597
becco-nyc.com
Lively spot with pastas from the pan and a large selection of Italian wines to enjoy.
🚻 150 🚇 A, C, E to 42nd St. ⏰ Closed Fri. L 💳 All major cards

🍴 DAWAT
$$$
210 E. 58TH ST.
(BET. 2ND & 3RD AVES.)
TEL 212/355–7555
dawatny.com
Haute Indian cuisine. Try bhindi masala, okra with onions and mangos.
🚻 130 🚇 N, Q, R, 4, 5, 6 to Lexington Ave./59th St. 💳 All major cards

🍴 ESTIATORIO MILOS
$$$
125 W. 55TH ST.
(BET. 6TH & 7TH AVES.)
TEL 212/245–7400
milos.ca

Elegant Greek seafood spot with umbrella tables in an airy space. Fish is served by the pound; crabs are excellent.
🚻 250 🚇 N, Q, R to 57th St./7th Ave. 💳 All major cards

🍴 JOE ALLEN
$$$
326 W. 46TH ST.
(BET. 8TH & 9TH AVES.)
TEL 212/581–6464
joeallenrestaurant.com
Things like burgers and chef's salads make this 40-year-old Theater District institution reliable for both audience and cast.
🚻 150 🚇 A, C, E to 42nd St. 💳 MC, V

🍴 LE COLONIAL
$$$
149 E. 57TH ST.
TEL 212/752–0808
lecolonialnyc.com
French-Vietnamese fare and luscious specialty drinks served in an intimate setting of velvet and teak.
🚻 195 🚇 N, Q, R, 4, 5, 6 to Lexington Ave./59th St. ⏰ Closed Sat. & Sun. L 💳 All major cards

🍴 LUCKY CHENG'S
$$$
240 W. 52ND ST.
TEL 212/995–5500
luckychengsnyc.com
A veritable transvestite sideshow with passable pan-Asian food; go for the fun and late-night cocktails.
🚻 200–350 🚇 C to 50th St. ⏰ Closed L 💳 All major cards

🍴 OYSTER BAR AT GRAND CENTRAL
$$$
GRAND CENTRAL TERMINAL, LOWER LEVEL (42ND ST. & VANDERBILT AVE.)
TEL 212/490–6650
oysterbarny.com
Classic 1913 setting in the historic station, with a huge raw bar, all sorts of seafood, steaks, and chicken. Make sure to ask

---

🚭 Nonsmoking ❄️ Air-Conditioning 🏊 Indoor Pool 🏊 Outdoor Pool 💪 Health Club 💳 Credit Cards

for the lunch menu.
🚇 500 🚈 S, 4, 5, 6, 7 to 42nd St.–Grand Central 🕒 Closed Sun. 💳 All major cards

🍴 PIGALLE
$$$
6TH AVE. (AT 40TH ST.)
TEL 212/489–7545
pigallenyc.com
Go for large portions of Parisian meat and seafood dishes, artisanal cheeses, and sumptuous brunches.
🚇 85 🚈 N, Q, R, W to Time Sq.–42 St. 💳 All major cards

🍴 ROSA MEXICANO
$$$
1063 1ST AVE. (AT 58TH ST.)
TEL 212/753–7407
rosamexicano.com
Haute Mexican cuisine, authentic dishes. Tableside guacamole, pomegranate margaritas, and *mixiote* (lamb shanks with chilies steamed in beer) are house specialties.
🚇 90 🚈 N, Q, R, 4, 5, 6 to Lexington Ave./59th St. 🕒 Closed L Mon.–Fri. 💳 All major cards

🍴 SHUN LEE PALACE
$$$
155 E. 55TH ST.
(BET. LEXINGTON & 3RD AVES.)
TEL 212/371–8844
shunleepalace.net
Finest upscale Chinese cuisine. The Cantonese wonton soup is in a class by itself and entrees have intriguing names like Ants Climb on Tree and Lily in the Woods (which aren't what they say) as well as Szechuan Style Alligator (which is).
🚇 350 🚈 N, Q, R, 4, 5, 6 to Lexington Ave./59th St. 💳 All major cards

🍴 THE SEA GRILL
$$$
19 W. 49TH ST.
(ROCKEFELLER PLAZA)
TEL 212/332–7610
patinagroup.com
This elegant seafood restaurant

with a remarkable selection of raw dishes, superb grilled fish, and crustaceans has been a guarantee of quality for its loyal Midtown clients for more than thirty years. The modern dining room offers splendid views.
🚈 B, D, F, M to 47th–50th St.–Rockefeller Center 🕒 Closed Sun. 💳 All majors cards

SOMETHING SPECIAL

🍴 THE PORTER HOUSE
$$–$$$$
10 COLUMBUS CIR., 4TH FL.
TEL 212/823–9500
porterhousenyc.com
The Porterhouse steak—from corn- and grass-fed Southern Californian cattle, and dry-aged to perfection—makes for a perfect carnivore's supper. Chef Michael Lomonaco's American restaurant also has a fine wine list. Or go in at lunchtime and you'll find one of the best deals in the city: a delicious three-course set meal (steak frites or Scottish salmon) for just $25. All served with a superb view of the Circle and Central Park West in a relaxing room by attentive, friendly service.
🚇 140 🚈 A, B, C, D, 1 to 59th St.–Columbus Circle 💳 All major cards

🍴 BAR VETRO
$$
222 E. 58TH ST.
TEL 212/308–0112
barvetro.com
Hot spot for contemporary Italian food, with particularly good pastas and seafood. Try the tasting dishes. Also popular for afternoon drinks and appetizers.
🚇 170 🚈 N, Q, R, 4, 5, 6 to Lexington Ave./59th St. 🕒 Closed L Sat. & all day Sun. 💳 All major cards

🍴 DELEGATES' DINING ROOM
$$
1ST AVE BET. 42ND & 48TH ST.
TEL 917/367–3314

ddr-reservations.com
Guests can enjoy a buffet of international food from 11:30 a.m. to 2:30 p.m.. Attire is formal and reservations are essential. No children under 12 are allowed.
🚇 350 🚈 4, 5, 6 to 42nd St. 🕒 Closed Sat.. & Sun. 💳 All major cards

🍴 GYU-KAKU
$$
805 3RD AVE.
TEL 212/702–8816
gyu-kaku.com
Japanese BBQ, with a varied and tasty menu. Also vegetarian.
🚇 100 🚈 4, 6, 6X to 51 St. 💳 All major card

🍴 JOHN'S OF TIMES SQUARE
$$
260 W. 44TH ST.
(BET. 7TH AVE. & 8TH AVE.)
TEL 212/391–7560
johnspizzerianyc.com
Pizza baked in coal-fire brick ovens and served in a 1950s atmosphere have made this a favorite with locals, VIPs, and tourists. There is an ATM available.
🚇 100 🚈 A, C, E to 42nd St./Port Authority 💳 Only cash

🍴 TRATTORIA DELL'ARTE
$$
900 7TH AVE.
(CNR. 57TH ST.)
TEL 212/245–9800
trattoriadellarte.com
The Italian menu at this popular restaurant near Carnegie Hall includes fantastic appetizers and thin-crust pizza.
🚇 75 🚈 N, Q, R to 57th St./7th Ave. 💳 All major cards

🍴 WHEELTAPPER
$$
141 E. 44TH ST.
(IN THE FITZPATRICK HOTEL)
TEL 212/351–6800
fitzpatrickhotels.com/fitzpatrick-grand-central-the-wheeltapper

---

🏨 Hotel 🍴 Restaurant 🛏 No. of Guest Rooms 🚇 No. of Seats 🅿 Parking 🚈 Subway 🕒 Closed 🛗 Elevator

Old World pub with an Irish railroad history theme, fireplace, and widescreen TV.

🛏 100 🚇 S, 4, 5, 6, 7 to 42nd St.–Grand Central
🚭 All major cards

🍴 ESS-A-BAGEL

$

831 3RD AVE.
TEL 212/980–1010
ess-a-bagel.com
Some of New York's finest bagels, hand rolled and cheerfully served along with great fillings, desserts, and coffee. Also in Midtown South.

🍴 25 tables 🚇 E to Lexington Ave.; 6 to 51st St.
🚭 All major cards

🍴 ORIGINAL SOUP MAN

$

259 W. 55TH ST.
TEL 212/956-0900
originalsoupman.com
This is the heritage of Al Yeganeh, the Soup Nazi of *Seinfeld* fame, with lines of New Yorkers claiming huge containers of lobster bisque, black bean soup, and gumbo.
🚇 A, B, C, D, 1 to 59th St.–Columbus Circle
🚭 AE, DC, MC, V

🍴 TONKATSU MATSUNOYA

$

131 E 45TH ST.
TEL 646/692-8143
www.matsunoyafoods-usa.com
Casual Japanese restaurant.
🚇 6 to 51st St.
🚭 All major cards

▶ UPPER EAST SIDE

Hotels

🏨 PLAZA ATHENÉE

$$$$$

37 E. 64TH ST. (BET. PARK & MADISON AVES.)
TEL 212/734–9100
plaza-athenee.com
Old World charm and Louis

XVI decor star at this New York version of the Paris original, distinguished by its smaller size and location on a quiet residential block. Deluxe suites have atriums and balconies.
🛏 149 🚇 6 to 68th St.–Hunter College 🏥
🚭 All major cards

SOMETHING SPECIAL

🏨 SHERRY–NETHERLAND
🍴 HOTEL

$$$$$

781 5TH AVE (AT 59TH ST.)
TEL 212/355–2800 OR
877/351–9744
sherrynetherland.com
This landmark 1927 Romanesque boutique hotel promises an experience of timeless elegance. Attention to detail and service are everywhere, from the crystal chandeliers and lobby modeled on the Vatican library, to attendants running the guest elevators that once graced the Vanderbilt Mansion. All rooms are spacious and individually decorated, with fresh flowers. The marble baths are divine, as is the daily complimentary continental breakfast. Suites include a separate living room and kitchenette. The fitness center is state-of-the-art, and legendary restaurant, **Harry Cipriani,** had a recent makeover. This intimate, extraordinary hotel at the edge of Central Park is one of the city's true grande dames.
🛏 53 🚇 N, R to 5th Ave/59th St. 🚭 All major cards

SOMETHING SPECIAL

🏨 THE CARLYLE
🍴

$$$$$

35 E. 76TH ST.
TEL 212/744–1600
thecarlyle.com
Since 1931 this gemlike hotel has welcomed the world's elite in a grand European style. Rooms have antiques, Audubon prints, marble bathrooms with whirlpools, and state-of-the-art electronics.

Nancy Reagan and President Kennedy were regular guests. Those who do not check in may still partake of romantic dining in the **Carlyle Restaurant,** bistro entertainment in the **Café Carlyle,** humorous murals in the **Bemelmans Bar,** or tea in the **Gallery,** modeled after Turkey's Topkapi Palace.
🛏 190 + 65 residential apartments 🚇 6 to 77th St.
🚭 All major cards

🏨 THE LOWELL

$$$$$

28 E. 63RD ST. (BET. PARK & MADISON AVES.)
TEL 212/838–1400
lowellhotel.com
A 1920s historic landmark on a quiet street, providing tasteful, Old World charm in an intimate setting. Many rooms have working fireplaces, kitchens, and libraries.
🛏 61 🚇 N, Q, R, 4, 5, 6 to Lexington Ave./59th St. 🏥
🚭 All major cards

🏨 THE MARK
🍴

$$$$$

25 E. 77TH ST.
(BET. 5TH & MADISON AVES.)
TEL 212/744–4300
themarkhotel.com
An elegant location with formal contemporary decor, large rooms with marble or Italian ceramic baths, high-quality artwork, and luxurious amenities. Popular are the **Mark's Bar** and the wood-paneled **Mark Restaurant**—perfect for indulgent afternoon teas.
🛏 180 🚇 6 to 77th St. 🏥
🚭 All major cards

🏨 THE PIERRE

$$$$$

2 E. 61ST ST. (AT 5TH AVE.)
TEL 212/838-8000
tajhotels.com
Elegance, antiques, and

opulent decor characterize this hotel and luxury co-op building overlooking Central Park. A $100 million renovation has added a Jiva spa.

ⓘ 206 🚇 N, R to 5th Ave./59th St. 🏧 🏧 All major cards

🏨 THE REGENCY
$$$$$
540 PARK AVE. (AT 61ST ST.)
TEL 877/878–6204
loewshotels.com/
Regency–Hotel
Named for its Regency decor, this hotel has both understated elegance and every amenity, including TVs and phones beside the marble bathtubs.

ⓘ 288 + 74 suites 🚇 N, Q, R, 4, 5, 6 to Lexington Ave./59th St. 🏧 🏧 All major cards

🏨 GRACIE INN
$$$
502 E. 81ST ST. (BET. YORK & EAST END AVES.)
TEL 212/628-1700 OR
800/404–2252
the-gracie-inn.
hotelinewyork.com
Located on a residential block, this B&B offers 13 rustic-style rooms of various sizes, each with kitchenette, full bath, and cable. Quiet location near park, museums. Elevator, free Wi-Fi.

ⓘ 12 🚇 4, 5, 6 to 86th St. 🏧 All major cards

🏨 HOTEL WALES
🍴 $$$
1295 MADISON AVE.
(AT 92ND ST.)
TEL 212/876–6000 OR
866/925–3746
hotelwalesnyc.com
Early-20th-century-style haven with spacious suites a block from Central Park and Museum Mile.

ⓘ 45 + 47 suites 🚇 6 to 96th St. 🏧 AE, MC, V

🏨 THE FRANKLIN
$$$

164 E. 87TH ST.
(BET. LEXINGTON & 3RD AVES.)
TEL 212/369–1000 OR
800/607–4009
franklinhotel.com
Pet friendly and romantic, the Franklin offers nicely decorated rooms with canopy beds, custom furniture, and photos of the city. Complimentary wine-and-cheese receptions nightly.

ⓘ 53 🚇 4, 5, 6 to 86th St. 🏧 AE, MC, V

Restaurants

SOMETHING SPECIAL

🍴 DANIEL
$$$$$
60 E. 65TH ST.
(BET. MADISON & PARK AVES.)
TEL 212/288–0033
danielnyc.com
This gastronomic palace opened in the old Mayflower Hotel (now private condos) in 1999. Owner/chef Daniel Boulud turned his former Restaurant Daniel (at 20 East 76th St.) into Café Boulud so he could open this larger "Venetian-Byzantine-Deco fantasy." Boulud is New York's longest-reigning four-star chef. His food is founded on ancient French farmhouse recipes that he re-creates with flair. Roasted saddle of lamb with black-truffle gnocchi, root vegetables with a satiny au jus, and other delights await.

🪑 100 🚇 6 to 68th St.– Hunter College 🏧 All major cards

🍴 THE MARK RESTAURANT BY JEAN-GEORGES
$$$$$
MARK HOTEL, 25 E. 77TH ST.
(BET. 5TH & MADISON AVES.)
TEL 212/744–4300 OR
212/606–3030
themarkrestaurantnyc.com
Hiding at the back of the Mark

Hotel is this innovative restaurant with a menu crafted by pre-eminent chef Jean-Georges Vongerichten. Fine eclectic eats for all hours of the day, from char-grilled octopus to pizza.

ⓘ 90 🚇 6 to 77th St. 🏧 All major cards

🍴 JO JO
$$$$
160 E. 64TH ST.
(BET. LEXINGTON & 3RD AVES.)
TEL 212/223–5656
jean-georges.com
Outstanding bistro fare by Jean-Georges Vongerichten. The lobster and the Vahlrona chocolate cake are recommended.

ⓘ 150 🚇 N, R, Q, 4, 5, 6 to Lexington Ave./59th St. 🏧 All major cards

🍴 PAOLA'S
$$$
1295 MADISON AVE.
(CNR. 92ND ST.)
TEL 212/794–1890
paolasrestaurant.com
Executive chef Paola Bottero and her son, Stefano, have brought traditional Italian cuisine to the Upper East

---

🏨 Hotel 🍴 Restaurant ⓘ No. of Guest Rooms 🪑 No. of Seats 🅿 Parking 🚇 Subway 🕐 Closed 🛗 Elevator

Side, with delicious dishes that include homemade pasta.

70 + 30 outdoors 6 to 96th St. All major cards

THE WRIGHT
$$$
1071 5TH AVE.
(IN GUGGENHEIM MUSEUM)
TEL 212/423–3665
guggenheim.org
Colored installations by Sarah Crowner and a menu of fish and meat proposed by the Michelin-starred chef Alejandro Cortez.

75 4, 5, 6 to 86th St. Closed Thur. & D All major cards

AFGHAN KEBAB HOUSE II
$$
1345 2ND AVE.
(BET. 70TH & 71ST STS.)
afghankebabhouseny.com
TEL 212/517–2776
Nicely flavored, reasonably priced foods; also good for vegetarians. Best value: the Combo Plate.

45 4, 5, 6 to 86th St. All major cards

HEIDELBERG
$$
1648 2ND AVE.
TEL 212/628–2332
heidelbergrestaurant.com
German beer hall with notable potato pancakes and wiener schnitzel, plus one- and two-liter boots of beer.

80–85 4, 5, 6 to 86th St. All major cards

SARABETH'S KITCHEN
$$
1295 MADISON AVE.
(AT 92ND ST.)
TEL 212/410–7335
sarabeth.com
Baked goods and popular brunches. Open for breakfast.

90 6 to 96th St. All major cards

SERENDIPITY 3
$$
225 E. 60TH ST.
(BET. 2ND & 3RD AVES.)
TEL 212/838–3531
serendipity3.com
Over-the-top ice-cream sundaes and casual fare. Known for frozen hot chocolate, celebrities, and kids of all ages.

165 N, R, Q, 4, 5, 6 to Lexington Ave./59th St. All major cards

▶ CENTRAL PARK

Restaurants

TAVERN ON THE GREEN
$$$$
CENTRAL PARK W.
(AT 67TH ST.)
TEL 212/877–8684
tavernonthegreen.com
A New York legend, currently being reinvented. Gorgeous, unique, fairy-tale setting right in the park. Due to reopen under new management at time of publication. Check website for latest contact details.

1,000+ 1 to 66th St.–Lincoln Center; A, B, C, D to 59th–Columbus Circle All major cards

CENTRAL PARK BOATHOUSE
$$$–$$$$
CENTRAL PARK
(EAST 72ND ST. & PARK DR. N. AT THE LAKE)
TEL 212/517–2233
thecentralparkboathouse.com
Nicely presented and extremely fresh seafood. Lovely for a weekend brunch watching the rowers on the lake. They also offer cheaper fare at their Bar and Grill and Express Cafe.

180 All major cards

▶ UPPER WEST SIDE

Hotels

TRUMP INTERNATIONAL HOTEL & TOWER
$$$$$
1 CENTRAL PARK W. (AT COLUMBUS CIR., BET. 60TH & 61ST STS.)
TEL 212/299–1000
trumpintl.com
Donald Trump's megaventure at the tip of Central Park, featuring floor-to-ceiling windows and personal attachés assigned to guests to coordinate their lives in New York. Dine downstairs at Nougatine or Jean Georges (see both, below), or have one of the chefs cook for you in your suite, if you prefer.

176 suites A, B, C, D, 1 to Columbus Circle–59th St. All major cards

BEACON HOTEL
$$$
2130 BROADWAY (AT 75TH ST.)
TEL 212/787–1100 OR
800/572–4969
beaconhotel.com
Generously sized rooms, great location, and family friendly are the buzz words for this hotel. Ideal for concertgoers with tickets to the legendary art deco Beacon Theater.

248 suites 1, 2, 3 to 72nd St. All major cards

EXCELSIOR
$$$
45 W. 81ST ST. (BET. COLUMBUS AVE. & CENTRAL PARK W.)
TEL 212/362–9200
excelsiorhotelny.com
Large, comfortable rooms with traditional decor, some views.

200 B, C to 81st St.–Museum of Natural History; 1 to 79th St. AE, MC, V

THE LUCERNE
$$$
201 W. 79TH ST.
TEL 212/875–1000
thelucernehotel.com

Nonsmoking Air-Conditioning Indoor Pool Outdoor Pool Health Club Credit Cards

Classic rooms in a gorgeously renovated 1904 landmark building, close to Central Park.
🛏 184 🚇 1 to 79th St.
💳 AE, MC, V

🏨 JAZZ ON THE PARK HOSTEL
$$
36 W. 106TH ST.
TEL 212/932–1600
jazzhostels.com
The hostel is located in front of Central Park and offers dormitories and private rooms.
🚇 1, 2, 3 per 79 St.

Restaurants

🍴 JEAN GEORGES
$$$$$
TRUMP INTERNATIONAL HOTEL, 1 CENTRAL PARK W. (SEE ABOVE)
TEL 212/299–3900
jean-georges.com
Top-class contemporary French-American cuisine by Jean-Georges Vongerichten. Try the tasting menu.
🪑 60 🚇 A, B, C, D, 1 to Columbus Circle–59th St.
💳 All major cards

🍴 CAFÉ LUXEMBOURG
$$$$
200 W. 70TH ST. (BET. AMSTERDAM & WEST END AVES.)
TEL 212/873–7411
cafeluxembourg.com
A classic hip destination with bistro fare.
🪑 107 🚇 1, 2, 3 to 72nd St.
💳 All major cards

🍴 NOUGATINE
$$$$
TRUMP INTERNATIONAL HOTEL, 1 CENTRAL PARK W. (SEE ABOVE)
TEL 212/299–3900
jean-georgesrestaurant.com
A more casual part of the Jean Georges restaurant. Open for breakfast, lunch, and dinner, with brunch on Sunday.
🪑 65–80 🚇 A, B, C, D, 1 to Columbus Circle–59th St.
💳 All major cards

🍴 CARMINE
$$$
2450 BROADWAY
TEL 212/362–2200
carminesnyc.com
Known for robust portions, it offers breakfast, lunch and dinner. Its outdoor tables are a great spot for people watching as you sample the excellent pasta, pizza, and spiced crustacean sauce. Open every day.
🪑 55 🚇 1, 2, 3 to 96th St., 1, 2 to 86th St.
💳 All major cards

🍴 OUEST
$$$
2315 BROADWAY (AT 84TH ST.)
TEL 212/580–8700
ouestny.com
See and be seen at this intimate foodie's paradise, popular with celebs, featuring Chef Tom Valenti's boldly layered style. Don't miss his signature lamb shanks. Sunday brunch.
🪑 135 🚇 1 to 86th St.
💳 All major cards

🍴 SHUN LEE CAFÈ
$$$
43 W. 65TH ST. (BET. COLUMBUS AVE. & CENTRAL PARK W.)
TEL 212/595–8895
shunleewest.com
First-rate Chinese dining, some of New York's finest.
🪑 300 🚇 1 to 66th St.–Lincoln Center 💳 All major cards

🍴 BARNEY GREENGRASS
$$
541 AMSTERDAM AVE. (BET. 86TH & 87TH STS.)
TEL 212/724–4707
barneygreengrass.com
Visit the "Sturgeon King" for a classic meal of smoked fish delights. Salmon and eggs and scallion cream cheese are recommended.
🪑 55 🚇 1 to 86th St.
🕐 B & L only; closed Mon.
💳 Cash only

▶ THE HEIGHTS & HARLEM

Restaurants

🍴 NEW LEAF
$$$–$$$$
1 MARGARET CORBIN DR., FORT TRYON PARK
TEL 212/568–5323
newleafrestaurant.com
Perfect after a visit to The Cloisters. In beautiful parkland surroundings, New Leaf offers a modern American menu inspired by local green markets. This elegantly renovated restaurant is now run by the nonprofit New York Restoration Project (NYRP) to aid its mission of creating a greener, more sustainable New York City.
🪑 200 with outdoor seating
🕐 Closes occasionally for special events; check website 🚇 A to 190th St. 💳 All major cards

🍴 RED ROOSTER
$$–$$$
310 LENOX AVE
TEL 212/792–9001
redroosterharlem.com
Chef Marcus Samuelsson's new place in Harlem serves amazing soul food and has proven an instant success. Bill Clinton, members of U2, and other notables are known to drop into this cool comfort food joint that takes its name from a legendary Harlem speakeasy. Try the spiced duck-liver pudding or the fried yard bird.
🪑 160 🚇 2, 3 to 125th St./ Lenox Ave. 💳 All major cards

🍴 DINOSAUR BBQ
$$
700 W 125TH ST.
TEL 212/694–1777
dinosaurbarbeque.com
Located under the Riverside Drive Viaduct by the Hudson. Awesome BBQ with insane portion sizes. Good live music and a children's menu as well.
🪑 90 🚇 1 to 125th St.
💳 All major cards

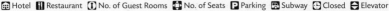

🏨 Hotel 🍴 Restaurant 🛏 No. of Guest Rooms 🪑 No. of Seats 🅿 Parking 🚇 Subway 🕐 Closed 🛗 Elevator

🍴 LONDEL'S
$$

2620 FREDERICK DOUGLASS
BLVD. (BET. 139TH & 140TH STS.)
TEL 212/234-6114
londelsrestaurant.com
Great Southern cooking with
classic fried chicken and greens.
🍴 150 🚇 B, C, 2, 3 to 135th
St. 🕐 Closed Sun. D & all day
Mon. 💳 All major cards

🍴 SYLVIA'S
$$

328 MALCOLM X BLVD.
(BET. 126TH & 127TH STS.)
TEL 212/996-0660
sylviasrestaurant.com
Famous soul food; brunch
Sun., and jazz 1 p.m.–4 p.m.
Sat. Try the barbecued ribs,
ham, and collard greens.
🍴 300 🚇 2, 3 to 125th St./
Lenox Ave. 🕐 Open until 8 p.m.
Sun. 💳 All major cards

▶ THE OUTER BOROUGHS

BROOKLYN

🍴 PETER LUGER'S STEAKHOUSE
$$$$

178 BROADWAY
(AT DRIGGS AVE.)
TEL 718/387-7400
peterluger.com
One of the city's finest steakhouses. No frills, just great por-
terhouse and creamed spinach.
🍴 150 🚇 J, M, Z to Marcy
Ave. 💳 Cash only

🍴 RIVER CAFÉ
$$$$

1 WATER ST.
(UNDER BROOKLYN BRIDGE)
TEL 718/522-5200
rivercafe.com
Spectacular view of Manhattan in an elegant setting—sit
outdoors in summer. Lobster,
lamb, and soft shells are great.
🍴 110 🚇 A to High St.–
Brooklyn Bridge; 2, 3 to
Clark St. 💳 All major cards

🍴 BAMCAFÉ
$$

BROOKLYN ACADEMY OF MUSIC,
30 LAFAYETTE AVE.
TEL 718/636-4100
bam.org
International cuisine at a cul-
tural landmark. Opens two
hours before performances.
🍴 300 🚇 2, 3, 4, 5 to Atlantic
Ave. 💳 All major cards

🍴 CAFÉ TATIANA
$$

3145 4TH ST.
TEL 718/646-4342
tatianagrill.com
Fine setting in Brooklyn
for Russian cuisine. Especially good are the soups
and dumplings. Open for
breakfast.
🍴 100 🚇 B, Q to Brighton
Ave. 💳 Cash only

🍴 GRIMALDI'S
$

1 FRONT ST.
TEL 718/858-4300
grimaldisnyc.com
One of New York's best pizza
places, with red-checkered
tablecloths and very long lines.
🍴 50 🚇 C to High St.
💳 Cash only

🍴 TOM'S RESTAURANT
$

782 WASHINGTON AVE.
TEL 718/636-9738
Quintessential neighborhood
diner, a few blocks from the
Brooklyn Museum; worth
the walk for breakfast and
lunch.
🍴 75 🚇 2, 3 to Eastern
Pkwy./Brooklyn Museum
🕐 Closed at 9 p.m. 💳 Cash
only

QUEENS

🏨 SHERATON LAGUARDIA EAST HOTEL
$$$–$$$$

135–20 39TH AVE.

TEL 718/460-6666
starwoodhotels.com/
sheraton
Airport hotel near the U.S.
Open Tennis Center and the
Mets' Citi Field. The restau-
rant serves fusion cuisine,
mixing Asian and Continen-
tal flavors.
🛏 173 rooms & suites
🚇 7 to Main St., Flushing
💪 💳 All major cards

🏨 CITY VIEW INN
$$$

3317 GREENPOINT AVE.,
LONG ISLAND CITY
TEL 718/392-8400
cityviewinn.net
Converted 19th-century
school near Citi Field and
U.S. Open Tennis Center.
Free shuttle to and from
LaGuardia.
🛏 72 rooms 🚇 7 to 40th St.
💳 All major cards

🍴 ELIAS CORNER
$$

24–02 31ST ST. (AT 24TH AVE.)
TEL 718/932-1510
eliascorner.com
Authentic Greek seafood joint.
🍴 100 🚇 N to Astoria Bou-
levard 🕐 Closed Mon.–Sun. L
💳 Cash only

🍴 JACKSON DINER
$$

37–47 74TH ST.
(BET. ROOSEVELT & 37TH AVES.)
TEL 718/672-1232
jacksondiner.com
Fine Indian food.
🍴 65 🚇 7 to 74th St.–Broadway 💳 Cash only

🍴 JOE'S SHANGHAI
$$

136–21 37TH AVE.
(BET. MAIN & UNION STS.)
TEL 718/539-3838
joeshanghairestaurants.com
Fantastic broth-filled
dumplings.
🍴 70 🚇 7 to Main St.
💳 Cash only

🍴 LA BOINA ROJA

$

80–22 37TH AVE.,
JACKSON HEIGHTS
TEL 718/424–6711

Small Colombian steakhouse,
with 23 different sauces for
your beef. Good choice of
Chilean and Argentinian wines.

🪑 100 🚇 7 to 82nd St.
💳 All major cards

🍴 TOURNESOL, BISTRO FRANÇAIS

$

50–12 VERNON BLVD.,
LONG ISLAND CITY
TEL 718/472–4355
tournesolnyc.com

A taste of France: mussels in
white wine, salad of lardons
with poached egg, and rab-
bit terrine with red onion
compote.

🪑 65 🚇 7 to Vernon Blvd.–
Jackson Ave. 🕐 Closed Mon.
L 💳 AE

▶ EXCURSIONS

WEST OF THE HUDSON

SOMETHING SPECIAL

🏨 SAUGERTIES LIGHTHOUSE

$$$

168 LIGHTHOUSE DR., SAUGERTIES
TEL 845/247–0656
saugertieslighthouse.com

This 1869 beacon guided steam-
boats, barges, and other vessels
safely along the Hudson River
for years. In the mid-1990s, the
lighthouse became a two-room
B&B, as well as a river museum,
where you can now stay over-
night in the middle of one of
America's great rivers. Reserve
well in advance as it's popular
for romantic getaways. Visitors
should note that the lighthouse is
accessible only by a half-mile (0.8
km) walking trail or by personal
boat. There is no ferry service.

🚪 2 💳 All major cards

🍴 SHIP TO SHORE

$$$$

15 WEST STRAND KINGSTON
TEL 845/334–8887
shiptoshorehudsonvalley.
com

Fine American bistro/old
New York steak house. Chef
Samir Hrichi offers tasty
variations to satisfy every
nationality of gourmet, from
bouillabaisse to New Zealand
rack of lamb. The tuna stack
is delicious.

🪑 70 💳 All major cards

🍴 MARINER'S HARBOR

$$

1 BROADWAY, KINGSTON
(ON THE WATERFRONT)
TEL 845/340–8051
marinersharbor.com

Relaxed indoor and outdoor
dining, specializing in seafood,
with great river views.

🪑 250 🕐 Closed Mon.
💳 All major cards

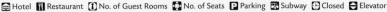

SHOPPING IN NEW YORK

Everything is available in New York at both the highest and the lowest prices. Many natives spend a good portion of their lives trying to stay on one end of the spectrum by doing their homework and shopping around. Department stores are best visited weekdays during mid-morning or early afternoon; some are open well into the evening. Many specialty stores do not open early in the morning. It may be worth calling specific destinations to verify hours, which can change seasonally (some places stay open later in the summer). Check websites for additional store locations.

Although Lower Manhattan is primarily a financial district, there are also many diversified shops in all price ranges. Nearly all of the chain stores are represented on or around Madison Avenue or Broadway. Tribeca is an up-and-coming shopping district, especially around Franklin Street and lower West Broadway. The Lower East Side is a fascinating area, originally Jewish but now multi-ethnic. Shopping there is a treat for the adventurous who will find a mix of old and new. It's a great Sunday destination, since everything is open (stores are closed Saturday for the Sabbath).

The area dubbed "NoLita" (North of Little Italy) stretches from Houston to Spring Streets and from Lafayette to Elizabeth Streets, and hosts many cute boutiques. Lafayette Street contains a number of "modern vintage" furniture sources. SoHo offers shopping galore. Go during the week when crowds of browsers are thinner.

In the West Village little places are tucked away here and there, and Bleecker Street and Christopher Street are good shopping spots. The East Village is a unique neighborhood, multi-ethnic and ever changing. Ninth Street between Second Avenue and Avenue A is a treasure trove. Bond Street, between Lafayette Street and Bowery, is a strip of old furniture stores, and the antiques zone is on 10th and 11th Streets, from University Place to Broadway.

While Fifth Avenue is the acknowledged shopping center of New York, Madison Avenue has many of the ritziest stores around. Columbus Circle's Time Warner Center is loaded with shops, and both Columbus and Amsterdam Avenues offer good shopping. Broadway is always booming uptown and down, and don't forget Midtown around Macy's; Chelsea's Seventh Avenue; and Harlem. The hottest shops have recently flocked to the Meatpacking District (see p. 79).

The largest concentrated area of shopping in New York is the Westfield World Trade Center shopping mall, opened in 2016, with 500,000 square feet (46,000 sq m) of retail space. Shopping options include such mall ever-presents as Apple, H&M, and Victoria's Secret, as well as plenty of dining options for shoppers in need of refreshment.

Accessories & Shoes

Dö Kham, 117 1st Ave., tel 212/966–2404, dokham.com. Subway: L to 1st Ave. Tibetan hats and crafts.

Harry's Shoes, 2299 Broadway, tel 855/642–7797, harrys-shoes .com. Subway: 1 to 86th St. Great family-owned store with shoes and apparel for men and women.

Hermès, 691 Madison Ave., at E. 62nd St, tel 212/751–3181. Subway: N, R to 5th Ave./59th St., 4, 5, 6 to Lexington Ave./59th St. Closed Sun. Upscale Parisian silk scarves, neckties, handbags.

Kiehl's, 109 3rd Ave. (at 13th St.), tel 212/677–3171, kiehls. com. Subway: N, Q, R, 4, 5, 6 to Union Sq.; L to 3rd Ave. High-end beauty products. Other location: 154 Columbus Ave. (bet. 66th & 67th Sts.), tel 212/799–3438. Subway: 1 to 66th St.–Lincoln Center

Manolo Blahnik, 31 W. 54th St., tel 212/582–3007, manolo blahnik.com. Subway: E, M to 5th Ave./53rd St. The Spanish designer's haute couture shoes are one of a kind, with heels and prices that will make you dizzy.

Nordstrom, 235 West 57th Street, tel 212/843–5100, shop. nordstrom.com. Subway: Q, R to 57th Street-Seventh Ave. The American department store has a new location in New York. Its men's store has a café, personal stylists, and exclusive toiletries.

T. O. Dey, 151 W. 46th St., tel 212/683–6300, todeyshoes.com. Subway: A, C, 1, 2, 3 to 42nd St. Call for hours. Custom shoes.

Antiques

Gill & Lagodich, 108 Reade St., tel 212/619–0631, gill-lagodich .com. Subway: 1, 2, 3 to Chambers St. Call for hours. Antique frames.

Manhattan Art & Antiques Center, 1050 2nd Ave. (bet. 55th & 56th Sts.), tel 212/355–4400, the-maac.com. Subway: E to 53rd/Lexington Ave. More than 100 galleries.

Pageant Book & Print Shop, 69 E. 4th St., tel 212/674–5296, pageantbooks.com. Subway: 6 to Bleecker St., F to 2nd Ave. Closed a.m. & Mon. Superior antique maps and prints.

Arts & Crafts

Jerry Ohlinger's, 253 W. 35th St. (bet. 7th & 8th Aves.), tel 212/989-0869, moviematerials.com. Subway: A, C, E to 34th St. Closed Sun. Movie stills and posters.

Tribeca Potters, 21–21 41st Ave., Long Island City, tel 212/431-7631, tribecapotters.com. Subway: F per 21st St.-Queensbridge. Call for hours. Ceramics for sale.

Triton Gallery, 690 8th Ave. (tra 43rd e 44th St.), tel 212/765-2472, broadwayposters.com. Subway: A, C, E to 42nd St. Closed Tues., Sat., & Sun. Broadway show posters.

Urban Archeology, 158 Franklin St., tel 212/431-4646, urban archeology.com. Subway: 1, 2 to Franklin St.. Closed Sat.–Sun. Amazing array of architectural elements as well as new fixtures.

Bags & Handbags

Altman Luggage, 135 Orchard St., tel 212/254-7275, altmanluggage.com. Subway: F to Delancey St. Closed Sat. Well-priced bags, backpacks, pens.

Big Drop, 174 Spring St., tel 212/966-4299, bigdropnyc.com. Subway: C, E to Spring St. Bags, caps, & trendy clothing.

Gucci, 725 5th Ave., tel 212/826-2600. Subway: E to 5th Ave./53rd St. Closed a.m. Sun. Expensive designer goods.

Il Bisonte, 120 Sullivan St., tel 212/966-8773, ilbisonte.com. Subway: C, E to Spring St.; A, C, E to Canal St. Closed a.m. Leather goods and bags.

Jutta Neumann, 355 E. 4th St., tel 212/982-7048, juttaneumann -newyork.com. Subway: J to Essex St. Closed a.m. & Sun. Leather accessories.

Kate Spade, 454 Broome St., tel 212/274-1991, katespade .com. Subway: C, E to Spring St. Chic handbags.

Books

Book Book, 266 Bleecker St., tel 212/807-8655, bookbooknyc. com. Subway: A, B, C, D to 4th St.

Central Park Kiosk, 60th St. & 5th Ave., daily 10 a.m. to dusk, April–Dec. For all your newspaper and magazine reading in the park.

Housing Works Used Book Café, 126 Crosby St., tel 212/334-3324. Subway: B, D, F to Broadway–Lafayette St. Comfortable book shop for café lounging and talks.

Kitchen Arts & Letters, 1435 Lexington Ave., tel 212/876-5550, kitchenartsandletters.com. Subway: 4, 5, 6 to 86th St.; 6 to 96th St. Closed Sun. & a.m. Mon. Outstanding cookbook collection.

Rizzoli, 31 W. 57th St. (bet. 5th & 6th Aves.), tel 212/759-2424, rizzoliusa.com. Subway: N, R to 57th St./7th Ave. Books and magazines in a distinguished environment.

Strand, 828 Broadway (at 12th St.), tel 212/473-1452, strand books.com. Subway: 4, 5, 6 to 14th St.–Union Sq. Ultimate new and used bookstore with "18 miles of books."

West Sider, 2246 Broadway (bet. 80th & 81st Sts.), tel 646/613-1100, westsiderbooks.com. Subway: 1 to 79th St. A wide variety includes rare art and fiction.

Clothes

Agnès B., 50 Howard St., tel 212/431-1335. Subway: A, C to Canal St. Designer clothing.

Anna Sui, 113 Greene St., tel 212/941-8406, annasui.com. Subway: N, R to Prince St. Women's designer clothing.

Bebe, 100 5th Ave., tel 646/949-2380, bebe.com. Subway: N, Q, R to 14th St.–Union Sq. Well-priced knockoffs of trendy clothing.

Ben Freedman, 137 Orchard St., tel 212/674-0854, benfreedman .com. Subway: F to Delancey. "Gents' furnishings," discounted

London Fog coats.

Brooks Brothers, 346 Madison Ave., tel 212/682-8800, brooks brothers.com. Subway: 4, 5, 6 to 42nd St. Classic menswear.

Calvin Klein, 654 Madison Ave., tel 212/292-9000, calvinklein .com. Subway: N, R to 5th Ave./59th St.; 4, 5, 6 to Lexington Ave./59th St. American chic.

Century 21, 22 Cortlandt St., tel 212/227-9092, c21stores.com. Subway: C, E to World Trade Center. Discount clothing.

Chanel, 15 E. 57th St., tel 212/355-5050, chanel.com. Subway: N, R, to 5th Ave./59th St. Designer wear.

Comme des Garçons, 520 W. 22nd St., tel 212/604-9200. Subway: C, E to 23rd St. Designer clothing.

Diane von Furstenberg, 440 W. 14th Street., tel 212/741-6607, dvf.com. Subway: L to 8th Ave.; A, C, E to 14th St. Classic fashions.

Diesel, 770 Lexington Ave., tel 212/308-0055, diesel.com. Subway: N, Q, R, 4, 5, 6 to Lexington Ave./59th St. Hip Italian fashion.

Gucci, 725 5th Ave. (bet. 56th & 57th Sts.), tel 212/826-2600, gucci.com. Subway: E to 53rd St. Hot and cool styles for every occasion.

Hermès, 15 Broad St., tel 212/785-3030, usa.hermes.com. Subway: J to Broad St. In the heart of the Financial District, the last word in Parisian élan with high-end fashions and luxury lifestyle goods.

Karl Lagerfeld, 420 W. Broadway, tel 212/785-3030, karl.com. Subway: A, C, E to Spring St. At his new American flagship store, opened in 2018, the designer proposes his clothing and accessories.

Infinity, 1116 Madison Ave., tel 212/517-4232. Subway: 4, 5, 6 to 86th St. Girls' and juniors' clothes and accessories paradise.

Levi's Store, 1501 Broadway,

us.levi.com. Subway: A, C, E, 1, 2, 3 to Times Sq.

Moschino, 73 Wooster Street, moschino.com. Subway: 1, 2 to Canal St., A, C, E to Spring St. Italian luxury fashion house in the Meatpacking District.

NY Fire Store, 17 Greenwich Ave., tel 212/226–3142. nyfirestore.com. Subway: A, B, C, D, E, F to W. 4th St. Clothes and toys.

Patricia Field, 200 East Broadway, tel 212/966–4066, patriciafield. com. Subway: B, D to Grand St., F to East Broadway. Destination for wild clothing and accessories.

Paul Smith, 108 5th Ave., tel 212/627–9770, paulsmith.co.uk. Subway: N, Q, R, 4, 5, 6 to Union Sq. Tasteful menswear.

Resurrection, 217 Mott St., tel 212/625–1374. resurrection vintage.com Subway: 6 to Spring St. Antique and vintage clothing.

Trash & Vaudeville, 4 Saint Mark's Pl., tel 212/982–3590, trashandvaudville.com Subway: 6 to Astor Pl., N, R to 8th St. Vaudeville upstairs and Trash down, loaded with vintage goods.

Versace, 647 5th Ave., tel 212/317–0224. Subway: E to 5th Ave./53rd St. Italian glitz.

Zara, 750 Lexington Ave., tel 212/754–1120. Subway: N, Q, R, 4, 5, 6 to Lexington Ave./59th St. Hip European styles for him and her (+ two branches downtown).

Department Stores

Barney's, 660 Madison at 61st St., tel 212/826–8900, barneys .com. Subway: N, R to 5th Ave./59th St.; 4, 5, 6 to Lexington Ave./59th St. Upscale department store with fashions, cosmetics, housewares. Popular with the in crowd. Also, try **Barney's Co-ops** for sportswear and casual clothes: 116 Wooster St., tel 212/965–9964; 236 W. 18th St., tel 212/593–7800; 2151 Broadway at 75th St., tel 646/335–0978.

Bergdorf Goodman, 754 5th Ave. at 57th St., tel 212/753–7300, bergdorfgoodman.com. Subway: N, R to 5th Ave./59th St. Elegant fashions.

Bergdorf Goodman Men, 745 5th Ave., tel 212/753–7300, bergdorfgoodman.com. Subway: E to 5th Ave./53rd St.; N, R to 5th Ave./59th St. High-end men's fashion.

Bloomingdale's, (two entrances) 1000 3rd Ave. or 59th & Lexington, tel 212/705–2000, bloomingdales.com. Subway: N, Q, R, 4, 5, 6 to Lexington Ave./59th St. Flagship store.

Century 21, 1972 Broadway, tel 212/518–2121. Brand names at reasonable prices attract NY professionals to Lincoln Square, and other Manhattan branches.

Henri Bendel, 712 5th Ave., tel 212/247–1100, henribendel.com. Subway: E to 5th Ave./53rd St.; N, R to 5th Ave./59th St. Boutique store.

Lord & Taylor, 424 5th Ave., tel 212/391–3344, lordandtaylor .com. Subway: B, D, F to 42nd St.; 7 to 5th Ave. Specializes in classic women's wear.

Macy's, 151 W. 34th St., tel 212/695–4400, macys.com. Subway: B, D, F, N, Q, R, 1, 2, 3 to 34th St. NYC's biggest.

Saks Fifth Avenue, 611 5th Ave., tel 212/940–2818, saksfifth avenue.com. Subway: B, D, F to 47th–50th Sts.–Rockefeller Center; E to 5th Ave./53rd St. Flagship store of fashion.

Food Stores

Dean & Deluca, 560 Broadway, tel 212/226–6800, deandeluca .com. Subway: N, R to Prince St. Where food is fashion.

Economy Candy, 108 Rivington St., tel 212/254–1531, economy candy.com. Subway: F to Delancey St. Candy and nuts.

Eli's Vinegar Factory, 431 E. 91st St. (bet. York & 1st Aves.), tel 212/987–0885, elizabar.com.

Subway: 4, 5, 6 to 86th or 96th Sts. Vast selection of vinegar and oils, produce and cheese, and weekend brunch.

Fairway, 2127 Broadway at 74th St., tel 212/595–1888, fairway market.com. Subway: 1, 2, 3 to 72nd. Gourmet food and excellent produce.

International Grocery and Meat, 543 9th Ave. (at 40th St.), tel 212/279–1000. Subway: A, C, E to 42nd St. Closed Sun. Amazing spice and dried goods selection, Greek dips, and cheeses.

Kalustyan's, 123 Lexington Ave., tel 212/685-3451, kalustyan.com. Subway: 6 to 28th St. The best spices, Indian foods.

Li-lac Chocolates, 40 8th Ave. (at Jane St.), tel 212/924–2280, li-lacchocolates.com. Subway: A, C, E to 14th St. Closed a.m. Handmade chocolates.

McNulty's, 109 Christopher St., tel 212/242–5351, mcnultys. com. Subway: 1 to Christopher St. Teas and coffees.

Murray's Cheese Shop, 254 Bleecker St., tel 212/243–3289, murrayscheese.com. Subway: A, B, C, D, E, F to W. 4th St. Great selection, knowledgeable staff.

Myer's of Keswick, 634 Hudson St., tel 212/691–4194, myersof keswick.com. Subway: A, C, E to 14th St. British foods.

New Kam Man, 200 Canal St. (at Mott St.), tel 212/571–0330, newkamman.com. Subway: J, M, Z, 6 to Canal St. Asian food and housewares emporium.

Russ & Daughters, 179 E. Houston St., tel 212/475–4880, russanddaughters.com. Subway: F to 2nd Ave. Some of NYC's best smoked fish and caviar.

Sullivan St. Bakery, 533 W. 47th St., tel 212/265–5580, sullivanstreetbakery.com. Subway: C, E to 50th St. Great breads and snacks.

Veniero's Pasticceria & Cafe, 342E. 11th St., tel 212/674 7070, venierospastry.com. Subway: L to 1st Ave.; 6 to Astor Pl. Italian pastries.

Zabar's, 2245 Broadway (at 80th St.), tel 212/787–2000, zabars. com. Subway: 1 to 79th St. Gourmet foods and housewares.

Furniture: Antique & Modern

Cathers & Dembrosky, 43 E. 10th St., tel 212/353–1244, cathers-dembrosky.com. Subway: R to 8th St; 6 to Astor Pl. Mission furniture. By appt. only.

Crate & Barrel, 611 Broadway, tel 212/780–0004, crateand barrel.com. Subway: B, D, F, M to Broadway-Lafayette. Simple furniture to kitchen ware.

Wyeth's, 315 Spring St., tel 212/243–3661, wyeth.nyc. Subway: C, E, to Spring St. Closed Sun. Modern and refurbished furniture, lighting, ceramics. By appt.

Household

ABC Carpet & Home, 888 Broadway, tel 212/473–3000, abchome. com. Subway: 6 to 23rd St.; N, Q, R, 4, 5, 6 to Union Sq. Unbelievable emporium of absolutely everything for the home, gifts, antiques, etc.

D. Porthault, 470 Park Ave., tel 212/688–1660, dporthault. com. Subway: N, Q, R, 4, 5, 6 to Lexington Ave./59th St. French luxury linens.

JB Prince, 36 E. 31st St., 11th floor, tel 212/683–3553, jbprince.com. Subway: 33rd St. Closed Sat.–Sun. Knives and kitchen gadgets.

New Kam Man, see above.

Le Fanion, 299 W. 4th St., tel 212/463–8760, lefanion.com. Subway: 1 to Christopher St. Closed Sun. French ceramics.

Shabby Chic, 83 Wooster St. (bet. Spring & Broome Sts.), tel 212/334–3500, shabbychic.com. Subway: N, R to Prince St.; C, E, to Spring St. Furnishings with multi-faceted fabrics.

Waterworks, 215 E. 58th St., tel 212/371–9266, waterworks.com. Subway: N, Q, R, 4, 5, 6 to Lexington Ave./59th St. Closed Sun. More than just a faucet shop.

Woodard & Greenstein, 506 E. 74th St. (bet. York Ave. & FDR Dr.), tel 212/794–9404, woodardweave.com. Subway: 6 to 77th St. Sat. by appt. only; closed Sun. Painted American country antiques, quilts.

Jewelry

Bulgari, 730 5th Ave, tel 212/315–9000, bulgari.com. Subway: E, M to 5 Ave./53th St. Forty years after the opening of its first New York boutique, Bulgari is boasting an exclusively designed restyling of its Fifth Avenue store. Luxury jewelry, watches, and leather goods.

Cartier, 653 5th Ave. (near 52nd St.), tel 212/753–0111, cartier .com. Subway: E to 53rd St. Closed Sun. Old favorites to new design jewelry in two turn-of-the-20th-century mansions.

David Baruch, 36 W. 47th St., tel 212/719–2884. Subway: B, D, F to 47th–50th Sts.–Rockefeller Center. Closed Fri.–Sun. Brand-name silver.

Fred Leighton, 773 Madison Ave., tel 212/288–1872, fred leighton.com. Subway: 6 to 68th St.–Hunter College. Closed Sun. Antique jewelry.

Gold Standard, 21 W. 47th St., tel 212/719–5656. Subway: B, D, F to 47th–50th Sts.–Rockefeller Center. Closed Sat.–Sun. Gold jewelry and objets d'art.

Greenwich Jewelers, 64 Trinity Place (near Rector St.), tel 212/964–7592, greenwichjewelers .com. Subway: R, 1 to Rector St. Wide selection of designer jewelry.

Jean's Silversmiths, 16 W. 45th St. (bet. 5th & 6th Aves.), tel 212/575–0723, jeanssilversmiths .com. Subway: B, D, F to 42nd St. Closed Sat.–Sun. Antique silverware and objects of value.

Jewelry 55 Exchange, 55 W. 47th St., Subway: B, D, F to 47th–50th Sts.–Rockefeller Center. Dizzying array of 30–40 jewelers' booths and shops.

Robert Lee Morris, 400 W. Broadway, tel 212/431–9405. Subway: C, E to Spring St.; 1 to Houston St.; N, R to Prince St. Original gold and silver jewelry.

Tiffany & Co., 727 5th Ave., tel 212/755–8000, tiffany.com. Subway: N, R to 5th Ave./59th St. Closed Sun. Jewelry, tabletop, and other fancy items. No breakfast. And if your stocks are rising, Tiffany & Co. are also at 37 Wall St., tel 212/514–8015.

Markets

Flea Market at P.S. 183, 419 E. 67th St. Subway: 6 to 68th St.–Hunter College. Sat. only.

Greenflea Market at M.S. 44, Columbus Ave (bet 76th & 77th Sts.), greenfleamarkets.com. Subway: 1 to 79th St. Sun. only.

SoHo Antiques Fair, corner of Broadway & Grand St. Subway: 6 to Canal St.–Broadway. Sat & Sun.

The Annex/Hell's Kitchen Flea Market, 39th St. (bet. 9th & 10th Ave.), hellskitchenfleamarket .com. Subway: A, C, E to Port Authority/42nd St. Sat & Sun. More than 100 vendors selling antiques, clothing, books, and rare and unusual things.

Union Square Greenmarket, Union Sq. Park. ny.com/dining/ green.html. Subway: N, Q, R, 4, 5, 6 to Union Sq. Mon., Wed., Fri., & Sat. Local farmers sell produce, flowers, cheeses, and ciders. Amazing selection with lots of unusual items and special events.

Museum Shops

If you are stuck for a gift or a unique memento for yourself, try any of the many excellent museum/institutional shops, including that of the New York Public Library. They offer a surprisingly wide selection of gift items in all price ranges, from the very inexpensive to fine textiles and exotic jewelry from throughout the world, as well as fine art works and art reproductions. You are guaranteed to find items in these places you will see nowhere else. Plus, a shop visit is a fascinating way to glimpse some of what the institution itself offers, even if you do not have time to tour.

Photography
Adorama Camera, 42 W. 18th St., tel 212/741–0052, 800/223–2500, adorama.com. Subway: 1 to 18th St.; 4, 5, N, Q, R to Union Sq. Closed Fri. at 2 p.m., all Sat.
B & H Photo, 420 9th Ave., tel 212/444–6615, 800/606–6969, bhphotovideo.com. Subway: A, C, E to 34th St. Closed Fri. at 1 p.m., all Sat. Well-priced photo/video supplies and equipment at this very large store.
K & M Camera, 385 Broadway (bet. Walker & White), kmcamera.com. Subway: J, N, Q, R, 6 to Canal St.

Records, CDs
Academy Records & CDs, 12 W. 18th St., tel 212/242–3000, academy-records.com. Subway: 1 to 18th St. Used items, specializing in classical music.
Bleecker St. Records, 188 W 4th St, 212/255–7899. A long-time

West Village independent CD and vinyl store, formerly on Bleecker Street, offering an amazing array from jazz to blues to gospel, to a superb range of live rock recordings. A browser's paradise, open till 10 p.m. every night.
Other Music, 15 E. 4th St., tel 212/477–8150, othermusic. com. Subway: 6, 4 to Bleecker St. Good, eclectic selection with an online shopping option and occasional in-store performance.

This & That
Apple, 767 5th Ave., tel 212/336–1440, apple.com/ retail/fifthavenue. Subway: N, Q, R, 4, 5, 6 to Lexington Ave./59th St. Computer megastore.
E.A.T., 1064 Madison Ave., tel 212/772–0022, elizabar.com. Subway: 6 to 77th St. Gifts for all.
Fountain Pen Hospital, 10 Warren St., tel 212/964–0580, fountainpenhospital.com. Subway: A, C to Chambers St. Closed Sat.–Sun. Well-priced vintage and new pens. For a treat, call this place to hear the recording.
Leo Kaplan Ltd., 114 E. 57th St. (bet. Park & Lexington Aves.), tel 212/355–7212, leokaplan.com. Subway: N, R, 4, 5, 6 to 59th St. Closed Sun. Antique and new paperweight collection.
The Art of Shaving, 141 E. 62nd St., tel 212/317–8436, theartof shaving.com. Subway: N, Q, R, 4,

5, 6 to Lexington Ave./59th St. Supplies or a shave.

Toys: Big Kids, Little Kids
American Girl Place 609 5th Ave., tel 212/371–2220, store.american girl.com. Subway: B, D, F, M to 47th–50th Sts.–Rockefeller Center. Doll grooming, studio photos, and a restaurant for brunch.
Chess Forum, 219 Thompson St., tel 212/475–2369, chessforum .com. Subway: A, B, C, D, E, F to W. 4th St. Long-established, in the West Village–with an unparalleled collection of chess sets; playing room two doors away.
Dinosaur Hill, 306 E. 9th St. (bet. 1st & 2nd Aves.), tel 212/473–5850, dinosaurhill.com. Subway: 6 to Astor Pl. Precious classics, from marionettes to craft kits. Wonderful and eclectic.
Forbidden Planet, 832 Broadway, tel 212/475–1576, fpnyc.com. Subway: L, N, R, Q, 4, 5, 6 to Union Sq. Sci-fi megastore, offering comics, graphic novels, apparel, games, and toys. Some material not for the younger set.
Nintendo World, 10 Rockefeller Plaza (at 48th St.), tel 646/459–0800, nintendoworld.com. Subway: B, D, F to 47th–50th Sts.–Rockefeller Center. Play the latest Nintendo games or get Pokémon trading cards.

ENTERTAINMENT & ACTIVITIES

Oh, can you be entertained in New York City! The only questions are how, and for how much? Just as with eating and shopping, there are options across the spectrum. Perhaps the most interesting time can be had by carefully scheduling anything you really have your heart set on doing, then leaving the rest to last-minute inspiration and serendipity. The real magic of the city often presents itself right on the street and out of the blue, and it is that element of exquisite randomness that native New Yorkers most enjoy talking about at the end of the day.

Official NYC Information Center, 810 7th Ave. (at 53rd St.), tel 800/ NYC-VISIT. Satellite locations: **Times Square Center,** 7th Ave. (bet. 46th & 47th Sts.), timessquarenyc.org; **City Hall Kiosk,** southern tip of City Hall Park; Times Square Plaza bet. 7th, Broadway, 44th, & 45th St.; and **Macy's Herald Sq.,** 151 W. 34 St. Literature on entertainment mailed to you, or speak to an agent (tel 212/484–1200, nycgo .com). For free tickets to concerts and TV tapings sometimes offered in person, **Theater Development Fund,** 520 8th Ave., tel 212/912–9770.

Useful Publications

Check out the New York Times, particularly Friday's Weekend section and Sunday's Arts and Leisure section, The New Yorker, New York magazine, the New York Observer, Time Out New York, and Paper (monthly).

Useful Websites

cityguidemagazine.com Activities, restaurants, and shopping suggestions.
newyorkmag.com New York magazine site with "best of" recommendations.
nytimes.com The New York Times, strong on cultural events.
timeout.com/newyork Time Out, large to small events listed by day and category.
timessquarenyc.org The Times Square Information Center, neighborhood deals, news, and activities.
villagevoice.com Website of

the historical culture and events magazine.

Theater

Theater, like other forms of entertainment in New York, runs the gamut: from Broadway blockbusters to the most experimental skits in an East Village cellar. All have appeal for different audiences or moods. Off-off Broadway is inexpensive but can still be soul-nurturing. There are officially 39 Broadway theaters, about 20 Off-Broadway (most fewer than 500 seats), and about 300 Off-off Broadway venues (most fewer than 100 seats).

Sources of Information

It's always worth stopping by or calling the theater box office of the show you would like to see. There may be house or single seats available, or cancellations. They are generally open from 10 a.m. until after the performance begins.

TKTS booths For 25–50 percent savings on Broadway and Off-Broadway tickets, try your luck here. **Lower Manhattan Center:** TKTS South Street Seaport, 190 Front Street at the corner of Front & John Sts., for evening and next-day matinee tickets only (11 a.m.–6 p.m. Mon.–Sat., 11 a.m.–4 p.m. Sun.). **Main branch,** TKTS Times Square, Theater District at 47th St. & Broadway, Duffy Sq., for evening and next-day matinee tickets (3 p.m.–8 p.m. for evening performances, 10 a.m.–2 p.m. Wed., Thur., Sat., & Sun. for matinees). **TKTS Lincoln Center,**

61 W. 62nd St., David Rubenstein Atrium, tickets for evening and same-day & next-day matinée (12 p.m.-7 p.m. Mon.-Sat., 12 p.m.–5 p.m. Sun.). Check the website for possible variations in opening hours (tdf.org). All booths accept credit cards, cash, and travelers' checks. Bring a list of theater reviews; it is unusual to get your first choice.
Broadway Inner Circle, tel 212/ 391–9621.
Broadway League, tel 212/764–1122, broadwayleague.com. Current show information and ticket sales.
Prestige Entertainment, tel 800/243–8849, prestige entertainment.com. Independent agent, may be able to find a seat.
Shakespeare in the Park, tel 212/539–8500, publictheater .org. After you've registered at the website, get in line in front of the theater (entrance between 81st St. and Central Park West, we recommend you arrive by 10). Distribution begins at 12 and each person can collect up to two tickets. Performances begin at 8 p.m. Tues.–Sun.
Telecharge, tel 212/239–6200 or 800/447–7400, telecharge.com. Ticket agency to reserve seats for Broadway and Off Broadway by credit card for a small handling fee.
Ticketmaster, tel 800/653–8000, ticketmaster.com. Same as above.

Broadway Venues

See pp. 117–118 for theater listings. **New Amsterdam,** 214 W. 42nd St. (bet. 7th & 8th Aves.), tel 866/870–2717. Subway: A, C, E,

N, R, 1, 2 to Times Sq. Acclaimed performances and outstanding productions. Site tours available.

Off–Broadway Venues

Astor Place Theater, 434 Lafayette St., tel 212/254–4371. Home of long-running Blue Man Group's *Tubes*.

Brooklyn Academy of Music, 30 Lafayette Ave., Brooklyn, tel 718/636–4100, bam.org. Established destination for innovative works.

Classic Stage Company, 136 E. 13th St. (bet. 3rd & 4th Aves.), tel 212/677–4210, classicstage.org. Subway: N. R, 4, 5, 6 to 14th St. Past works find influence again in today's audiences.

La Mama E.T.C., 74A E. 4th St., tel212/475–7710, lamama.org. Off–Broadway groundbreaker.

Lincoln Center Theater, 150 W. 65th St., tel 212/239–6200, lct.org. Top-class productions.

Manhattan Theatre Club, 131 W. 55th St., and 261 W. 47th St. (Samuel J. Friedman Theater) tel 212/397–2420, mtc-nyc.org. Three theaters, including the works of new and established playwrights, readings, and workshops.

New York Theater Workshop, 79 E. 4th St., tel 212/780–9037, nytw.org. New plays by young, up-and-coming directors.

The Culture Project, 49 Bleecker St., tel 212/925–1806, culture project.org. Subway: 6 to Bleecker St. Top short-run dramas with a sociopolitical edge. Meryl Streep has co-produced here.

The Public Theater, 425 Lafayette St., tel 212/539–8500, publictheater.org. One of the finest theaters in New York, founded by Joseph Papp.

Dance

Performance tickets can be available to certain dance events at TKTS (see p. 262).

Ballet

New York City Ballet, David H. Koch Theater, Columbus Ave. & 63rd St., tel 212/496–0600, nycballet.com. World-famous company, highlights works by founder George Balanchine, Jerome Robbins, Peter Martins, and other choreographers. Two seasons: before Thanksgiving to beginning of March, then beginning late April/May for 8 weeks.

The American Ballet Theatre, Metropolitan Opera House, 65th & Broadway, tel 212/477–3030, abt.org. Classics and works created in traditional style. Large theater, so top tiers are far from stage. Also visiting foreign ballet companies.

Contemporary Dance

Brooklyn Academy of Music, see Off–Broadway Venues. Excellent modern dance companies, lovely stage. Next Wave festival every fall, featuring renowned artists and experimental dance, other festivals.

Joyce Theater, 175 8th Ave. (at 19th St.), tel 212/691–9740, joyce.org. One of the best dance destinations, with great variety and an emphasis on newer artists.

New York City Center, 130 W. 55th St., tel 212/581–1212, nycitycenter.org. Regular performances by famous, lesser known, and visiting troupes.

Other Troupes & Venues

Alvin Ailey American Dance Theater, 405 W. 55th St. (9th Ave.), tel 212/405–9000, alvinailey.org. American modern dance.

Dance Theatre of Harlem, 466 W. 152nd St., tel 212/690-2800, dancetheatreofharlem.org. Rarely in town; try to catch them.

Juilliard, 155 W. 65th St, tel 212/769–7406 or 212/721–6500, juilliard.edu. The Juilliard School performs at the Peter Jay Sharp Theater (*416 W. 42nd St.*).

Mark Morris Dance Group, 3 Lafayette Ave., Brooklyn,

tel 718/624–8400, markmorris dancegroup.org. Modern dance.

Movement Research, 219 W. 19th St., tel 212/598–0551, movementresearch.org. Free and low-cost dance series since 1960s.

New York Live Arts, 219 W. 19th St., tel 212/924–0077, newyorklivearts.org. Alternative dance performances.

Outdoor Summer Dance Events

Central Park SummerStage, Rumsey Playfield at 72nd St., tel 212/360–2777, cityparks foundation.org/summerstage. Free dance program Fridays in July and early August.

Lincoln Center Out of Doors, 70 Lincoln Plaza, 212/546–2656, lcoutofdoors.org. Free dance events on plaza.

Cabaret

Bemelmans Bar, Carlyle Hotel, 35 E. 76th St., tel 212/744–1600, thecarlyle.com. Great ambience with fine pianists.

Café Carlyle, 35 E. 76th St., tel 212/744–1600, thecarlyle.com. Classic shows (Woody Allen Ensemble plays Dixieland Mon.).

Don't Tell Mama, 343 W. 46th St., tel 212/757–0788, donttell mamanyc.com. Cabaret, emerging acts, revues.

Joe's Pub, see p. 264.

The Duplex, 61 Christopher St., tel 212/255–5438, theduplex .com. A piano bar and cabaret theater in the West Village.

Clubs

(See sidebar p. 214)

Comedy

(See also sidebar p. 116)

Broadway Comedy Club, 318 W. 53rd (bet. 8th and 9th Aves.), tel 212/757–2323, broadwaycomedyclub.com.

Caroline's Comedy Club, 1626 Broadway at 49th St., tel

212/757–4100, carolines.com.
Comedy Cellar, 117 MacDougal St., tel 212/254–3480, comedycellar.com.
Comic Strip, 1568 2nd Ave. (bet. 81st and 82nd Sts.), tel 212/861–9386, comicstriplive.com.
Dangerfield's, 1118 1st Ave. (61st St.), tel 212/593–1650, dangerfields.com.
Gotham Comedy Club, 208 W. 23rd St., tel 212/367–9000, gothamcomedyclub.com.
Stand Up NY, 236 W. 78th St., tel 212/595–0850, standupny.com. Small venue for up-and-coming as well as established acts.
Upright Citizens Brigade Theatre, 307 W. 26th St., tel 212/366–9176, ucbtheatre.com

Electronics
Sony Building, at 550 Madison Ave., tel 212/833-8100. Closed Sun.–Mon. A "techie heaven" with state-of-the-art interactive games for kids of all ages.

Film
In addition to regular Hollywood fare, this most cosmopolitan city offers unparalleled film selections, from small independent premieres and foreign film seasons, to outdoor movies in Bryant Park in the summer. Many museums sponsor film festivals, and there are fine collections open to the public in libraries and museums. Some of the world's best film-making programs and schools are here as well.

MovieFone, moviefone.com. A ticket-buying system with recorded information on all films showing and nearest locations.
The New York Film Festival, tel 212/875–5600, filmlinc.org. Presented by the Film Society of Lincoln Center, begins in late Sept. and consists of two weeks of new American and foreign films.
Tribeca Film Festival, tribecafilm .com. Premieres, screenings, panels, city events, and a Tribeca Family

Street Fair. Focus on independent films. April–May for two weeks (see sidebar p. 71).

Classic Film Venues
Anthology Film Archives, 32 2nd Ave., tel 212/505–5181, anthologyfilmarchives.org.
Film Forum, 209 W. Houston St., tel 212/727–8110, filmforum.org.
Museum of Modern Art, 11 W. 53rd St., tel 212/708–9480, moma.org. Year-round.
Museum of the Moving Image, 35th Ave. at 37th St., Astoria, Queens, tel 718/784–0077, movingimage.com.
Public Theater, 425 Lafayette St., tel 212/539–8500, publictheater .org.
The Paley Center for Media, 25 W. 52nd St., tel 212/621–6800, paleycenter.org.
Whitney Museum of American Art, 945 Madison Ave. (at 75th St.), tel 212/570–3600, whitney. org.

Children's Cinema
IMAX Theater, at the American Museum of Natural History, Central Park W. at 79th St., tel 212/769–5100, amnh.org/ exhibitions/imax-and-3d.
Walter Reade Theater/Film Society of Lincoln Center, see Foreign & Independent Film Houses. Children's series on Sat. Morning.

Foreign & Independent Film Houses
Angelika Film Center, 18 W. Houston St., tel 212/995–2570, angelikafilmcenter.com.
Asia Society, 725 Park Ave., tel 212/288–6400, asiasociety.org.
Cinema Village, 22 E. 12th St., tel 212/924–3363, cinemavillage .com.
Film Forum, 209 W. Houston St., tel 212/727–8110, filmforum.org.
French Institute, 22 E. 60th St., tel 212/355–6100, fiaf.org.
IFC Center, 323 6th Ave. (at W.

3rd St.), tel 212/924–7771.
Lincoln Plaza Cinema, Broadway (bet. 62nd & 63rd Sts.), tel 212/ 757–2280, lincolnplazacinema.com.
Paris Theatre, 4 W. 58th St., tel 212/688–3800, theparistheatre. com.
Quad Cinema, 34 W. 13th St., tel 212/255–2243, quadcinema .com.
Walter Reade Theater, 165 W. 65th St. (bet. Broadway & Amsterdam Ave.), tel 212/875–5600.

Ultra Movie Experiences
AMC Loews Lincoln Square, 1998 Broadway (at 68th St.), tel 212/336–5020. Multistory screen with 3-D offerings. Short subjects.
The Ziegfeld, 141 W. 54th St., tel 212/765–7600, bowtiecinemas .com. 1,400-seat, velvet-cushioned palace. A throwback and a classic venue no matter what's playing.

Music
Tickets are available directly from venues or can be booked through Ticketmaster for a fee (see p. 262). An option, for discounted same-day tickets, is TKTS (see p. 262).

Classical Music
Alice Tully Hall, tel 212/671–4050.
Home of Chamber Music Society.
Avery Fisher Hall, tel 212/875–5030. Home of the New York Philharmonic.
Bargemusic, Fulton Ferry Landing, Brooklyn, tel 718/718/624–4924, bargemusic.org. Chamber music Thurs.–Sun. on a barge with great view of Manhattan.
Brooklyn Academy of Music, see above. Home of Brooklyn Philharmonic Orchestra, specializing in contemporary classical composers.
Carnegie Hall, 881 7th Ave., 154 W. 57th St., tel 212/247–7800, carnegiehall.org. One of the world's greatest venues.
Damrosch Park, tel 212/875–

5000. Free outdoor concerts in summer.

Juilliard School of Music, tel 212/799–5456. Many free recitals.

Kaufmann Concert Hall, 92nd St. Y, 1395 Lexington Ave., tel 212/415–5780, 92y.org. Great acoustics, interesting series.

Lincoln Center for the Performing Arts, Columbus Ave. bet. 62nd & 65th Sts., tel 212/875–5000 or 212/LINCOLN (hotline), lincolncenter.org.

Metropolitan Museum of Art, 5th Ave. & 82nd St., Grace Rainey Rogers Auditorium, tel 212/535–7710. Chamber music.

Other Classical Music Venues
Cathedral Church of St. John the Divine, Amsterdam Ave. at 112th St., tel 212/316–7540, stjohndivine.org.

Central Park Summerstage, tel 212/360–1399, summerstage.org. Summertime concerts.

Church of St. Ignatius Loyola, 980 Park Ave., tel 212/288–3588, stignatiusloyola.org.

Church of the Ascension, 12 W. 11th St., tel 212/254–8620.

The Cloisters, Fort Tryon Park, Inwood, tel 212/923–3700, metmuseum.org.

Jazz & Blues
Birdland, 315 W. 44th St., tel 212/581–3080, birdlandjazz.com. A classy spot for top jazz.

Blue Note, 131 W. 3rd St., tel 212/475–8592, bluenote.net. Big names.

Blue Smoke Flatiron/Jazz Standard, 116 E. 27th St., tel 212/447–7733, bluesmoke.com. BBQ joint upstairs, great jazz downstairs.

Dizzy's Club Coca–Cola, Time Warner Center, 5th fl., Broadway at 60th St., tel 212/258–9595, jalc.org/dizzys. Affordable hot spot for Midtown jazz; soul food menu, Central Park views.

Iridium, 1650 Broadway at 51st

St., tel 212/582–2121, theiridium.com. Top performers.

Jazz Standard, 116 E. 27th St., tel 212/576–2232, jazzstandard.net. Restaurant/jazz club combo.

Knickerbocker, 33 University Place, tel 212/228–8490, knickerbockerbarandgrill.com. Good lineups of blues players.

Smalls, 183 W. 10th St., tel 212/252–5091, smallsjazzclub.com. Emerging artists in a casual all-night spot.

Swing 46, 349 W. 46th St., tel 212/262–9554, swing46.com. Jazz, blues, and swing on Restaurant Row.

Village Vanguard, 178 7th Ave. South (at 11th St.), tel 212/ 255–4037, villagevanguard.com. A basement club—the best.

Zinc Bar, 82 W. 3rd St. (bet. Thompson & Sullivan Sts), tel 212/477–9462, zincbar.com. Preeminent spot for jazz, Latin, and Brazilian sounds. Micro stage.

Music Venues
Many do not accept credit cards.

Apollo Theater, 253 W. 125th St., tel 212/531–5300 or 212/531–5337, apollotheater.org. Variety of African-American musical acts.

Beacon Theatre, 2124 Broadway (at 74th St.), tel 212/465–6500, beacontheatrenyc.com. Mainstream and unusual groups in a beautiful art deco theater.

Bitter End, 147 Bleecker St., tel 212/673–7030, bitterend.com. Singer-songwriter joint.

Cafe wha?, 115 Mcdougal, tel 212/254–3706, cafewha.com. In the heart of Greenwich Village since 1959, frequented by artists who later became famous.

Central Park Summerstage, see p. 263.

Gramercy Theatre, 127 E. 23rd St., tel 212/614–6932, the gramercytheatre.com. Important shows.

Irving Plaza, 17 Irving Pl., tel 212/777–6800, irvingplaza.com. Nearly big-time acts.

Joe's Pub, 425 Lafayette St., tel 212/967–75555, joespub.com. Wide range of music and a hip scene. Italian menu at night.

Jones Beach Theater, 895 Bay Pkwy., Wantagh, Long Island, tel 516/221–1000, jonesbeach.com. Summertime open amphitheater for top performances.

Knitting Factory, 361 Metropolitan Ave., Brooklyn, tel 347/529–6696, knittingfactory.com. Progressive rock, experimental music, etc.

Madison Square Garden, 7th Ave. at 33rd St., tel 212/465–6741, thegarden.com. Biggest rock acts, and more. See sidebar p. 99.

Mercury Lounge, 217 E. Houston St., tel 212/260–4700, mercury loungenyc.com. Hip spot for new bands.

Nassau Coliseum, 1255 Hempstead Turnpike, Uniondale, N.Y., tel 516/794–9300, nassau coliseum.com. Rock's big tickets.

Paddy Reilly's, 519 2nd Ave., tel 212/686–1210. Irish rock.

Radio City Music Hall, 6th Ave. (at 50th St.), tel 212/247–4777, radiocity.com. Art deco hall with huge acts.

S.O.B's, 204 Varick St., tel 212/243–4940, sobs.com. Premier world music venue.

Webster Hall, 125 E. 11th St., tel 212/353–1600. websterhall.com. Big downtown dance bar.

Opera
David H. Koch Theater, Lincoln Center, tel 212/ 870–5570. Variety of productions.

Juilliard Opera Center, see p. 263,tel 212/769–7406. Student shows.

Metropolitan Opera House, Lincoln Center, tel 212/362–6000, metoperafamily.org. Its own company and hosts visiting performers, world-class productions.

New York City Center, 131 W. 55th St., tel 212/581–1212, nycitycenter.org.

INDEX

Bold page numbers indicate illustrations. CAPS indicates thematic categories.

National Geographic
TRAVELER
New York
FIFTH EDITION

Since 1888, the National Geographic Society has funded more than 13,000 research, exploration, and preservation projects around the world. National Geographic Partners distributes a portion of the funds it receives from your purchase to National Geographic Society to support programs including the conservation of animals and their habitats.

National Geographic Partners, LLC
1145 17th Street NW
Washington, DC 20036-4688 USA

Get closer to National Geographic explorers and photographers, and connect with our global community. Join us today at nationalgeographic.com/join

For information about special discounts for bulk purchases, please contact National Geographic Books Special Sales: specialsales@natgeo.com

For rights or permissions inquiries, please contact National Geographic Books Subsidiary Rights: bookrights@natgeo.com

Drive maps drawn by Chris Orr Associates, Southampton, England
Cutaway illustrations drawn by Maltings Partnership, Derby, England

Fifth edition edited by White Star s.r.l. Licensee of National Geographic Partners, LLC. Update by Iceigeo, Milan (Francesco Filippini, Cynthia Anne Koeppe, Max Rankenburg)

The information in this book has been carefully checked and to the best of our knowledge is accurate. However, details are subject to change, and the publisher cannot be responsible for such changes, or for errors or omissions. Assessments of sites, hotels, and restaurants are based on the author's subjective opinions, which do not necessarily reflect the publisher's opinion.

ISBN: 978-88-544-1679-6

Printed by
Rotolito S.p.A. - Seggiano di Pioltello (MI) - Italy

ILLUSTRATIONS CREDITS